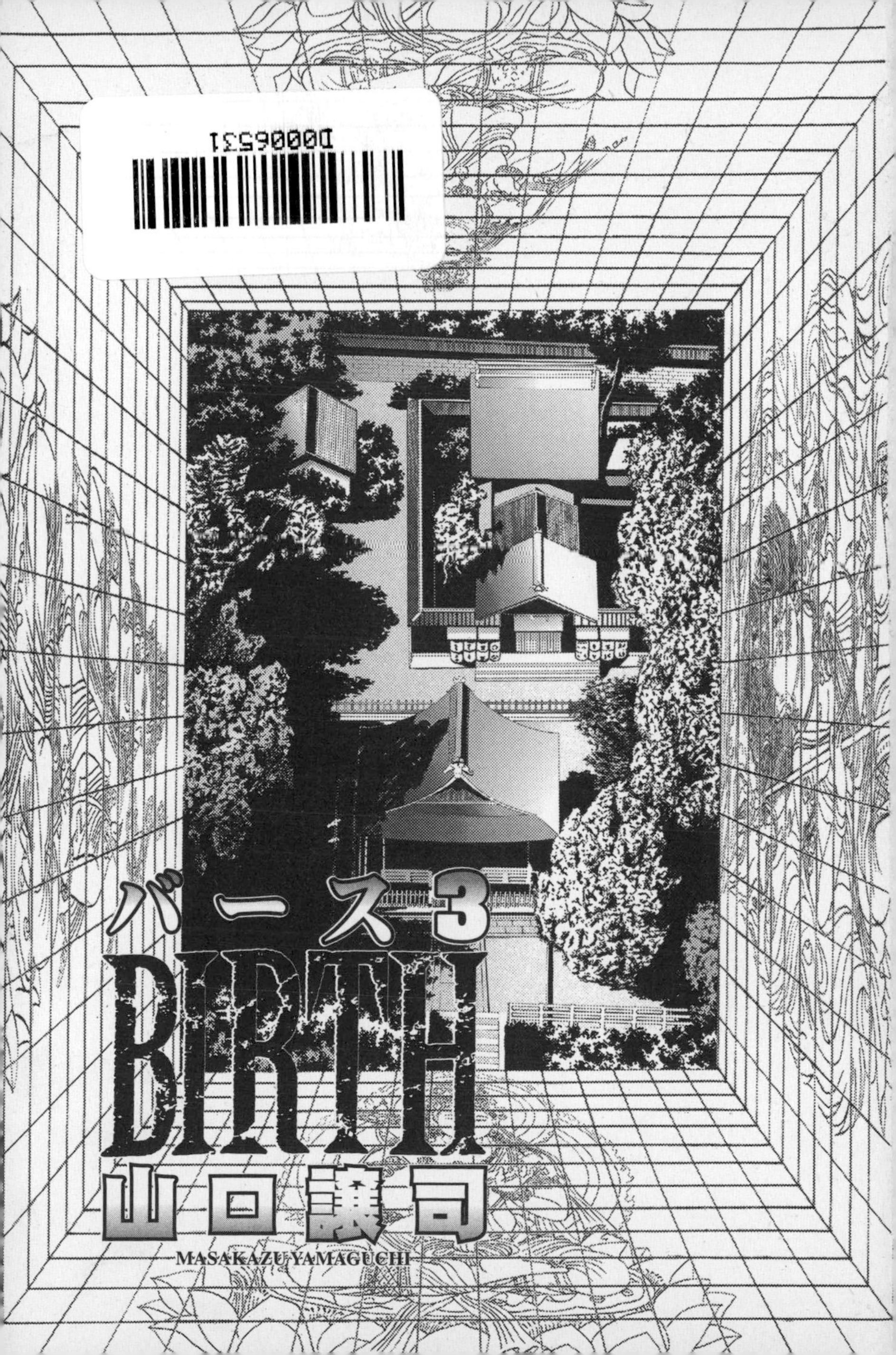
バース 3
BIRTH
山口譲司
MASAKAZU YAMAGUCHI

Arm of Kannon Vol. 3
created by Masakazu Yamaguchi

Translation - Takae Brewer
English Adaptation - Jordan Capell
Retouch and Lettering - Eric Botero
Production Artist - Yoohae Yang
Cover Artist - Raymond Makowski

Editor - Luis Reyes
Digital Imaging Manager - Chris Buford
Pre-Press Manager - Antonio DePietro
Production Managers - Jennifer Miller and Mutsumi Miyazaki
Art Director - Matt Alford
Managing Editor - Jill Freshney
VP of Production - Ron Klamert
President and C.O.O. - John Parker
Publisher and C.E.O. - Stuart Levy

A TOKYOPOP® Manga

TOKYOPOP Inc.
5900 Wilshire Blvd. Suite 2000
Los Angeles, CA 90036

E-mail: info@TOKYOPOP.com
Come visit us online at www.TOKYOPOP.com

ISBN: 1-59182-812-0

First TOKYOPOP printing: September 2004

10 9 8 7 6 5 4 3 2 1
Printed in the USA

ARM OF KANNON

Volume 3
Masakazu Yamaguchi

HAMBURG // LONDON // LOS ANGELES // TOKYO

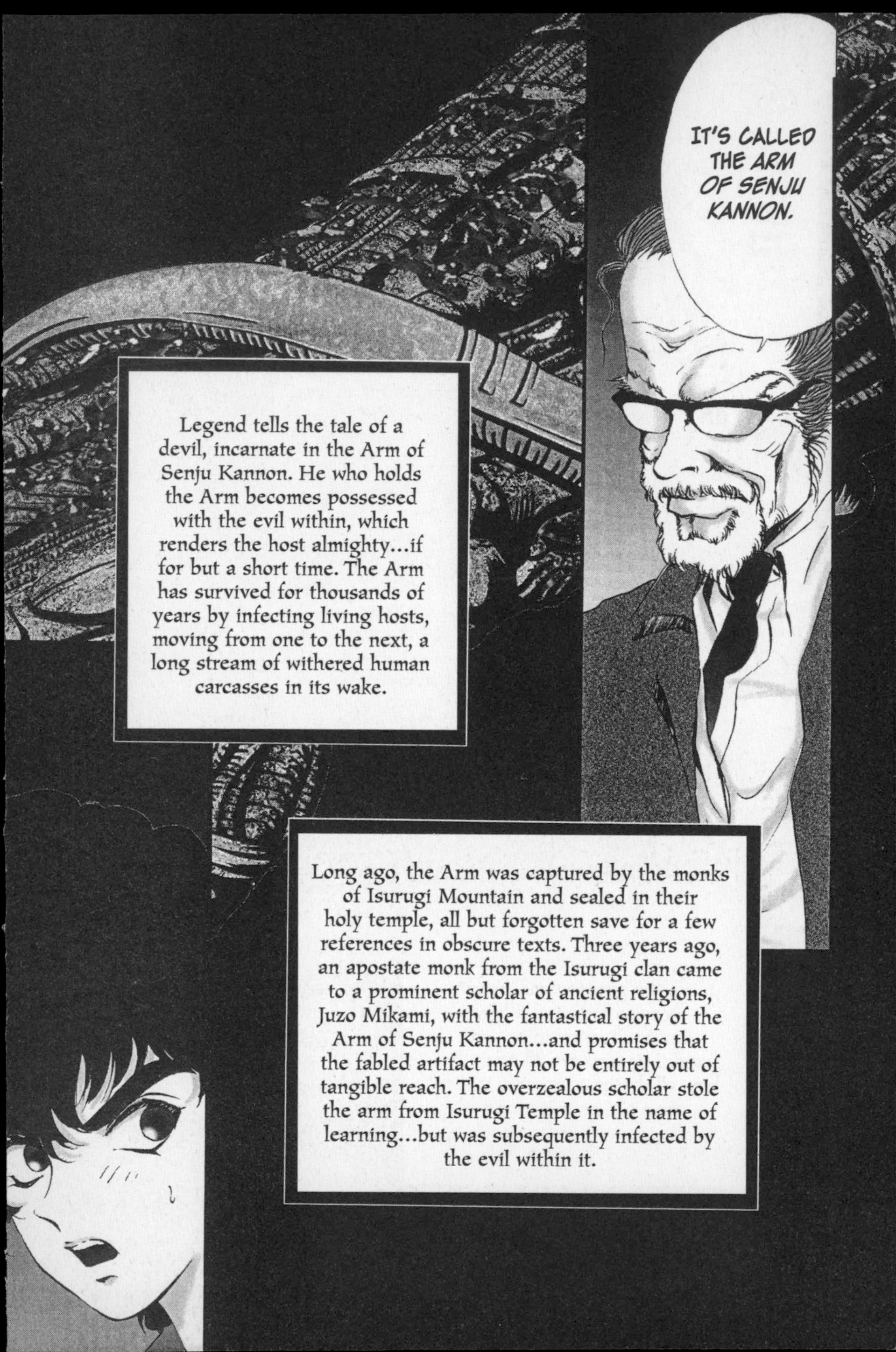
IT'S CALLED THE ARM OF SENJU KANNON.
Legend tells the tale of a devil, incarnate in the Arm of Senju Kannon. He who holds the Arm becomes possessed with the evil within, which renders the host almighty...if for but a short time. The Arm has survived for thousands of years by infecting living hosts, moving from one to the next, a long stream of withered human carcasses in its wake.
Long ago, the Arm was captured by the monks of Isurugi Mountain and sealed in their holy temple, all but forgotten save for a few references in obscure texts. Three years ago, an apostate monk from the Isurugi clan came to a prominent scholar of ancient religions, Juzo Mikami, with the fantastical story of the Arm of Senju Kannon...and promises that the fabled artifact may not be entirely out of tangible reach. The overzealous scholar stole the arm from Isurugi Temple in the name of learning...but was subsequently infected by the evil within it.

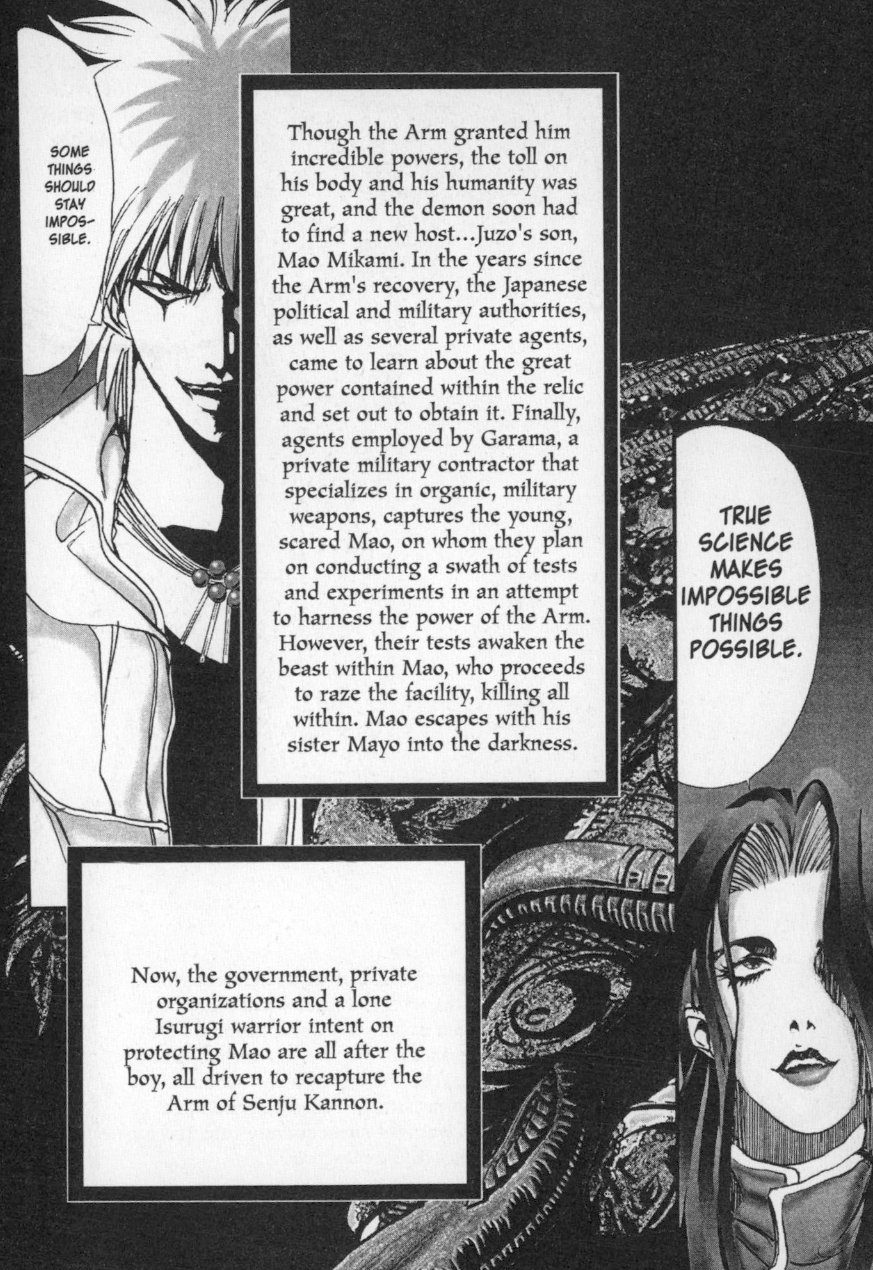
Though the Arm granted him incredible powers, the toll on his body and his humanity was great, and the demon soon had to find a new host...Juzo's son, Mao Mikami. In the years since the Arm's recovery, the Japanese political and military authorities, as well as several private agents, came to learn about the great power contained within the relic and set out to obtain it. Finally, agents employed by Garama, a private military contractor that specializes in organic, military weapons, captures the young, scared Mao, on whom they plan on conducting a swath of tests and experiments in an attempt to harness the power of the Arm. However, their tests awaken the beast within Mao, who proceeds to raze the facility, killing all within. Mao escapes with his sister Mayo into the darkness.
TRUE SCIENCE MAKES IMPOSSIBLE THINGS POSSIBLE.
SOME THINGS SHOULD STAY IMPOS-SIBLE.
Now, the government, private organizations and a lone Isurugi warrior intent on protecting Mao are all after the boy, all driven to recapture the Arm of Senju Kannon.

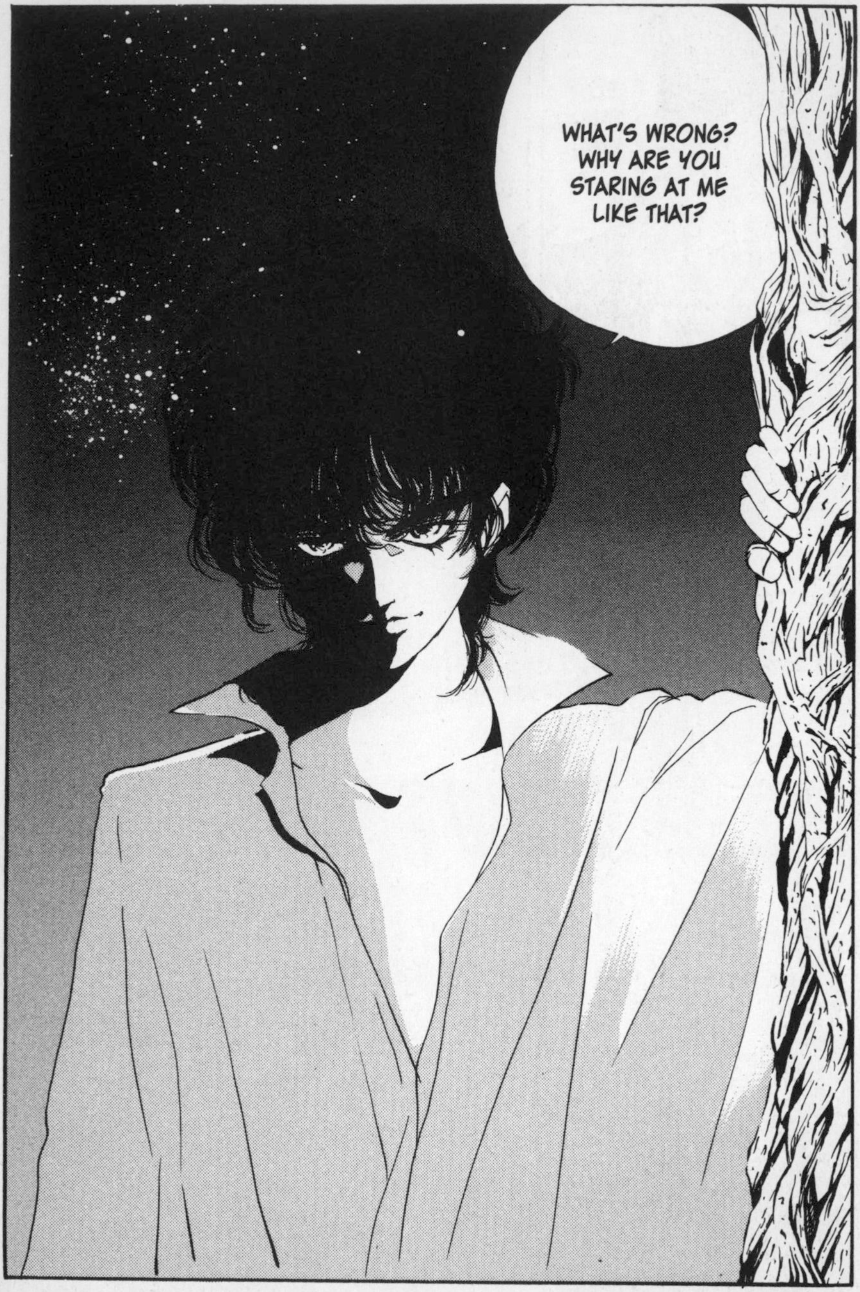
WHAT'S WRONG? WHY ARE YOU STARING AT ME LIKE THAT?

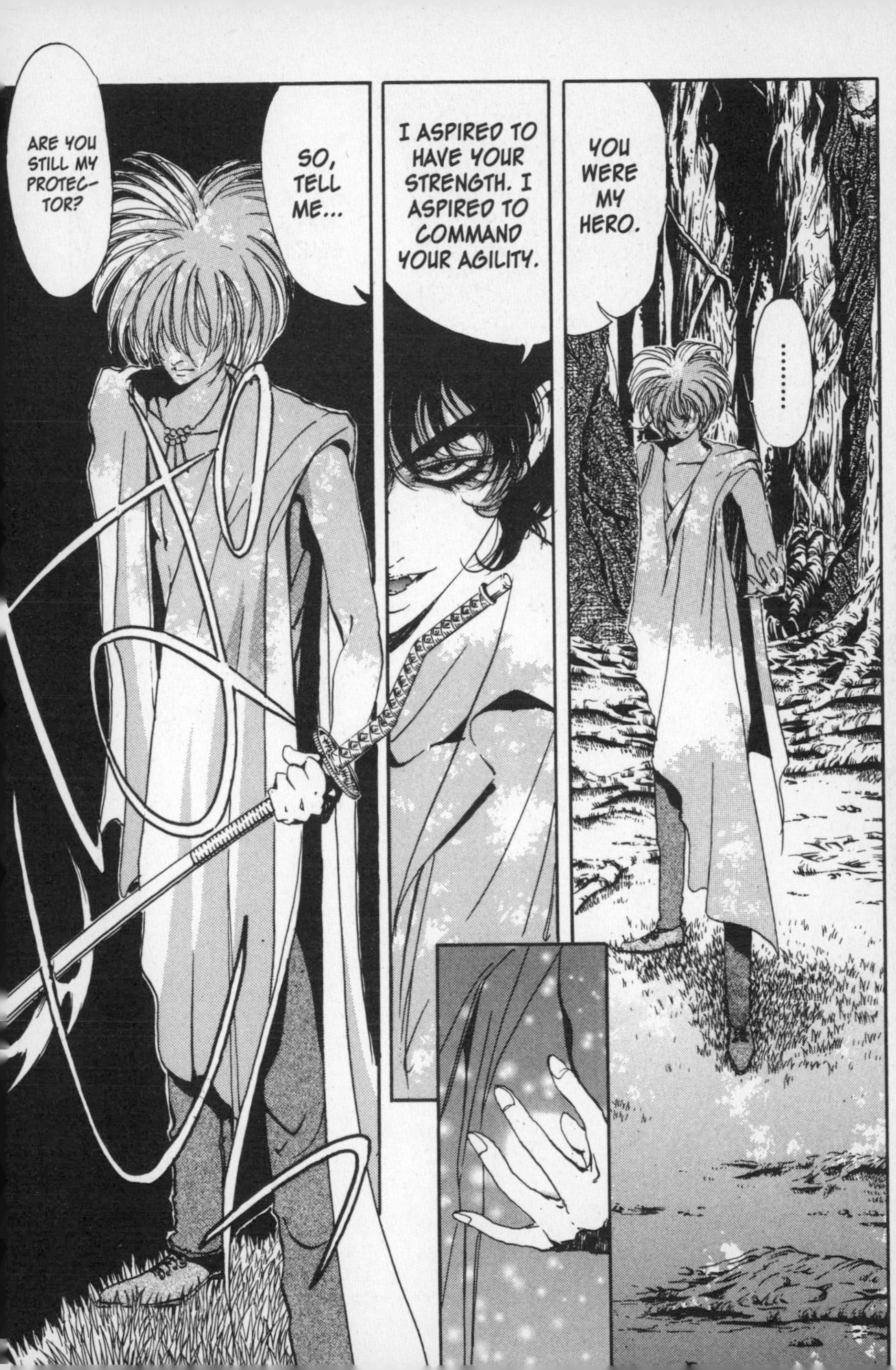
YOU WERE MY HERO.
......
I ASPIRED TO HAVE YOUR STRENGTH. I ASPIRED TO COMMAND YOUR AGILITY.
SO, TELL ME...
ARE YOU STILL MY PROTECTOR?

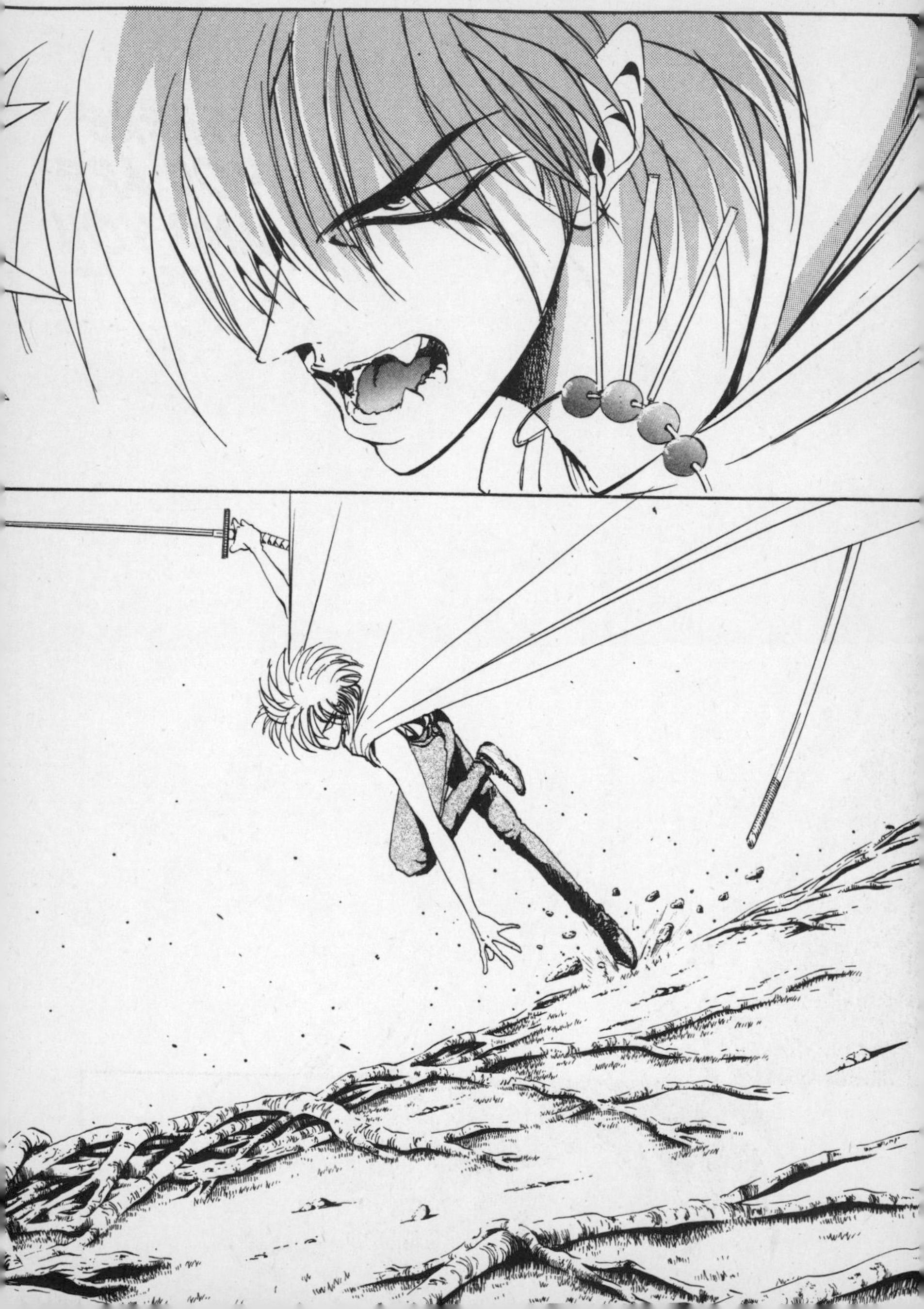

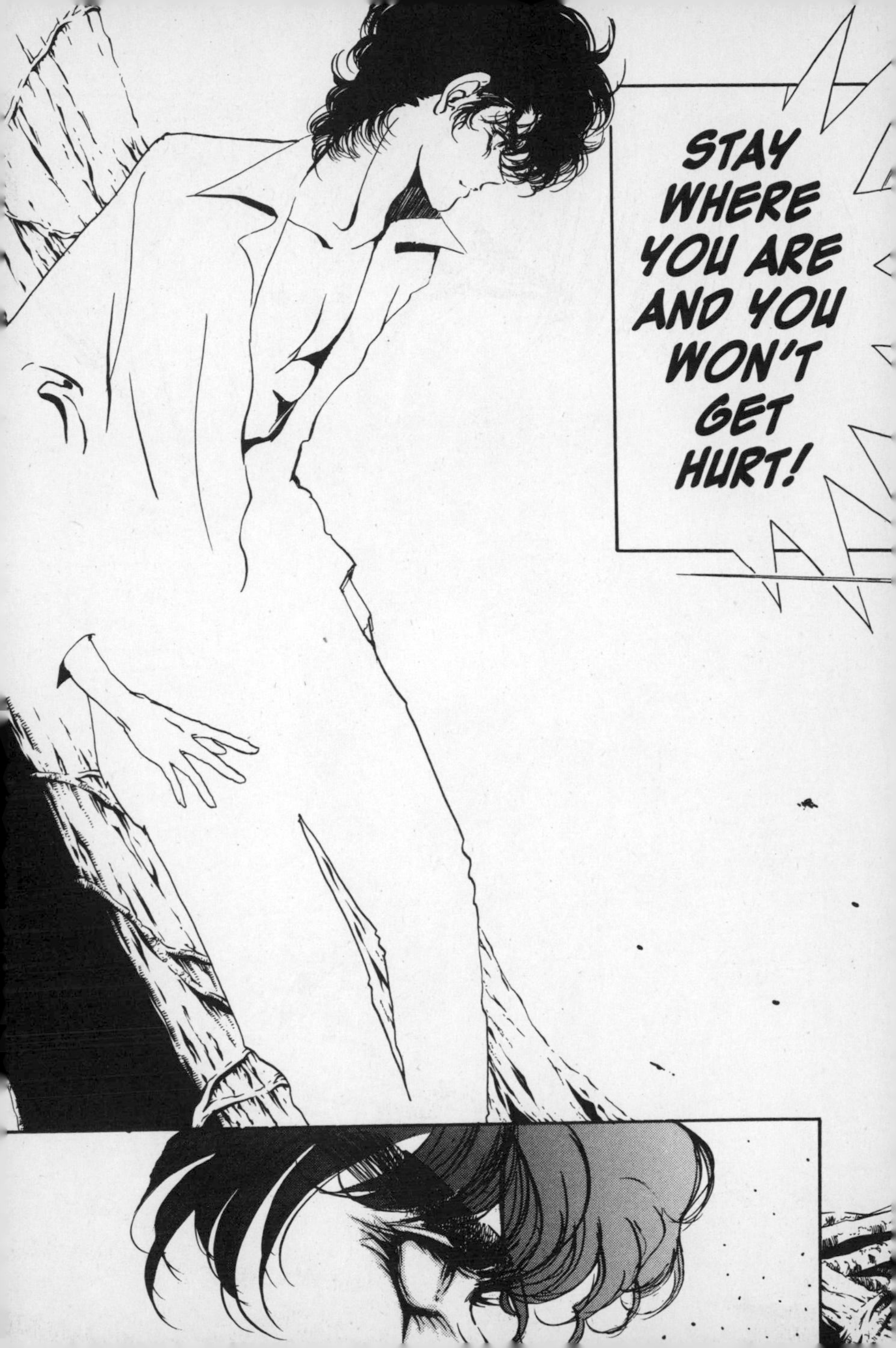
STAY WHERE YOU ARE AND YOU WON'T GET HURT!

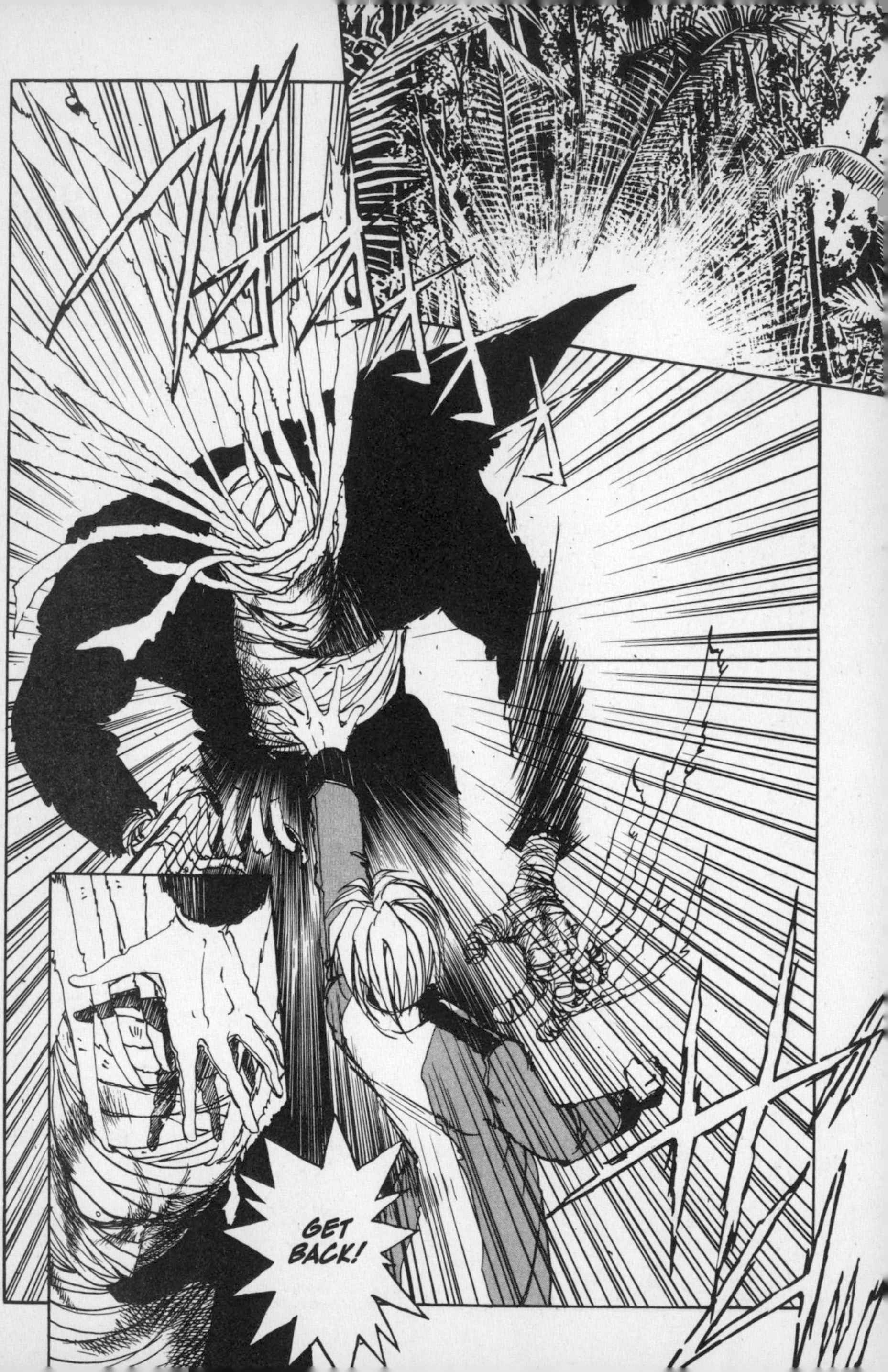
GET BACK!

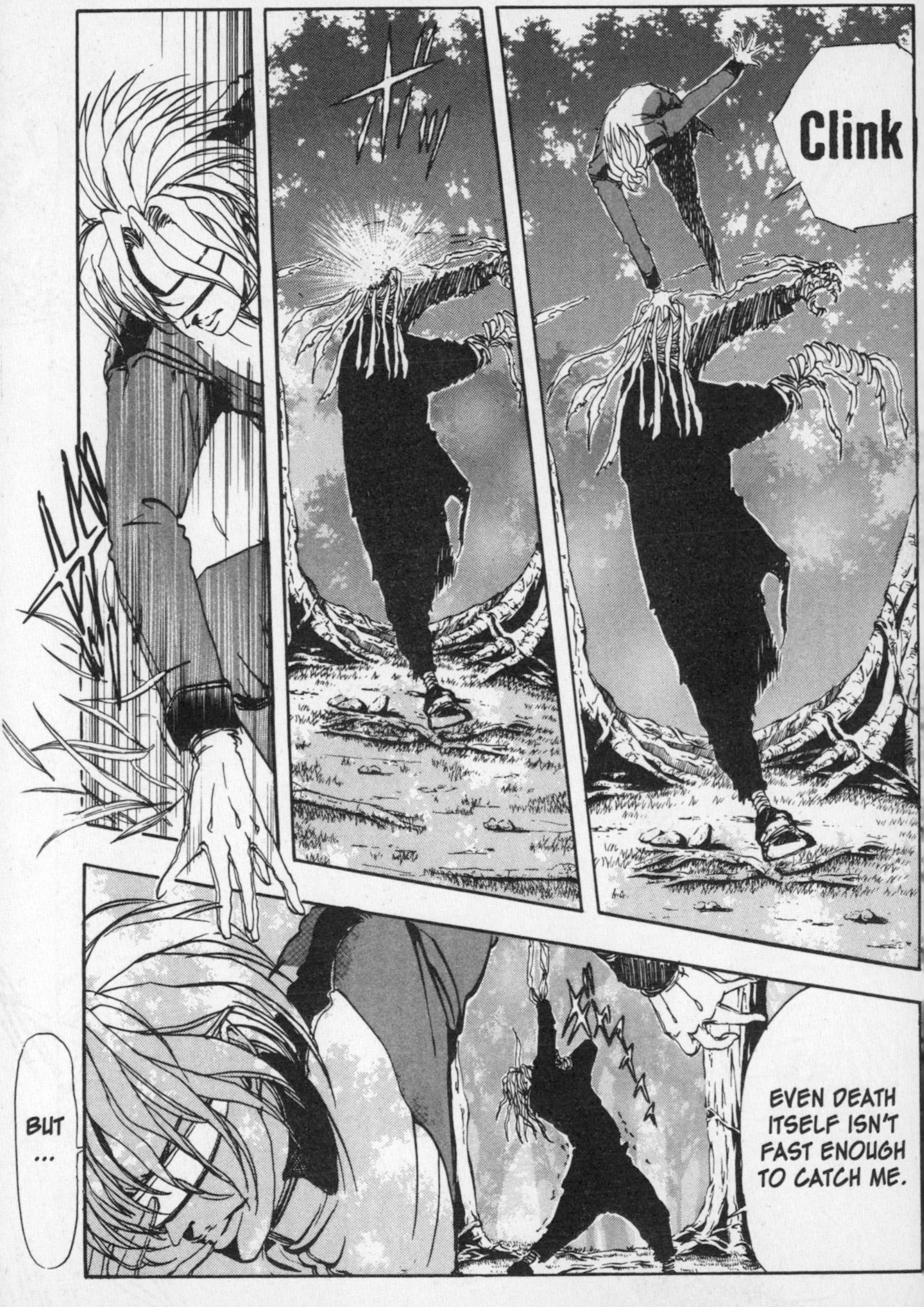
Clink
EVEN DEATH ITSELF ISN'T FAST ENOUGH TO CATCH ME.
BUT ...

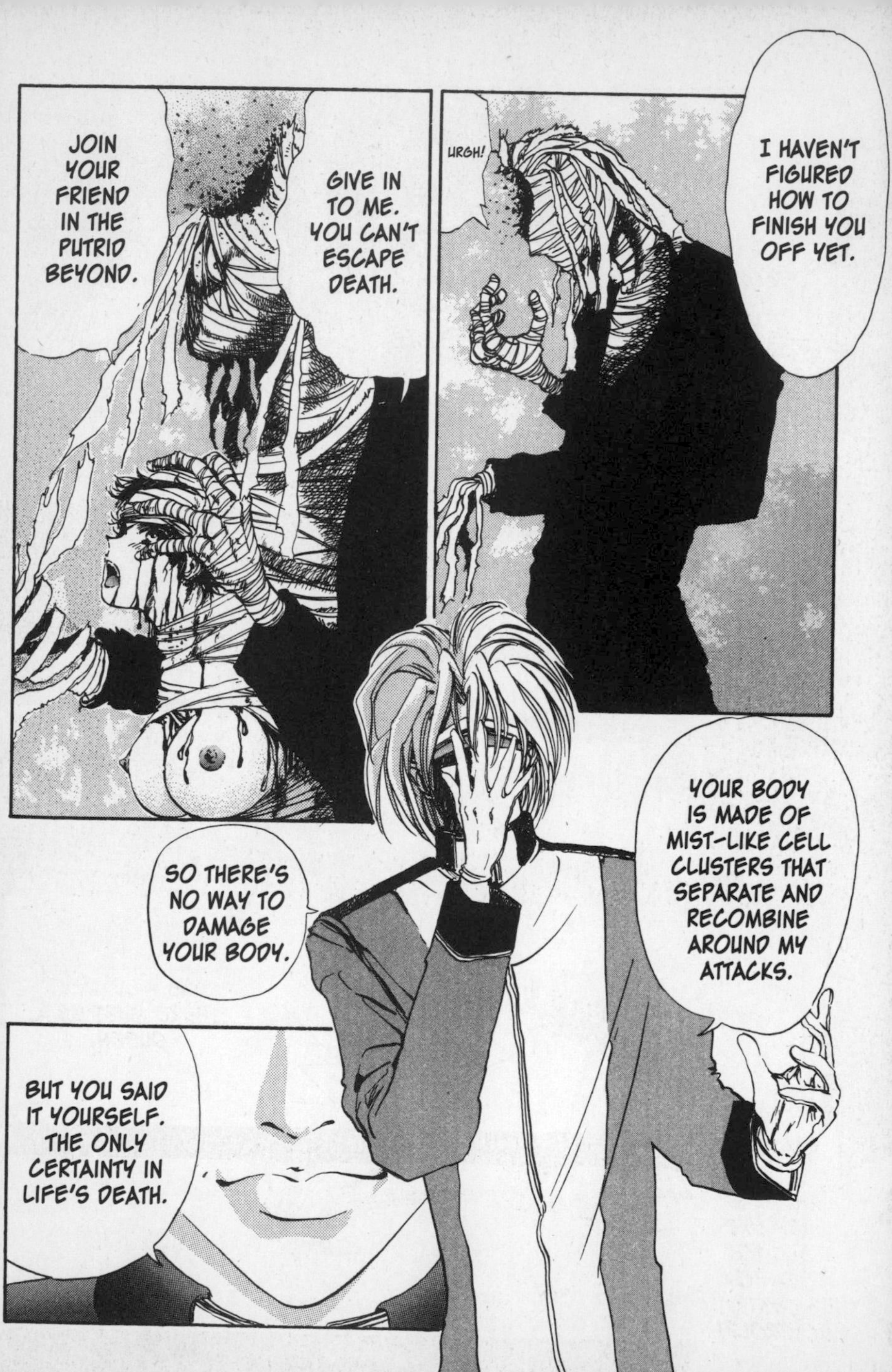
I HAVEN'T FIGURED HOW TO FINISH YOU OFF YET.
URGH!
GIVE IN TO ME. YOU CAN'T ESCAPE DEATH.
JOIN YOUR FRIEND IN THE PUTRID BEYOND.
YOUR BODY IS MADE OF MIST-LIKE CELL CLUSTERS THAT SEPARATE AND RECOMBINE AROUND MY ATTACKS.
SO THERE'S NO WAY TO DAMAGE YOUR BODY.
BUT YOU SAID IT YOURSELF. THE ONLY CERTAINTY IN LIFE'S DEATH.

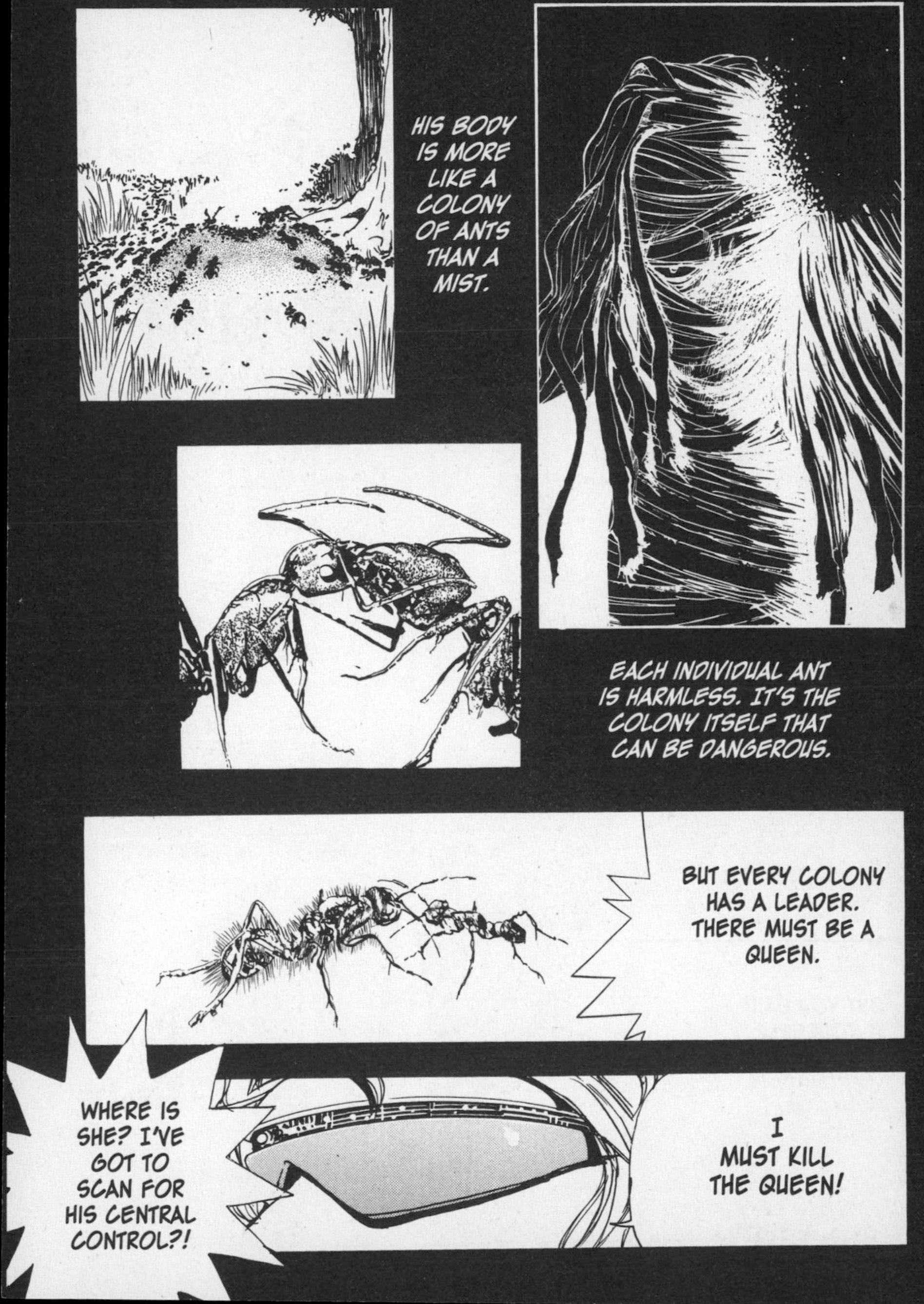
HIS BODY IS MORE LIKE A COLONY OF ANTS THAN A MIST.
EACH INDIVIDUAL ANT IS HARMLESS. IT'S THE COLONY ITSELF THAT CAN BE DANGEROUS.
BUT EVERY COLONY HAS A LEADER. THERE MUST BE A QUEEN.
I MUST KILL THE QUEEN!
WHERE IS SHE? I'VE GOT TO SCAN FOR HIS CENTRAL CONTROL?!

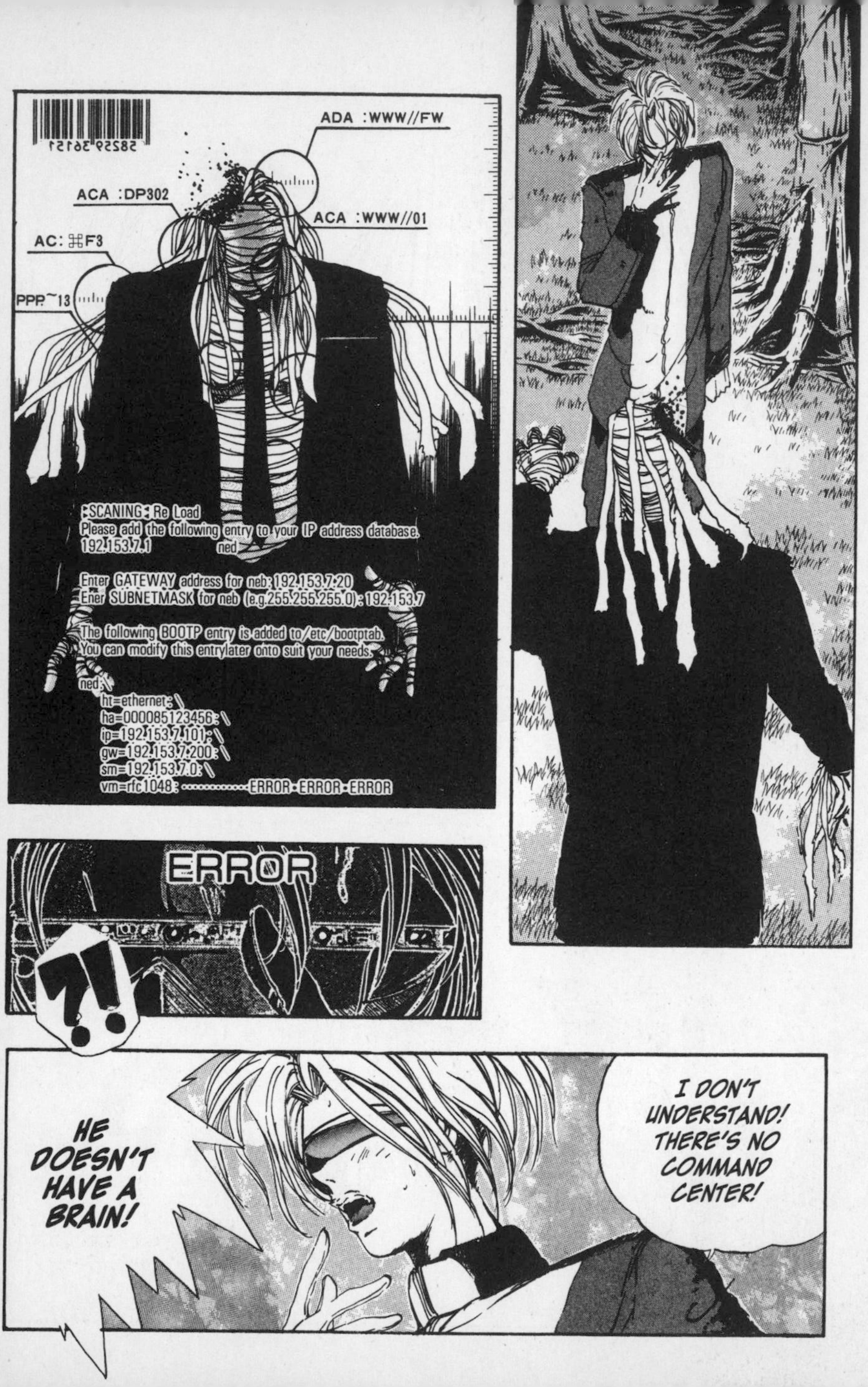
ADA :WWW//FW
ACA :DP302
ACA :WWW//01
AC: ⌘F3
PPP.~13
:SCANING: Re Load
Please add the following entry to your IP address database.
192.153.7.1 ned
Enter GATEWAY address for neb: 192.153.7.20
Ener SUBNETMASK for neb (e.g.255.255.255.0): 192.153.7
The following BOOTP entry is added to/etc/bootptab.
You can modify this entrylater onto suit your needs.
ned:\
ht=ethernet:\
ha=000085123456:\
ip=192.153.7.101:\
gw=192.153.7.200:\
sm=192.153.7.0:\
vm=rfc1048:...............ERROR-ERROR-ERROR
ERROR
?!
I DON'T UNDERSTAND! THERE'S NO COMMAND CENTER!
HE DOESN'T HAVE A BRAIN!

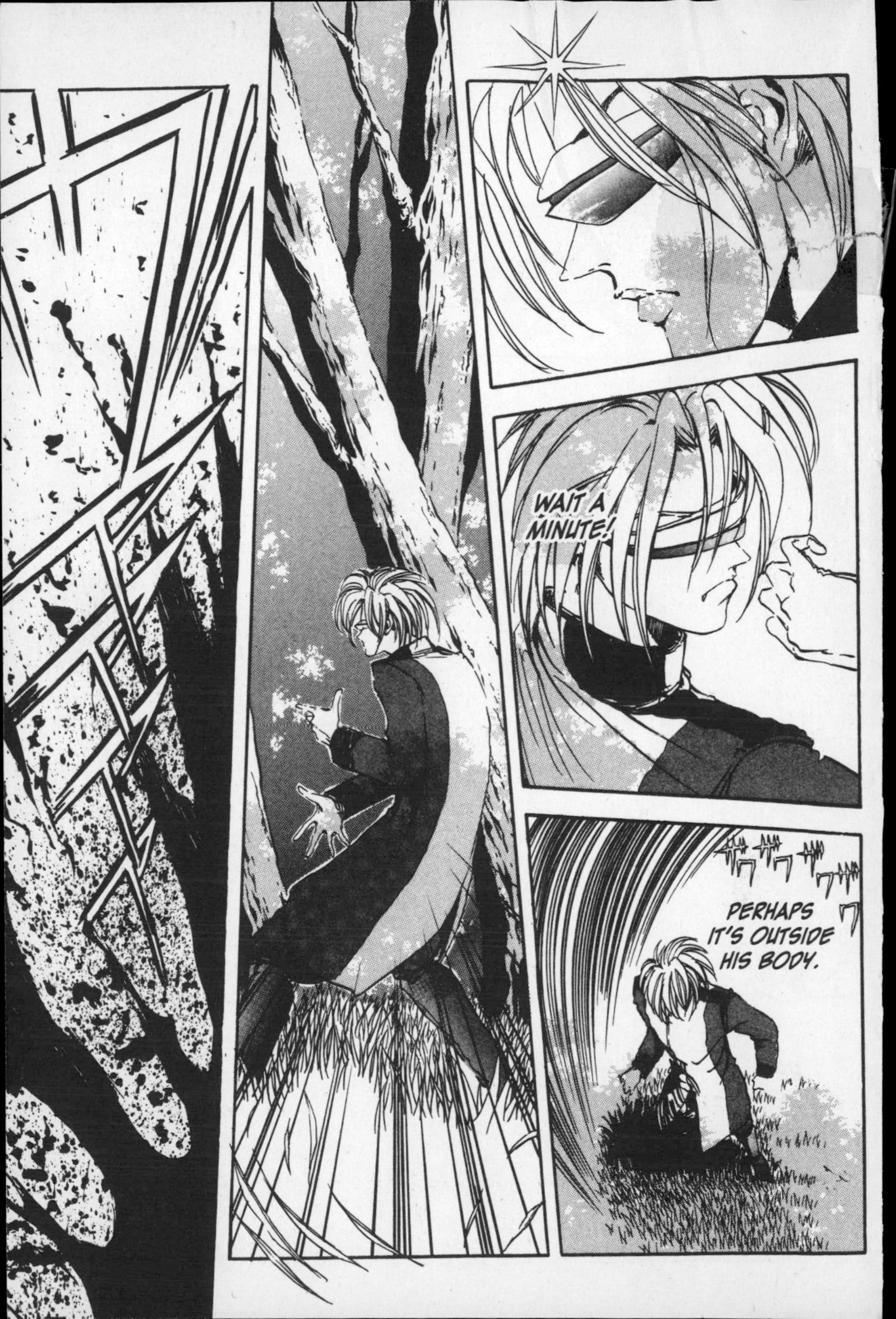
WAIT A MINUTE!
PERHAPS IT'S OUTSIDE HIS BODY.

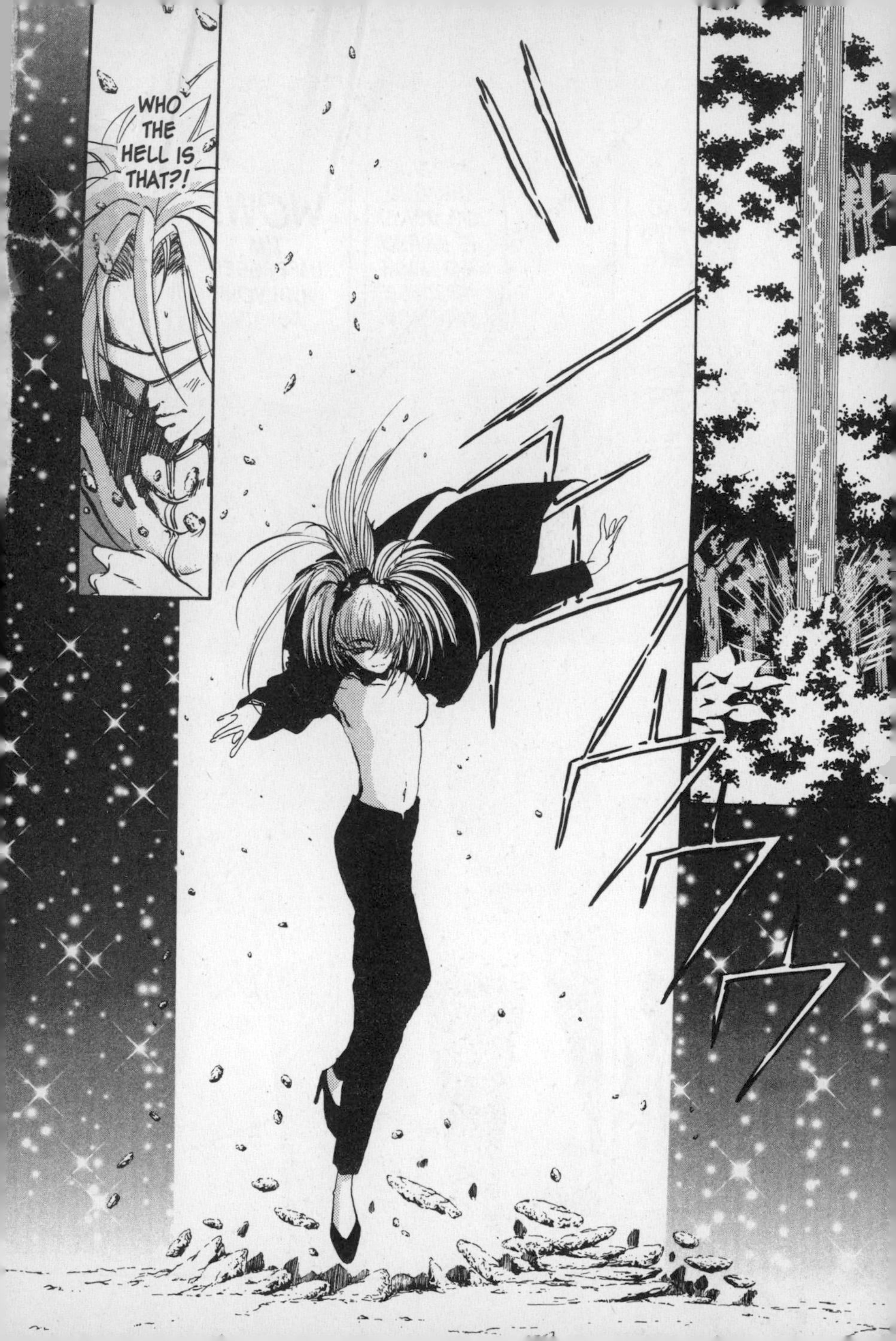
WHO THE HELL IS THAT?!

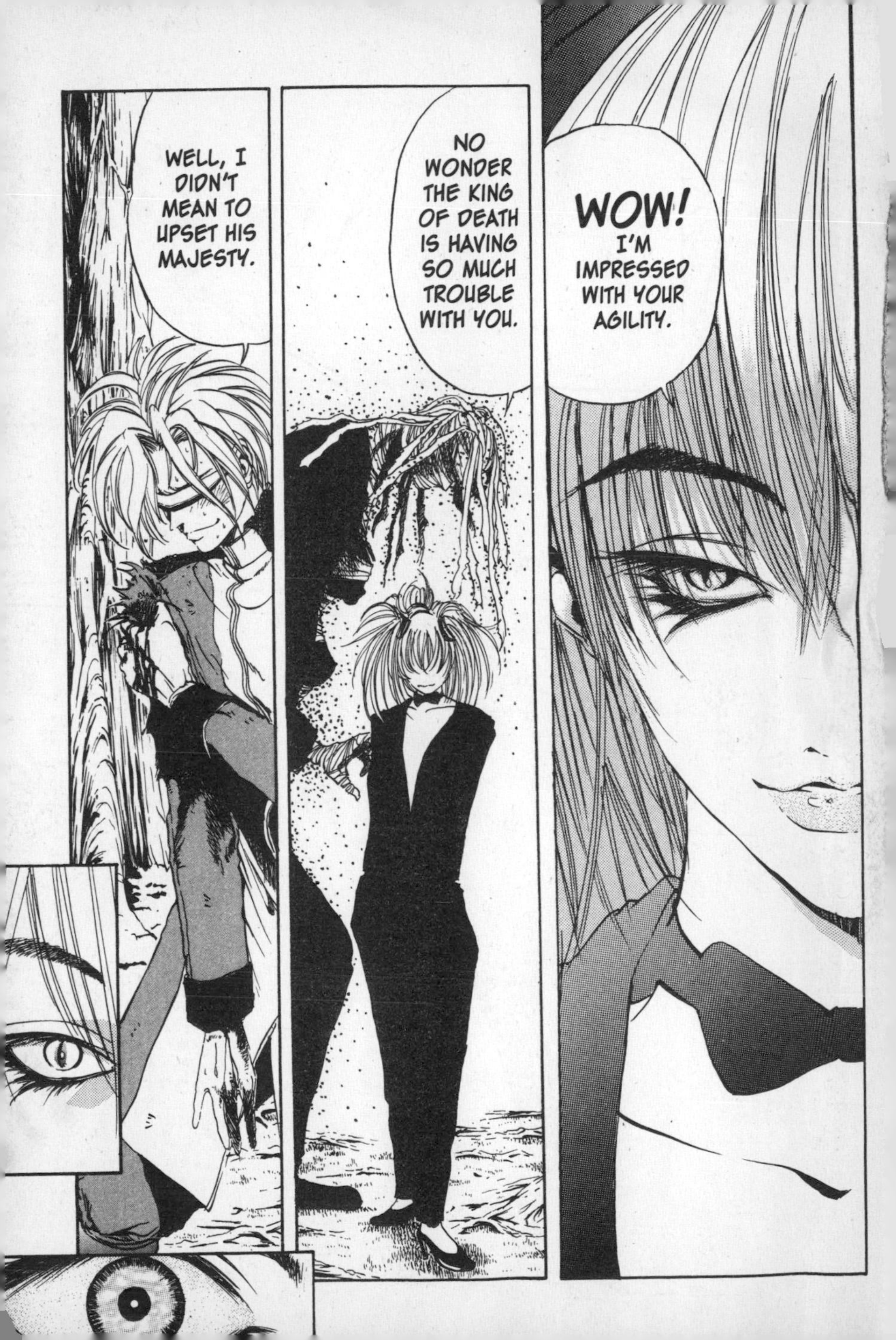
WOW! I'M IMPRESSED WITH YOUR AGILITY.
NO WONDER THE KING OF DEATH IS HAVING SO MUCH TROUBLE WITH YOU.
WELL, I DIDN'T MEAN TO UPSET HIS MAJESTY.

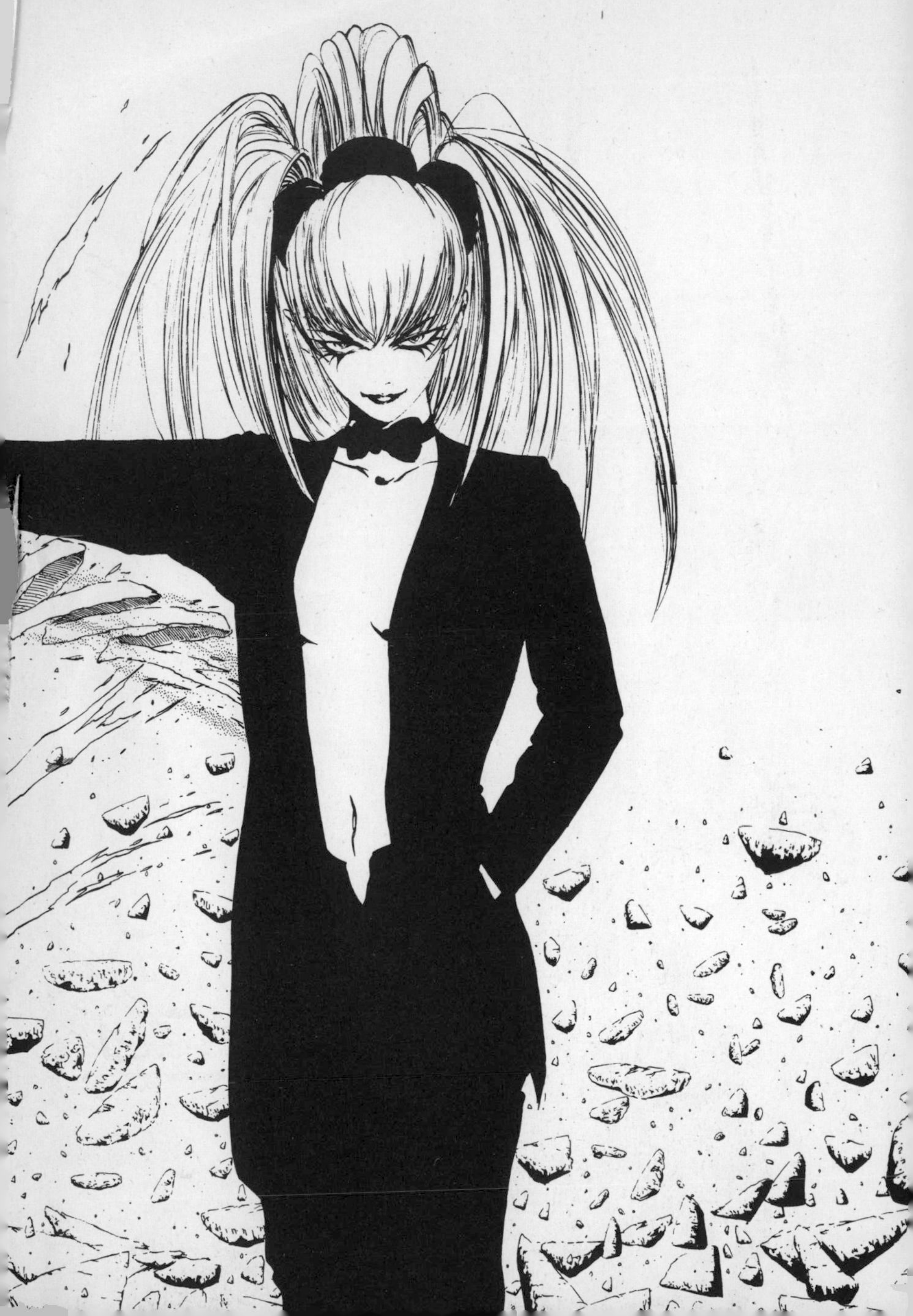

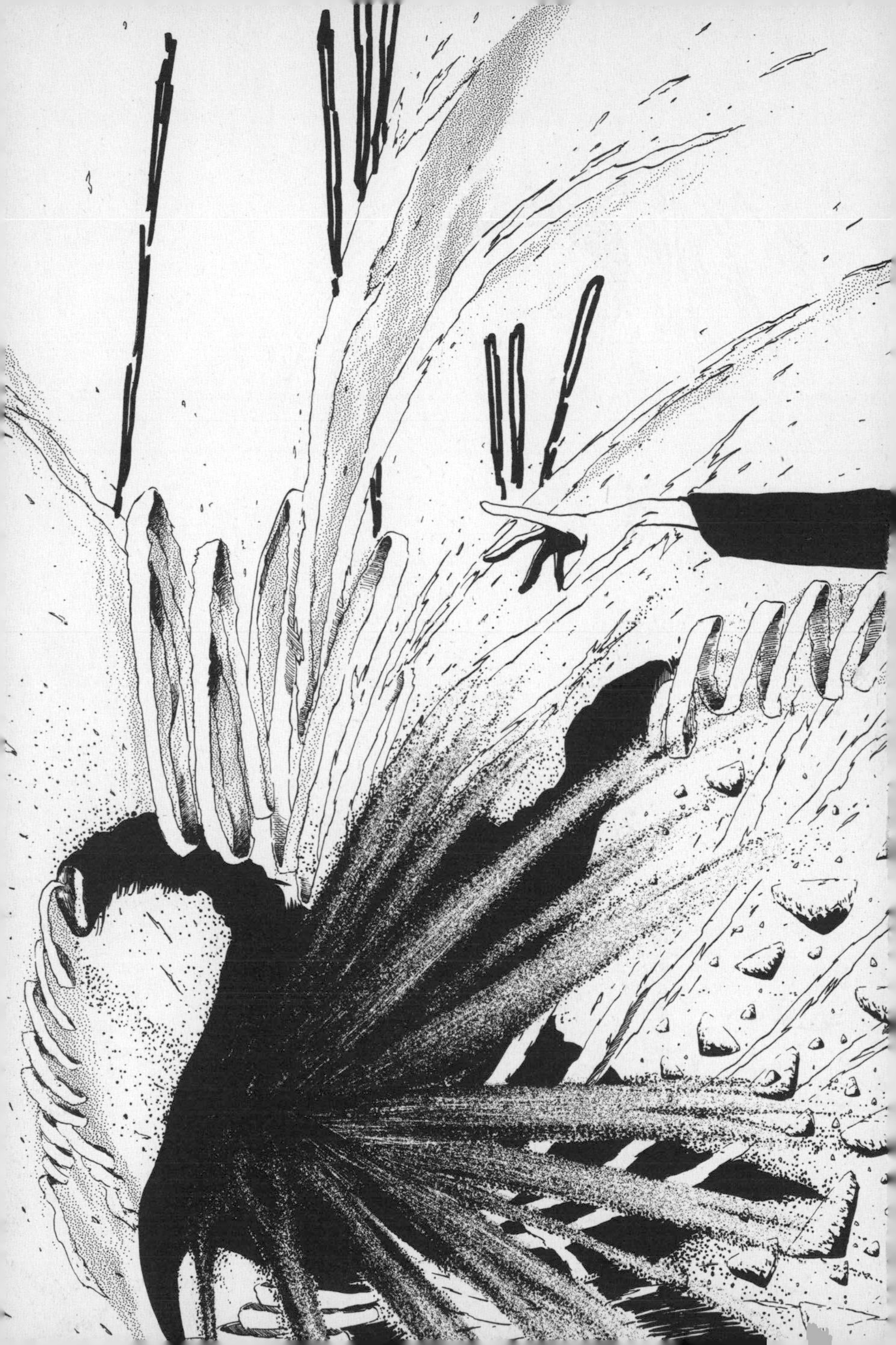

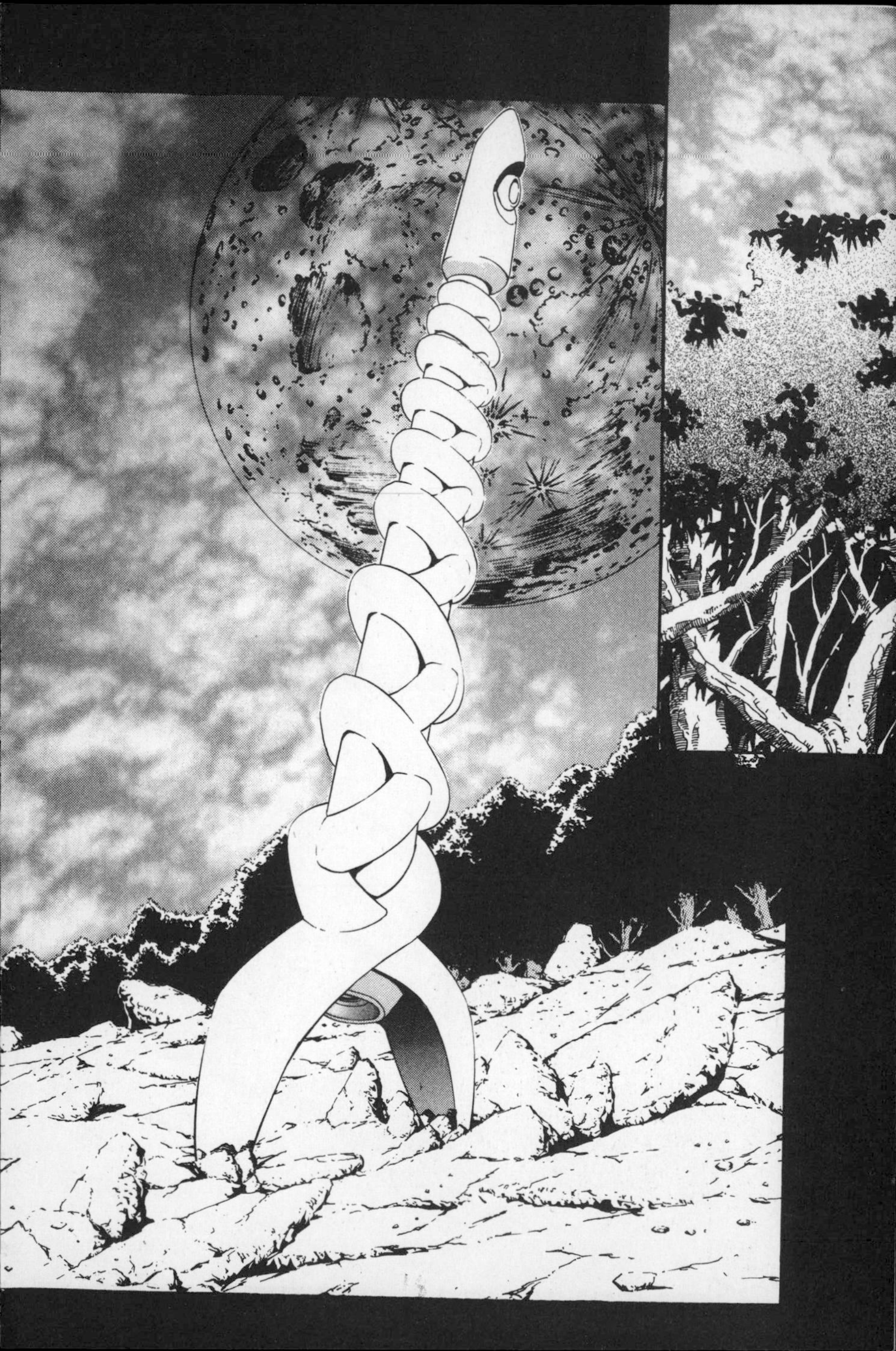

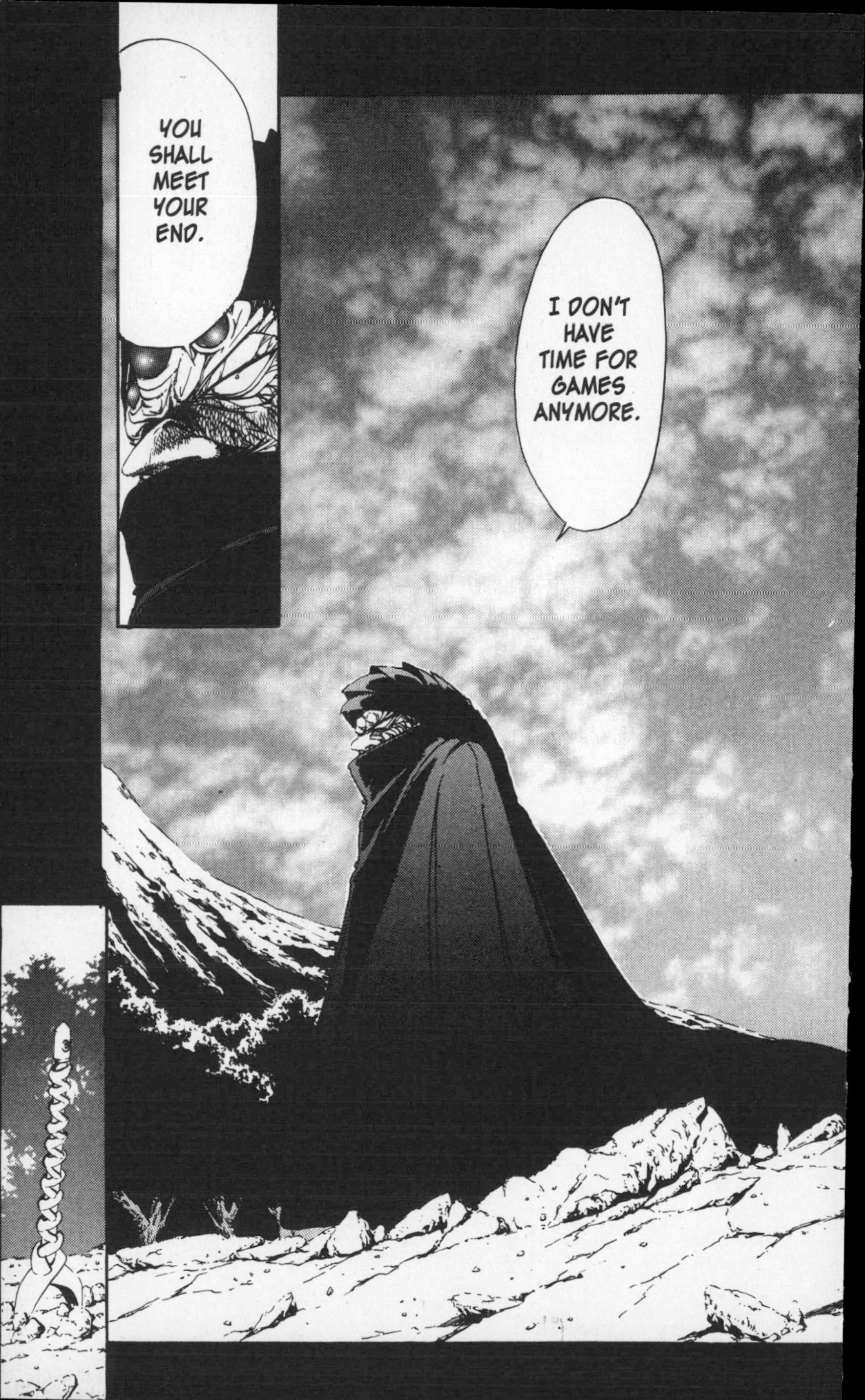
I DON'T HAVE TIME FOR GAMES ANYMORE.
YOU SHALL MEET YOUR END.

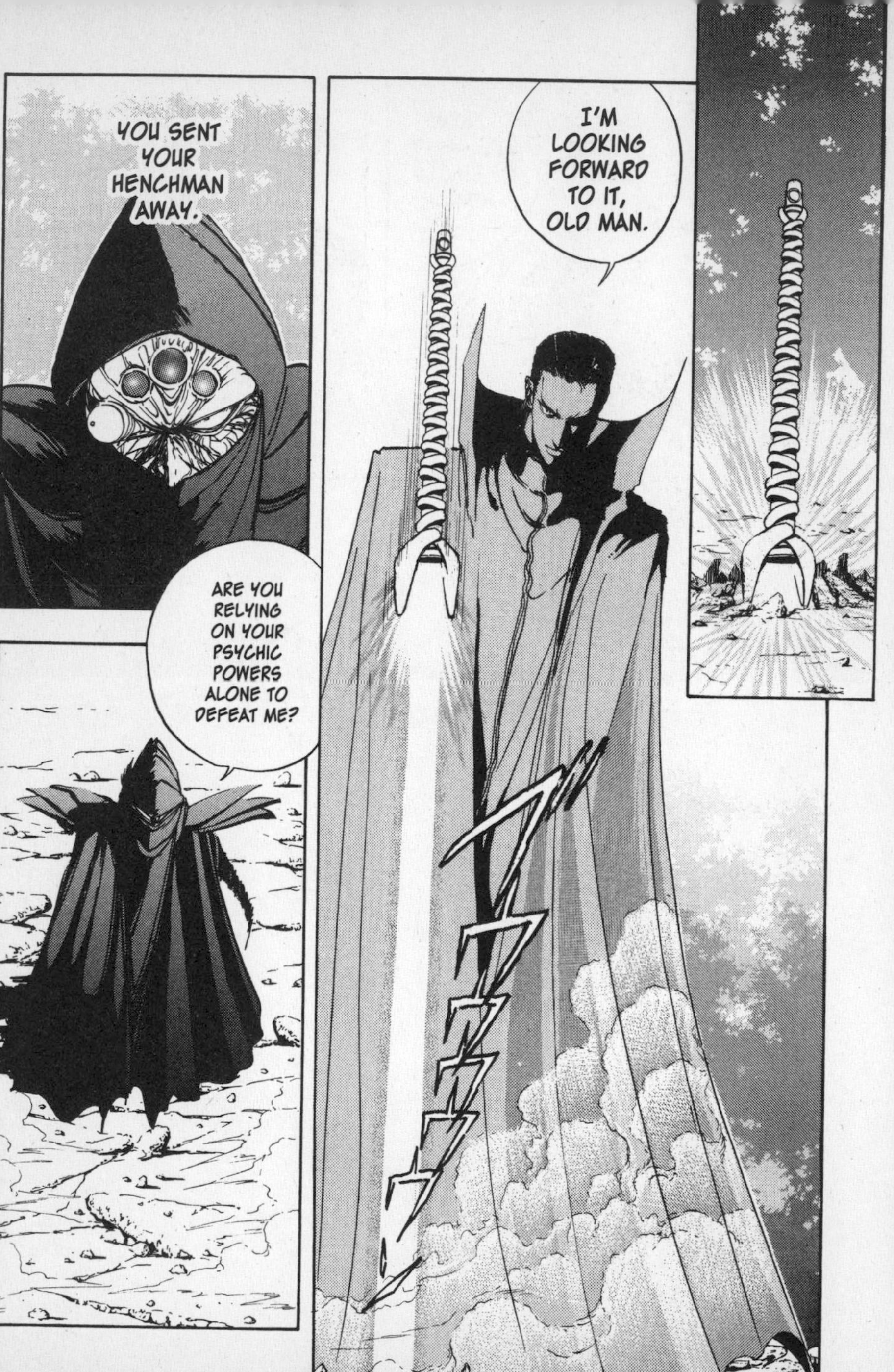
I'M LOOKING FORWARD TO IT, OLD MAN.
YOU SENT YOUR HENCHMAN AWAY.
ARE YOU RELYING ON YOUR PSYCHIC POWERS ALONE TO DEFEAT ME?

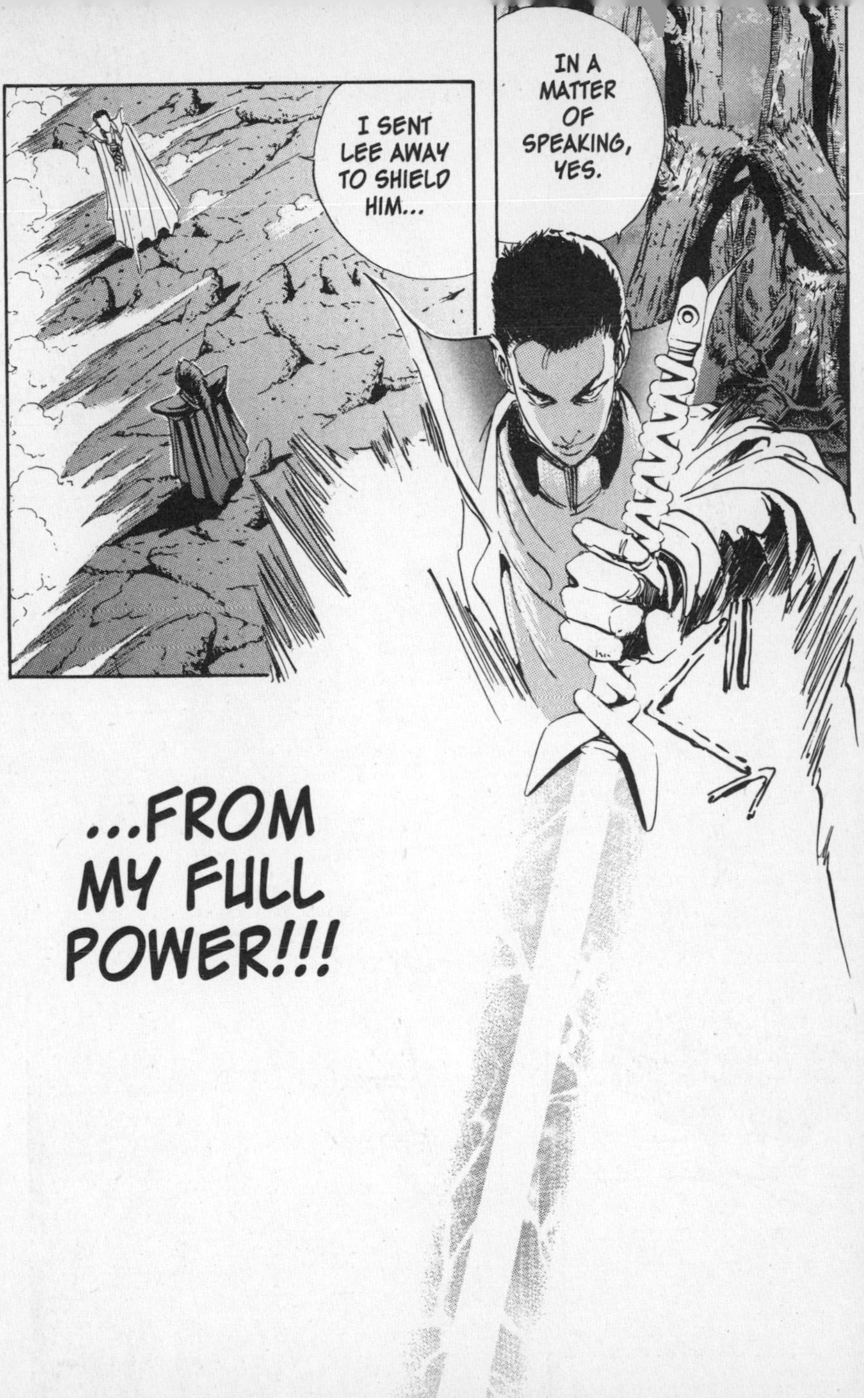
IN A MATTER OF SPEAKING, YES.
I SENT LEE AWAY TO SHIELD HIM...
...FROM MY FULL POWER!!!

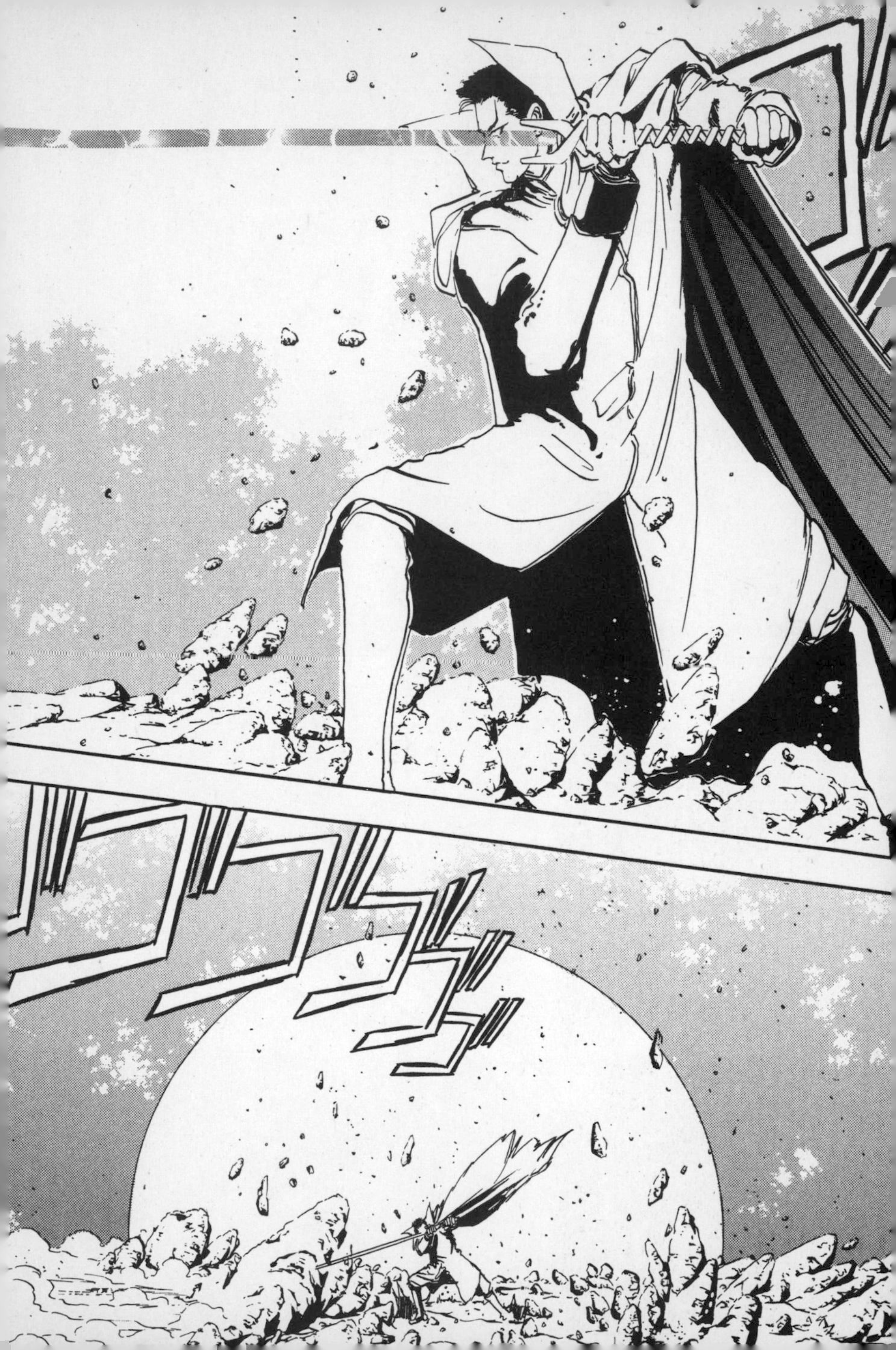

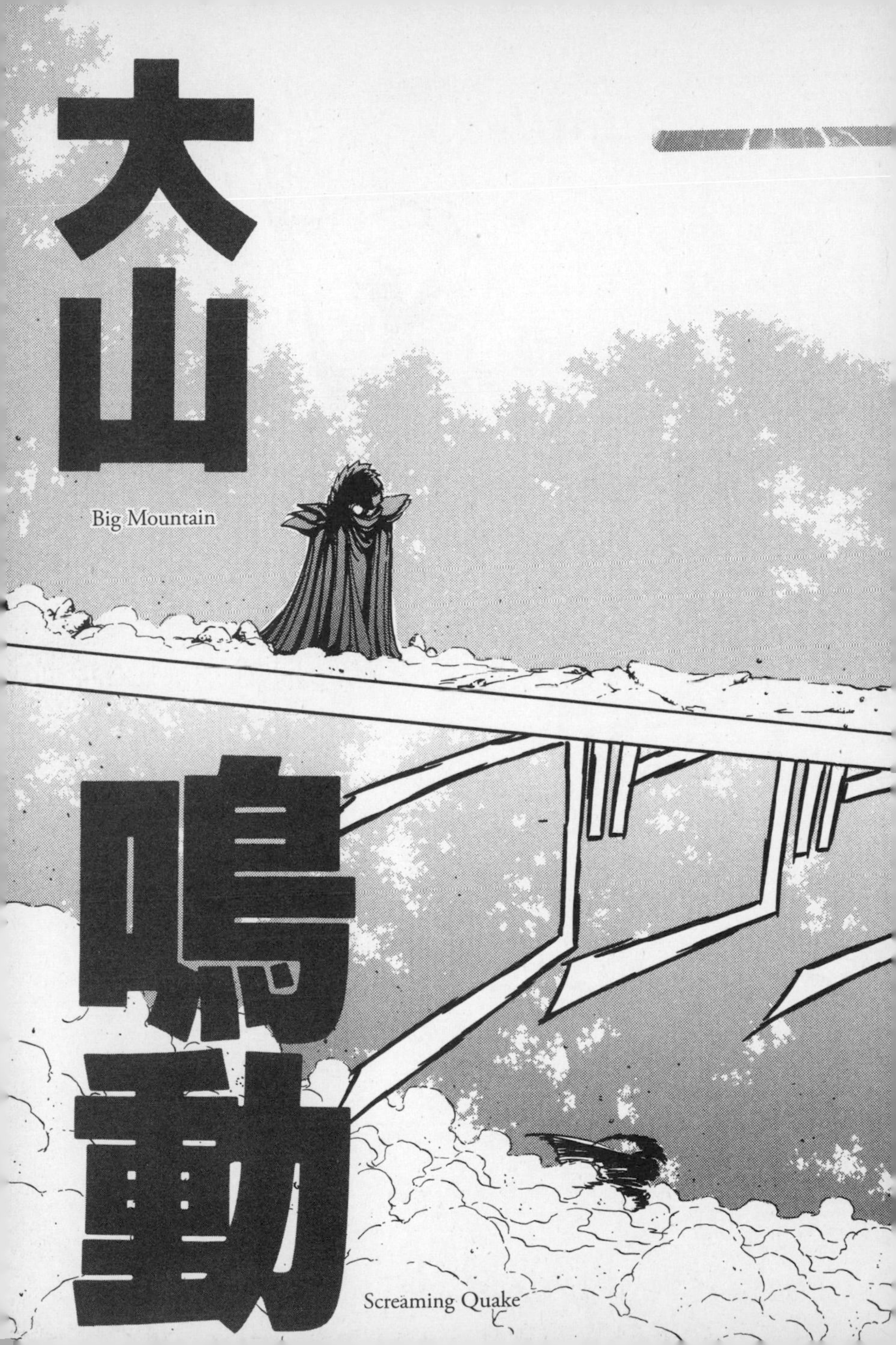

大山
Big Mountain
鳴動
Screaming Quake

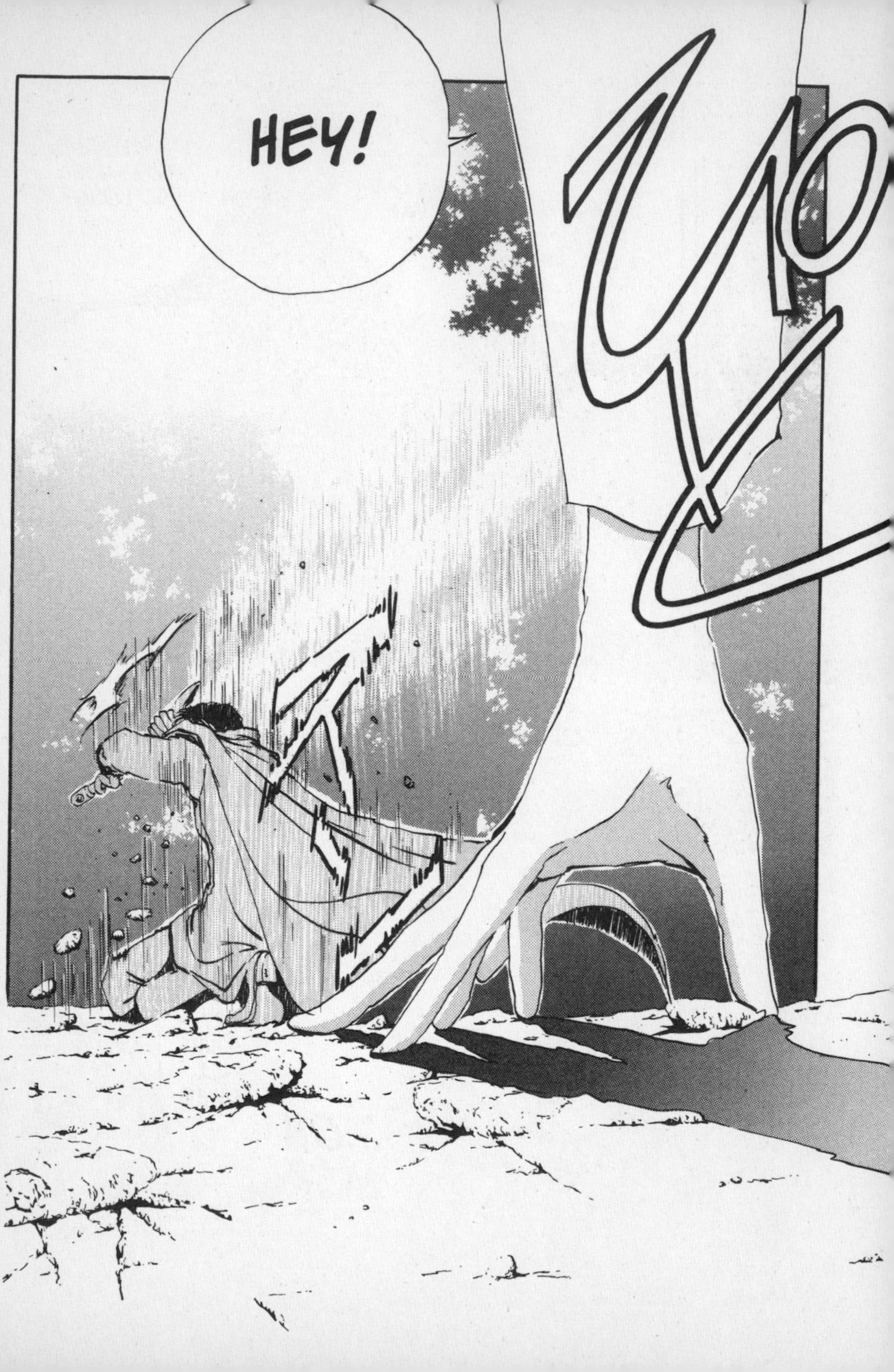
HEY!

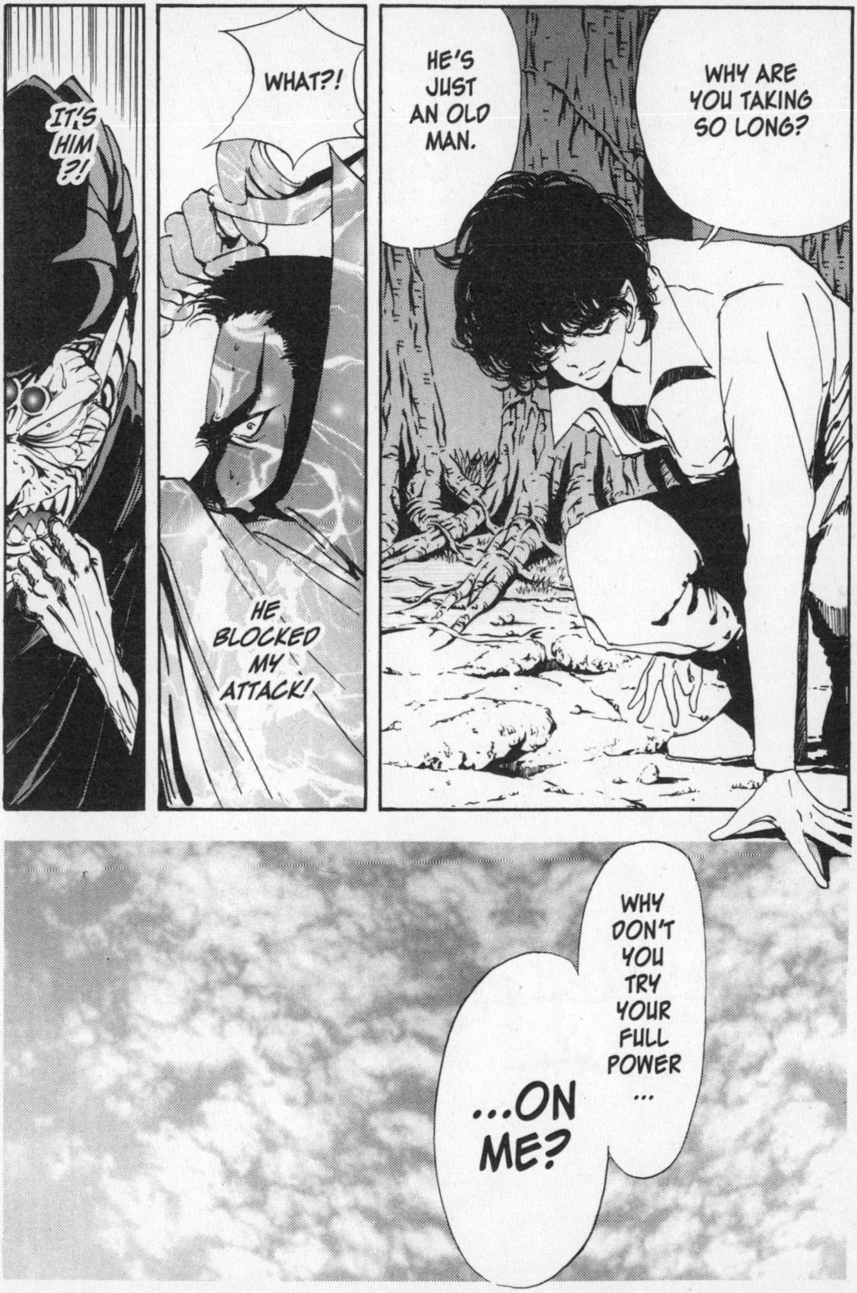
WHY ARE YOU TAKING SO LONG?
HE'S JUST AN OLD MAN.
WHAT?!
HE BLOCKED MY ATTACK!
IT'S HIM ?!
WHY DON'T YOU TRY YOUR FULL POWER ...
...ON ME?

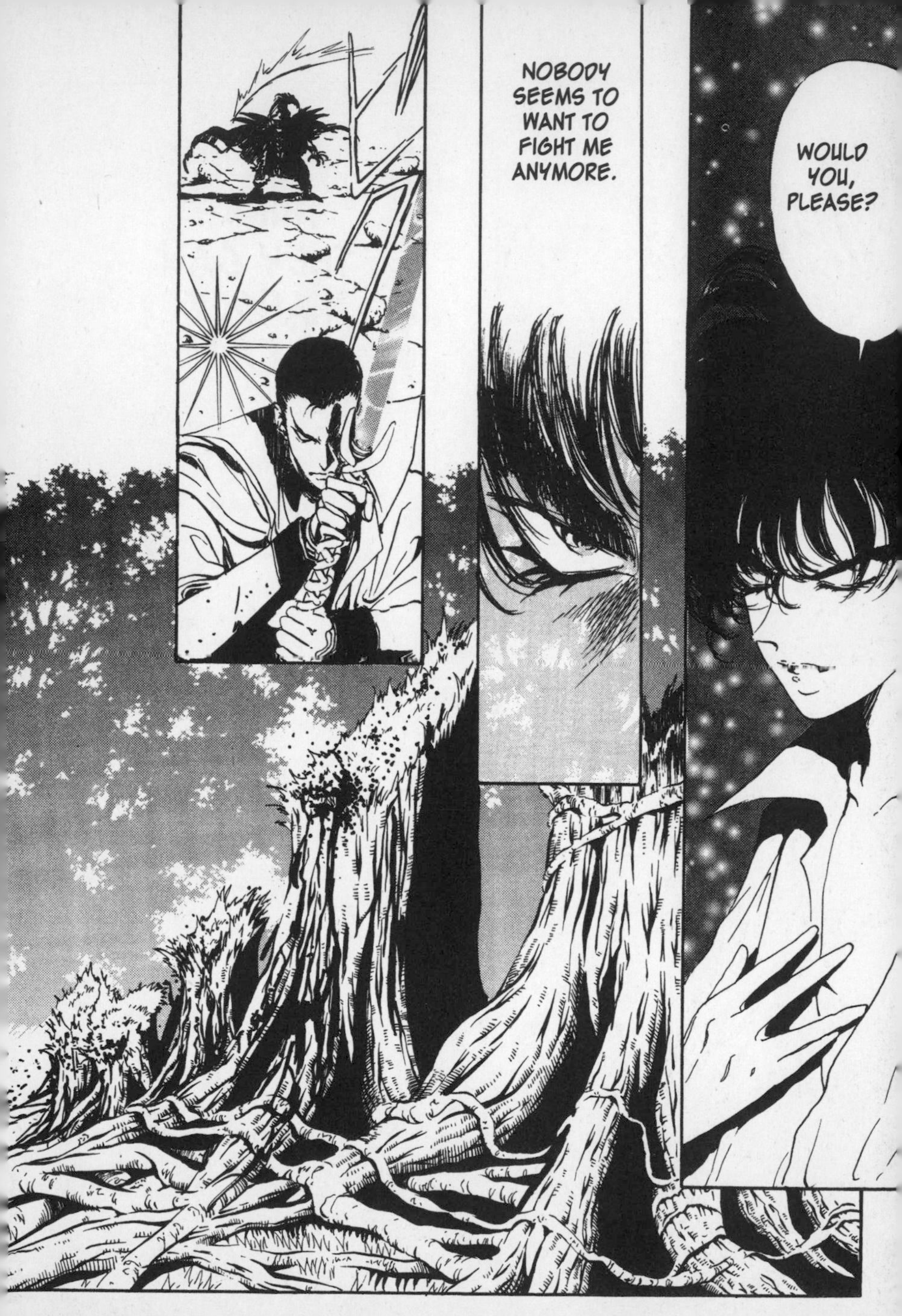
WOULD YOU, PLEASE?
NOBODY SEEMS TO WANT TO FIGHT ME ANYMORE.

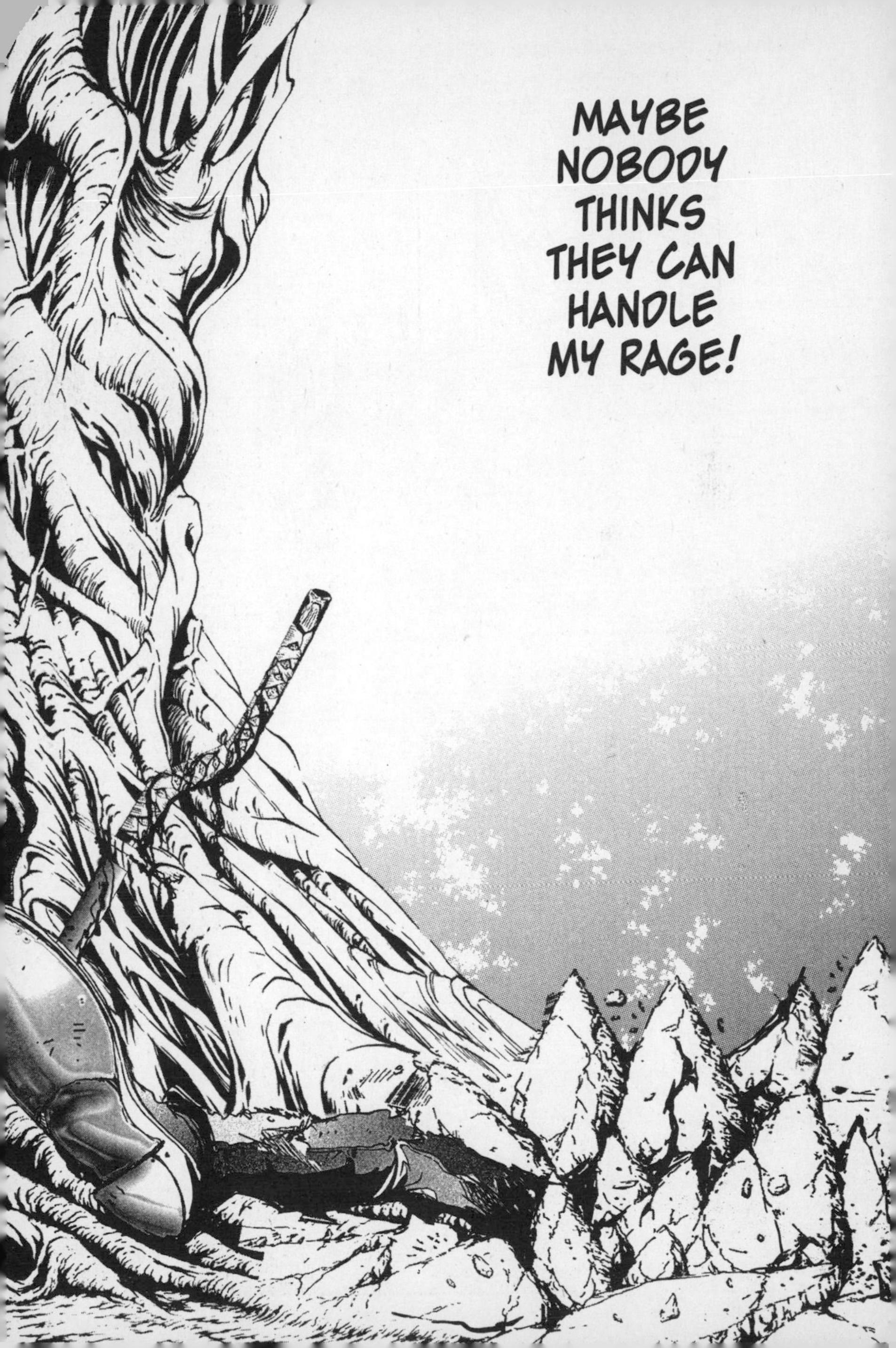
MAYBE NOBODY THINKS THEY CAN HANDLE MY RAGE!

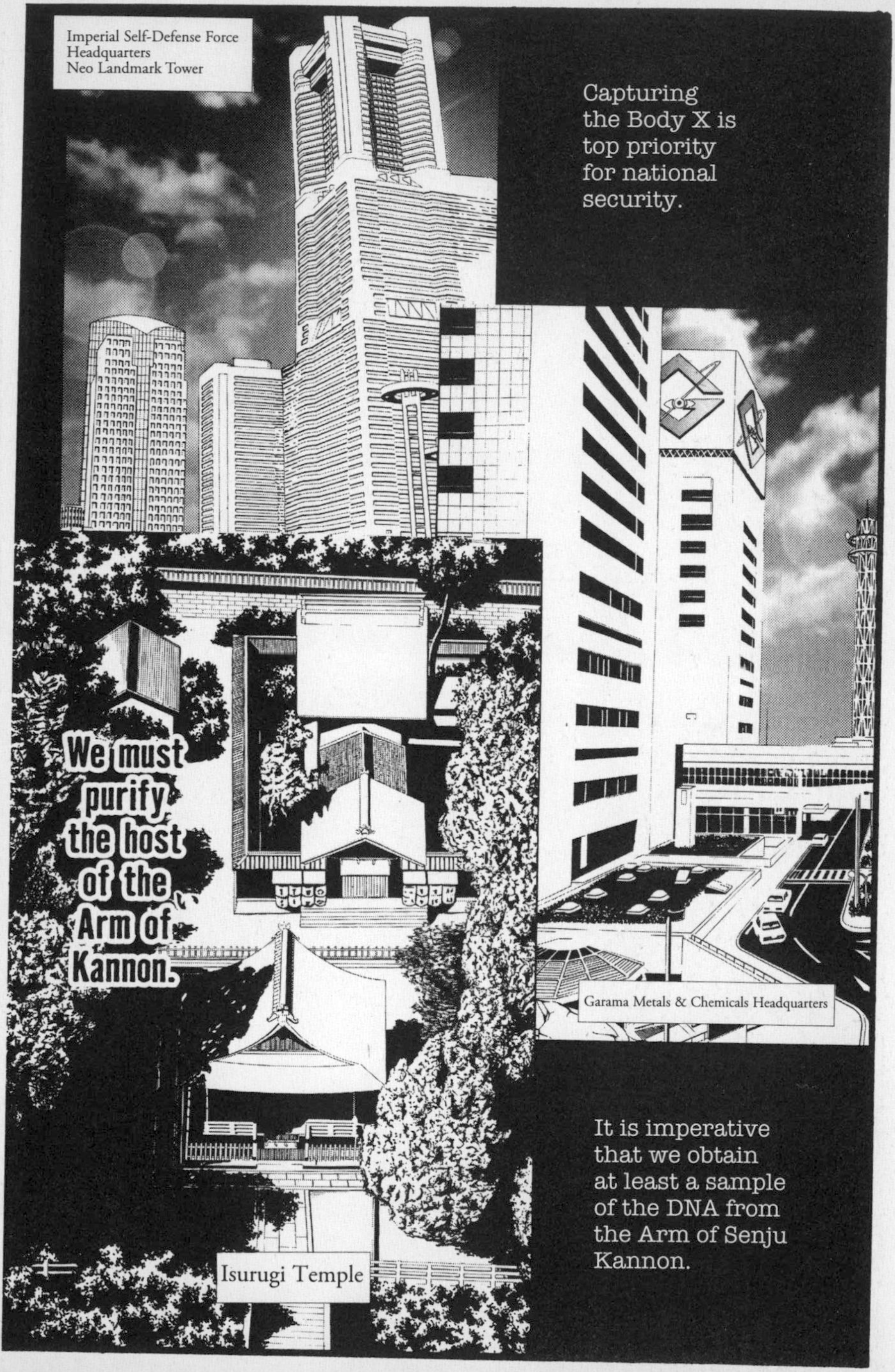
Imperial Self-Defense Force Headquarters Neo Landmark Tower
Capturing the Body X is top priority for national security.
Garama Metals & Chemicals Headquarters
It is imperative that we obtain at least a sample of the DNA from the Arm of Senju Kannon.
We must purify the host of the Arm of Kannon.
Isurugi Temple

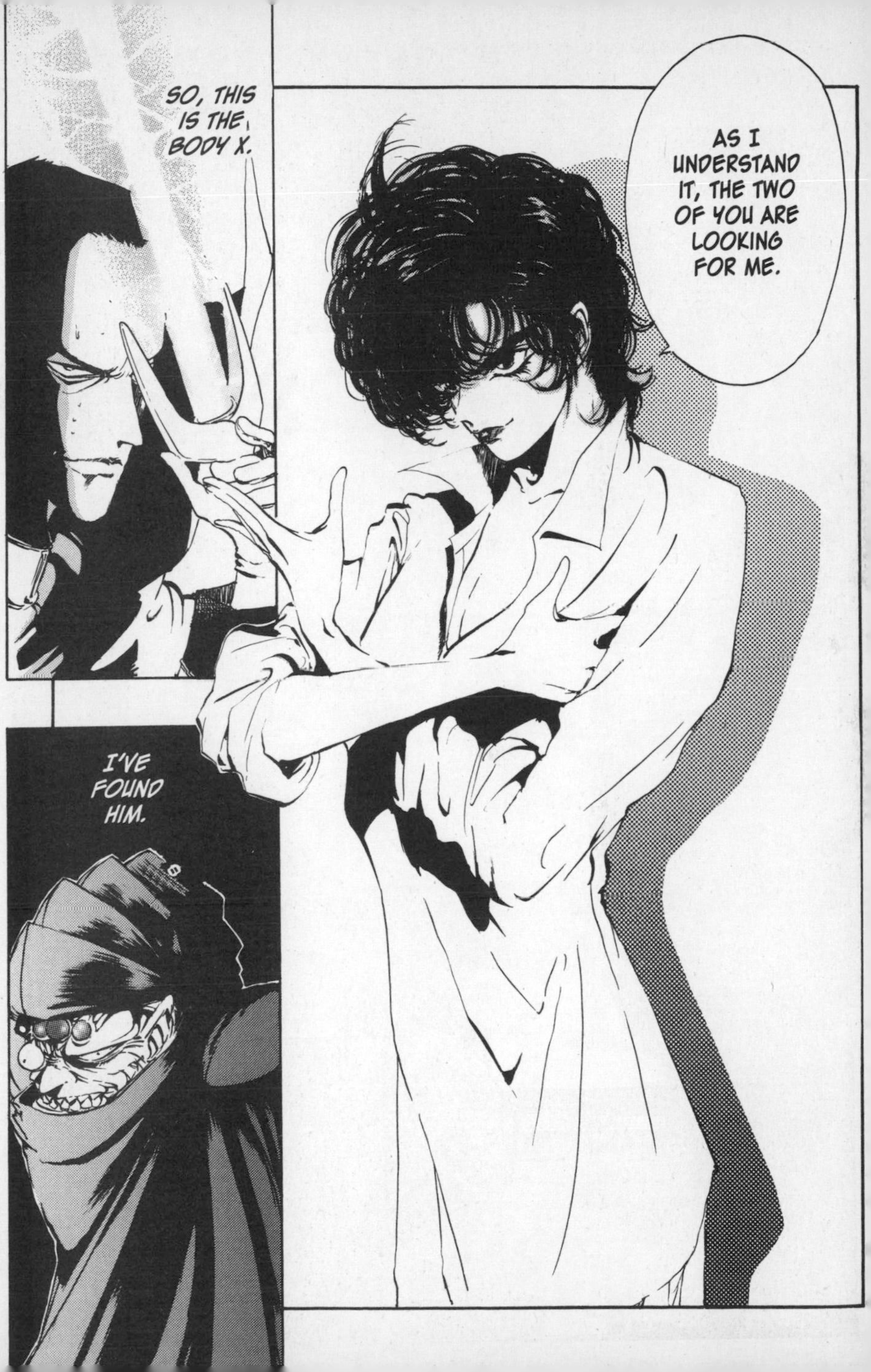
AS I UNDERSTAND IT, THE TWO OF YOU ARE LOOKING FOR ME.
SO, THIS IS THE BODY X.
I'VE FOUND HIM.

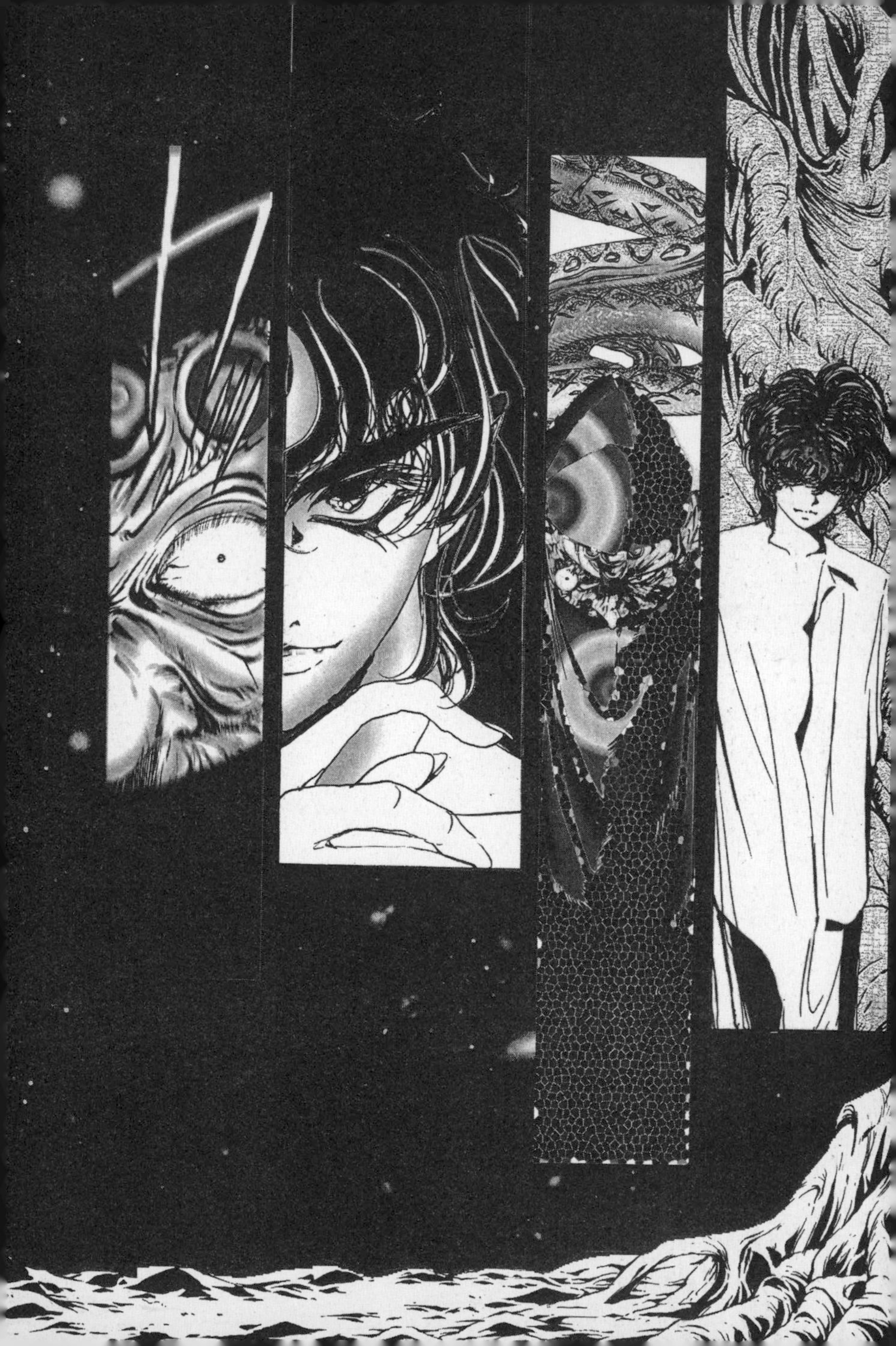

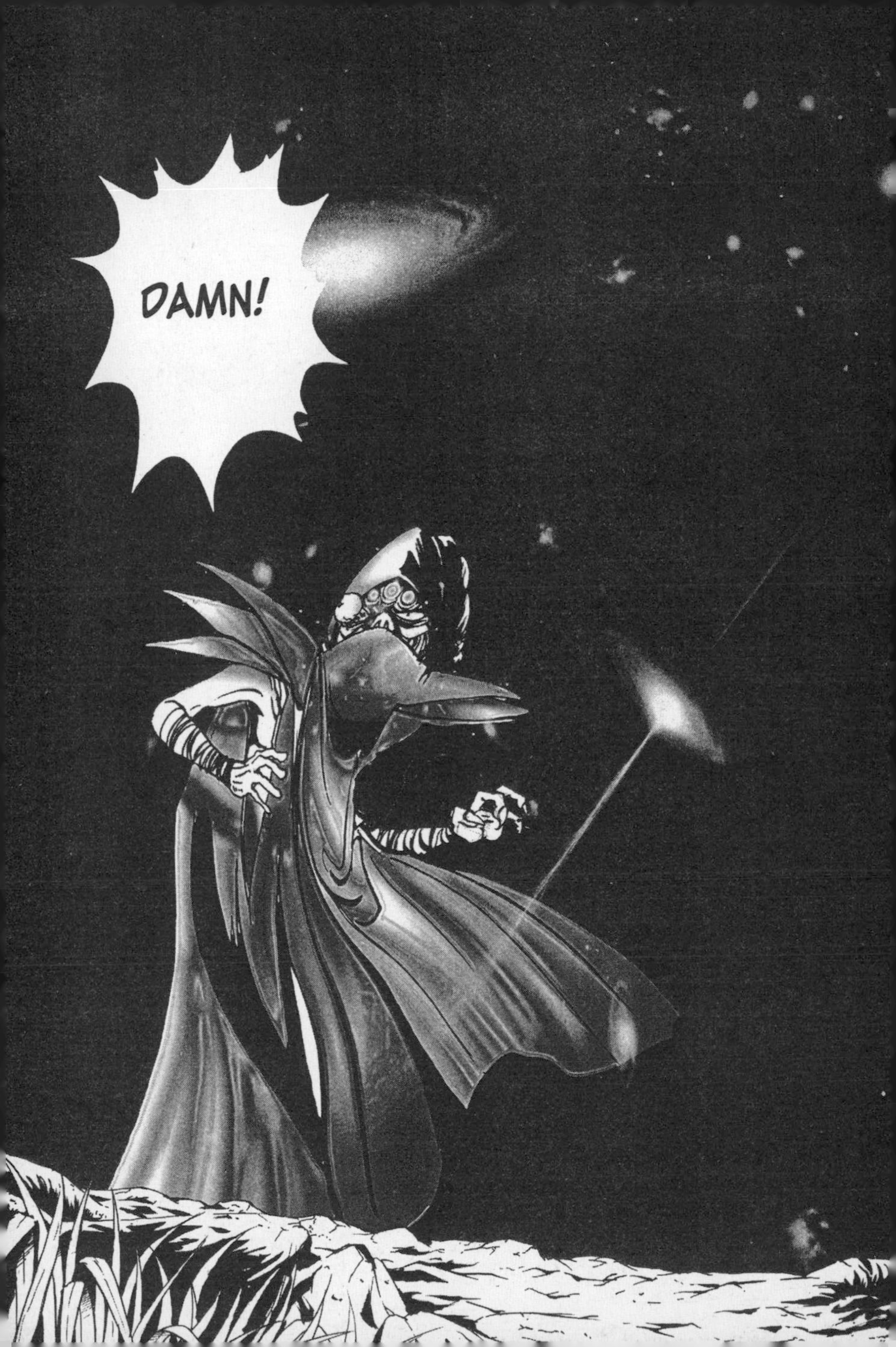
DAMN!

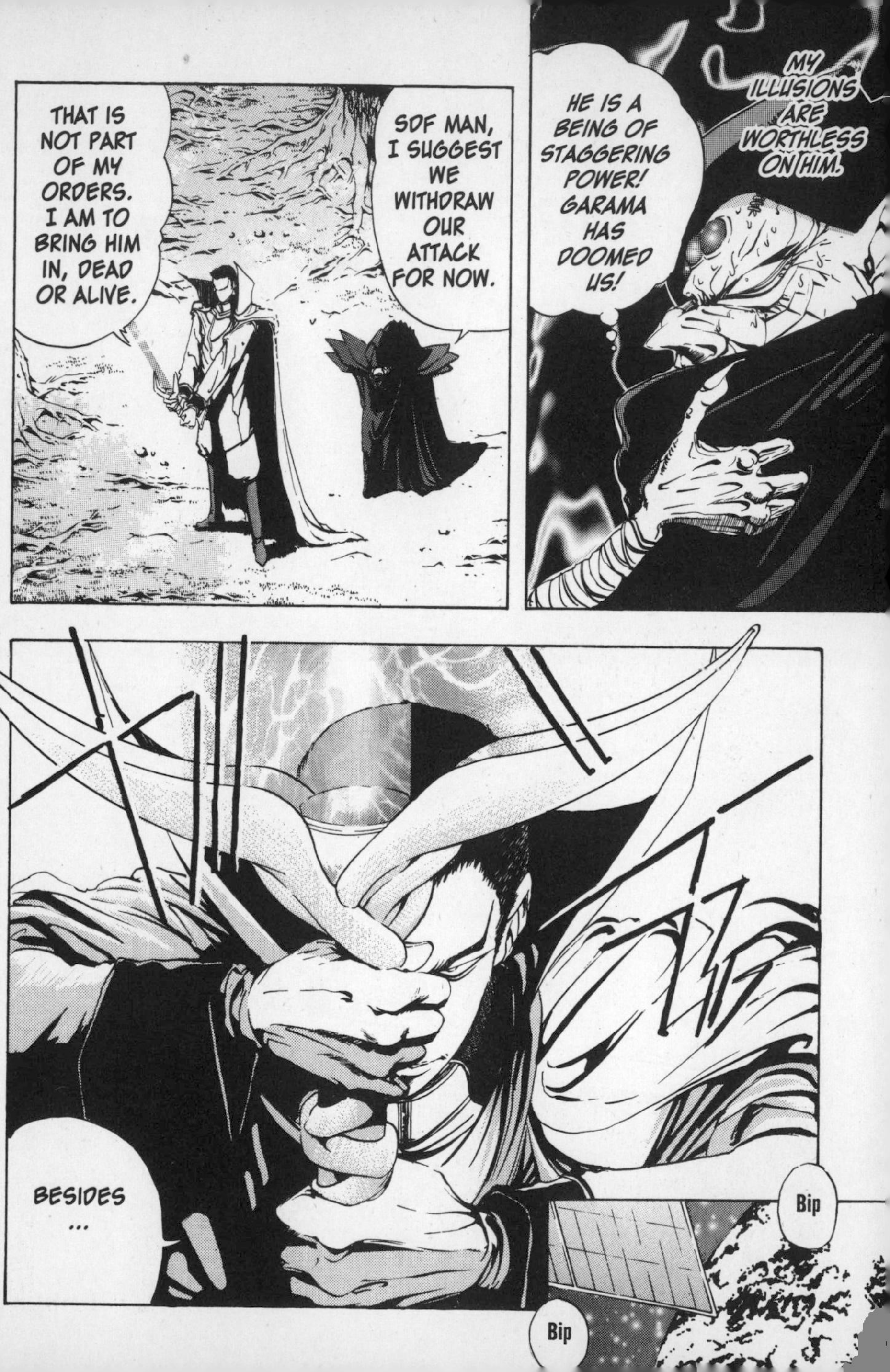
MY ILLUSIONS ARE WORTHLESS ON HIM.
HE IS A BEING OF STAGGERING POWER! GARAMA HAS DOOMED US!
SDF MAN, I SUGGEST WE WITHDRAW OUR ATTACK FOR NOW.
THAT IS NOT PART OF MY ORDERS. I AM TO BRING HIM IN, DEAD OR ALIVE.
Bip
Bip
BESIDES ...

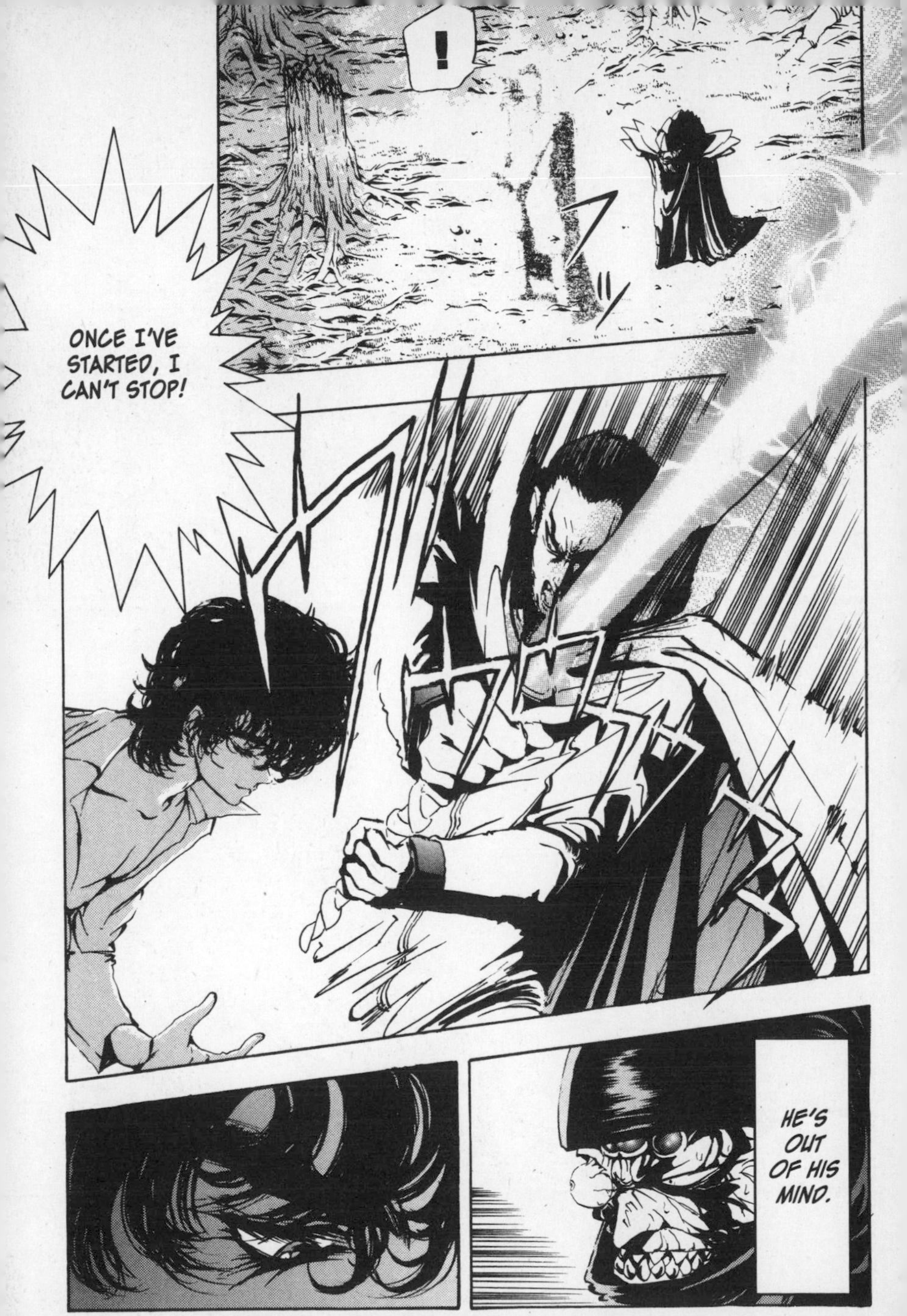
!
ONCE I'VE STARTED, I CAN'T STOP!
HE'S OUT OF HIS MIND.

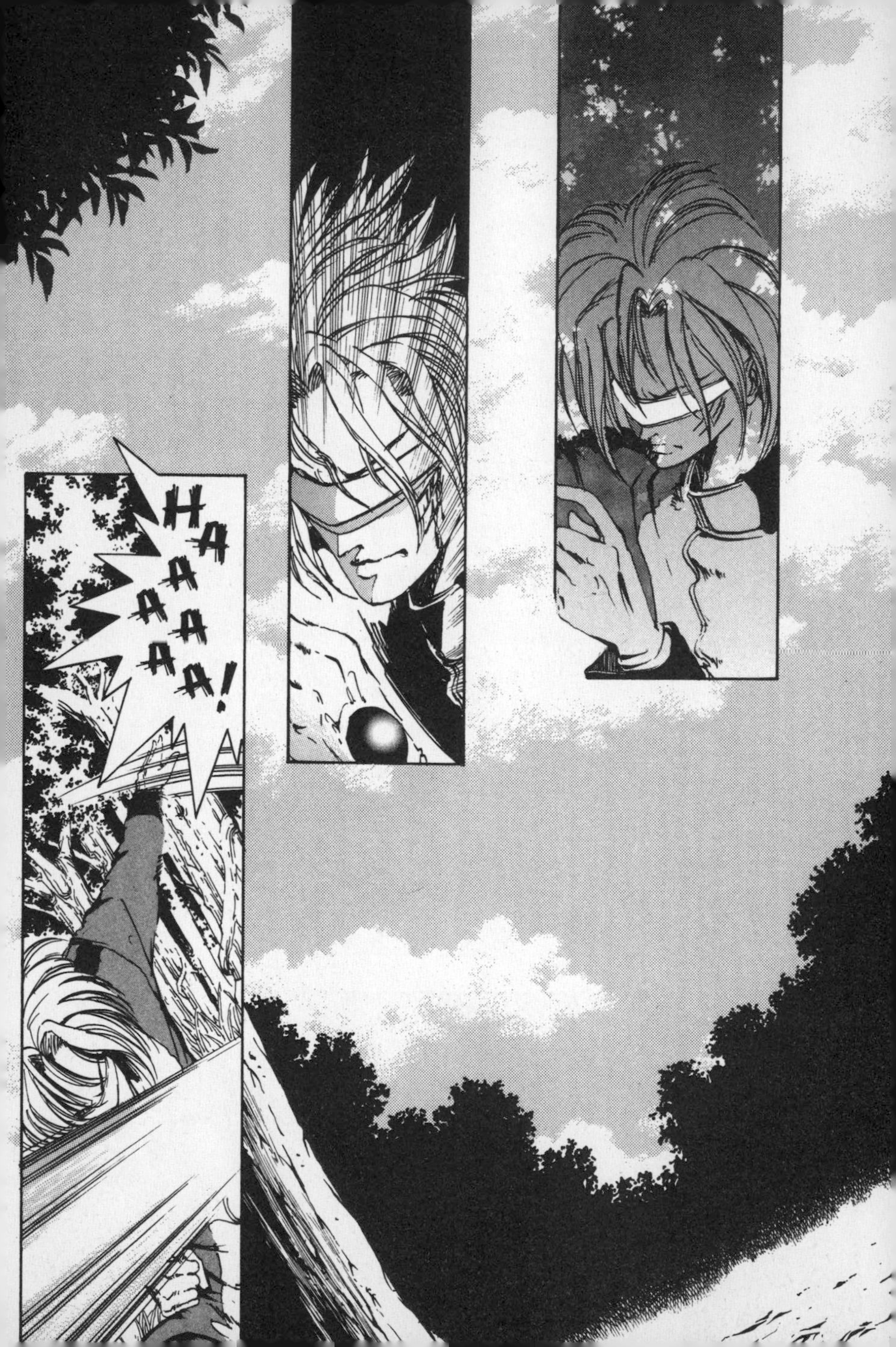
HAAAAAAA!

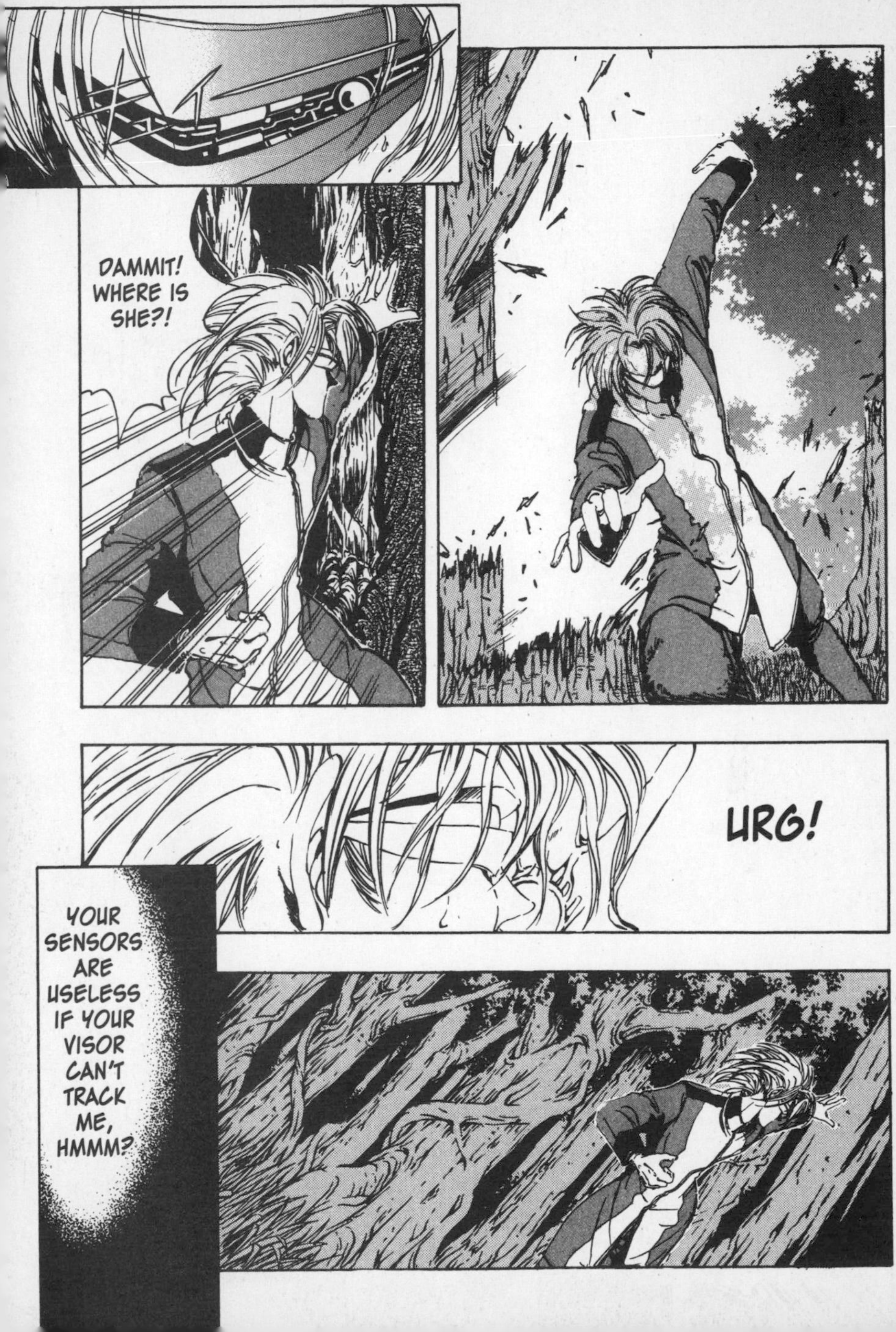
DAMMIT! WHERE IS SHE?!
URG!
YOUR SENSORS ARE USELESS IF YOUR VISOR CAN'T TRACK ME, HMMM?

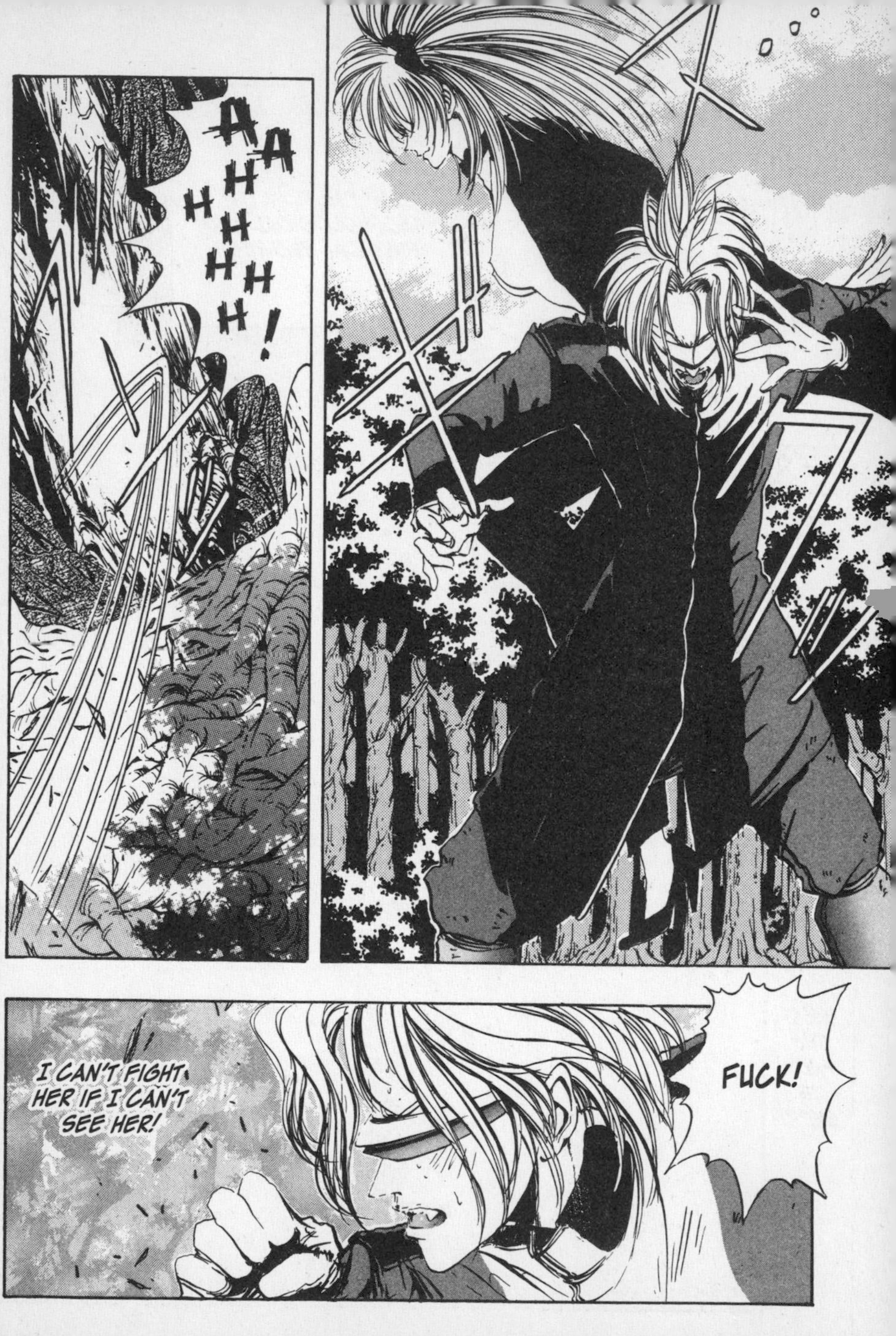
AAHHHHHHHH!
FUCK!
I CAN'T FIGHT HER IF I CAN'T SEE HER!

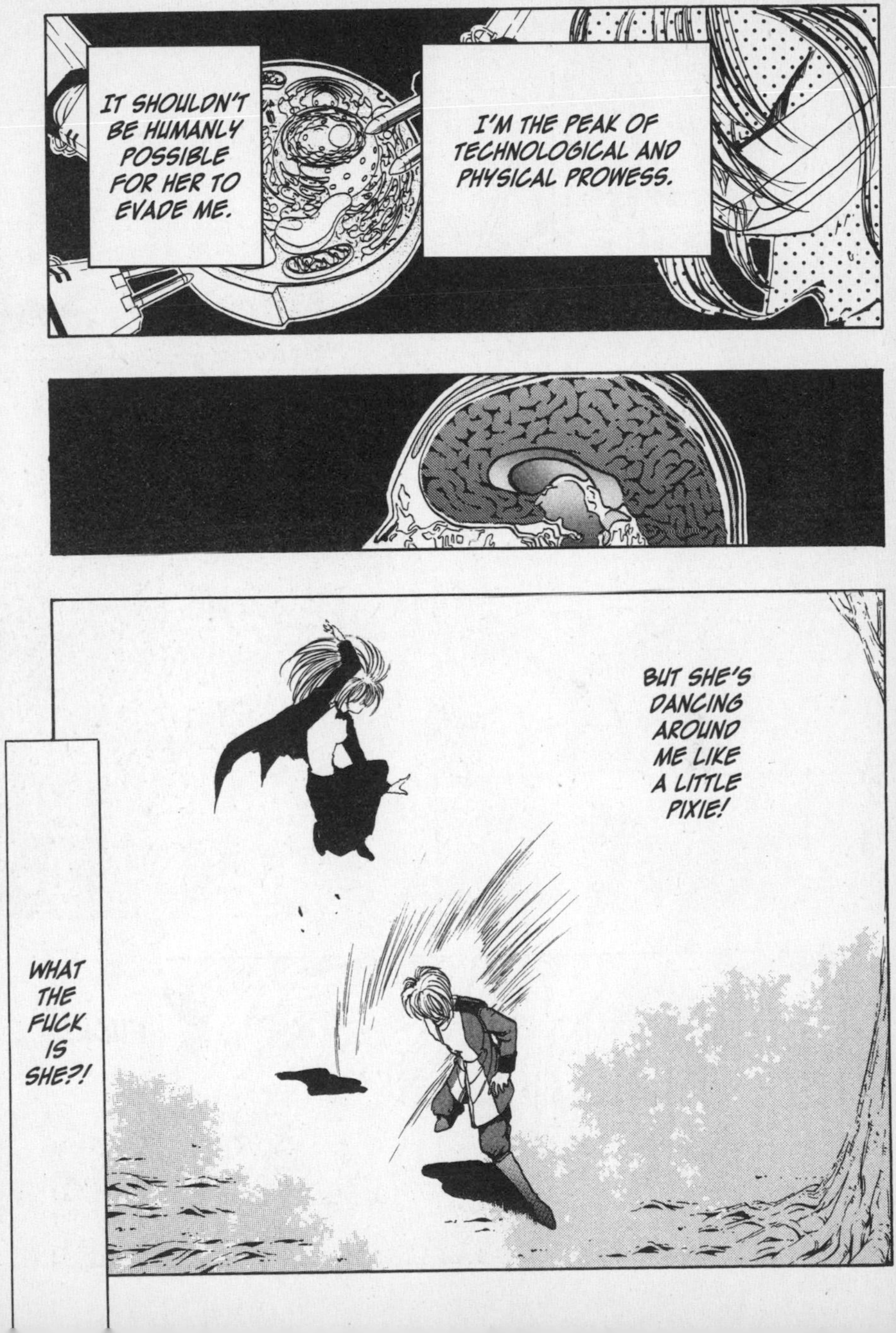
I'M THE PEAK OF TECHNOLOGICAL AND PHYSICAL PROWESS.
IT SHOULDN'T BE HUMANLY POSSIBLE FOR HER TO EVADE ME.
BUT SHE'S DANCING AROUND ME LIKE A LITTLE PIXIE!
WHAT THE FUCK IS SHE?!

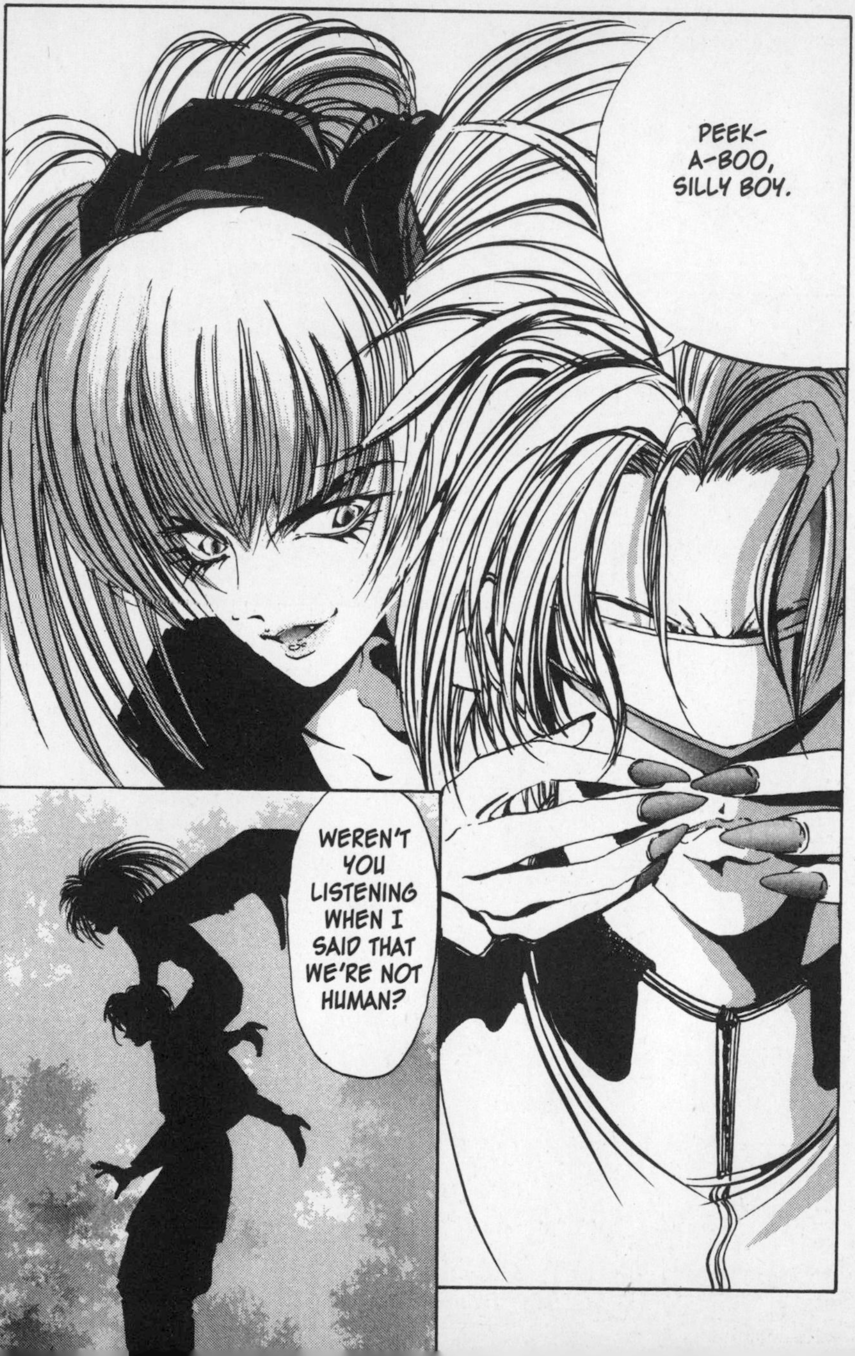
PEEK-A-BOO, SILLY BOY.
WEREN'T YOU LISTENING WHEN I SAID THAT WE'RE NOT HUMAN?

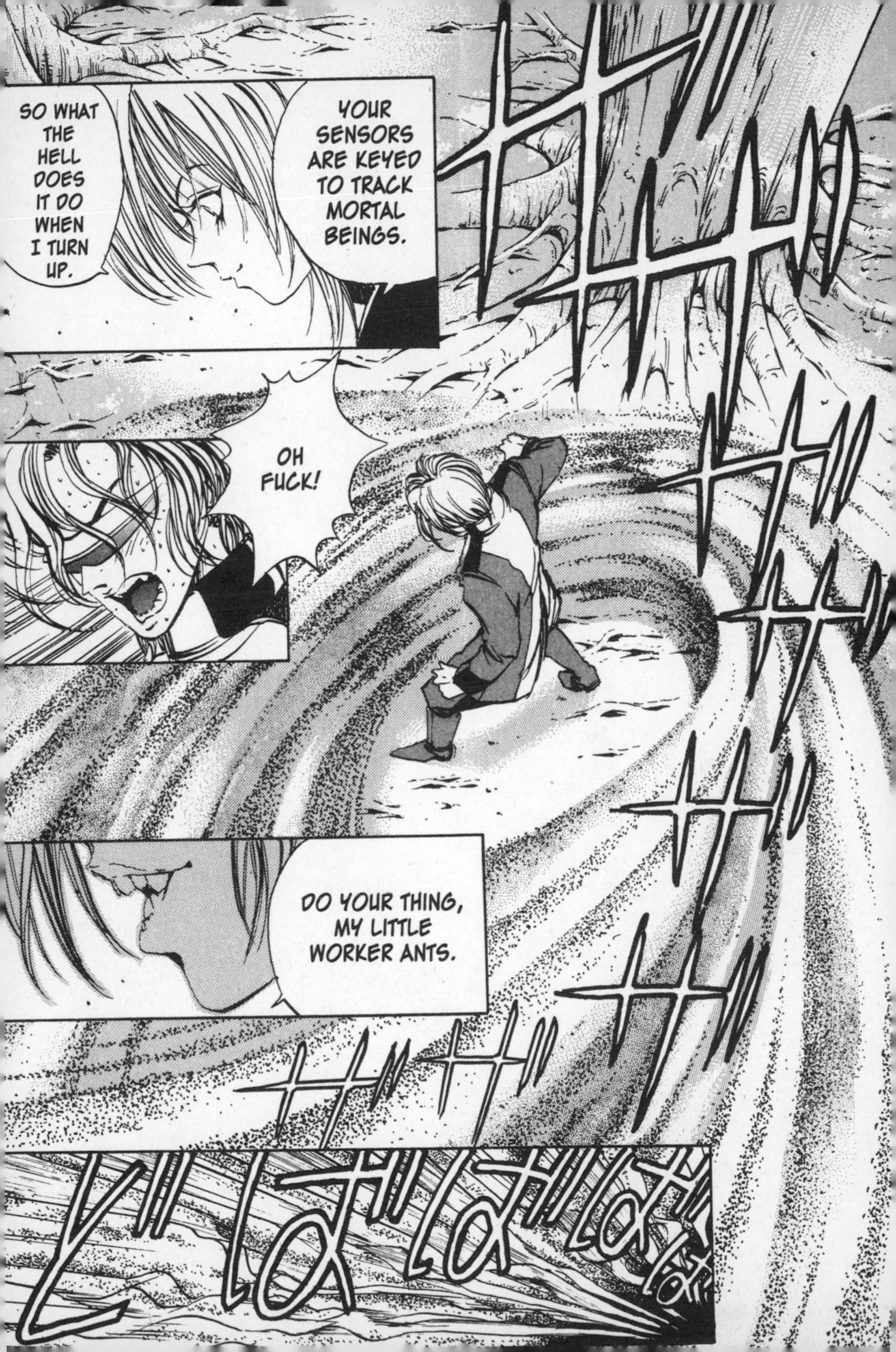
YOUR SENSORS ARE KEYED TO TRACK MORTAL BEINGS.
SO WHAT THE HELL DOES IT DO WHEN I TURN UP.
OH FUCK!
DO YOUR THING, MY LITTLE WORKER ANTS.

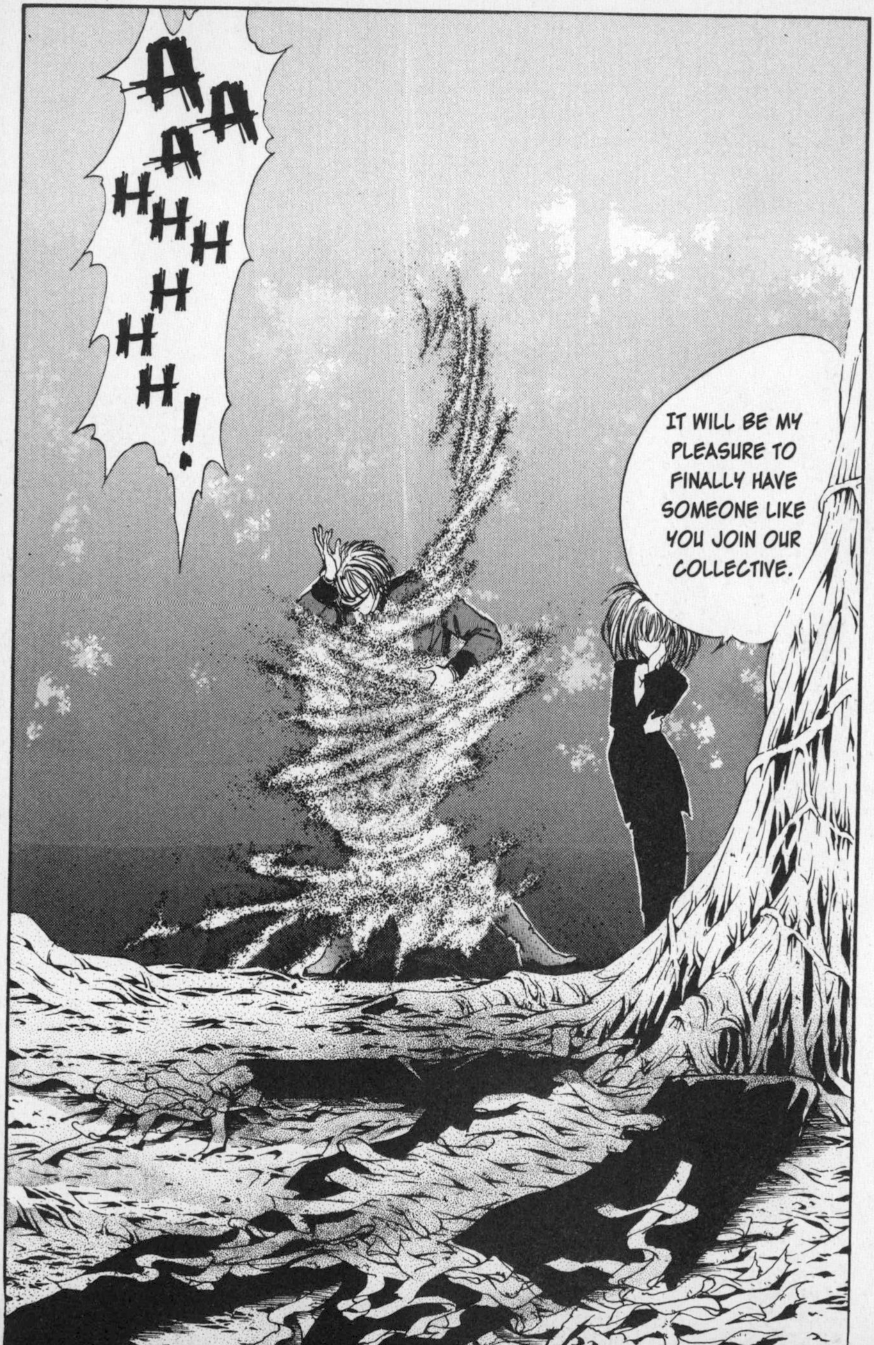
IT WILL BE MY PLEASURE TO FINALLY HAVE SOMEONE LIKE YOU JOIN OUR COLLECTIVE.
AAAAHHHHHHHH!

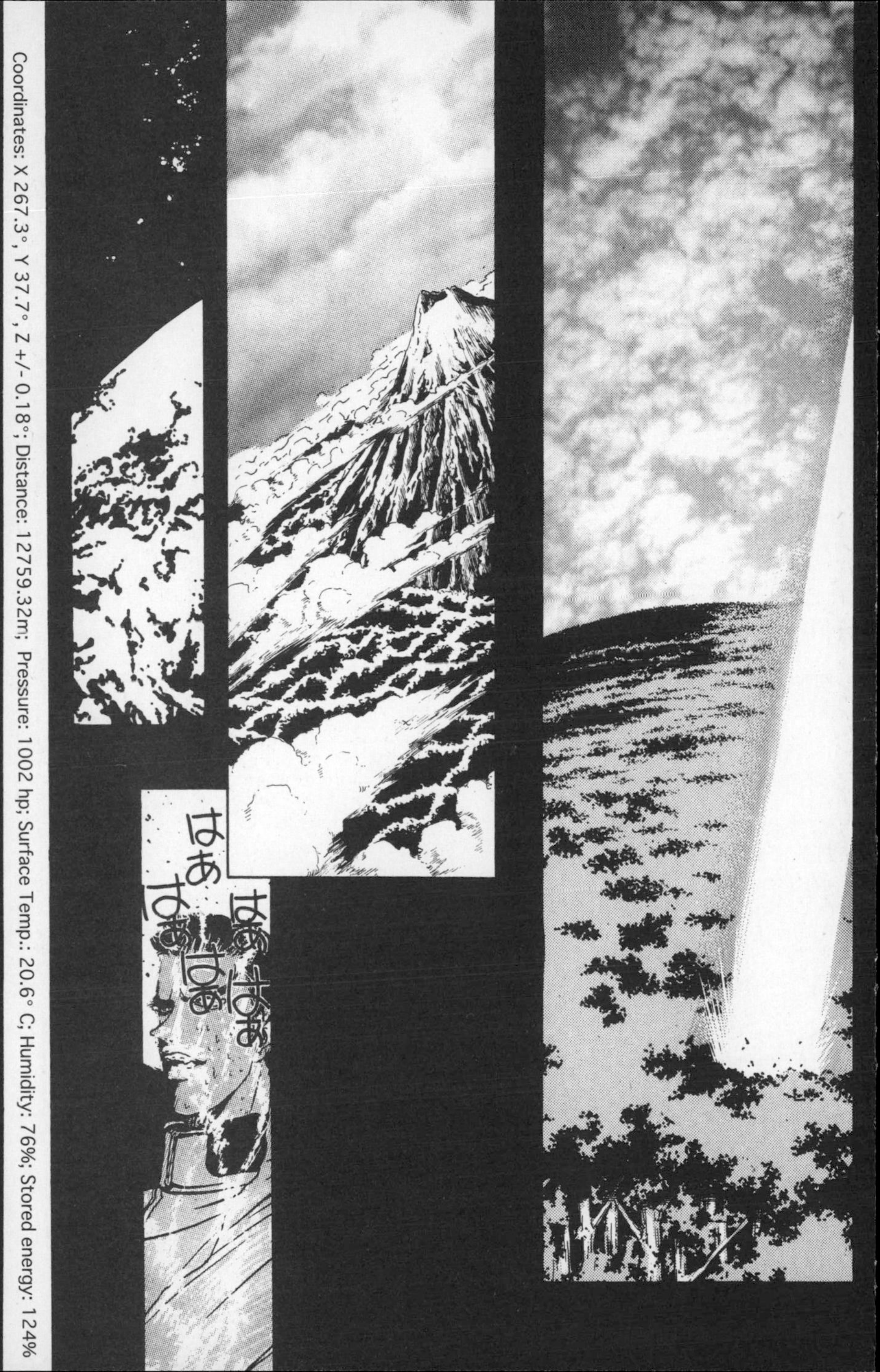
はぁ はぁ
はぁ はぁ
はぁ はぁ
Coordinates: X 267.3°, Y 37.7°, Z +/- 0.18°; Distance: 12759.32m; Pressure: 1002 hp; Surface Temp.: 20.6° C; Humidity: 76%; Stored energy: 124%

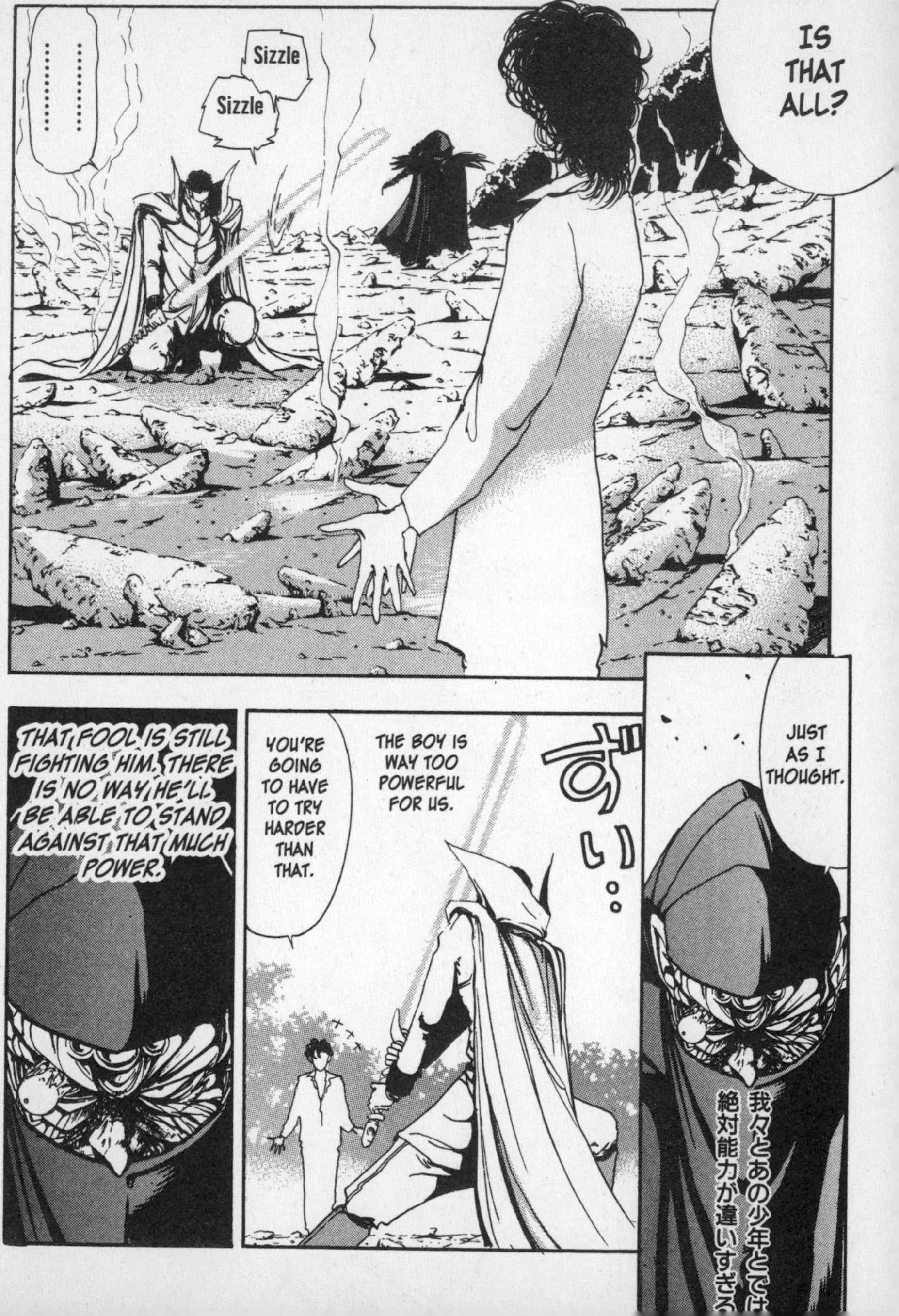
IS THAT ALL?
Sizzle
Sizzle
......
JUST AS I THOUGHT.
我々とあの少年とでは
絶対能力が違いすぎる
ずい。。
THE BOY IS WAY TOO POWERFUL FOR US.
YOU'RE GOING TO HAVE TO TRY HARDER THAN THAT.
THAT FOOL IS STILL FIGHTING HIM. THERE IS NO WAY HE'LL BE ABLE TO STAND AGAINST THAT MUCH POWER.

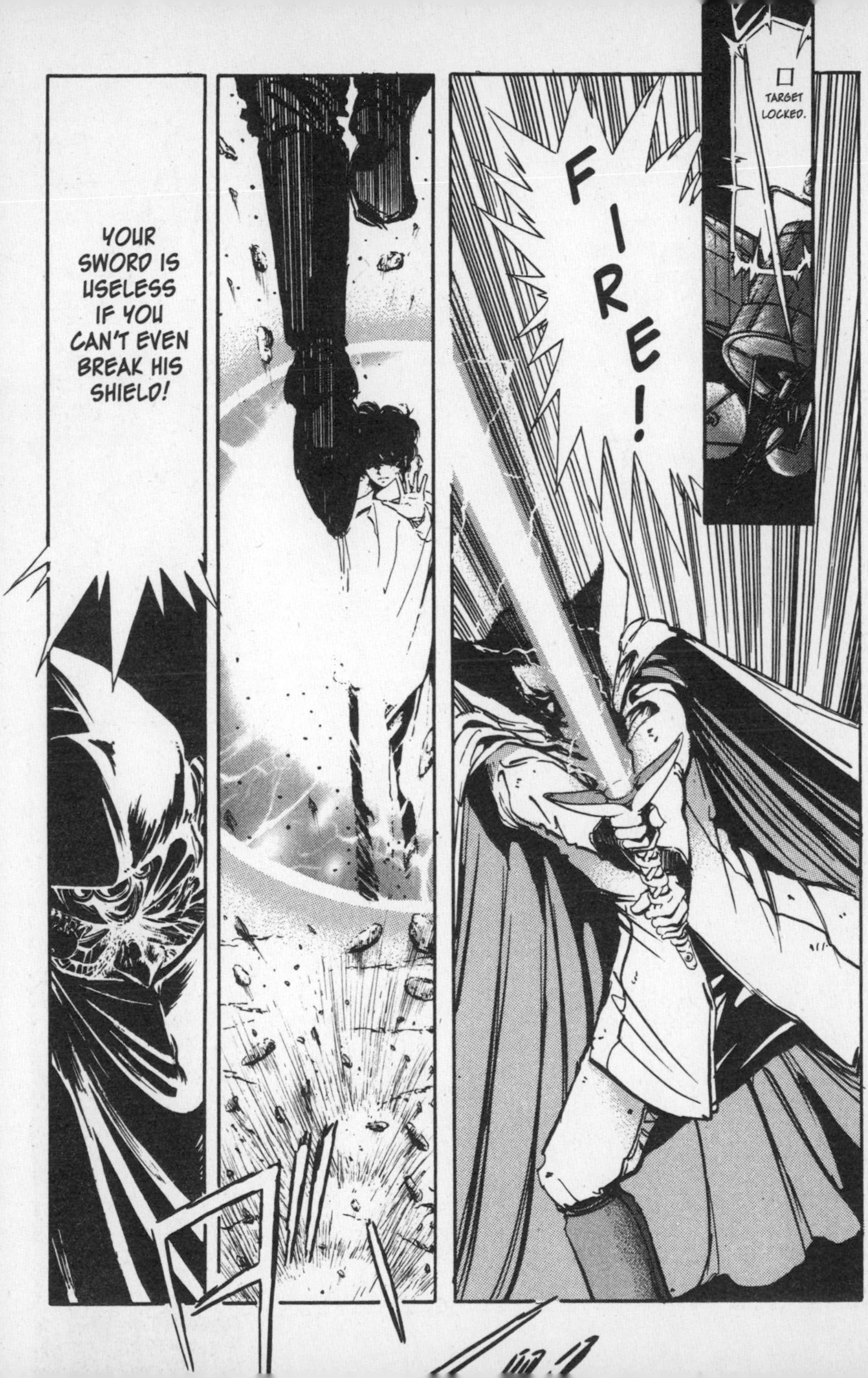
TARGET LOCKED.
FIRE!
YOUR SWORD IS USELESS IF YOU CAN'T EVEN BREAK HIS SHIELD!

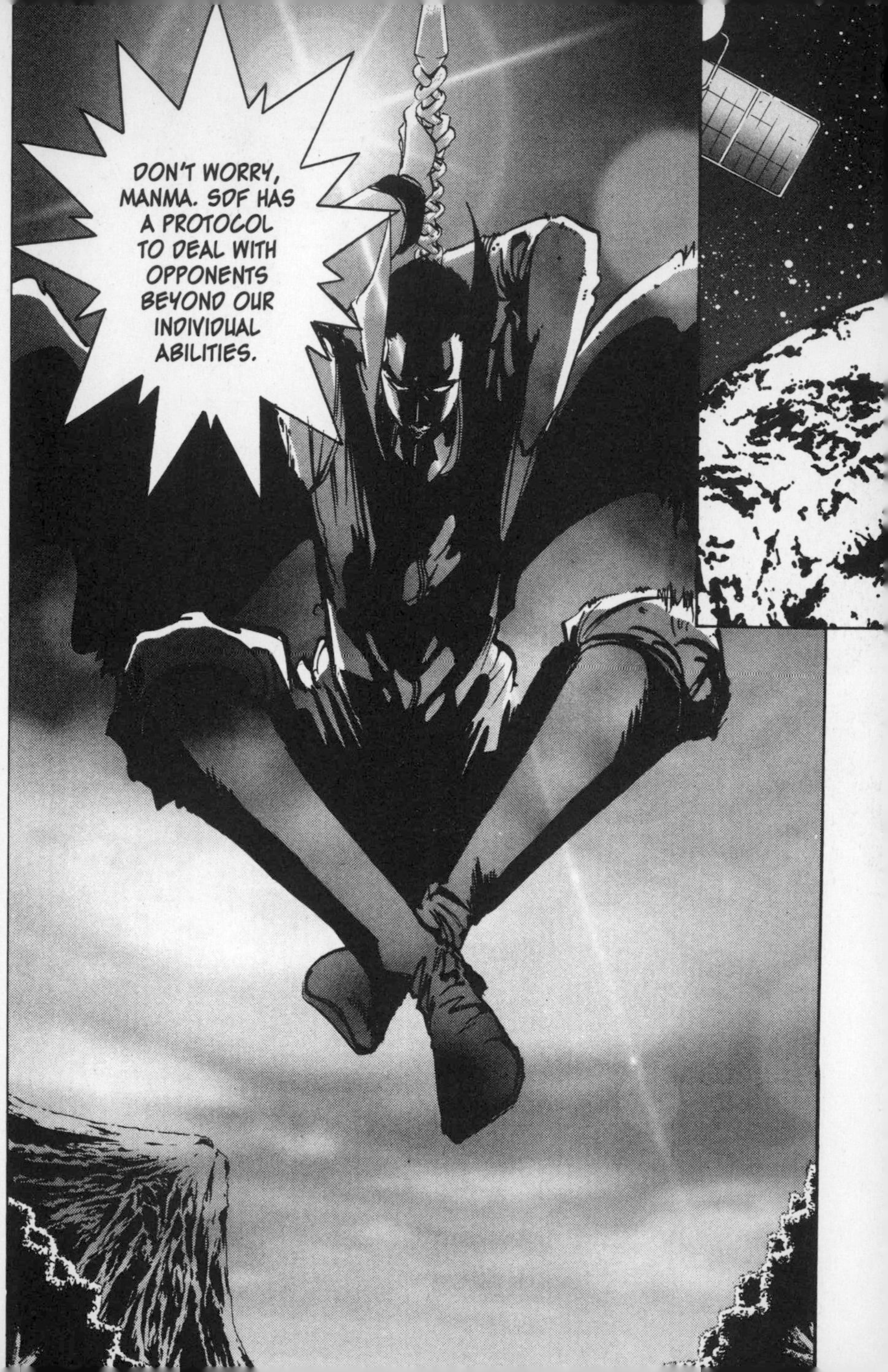
DON'T WORRY, MANMA. SDF HAS A PROTOCOL TO DEAL WITH OPPONENTS BEYOND OUR INDIVIDUAL ABILITIES.

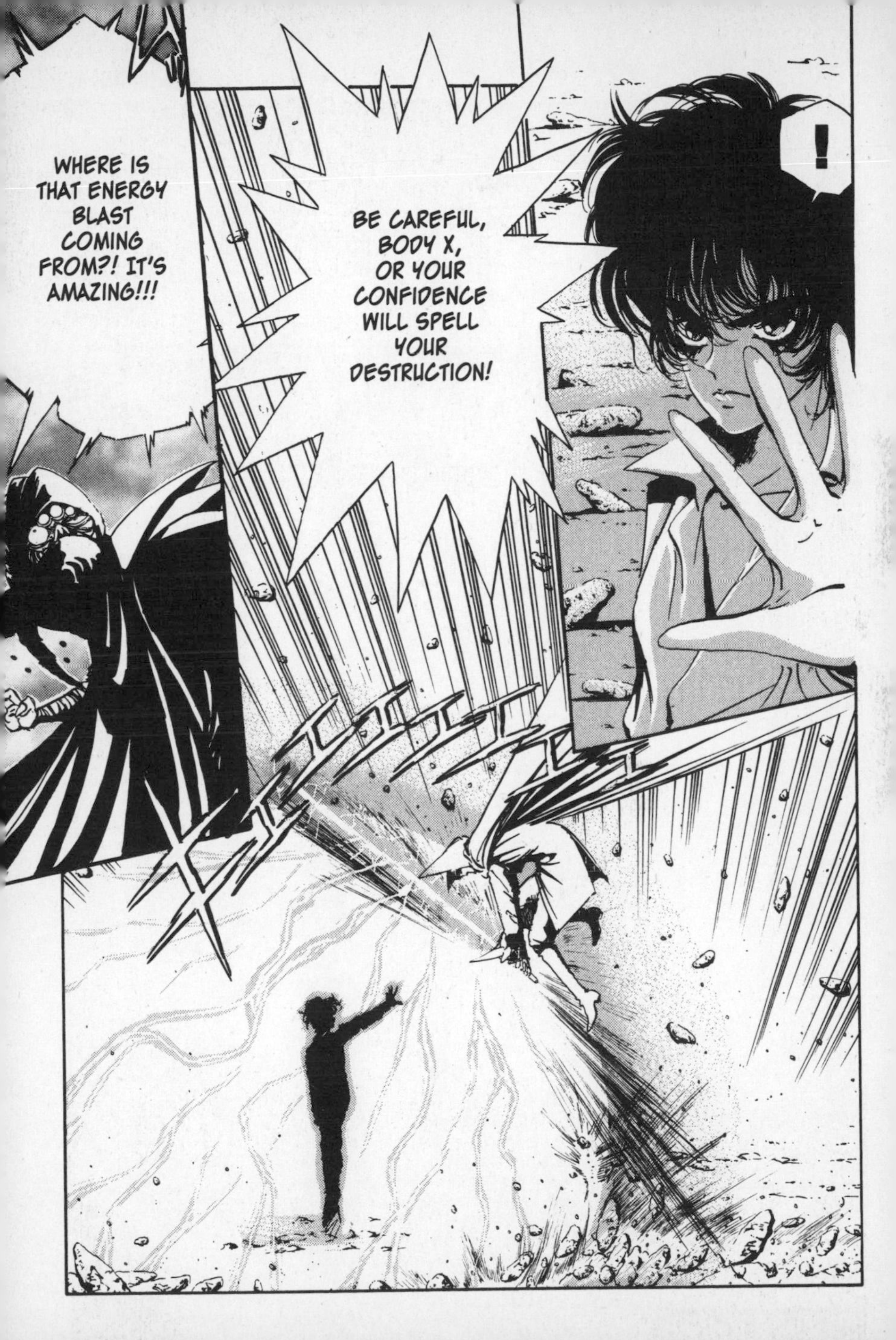
!
BE CAREFUL, BODY X, OR YOUR CONFIDENCE WILL SPELL YOUR DESTRUCTION!
WHERE IS THAT ENERGY BLAST COMING FROM?! IT'S AMAZING!!!

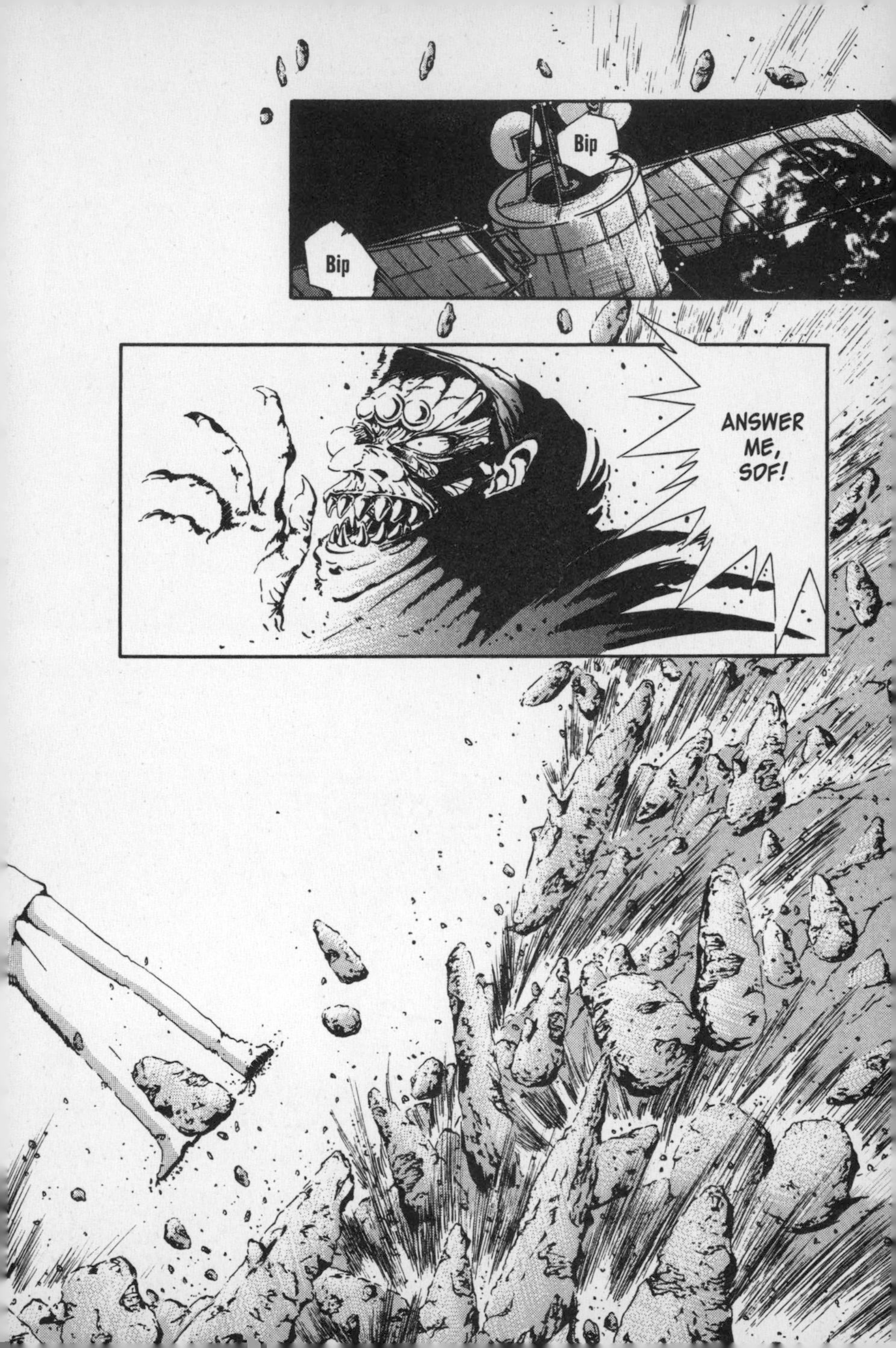
Bip
Bip
ANSWER ME, SDF!

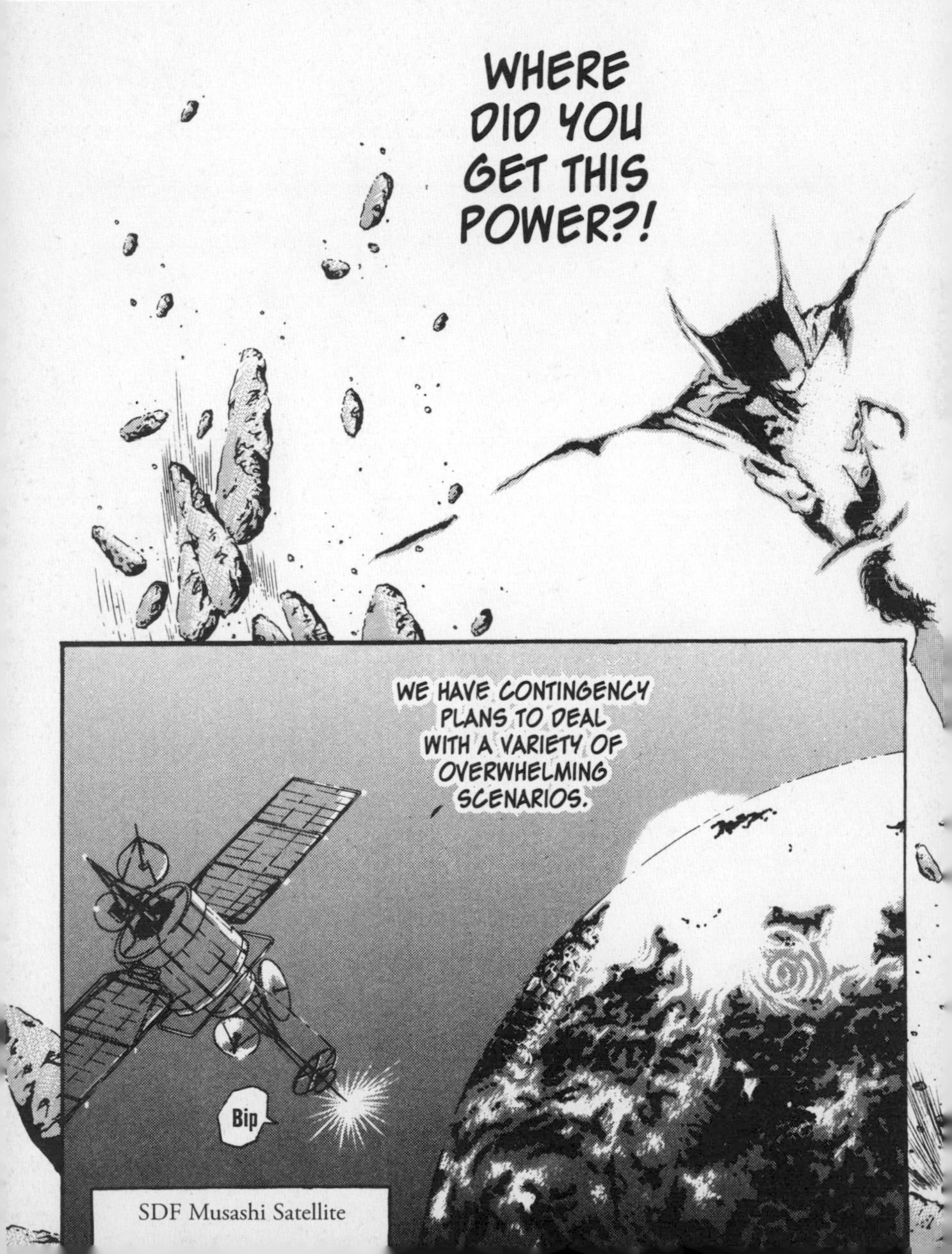
WHERE DID YOU GET THIS POWER?!
WE HAVE CONTINGENCY PLANS TO DEAL WITH A VARIETY OF OVERWHELMING SCENARIOS.
Bip
SDF Musashi Satellite

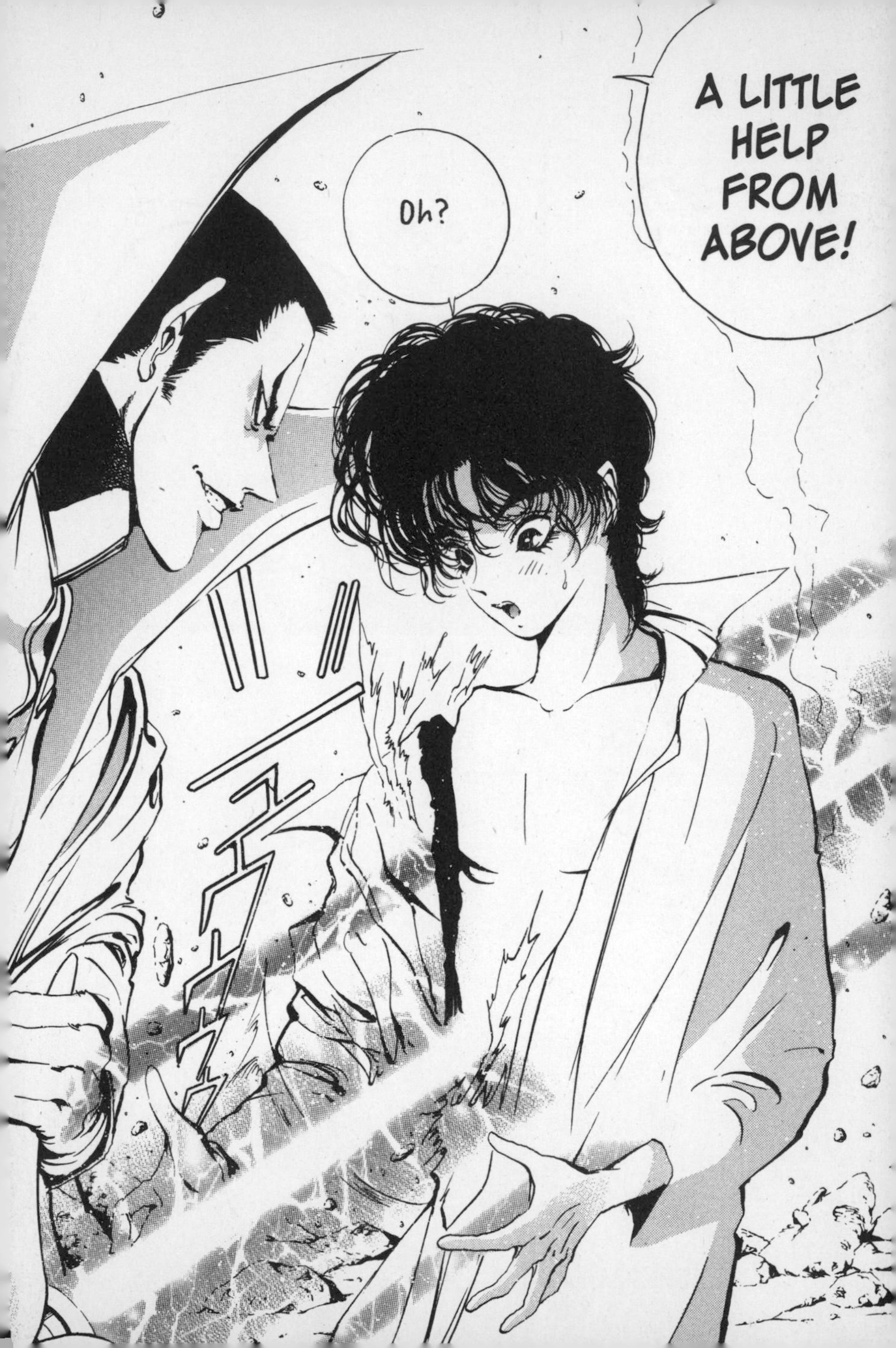
A LITTLE HELP FROM ABOVE!
Oh?

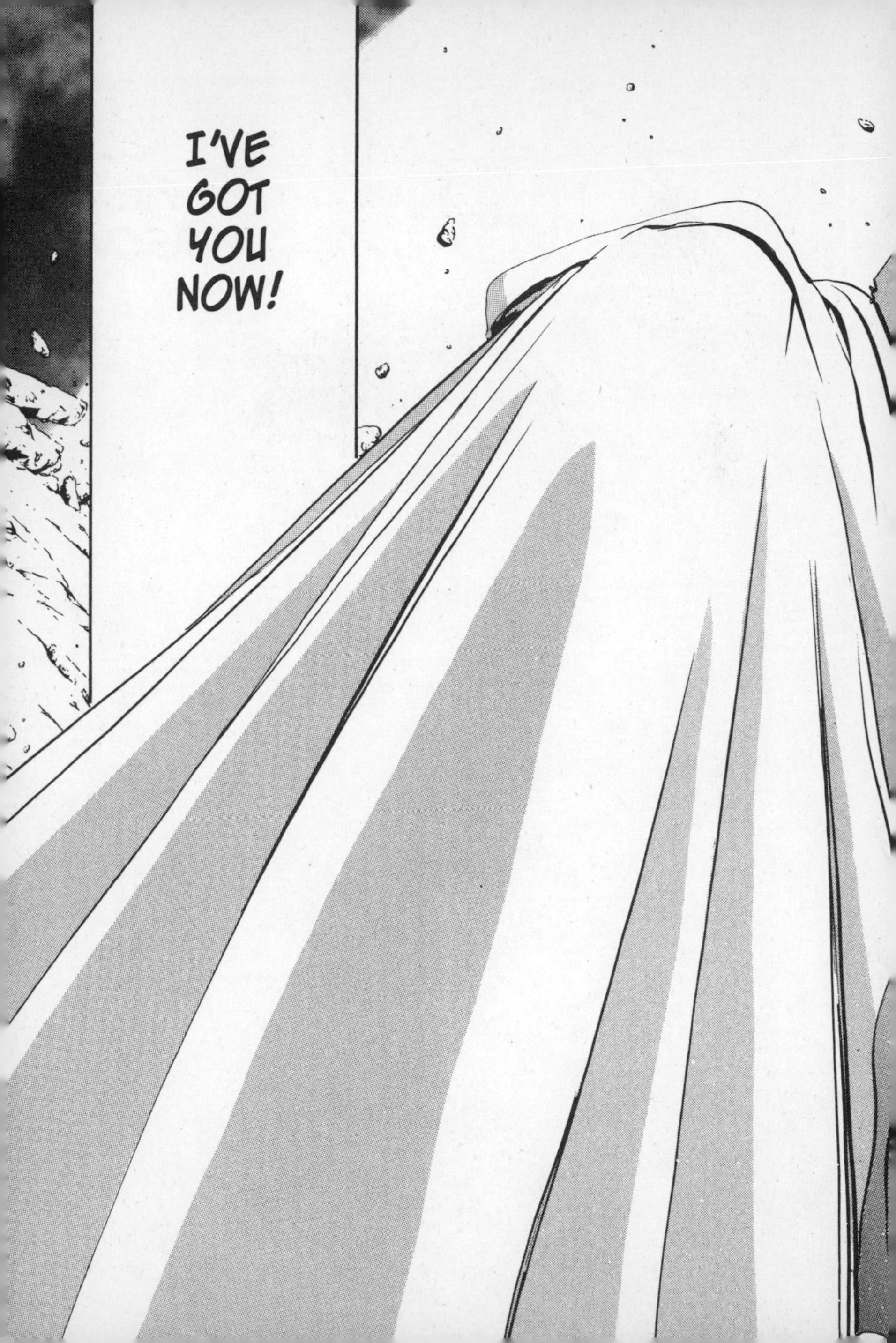
I'VE GOT YOU NOW!

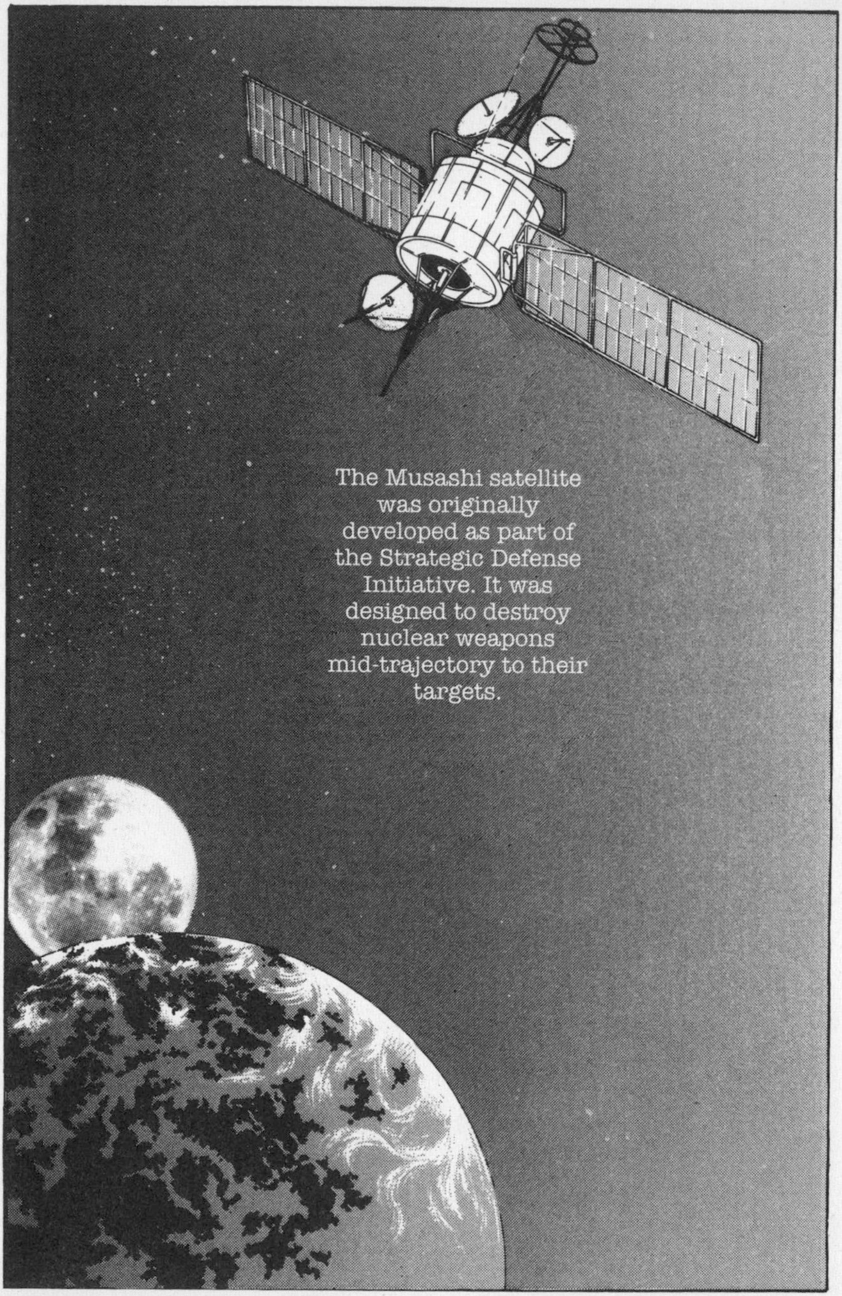
The Musashi satellite was originally developed as part of the Strategic Defense Initiative. It was designed to destroy nuclear weapons mid-trajectory to their targets.

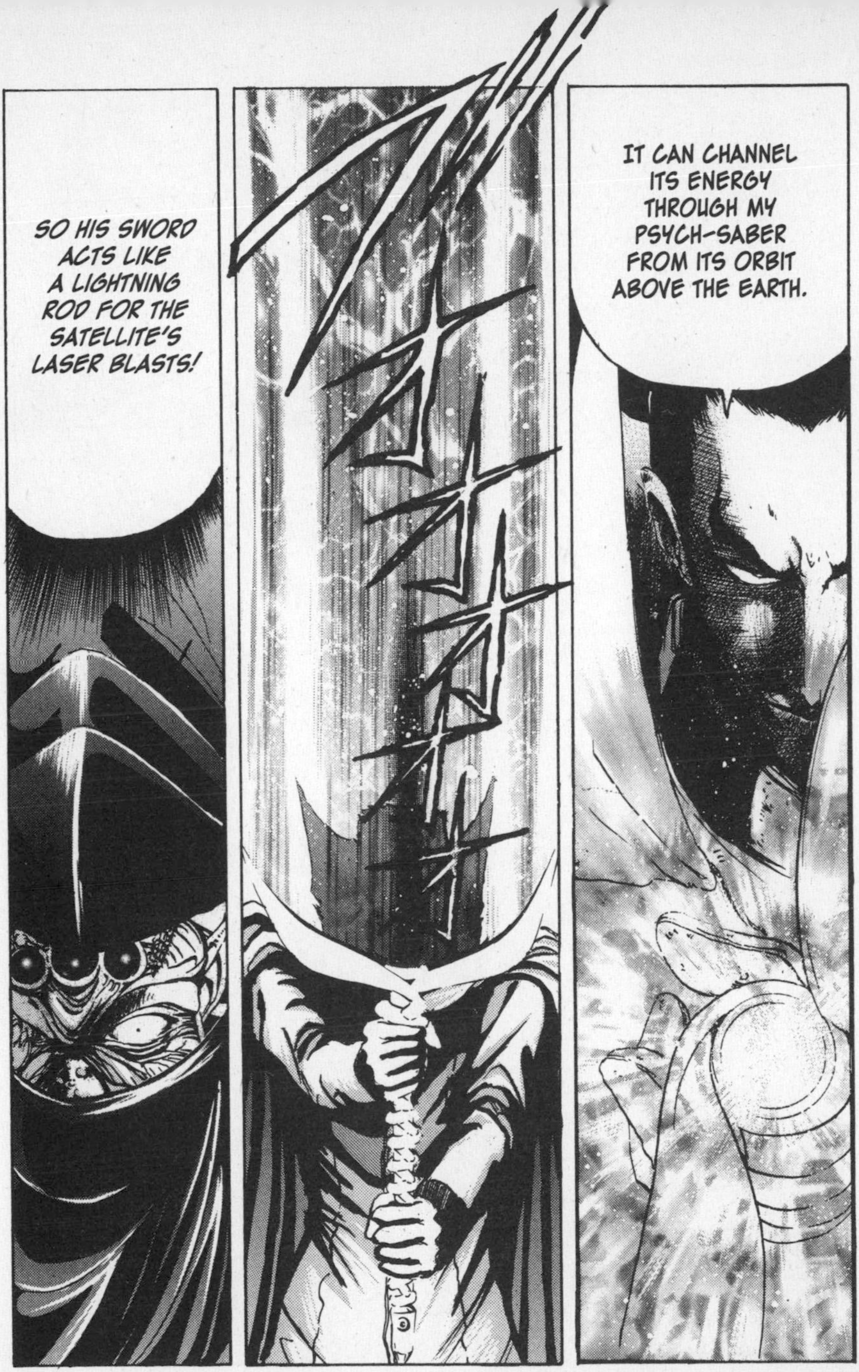
IT CAN CHANNEL ITS ENERGY THROUGH MY PSYCH-SABER FROM ITS ORBIT ABOVE THE EARTH.
SO HIS SWORD ACTS LIKE A LIGHTNING ROD FOR THE SATELLITE'S LASER BLASTS!

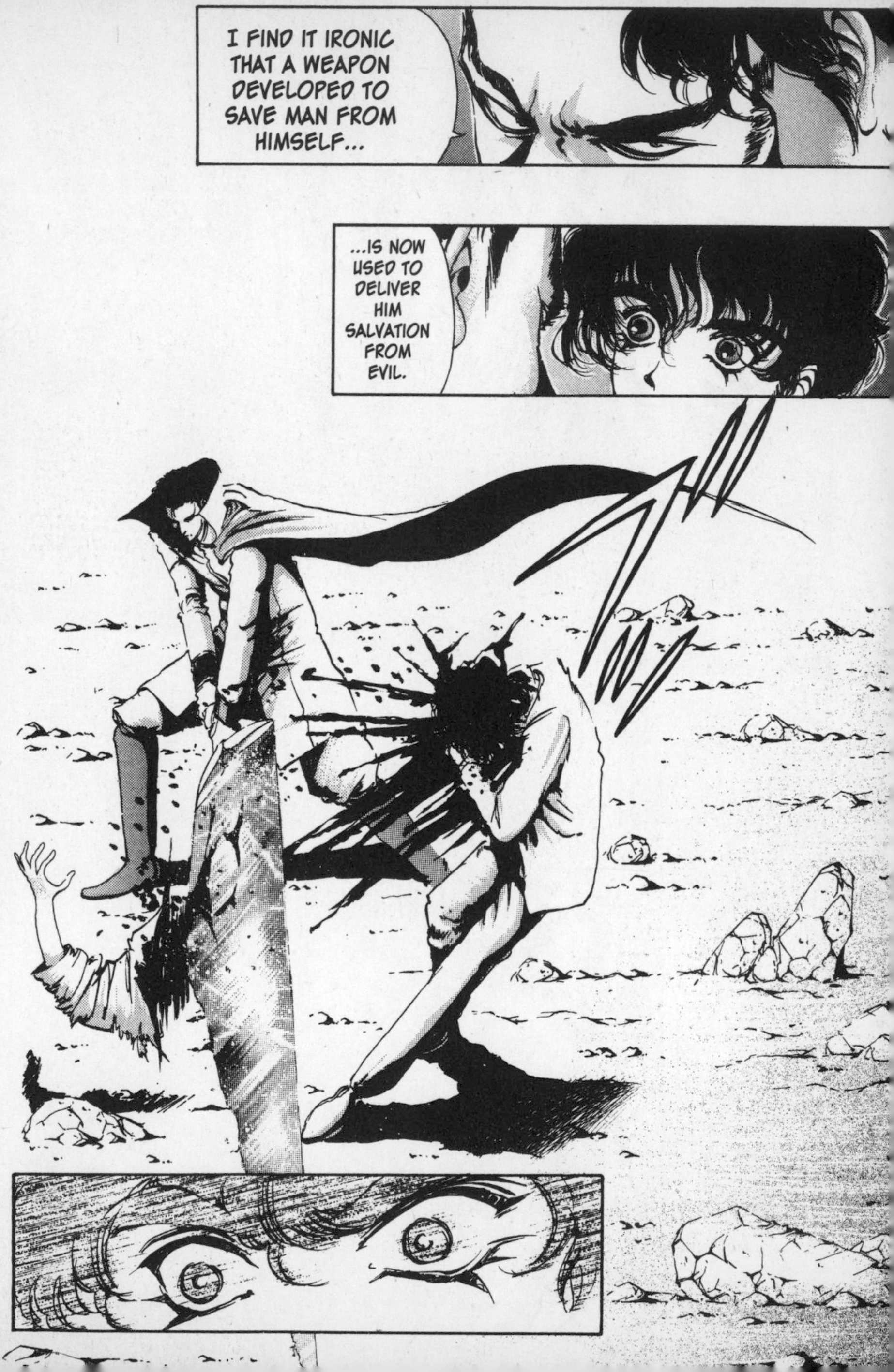
I FIND IT IRONIC THAT A WEAPON DEVELOPED TO SAVE MAN FROM HIMSELF...
...IS NOW USED TO DELIVER HIM SALVATION FROM EVIL.

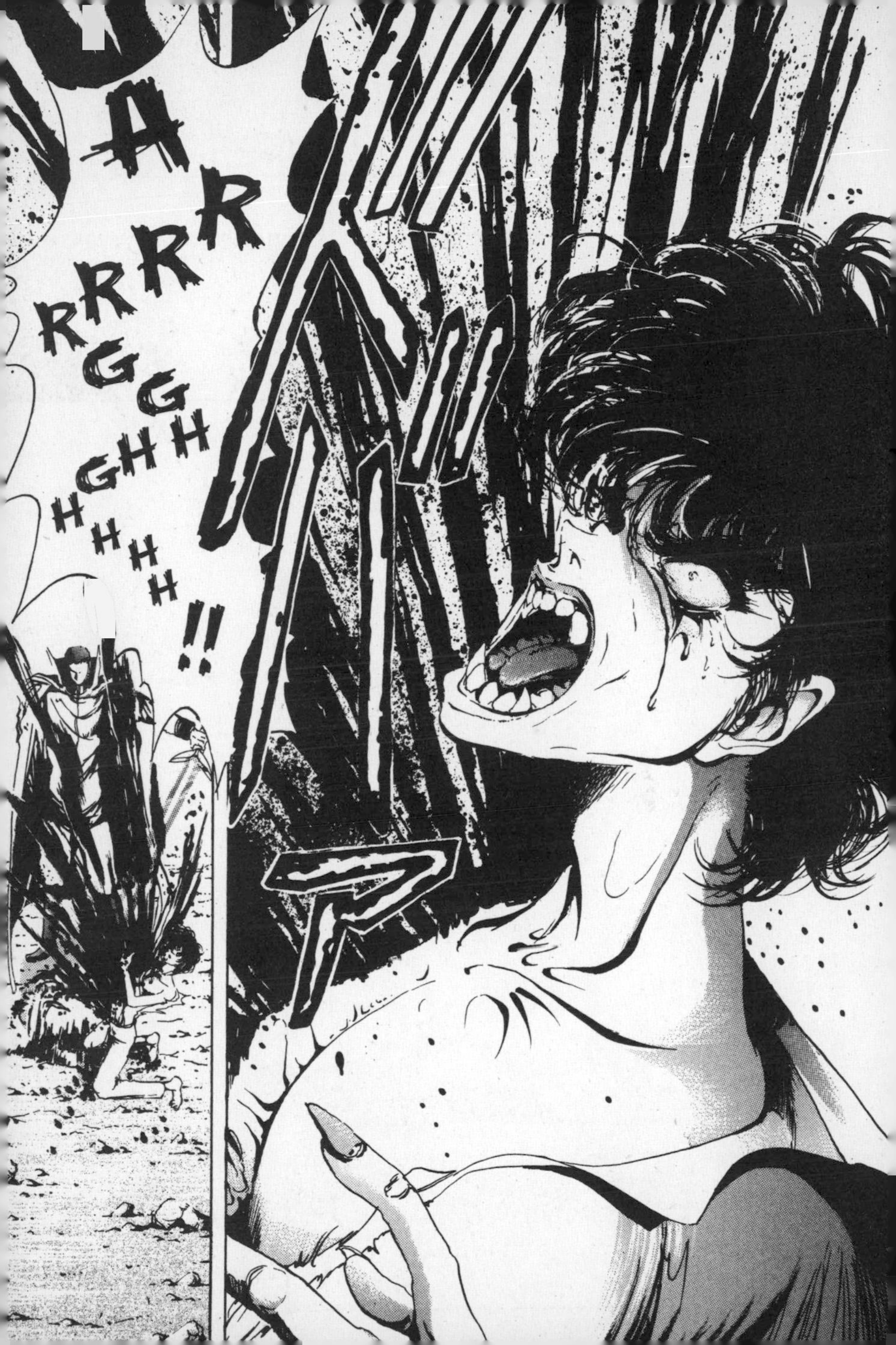

ARRRRRRGGGHHHHHH!!

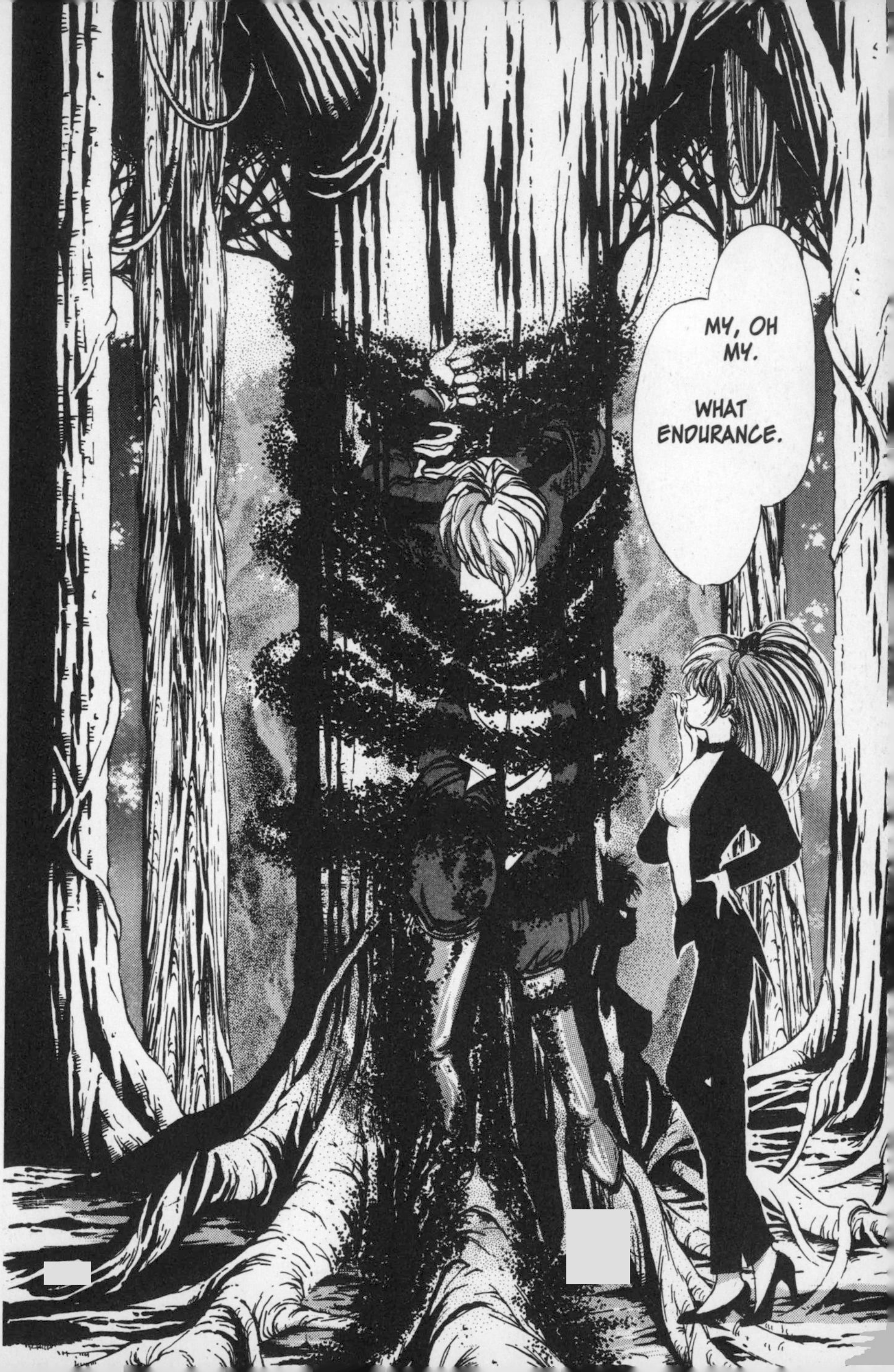
MY, OH MY.
WHAT ENDURANCE.

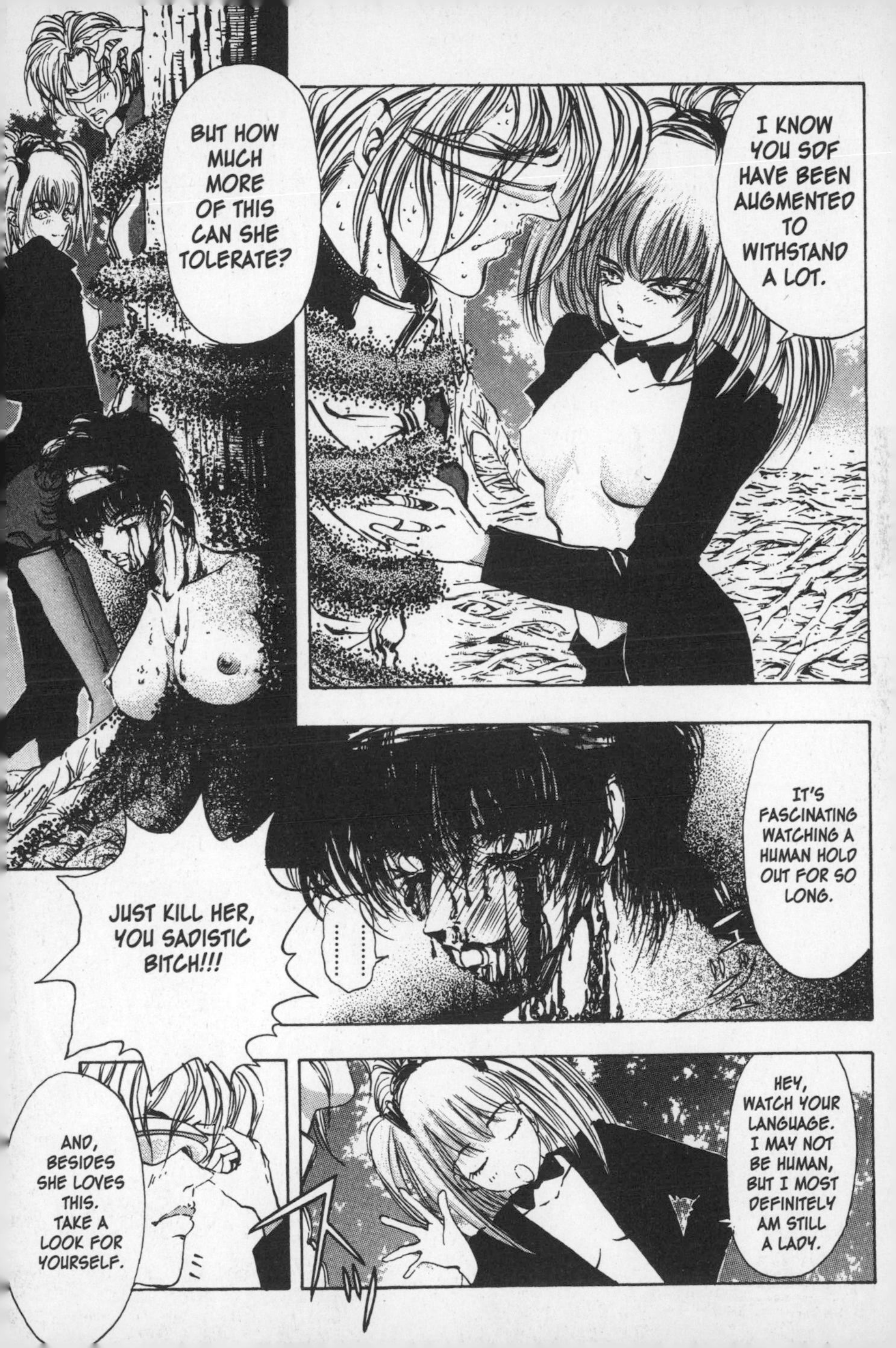
I KNOW YOU SDF HAVE BEEN AUGMENTED TO WITHSTAND A LOT.
BUT HOW MUCH MORE OF THIS CAN SHE TOLERATE?
IT'S FASCINATING WATCHING A HUMAN HOLD OUT FOR SO LONG.
......
JUST KILL HER, YOU SADISTIC BITCH!!!
HEY, WATCH YOUR LANGUAGE. I MAY NOT BE HUMAN, BUT I MOST DEFINITELY AM STILL A LADY.
AND, BESIDES SHE LOVES THIS. TAKE A LOOK FOR YOURSELF.

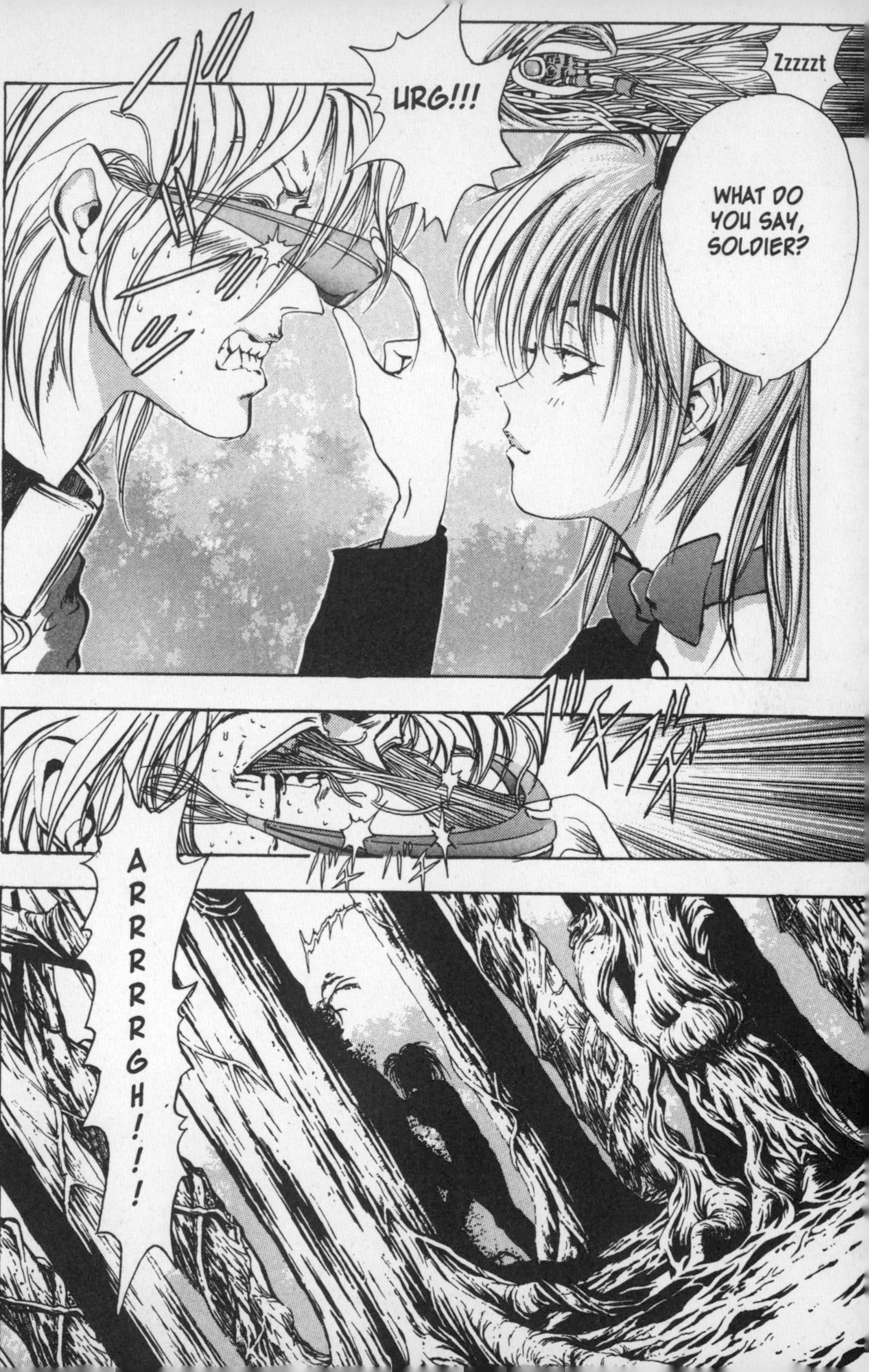
Zzzzzt
WHAT DO YOU SAY, SOLDIER?
URG!!!
ARRRRRGH!!!

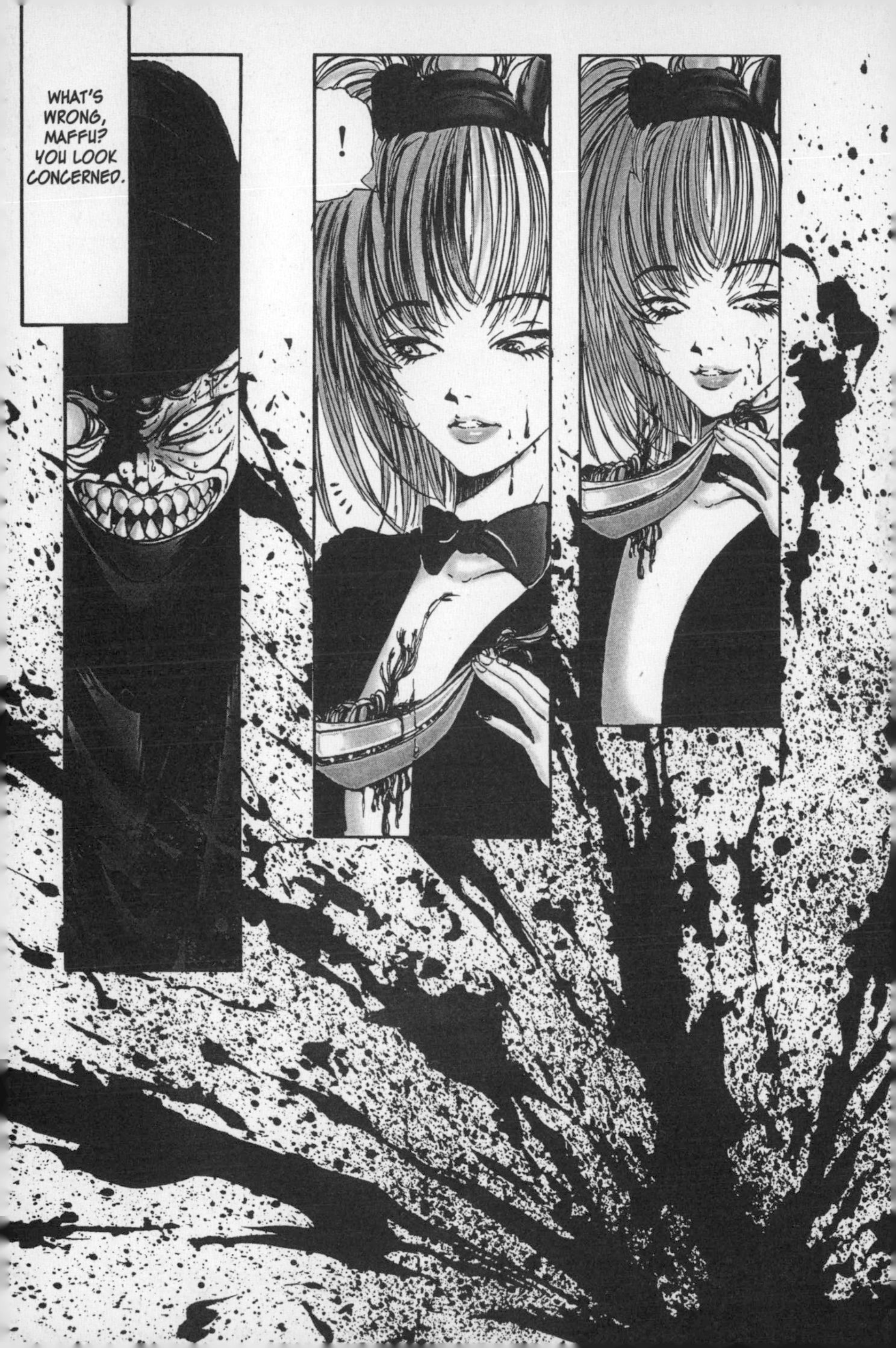
!
WHAT'S WRONG, MAFFU? YOU LOOK CONCERNED.

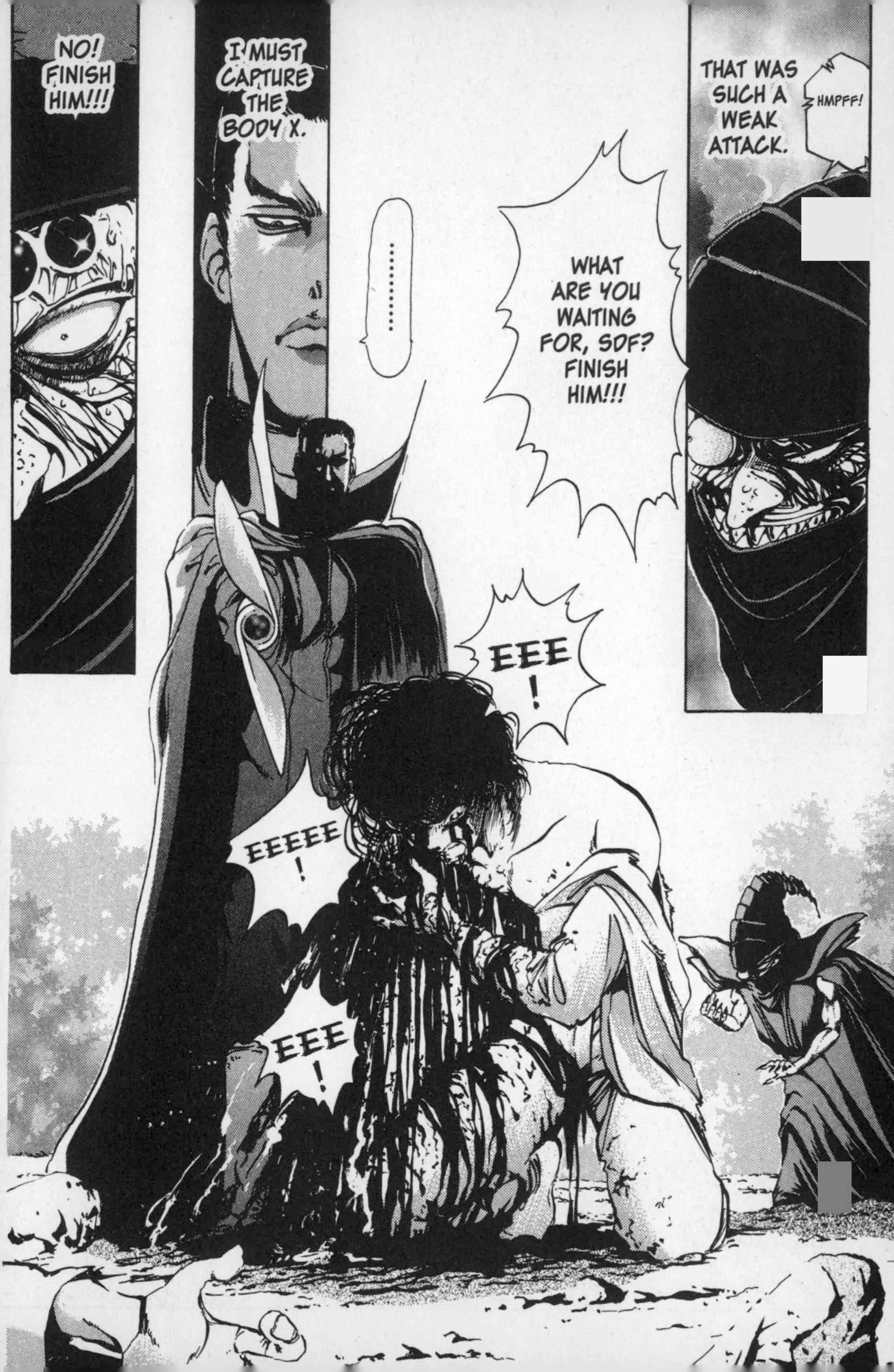
HMPFF!
THAT WAS SUCH A WEAK ATTACK.
WHAT ARE YOU WAITING FOR, SDF? FINISH HIM!!!
......
I MUST CAPTURE THE BODY X.
NO! FINISH HIM!!!
EEE!
EEEEE!
EEE!

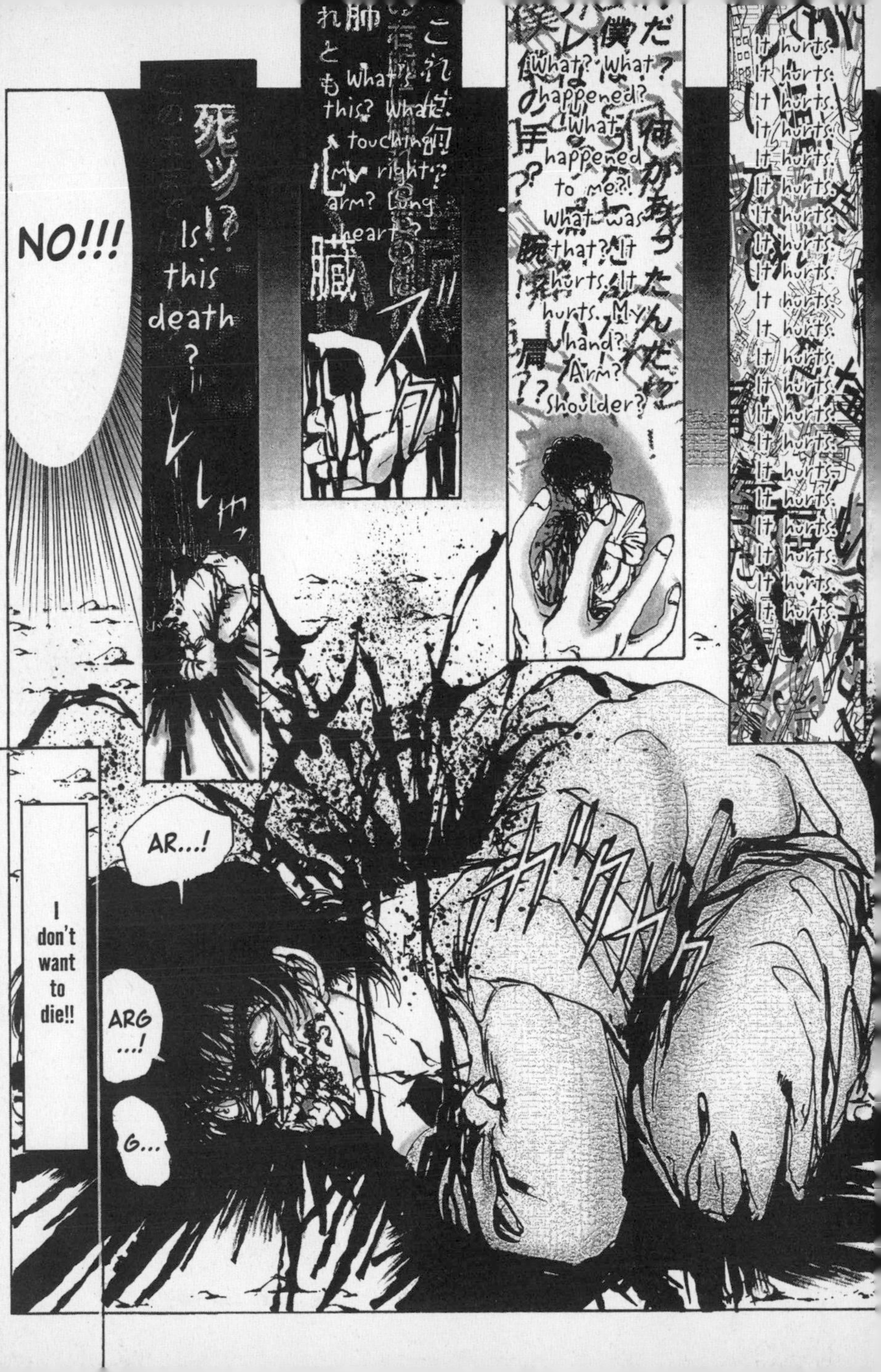
It hurts. It hurts.
What? What? happened? What happened to me?! What was that? It hurts. It hurts. My hand? Arm? Shoulder?
What's this? What's touching my right arm? Lung heart?
Is this death?
NO!!!
AR...!
I don't want to die!!
ARG...!
G...

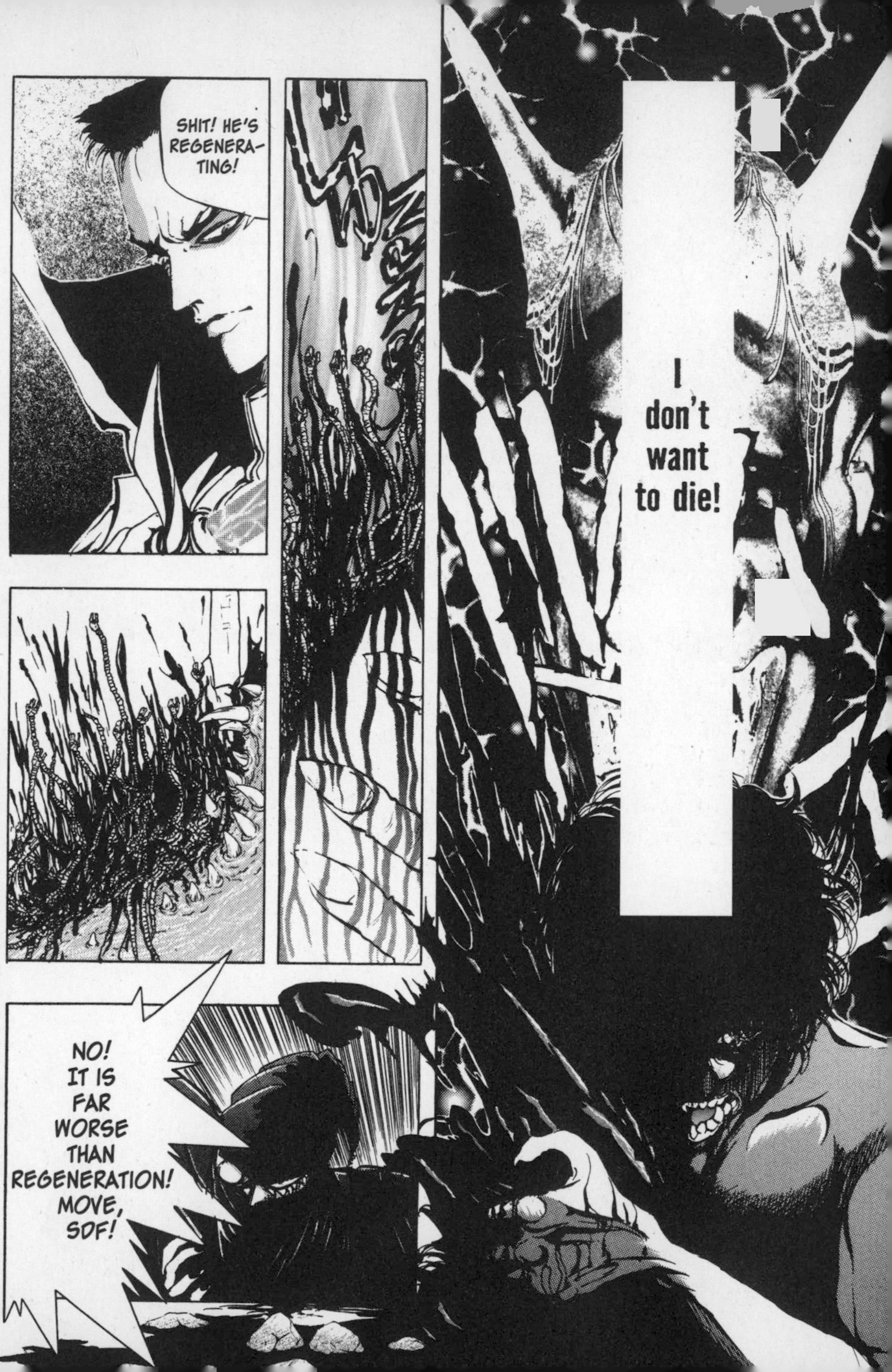
I don't want to die!
SHIT! HE'S REGENERA-TING!
NO! IT IS FAR WORSE THAN REGENERATION! MOVE, SDF!

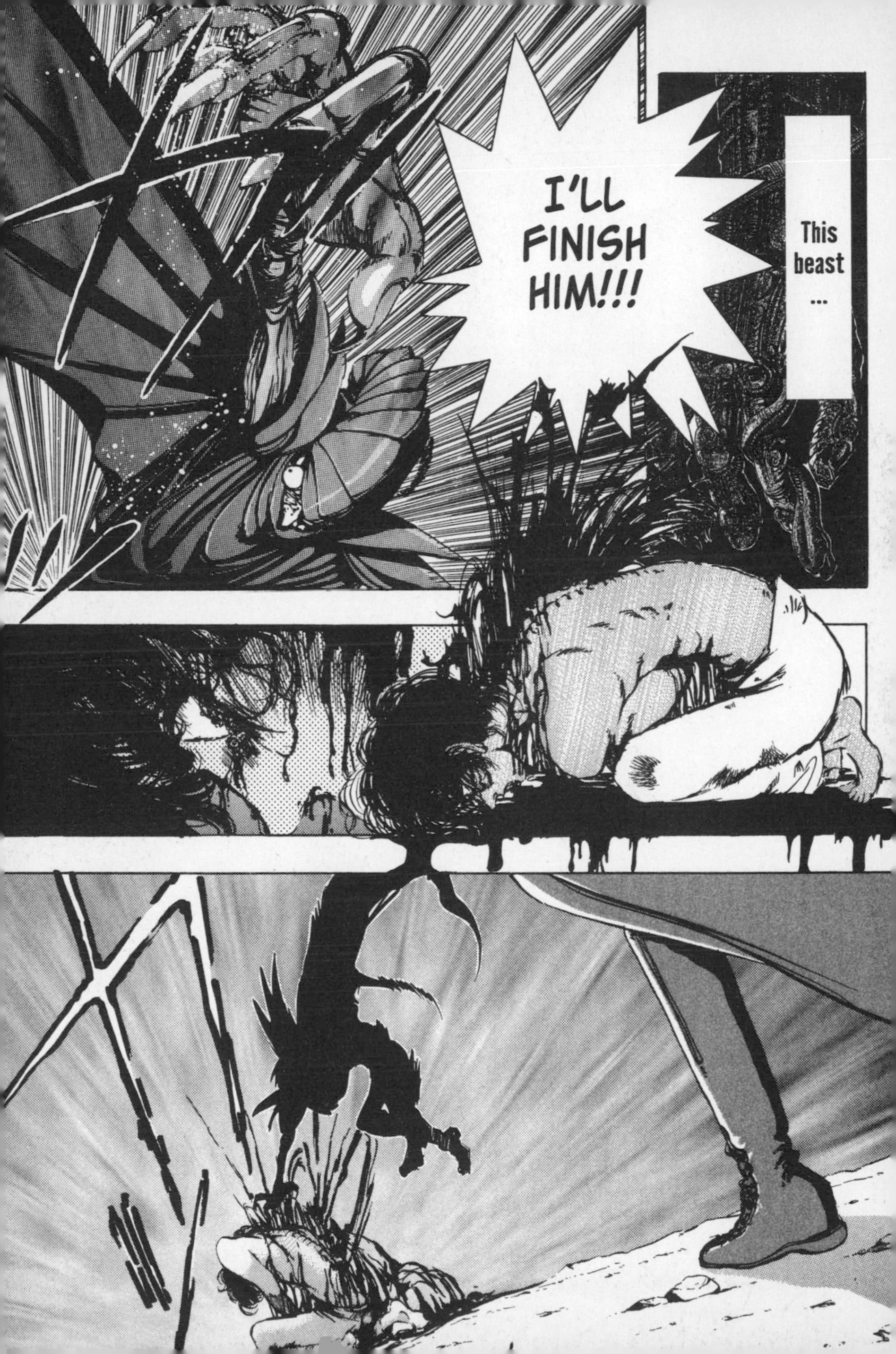
This beast …
I'LL FINISH HIM!!!

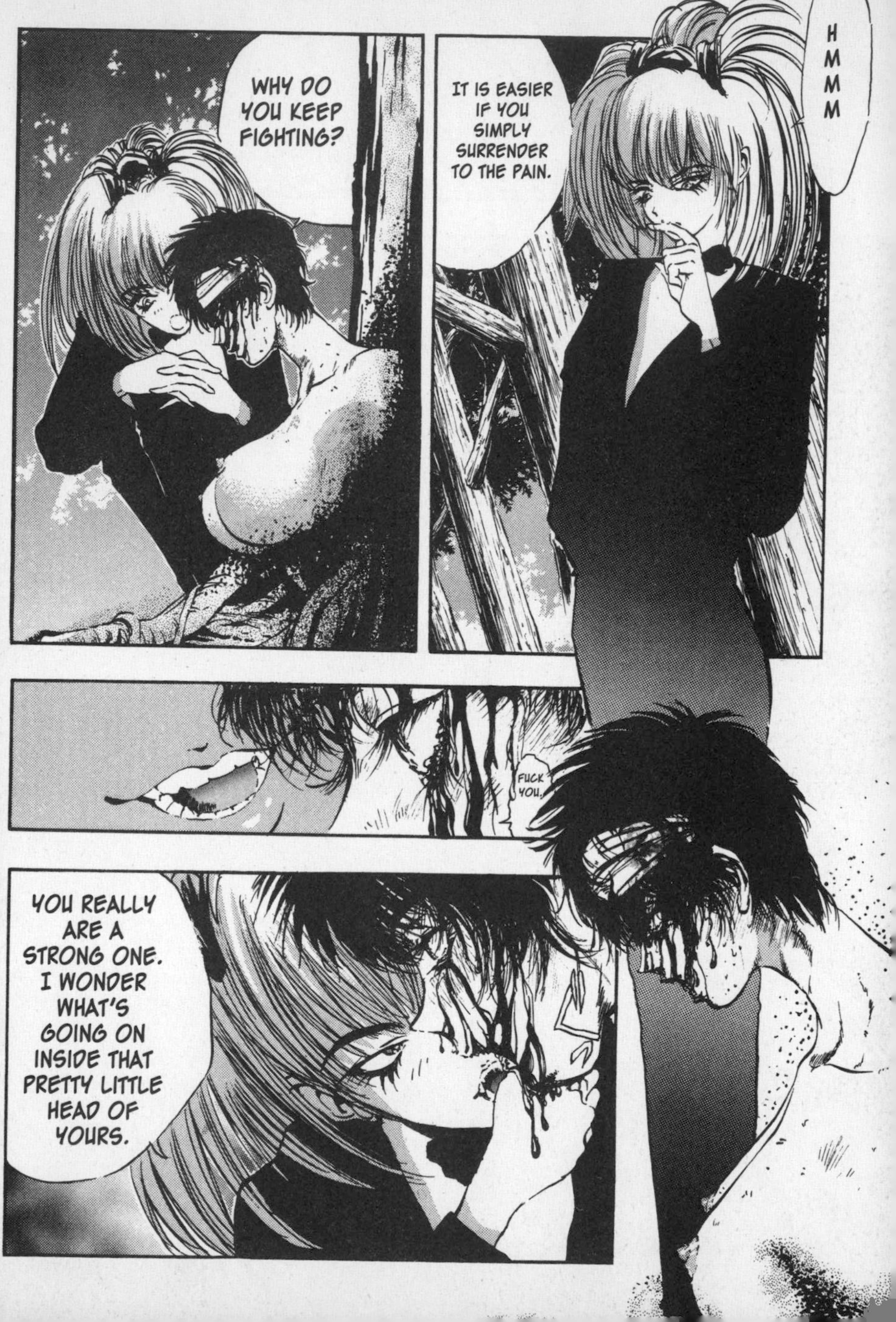
HMMM
IT IS EASIER IF YOU SIMPLY SURRENDER TO THE PAIN.
WHY DO YOU KEEP FIGHTING?
FUCK YOU.
YOU REALLY ARE A STRONG ONE. I WONDER WHAT'S GOING ON INSIDE THAT PRETTY LITTLE HEAD OF YOURS.

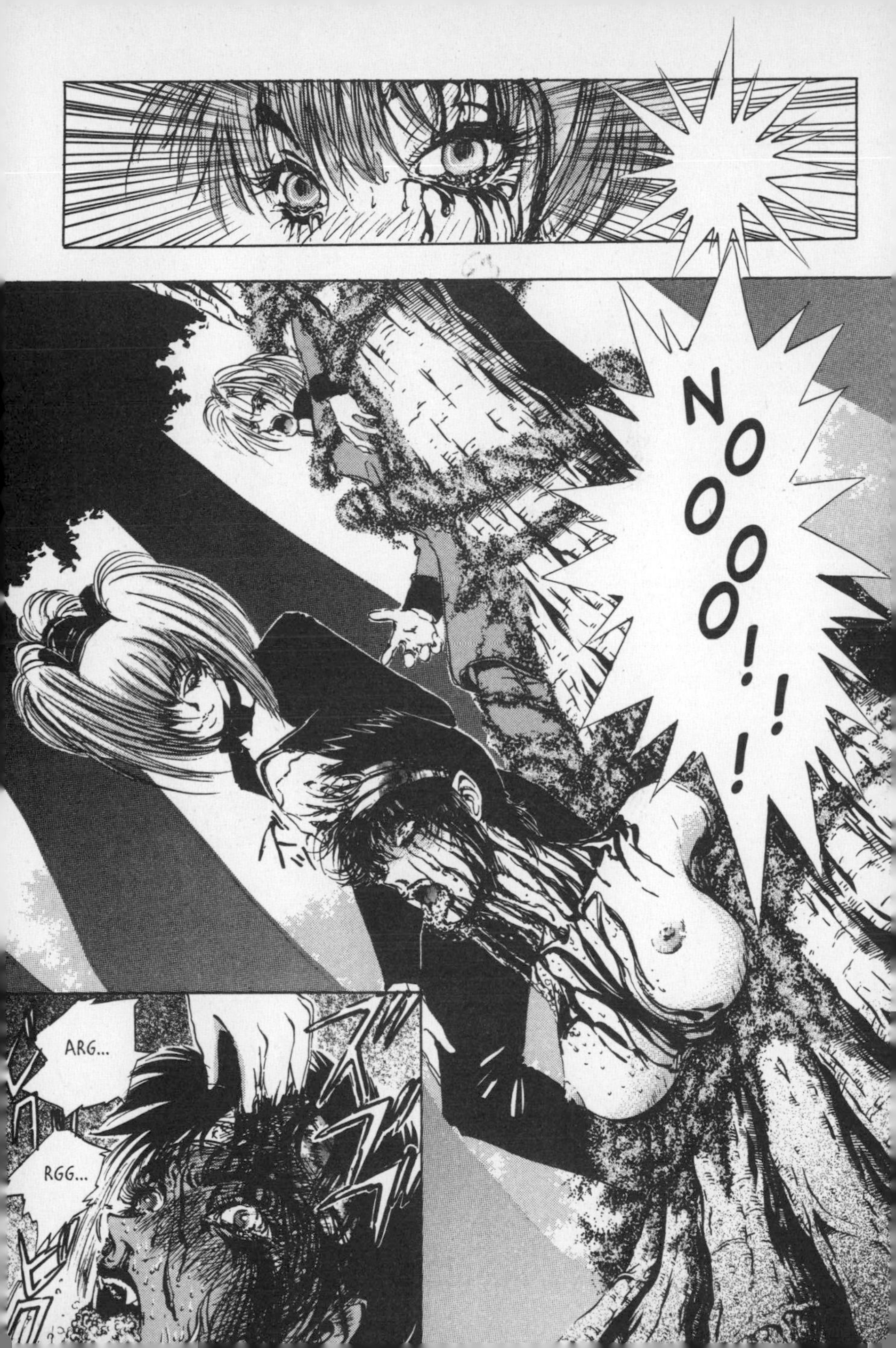
NOOOO!!!
ARG...
RGG...

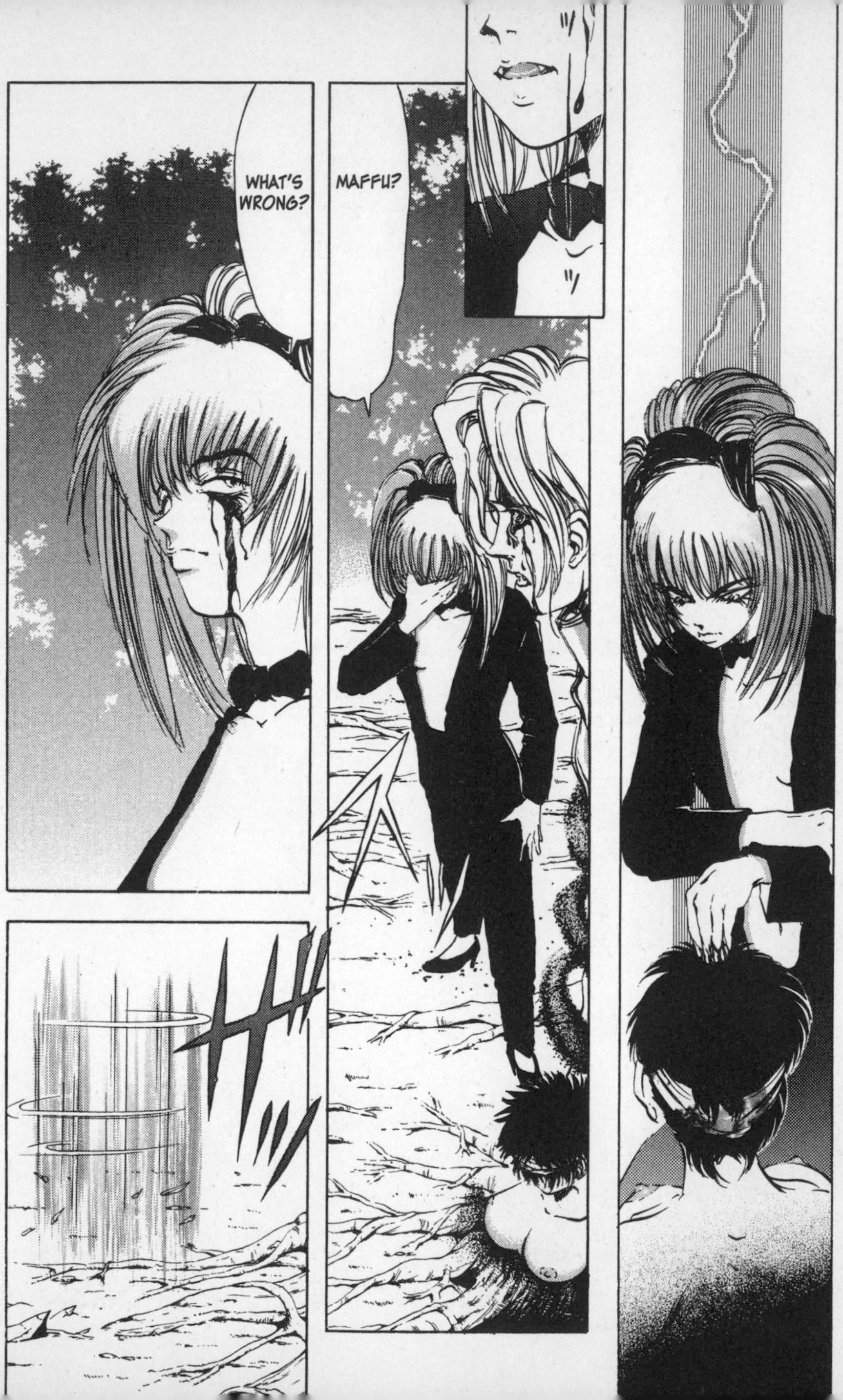
MAFFU?
WHAT'S WRONG?

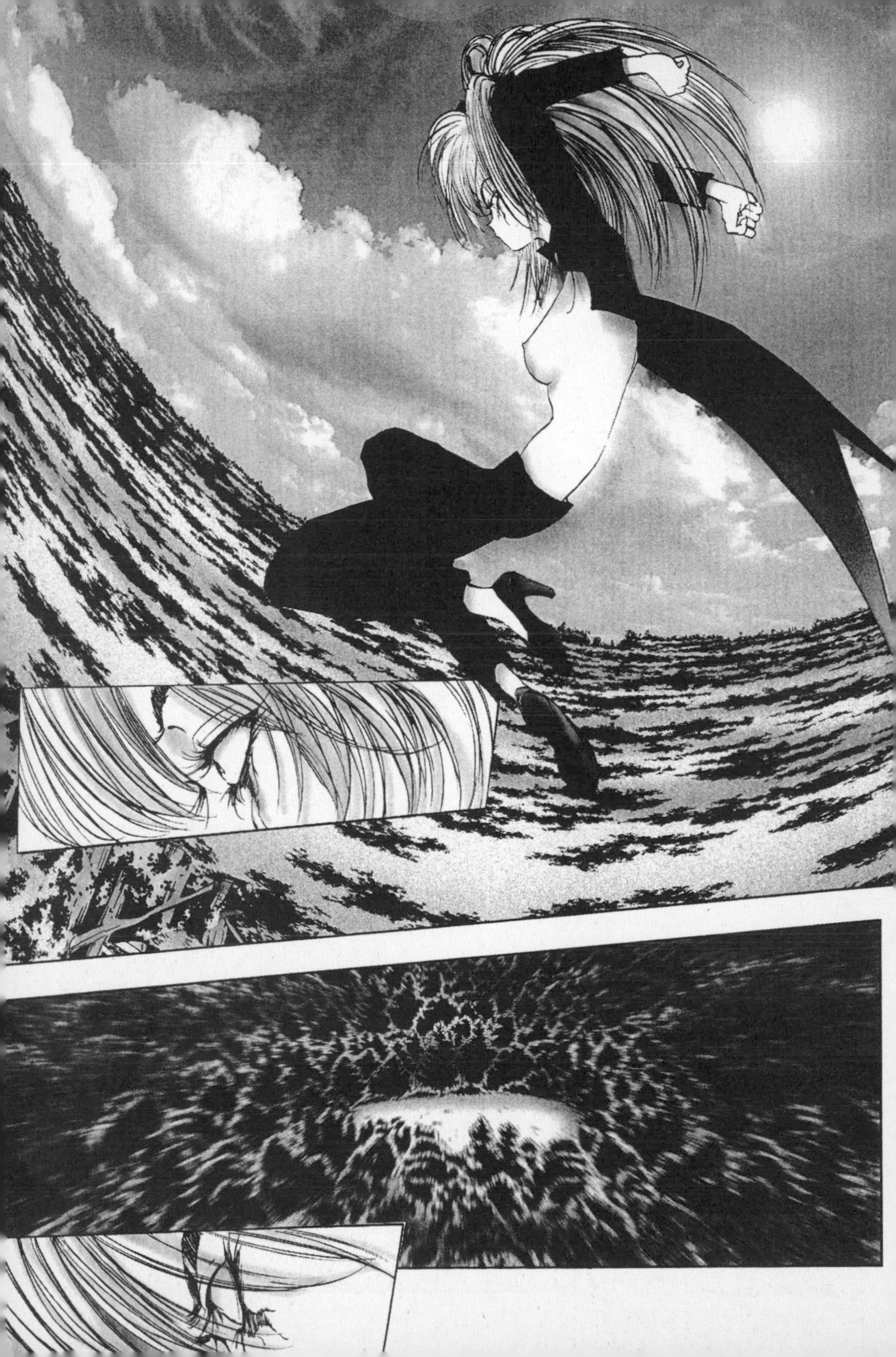

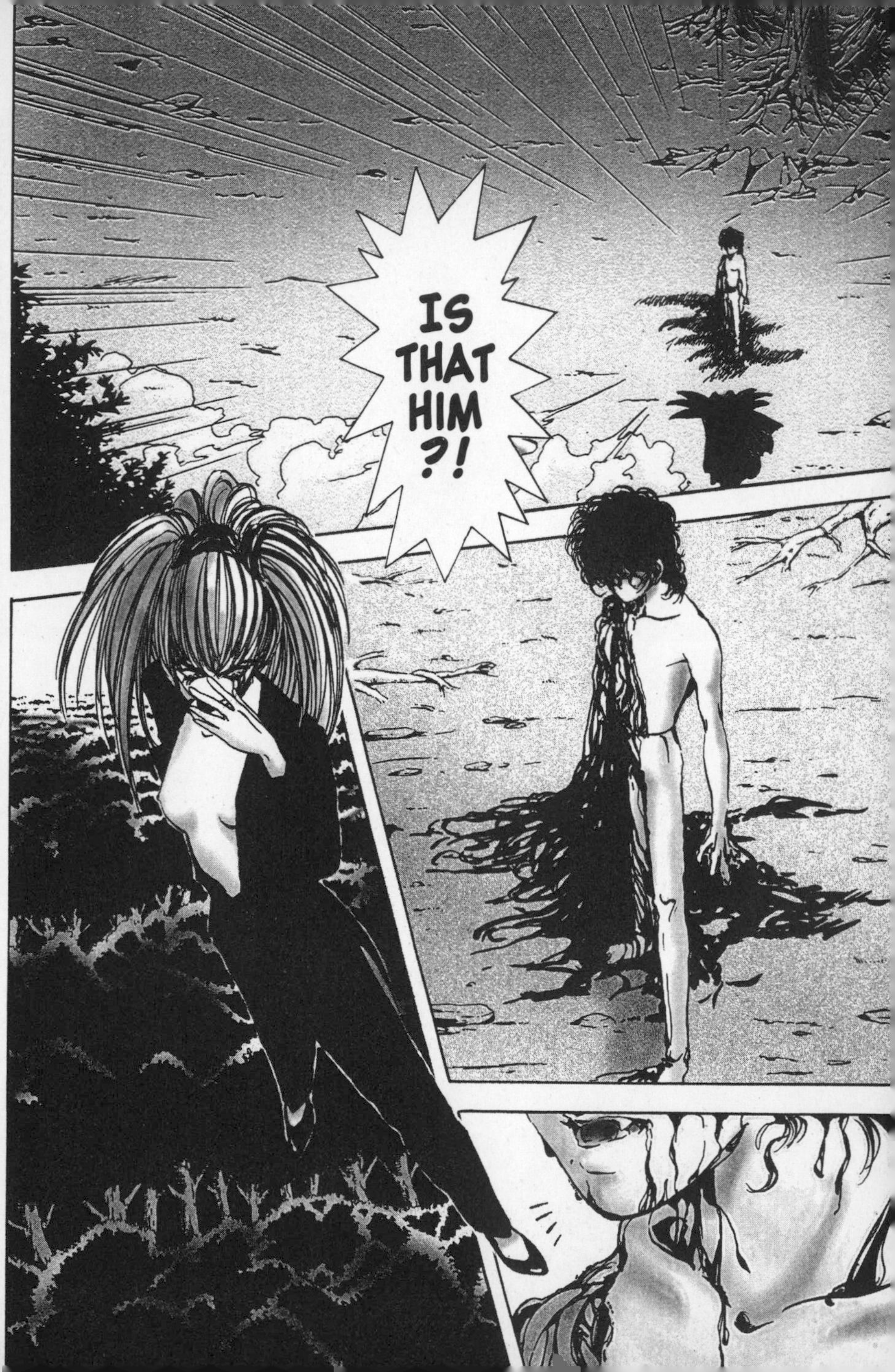
IS THAT HIM ?!

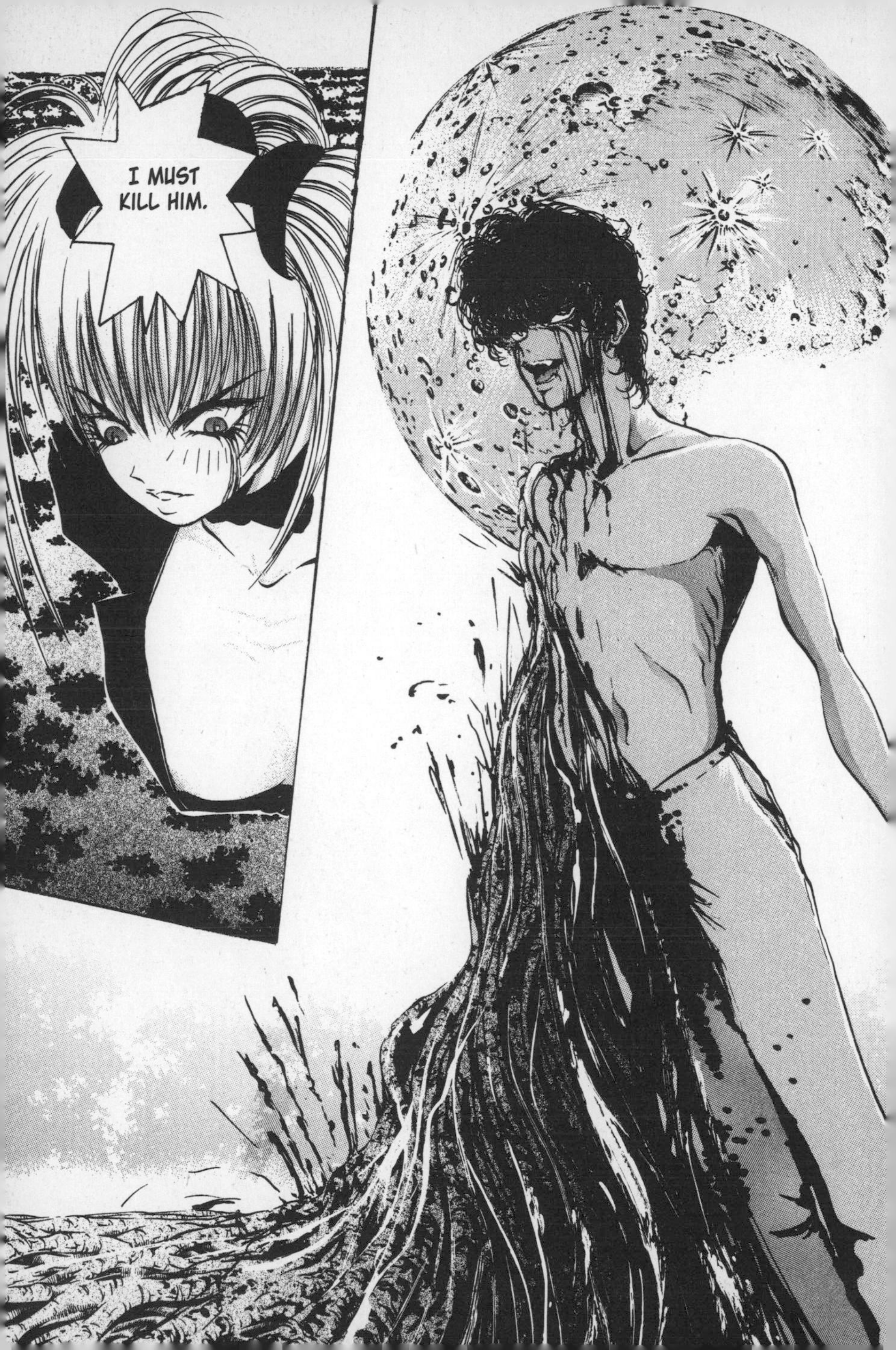
I MUST KILL HIM.

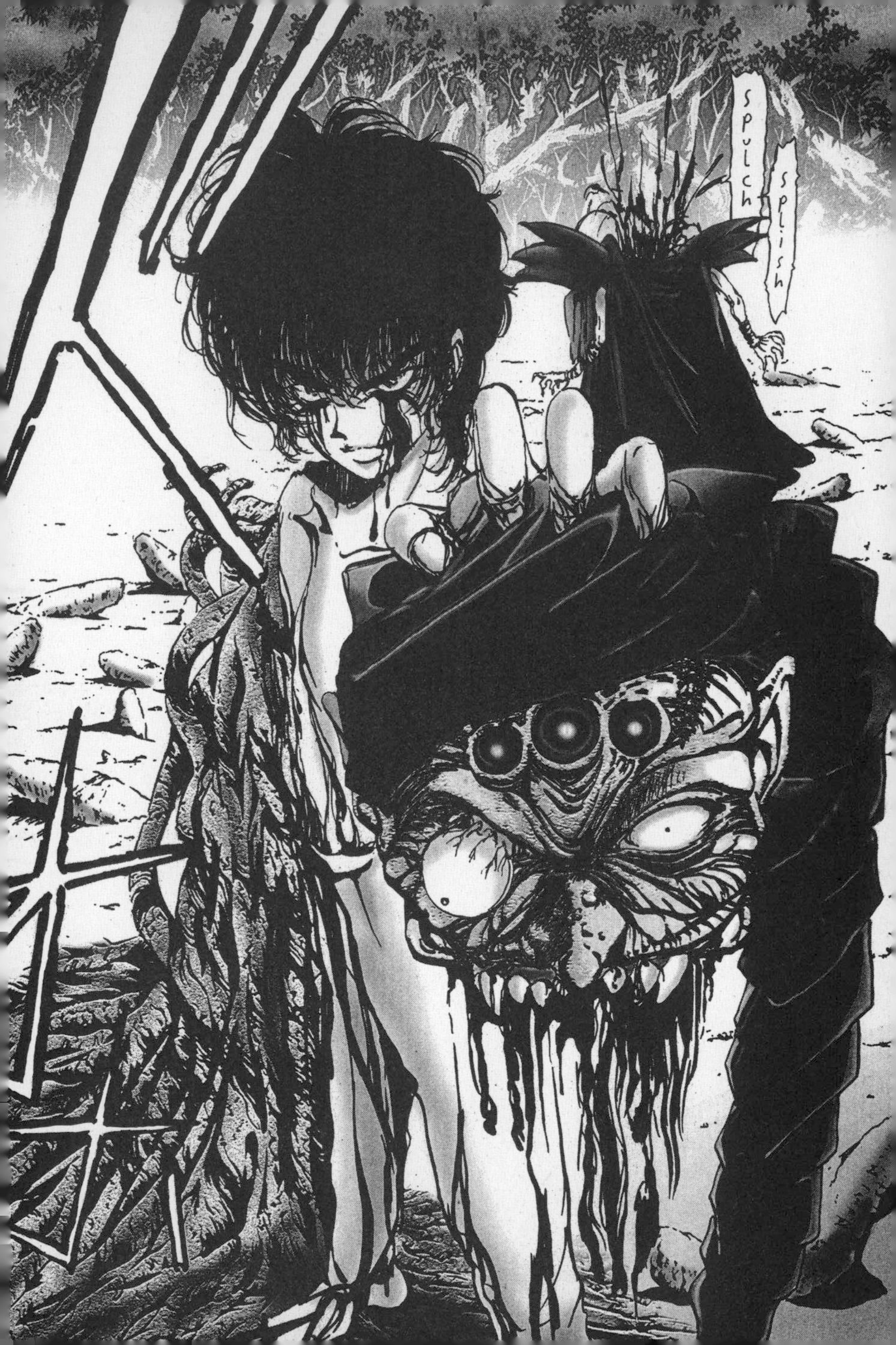
splish
spulch

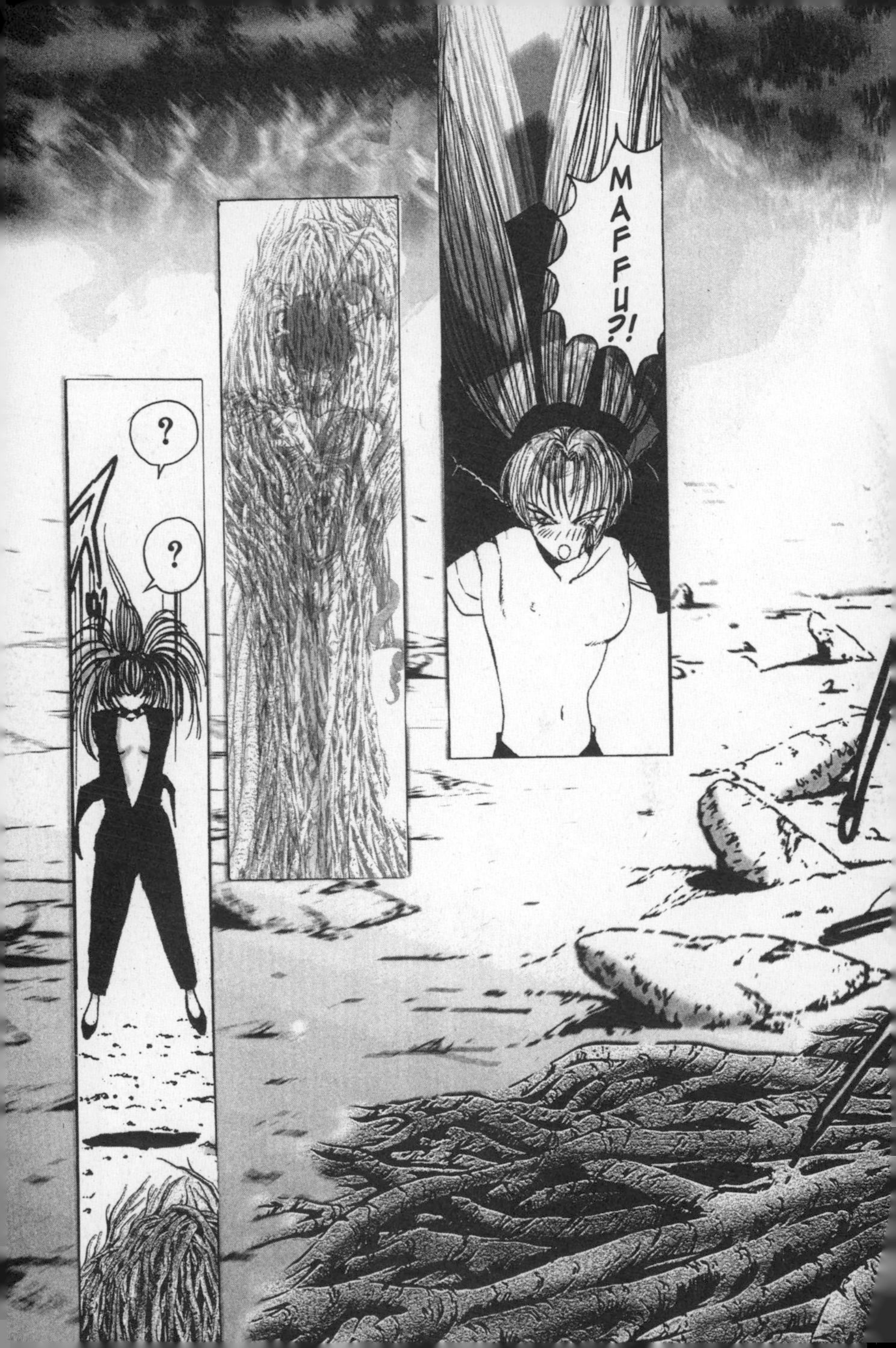
MAFFU?!
?
?

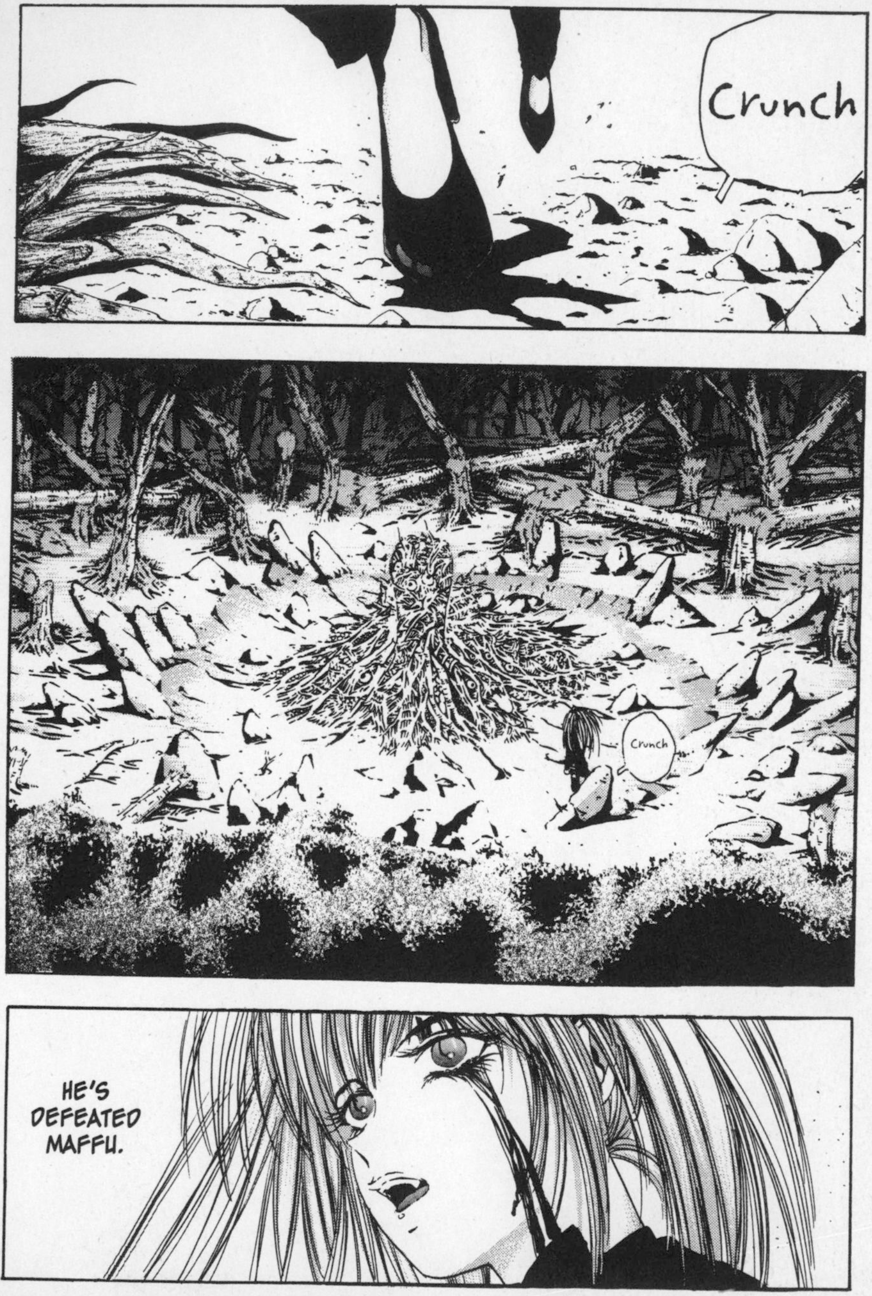
Crunch
Crunch
HE'S DEFEATED MAFFU.

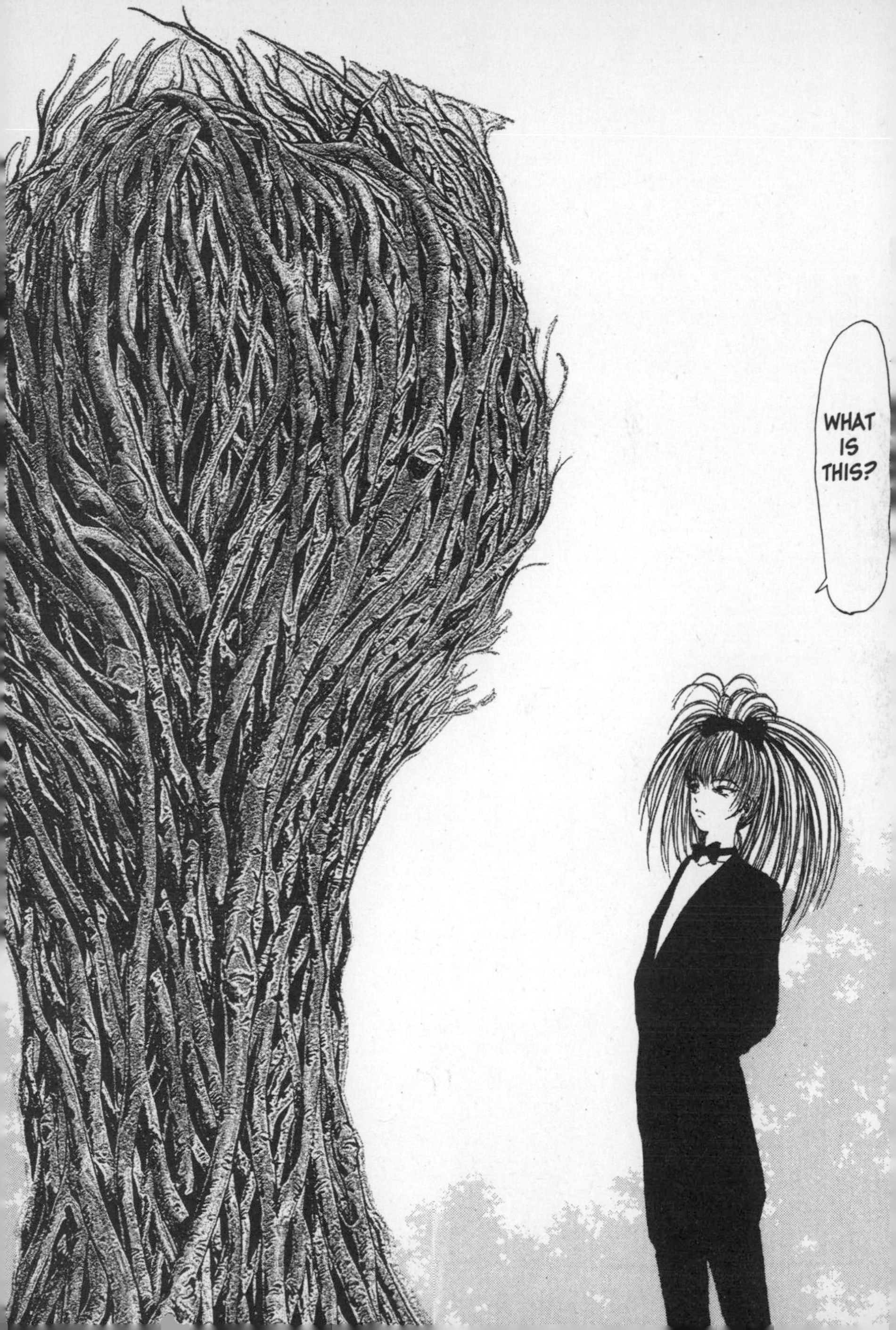
WHAT IS THIS?

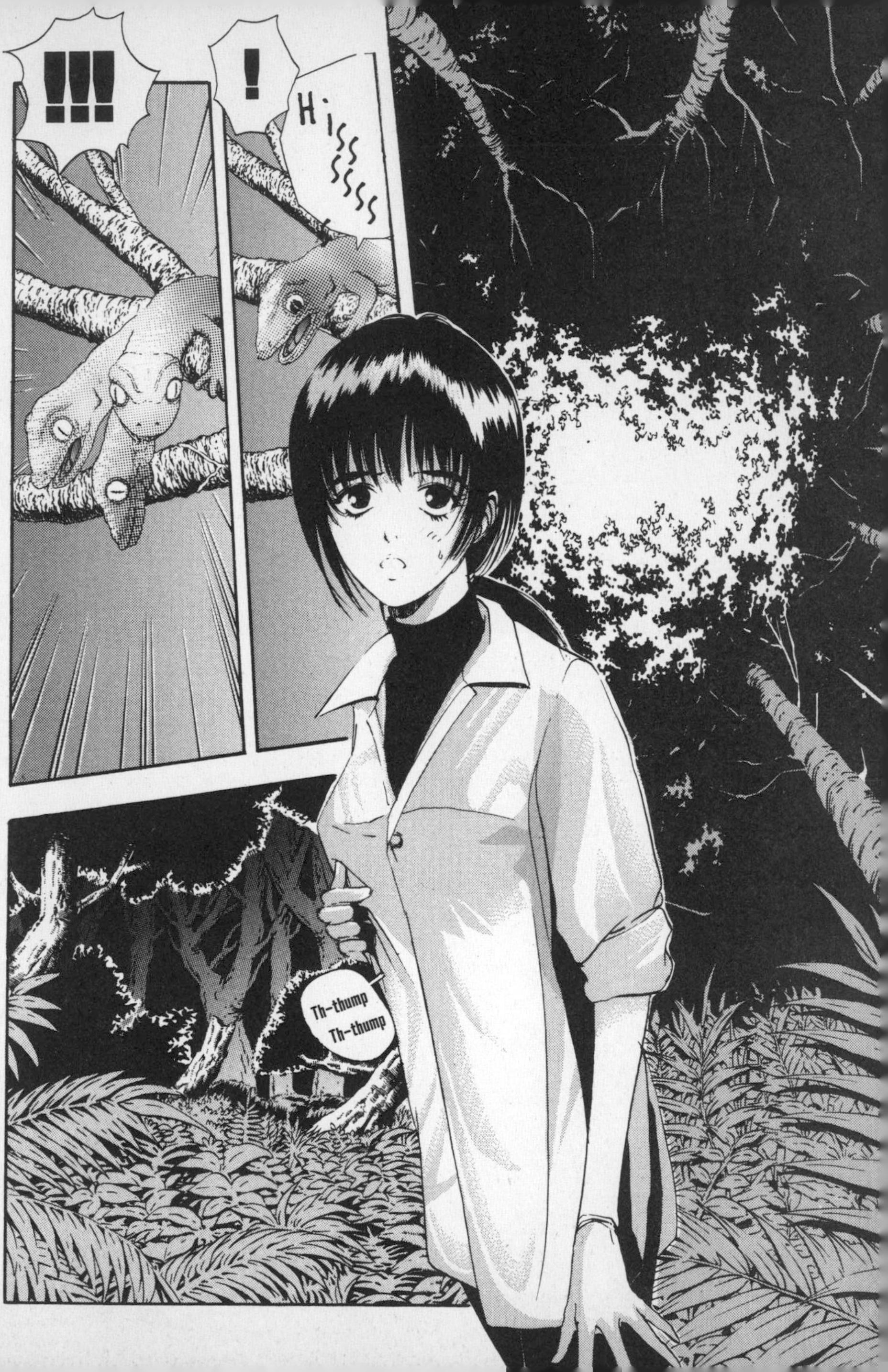
!
Hisssss
!!!
Th-thump
Th-thump

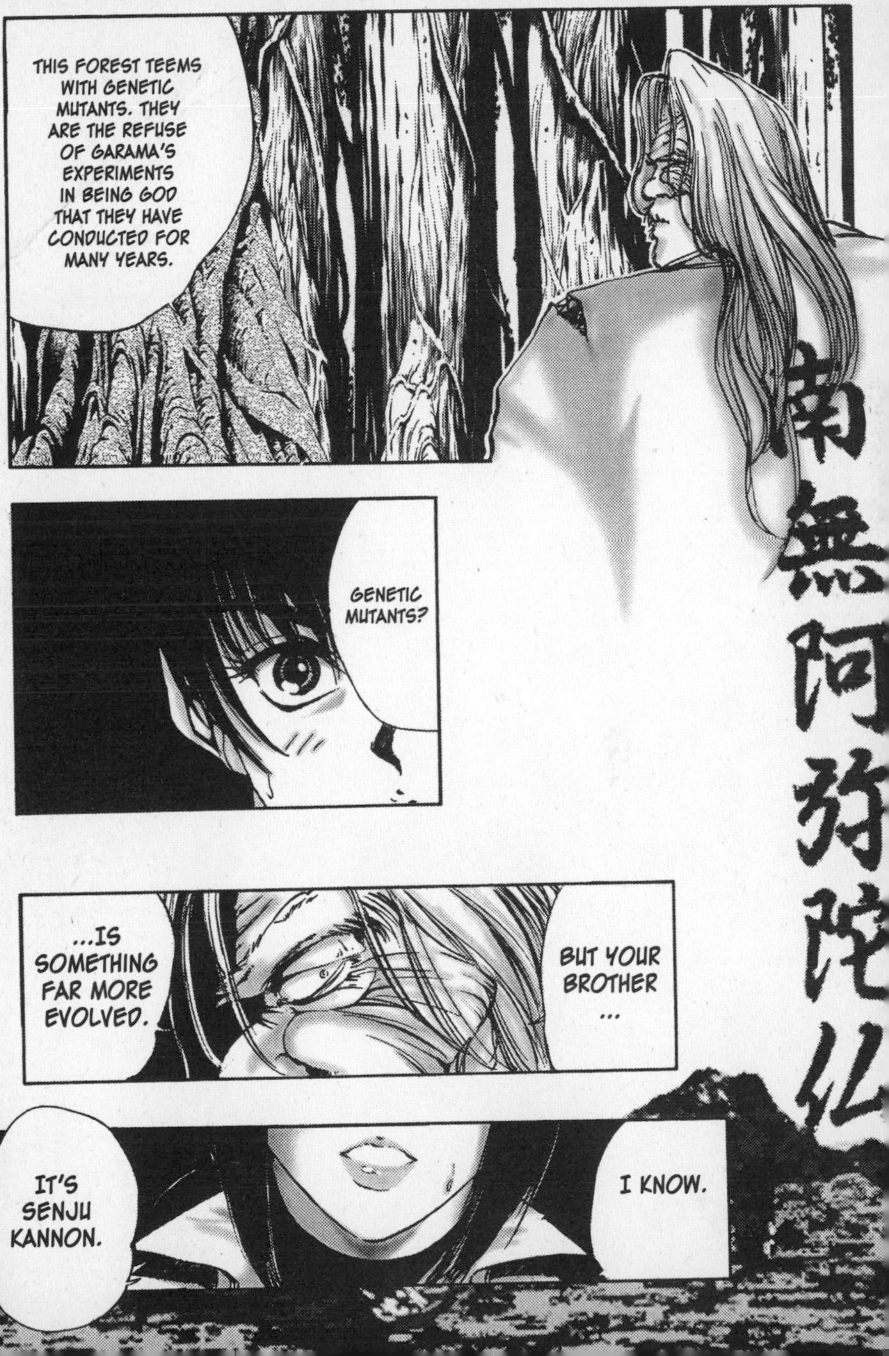
南無阿弥陀仏
THIS FOREST TEEMS WITH GENETIC MUTANTS. THEY ARE THE REFUSE OF GARAMA'S EXPERIMENTS IN BEING GOD THAT THEY HAVE CONDUCTED FOR MANY YEARS.
GENETIC MUTANTS?
BUT YOUR BROTHER ...
...IS SOMETHING FAR MORE EVOLVED.
I KNOW.
IT'S SENJU KANNON.

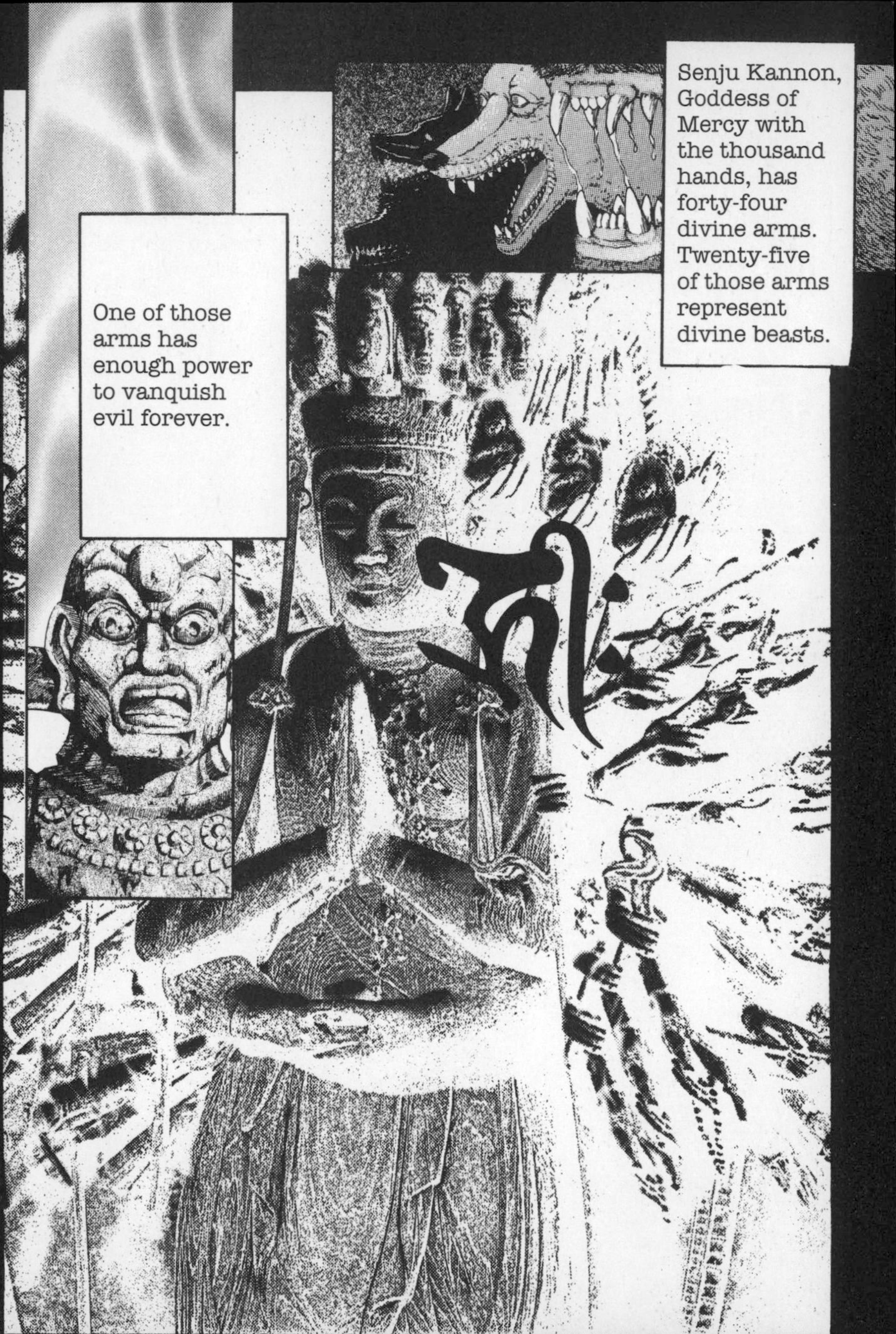
Senju Kannon, Goddess of Mercy with the thousand hands, has forty-four divine arms. Twenty-five of those arms represent divine beasts.
One of those arms has enough power to vanquish evil forever.

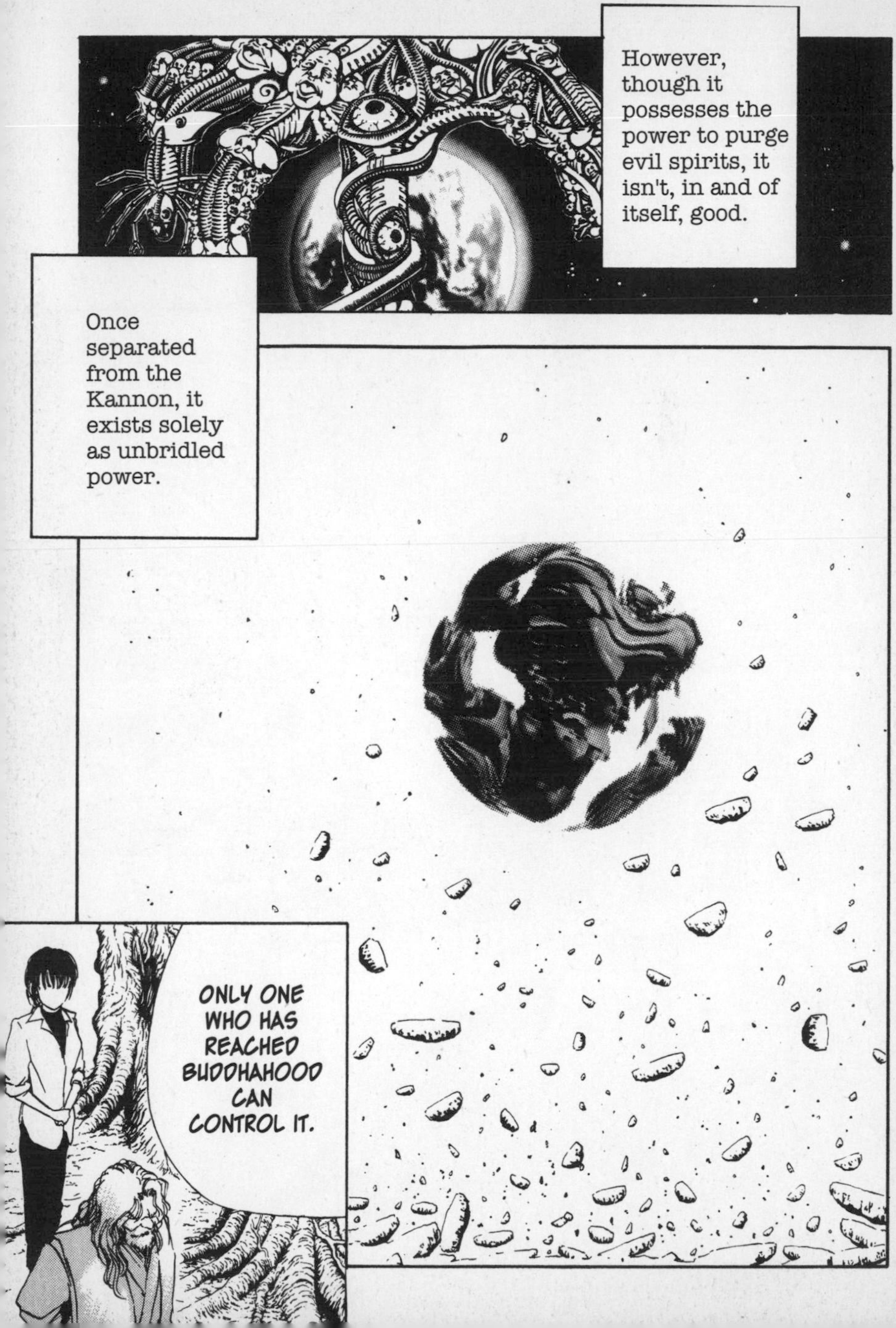
However, though it possesses the power to purge evil spirits, it isn't, in and of itself, good.
Once separated from the Kannon, it exists solely as unbridled power.
ONLY ONE WHO HAS REACHED BUDDHAHOOD CAN CONTROL IT.

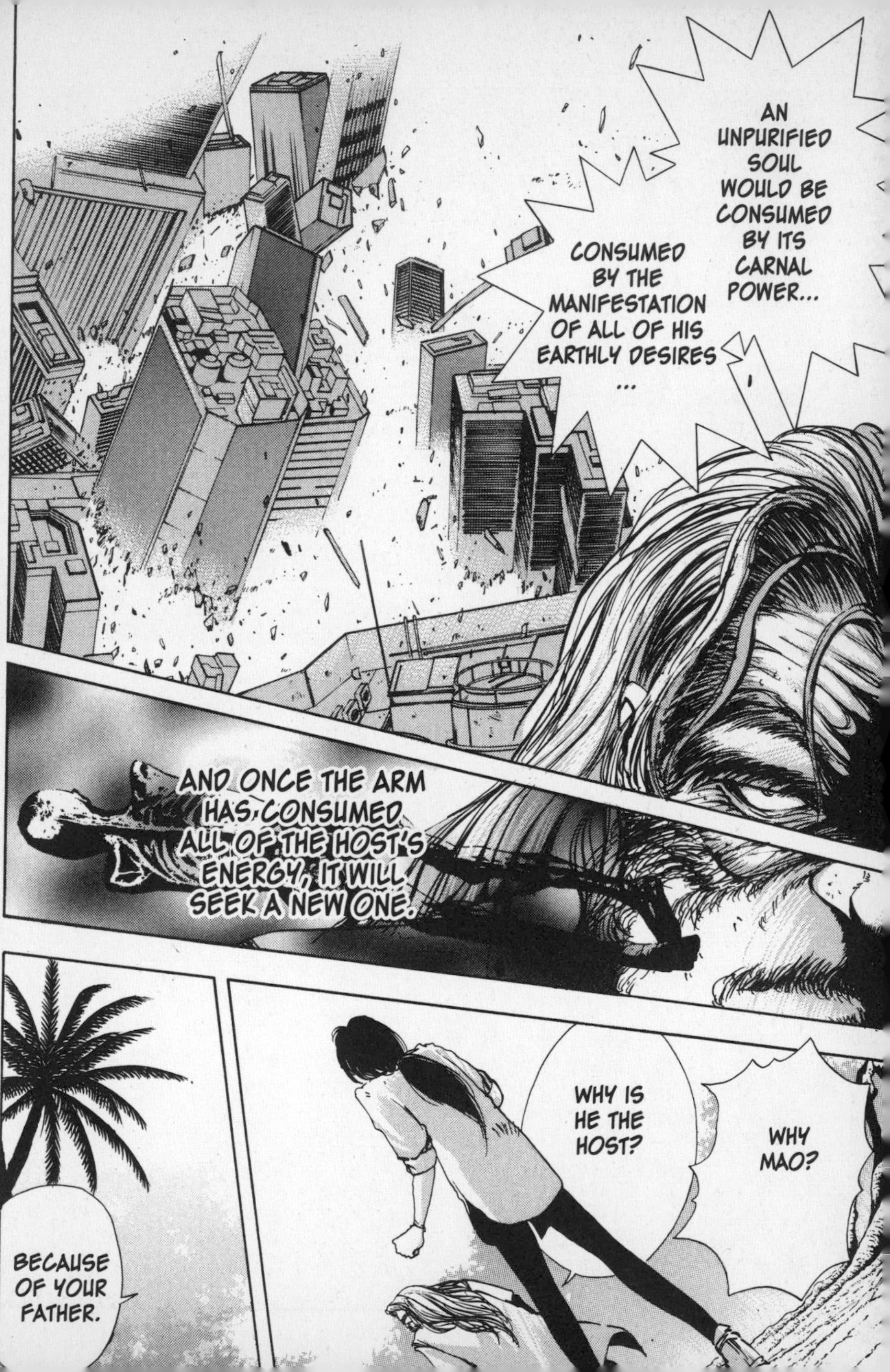
AN UNPURIFIED SOUL WOULD BE CONSUMED BY ITS CARNAL POWER...
CONSUMED BY THE MANIFESTATION OF ALL OF HIS EARTHLY DESIRES ...
AND ONCE THE ARM HAS CONSUMED ALL OF THE HOST'S ENERGY, IT WILL SEEK A NEW ONE.
WHY MAO?
WHY IS HE THE HOST?
BECAUSE OF YOUR FATHER.

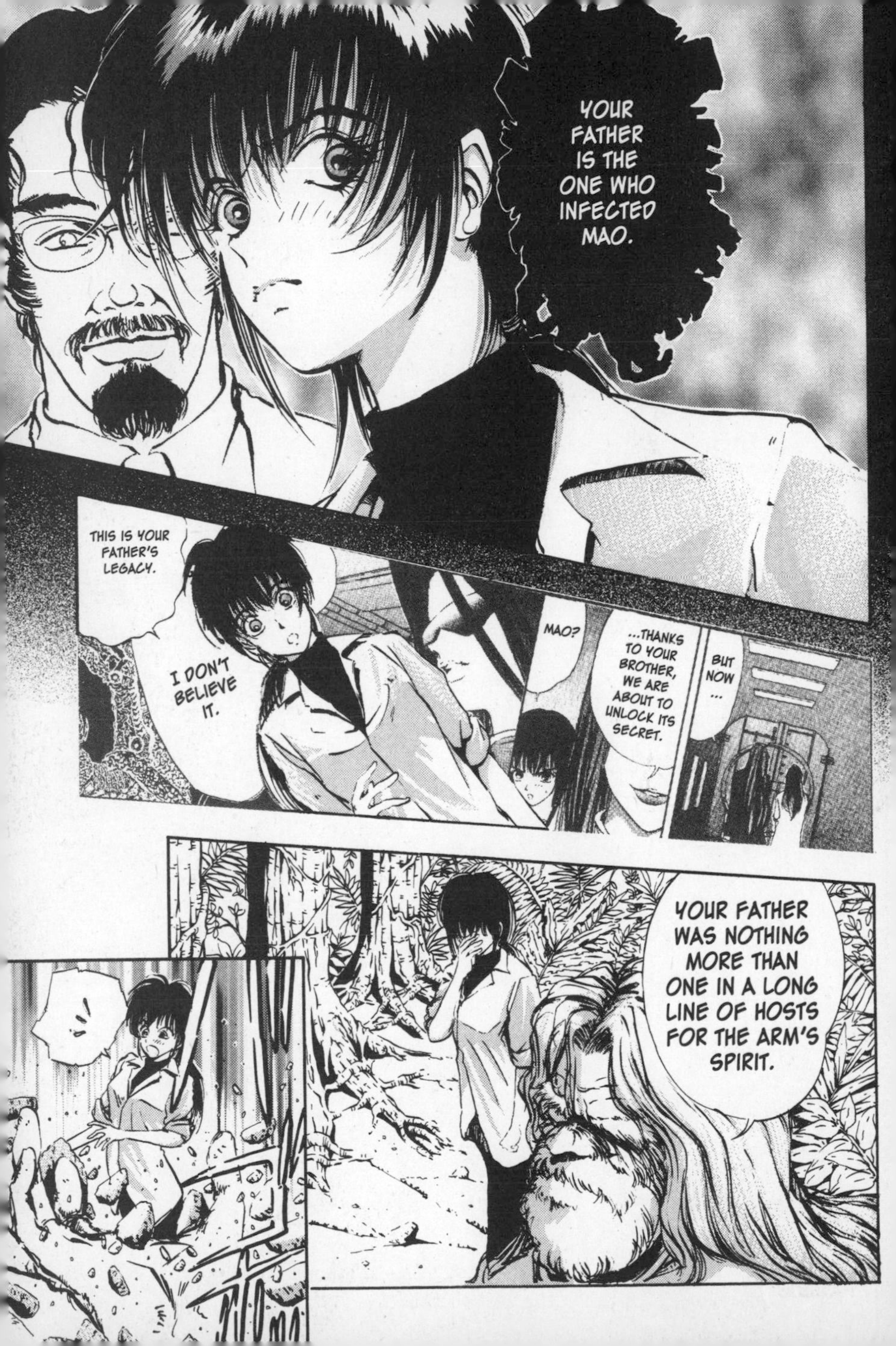
YOUR FATHER IS THE ONE WHO INFECTED MAO.
BUT NOW ...
...THANKS TO YOUR BROTHER, WE ARE ABOUT TO UNLOCK ITS SECRET.
MAO?
THIS IS YOUR FATHER'S LEGACY.
I DON'T BELIEVE IT.
YOUR FATHER WAS NOTHING MORE THAN ONE IN A LONG LINE OF HOSTS FOR THE ARM'S SPIRIT.
!

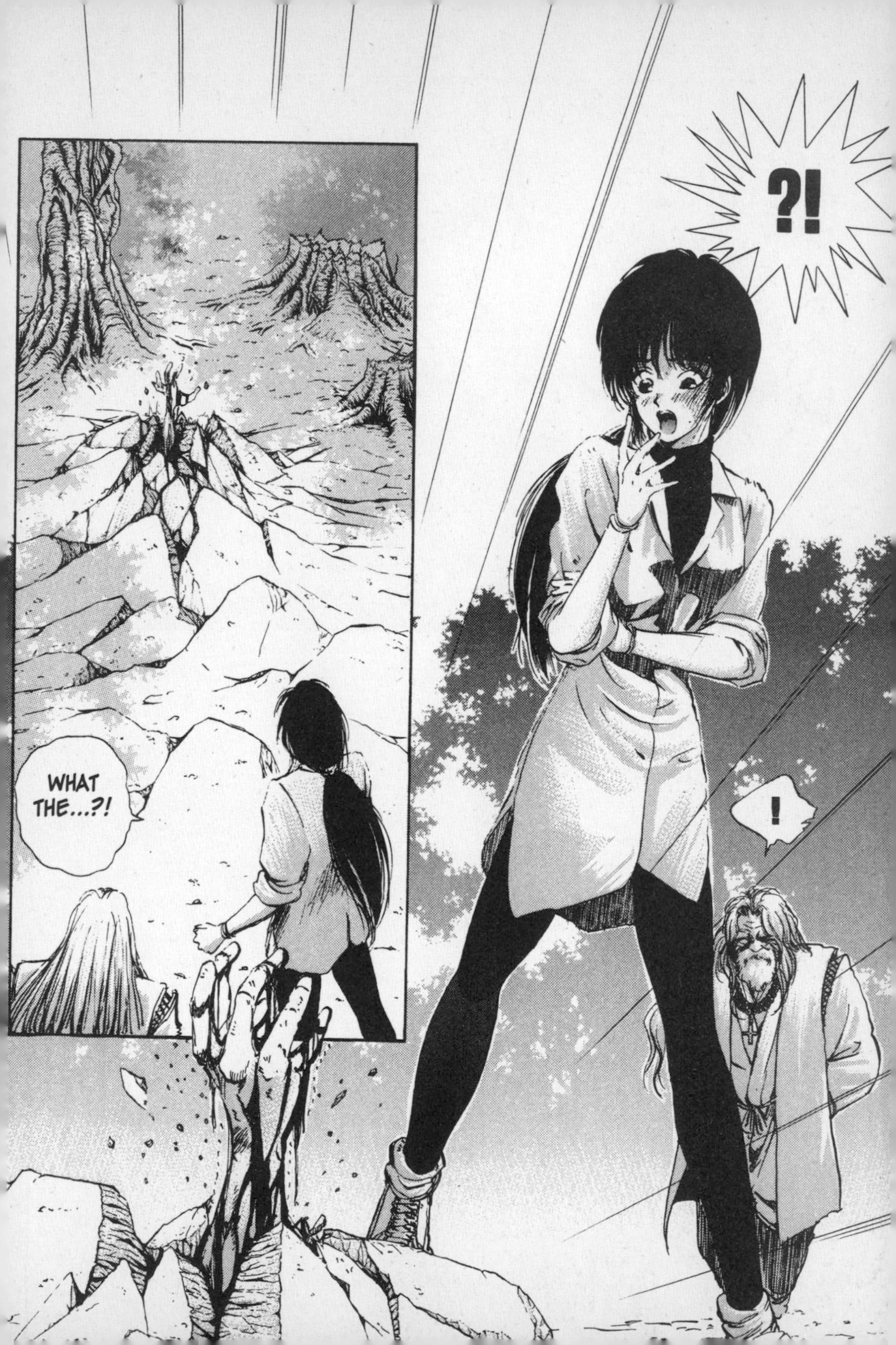
?!
!
WHAT THE...?!

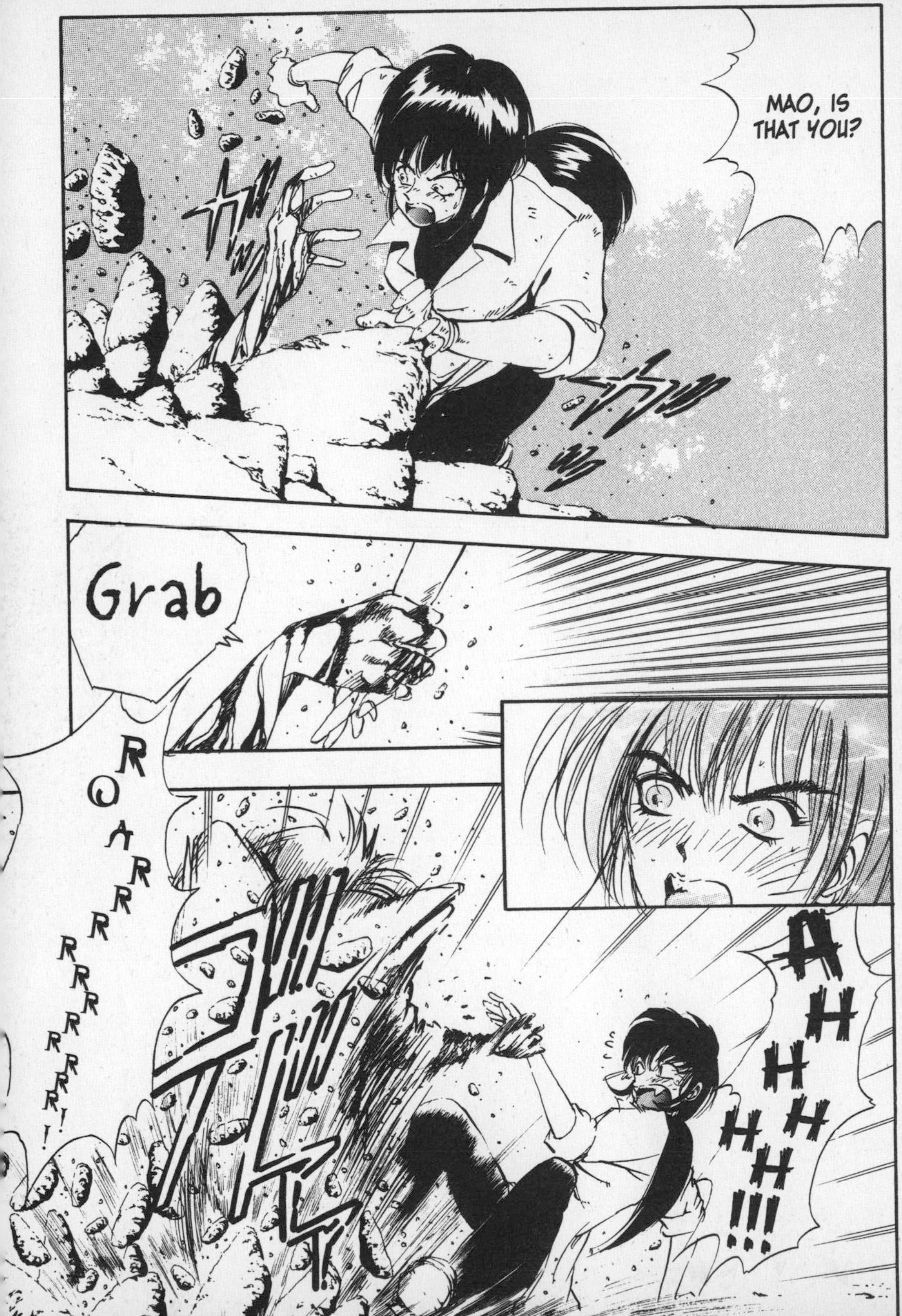

MAO, IS THAT YOU?
Grab
AHHHHH!!!
ROARRRRRRRRRRRR!

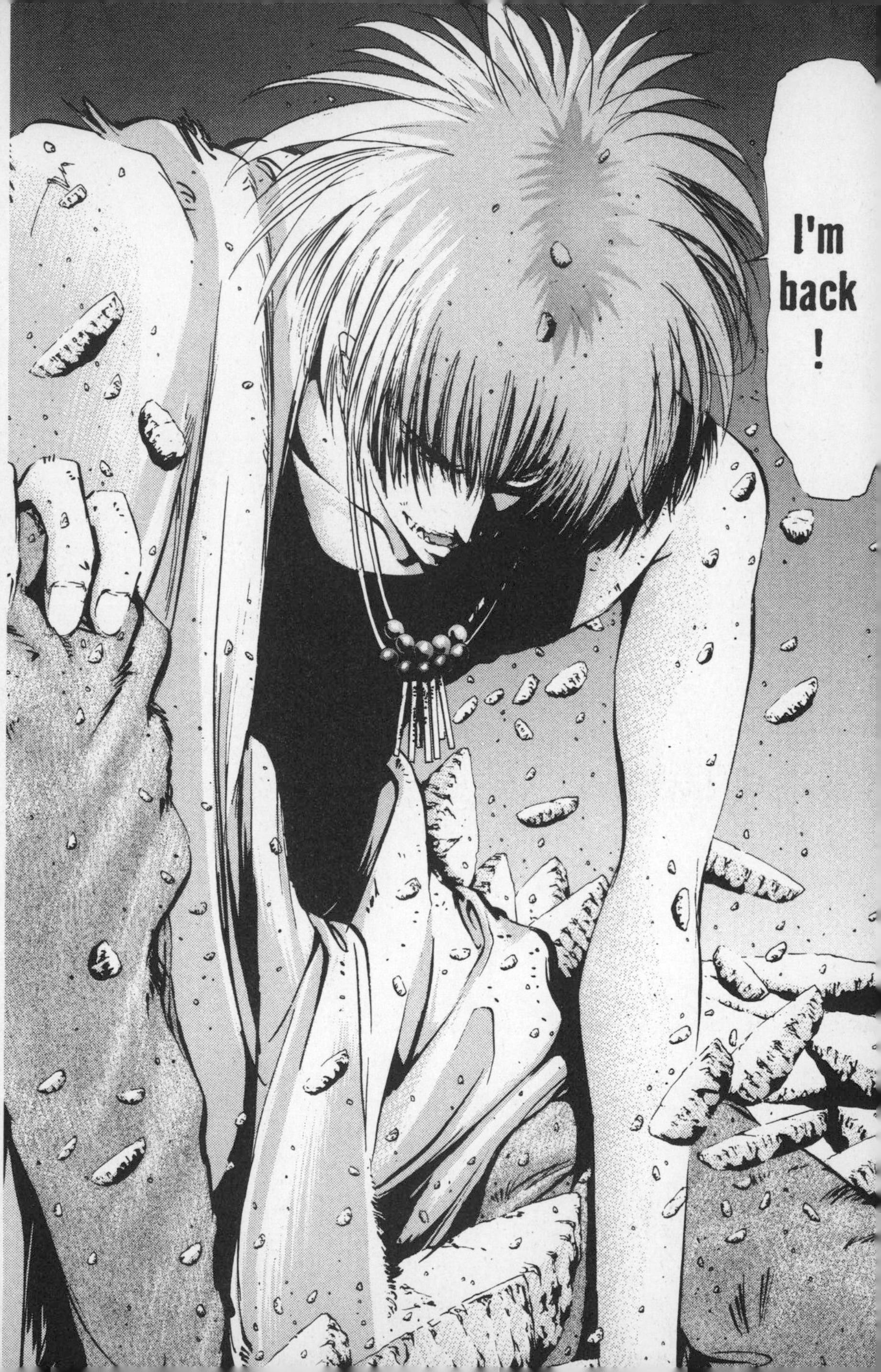
I'm back !

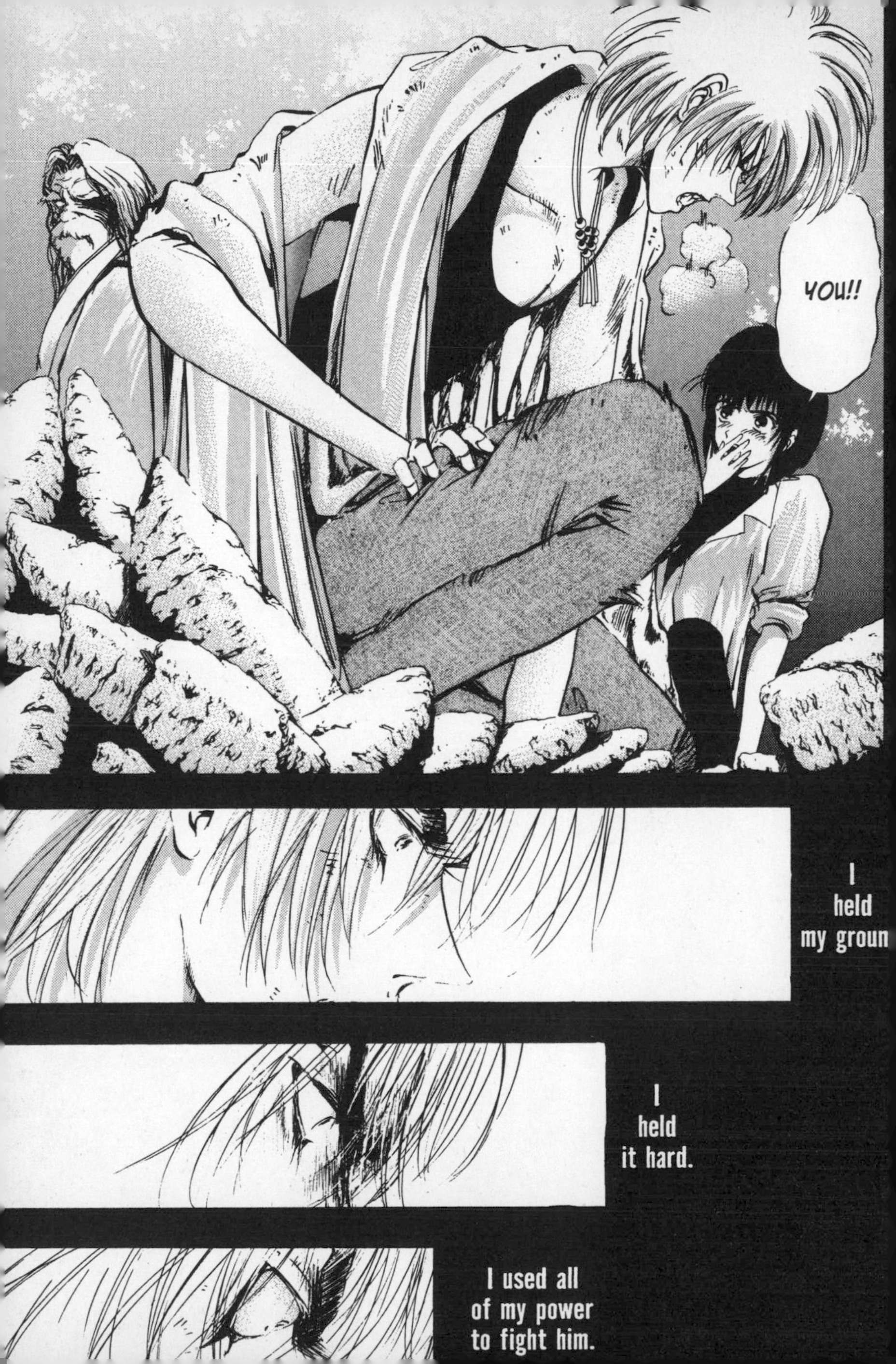
YOU!!
I held my groun
I held it hard.
I used all of my power to fight him.

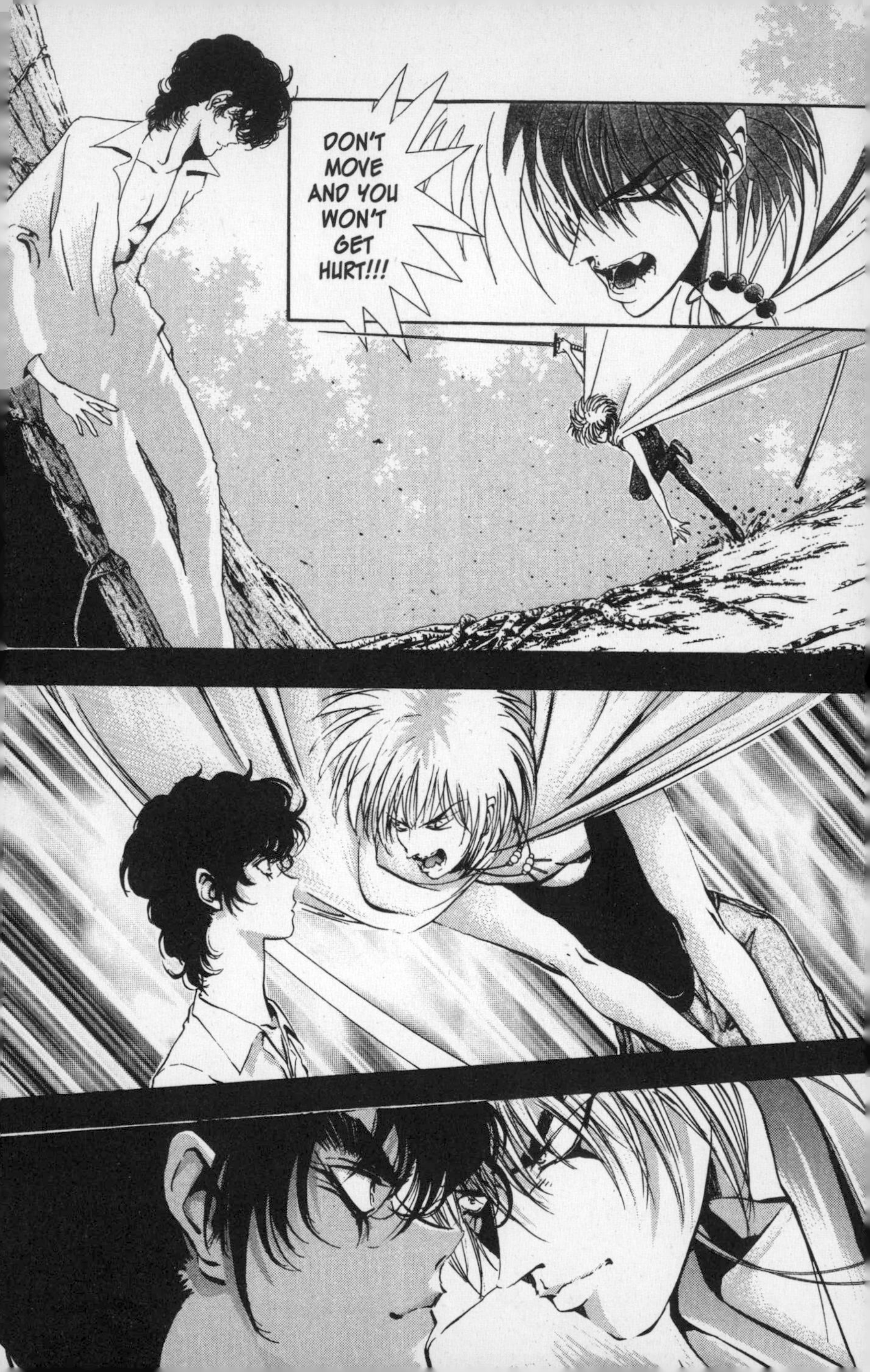
DON'T MOVE AND YOU WON'T GET HURT!!!

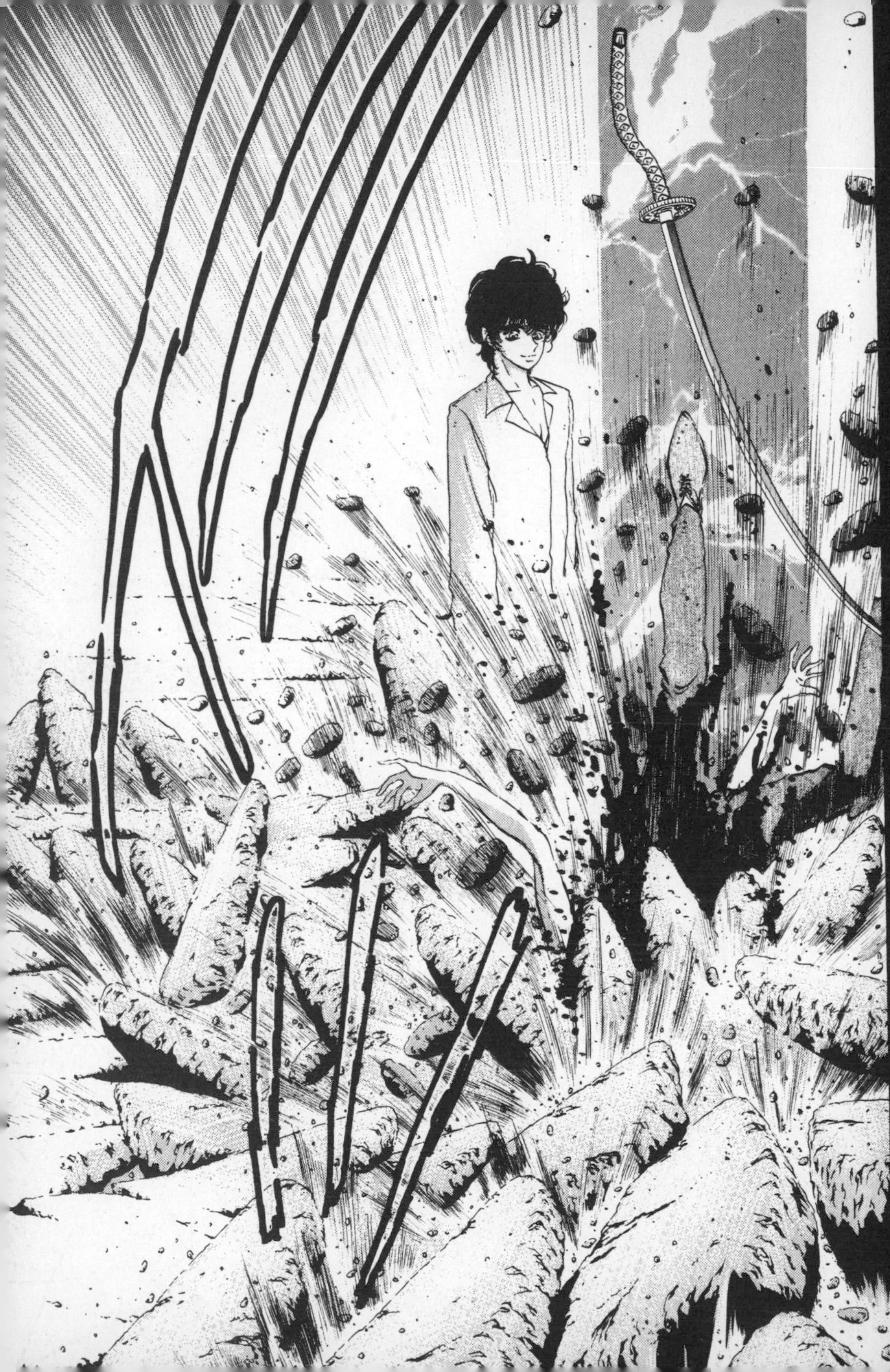

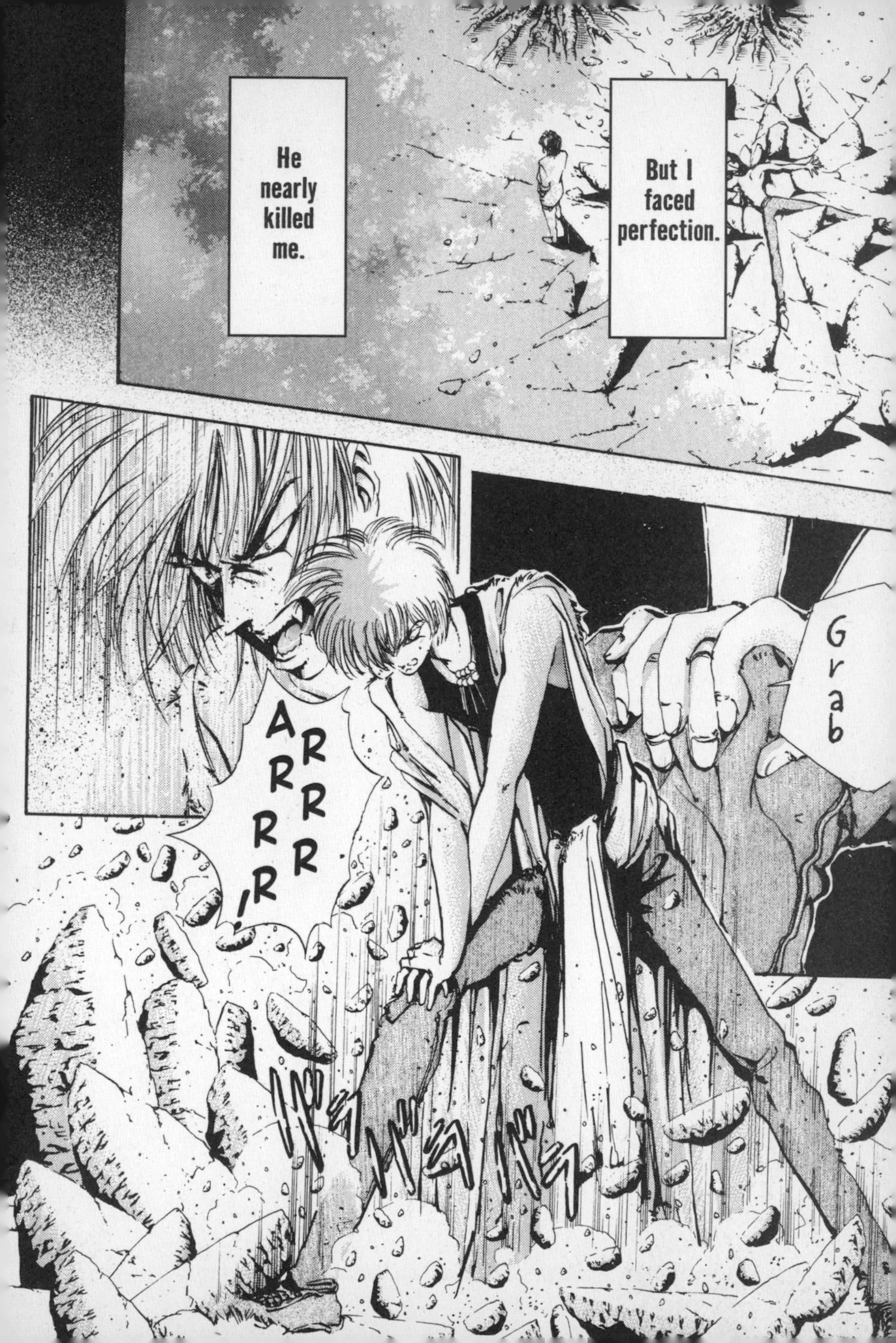

But I faced perfection.
He nearly killed me.
Grab
ARRRRRR!

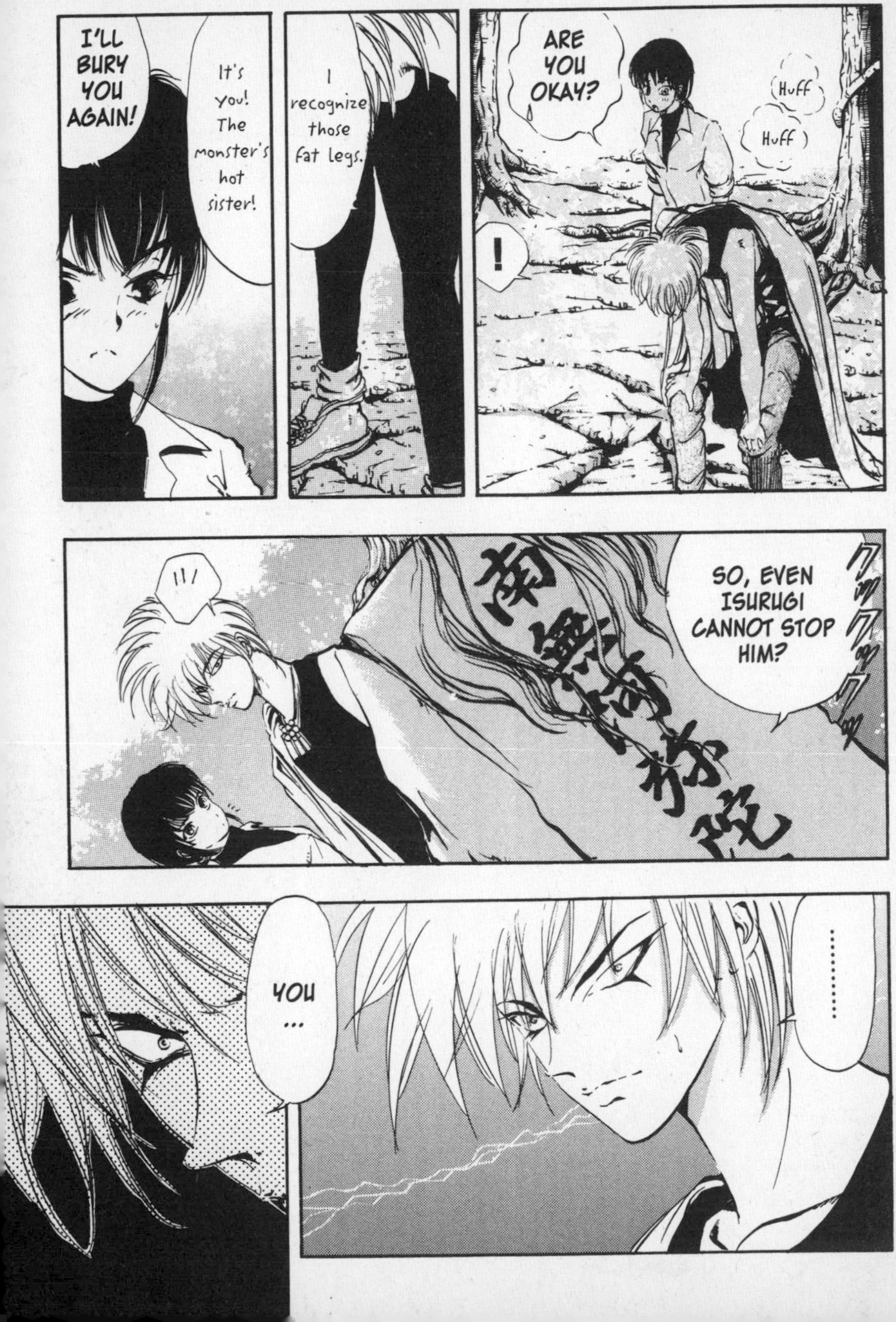
Huff
Huff
ARE YOU OKAY?
!
I recognize those fat legs.
It's you! The monster's hot sister!
I'LL BURY YOU AGAIN!
SO, EVEN ISURUGI CANNOT STOP HIM?
!!!
......
YOU ...

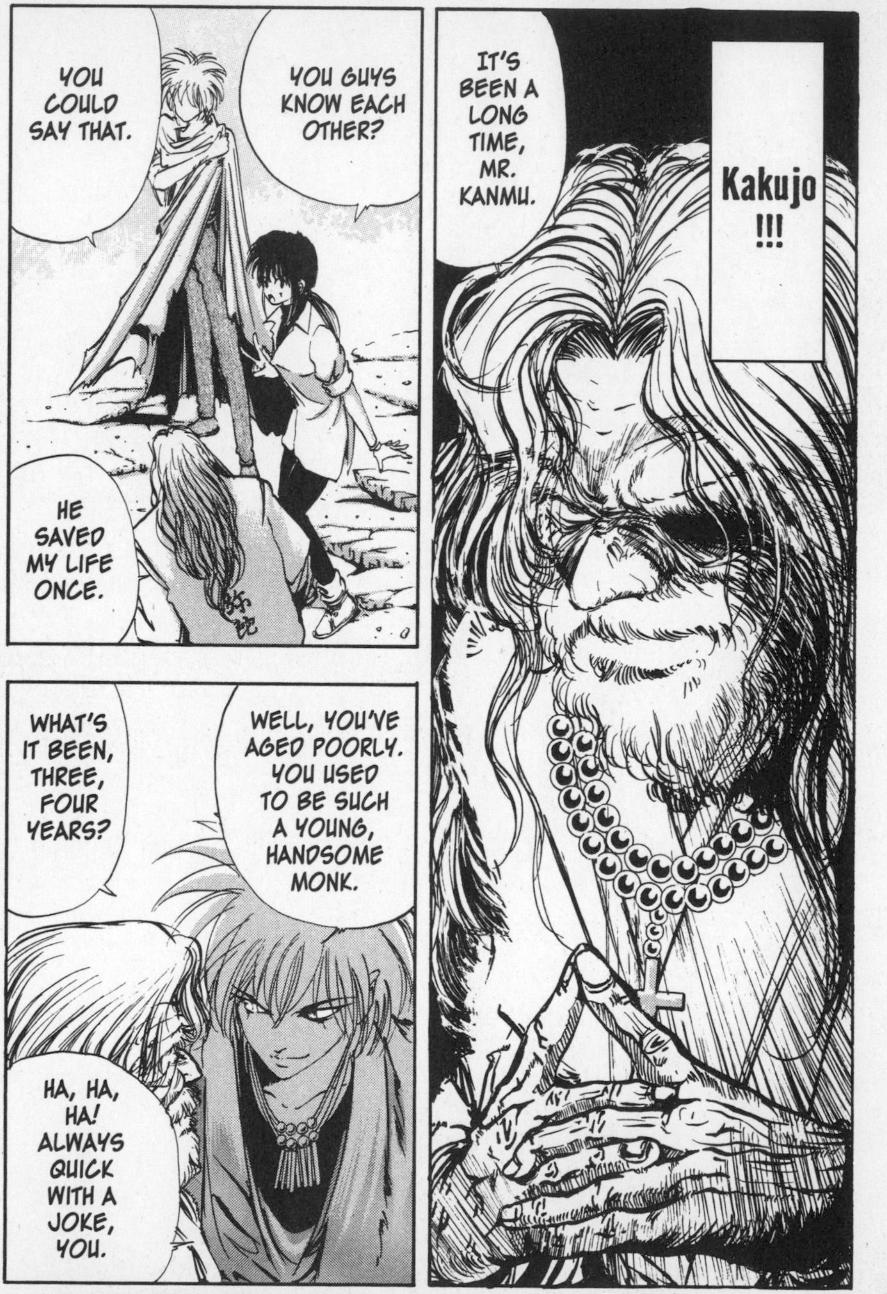
Kakujo !!!
IT'S BEEN A LONG TIME, MR. KANMU.
YOU GUYS KNOW EACH OTHER?
YOU COULD SAY THAT.
HE SAVED MY LIFE ONCE.
WELL, YOU'VE AGED POORLY. YOU USED TO BE SUCH A YOUNG, HANDSOME MONK.
WHAT'S IT BEEN, THREE, FOUR YEARS?
HA, HA, HA! ALWAYS QUICK WITH A JOKE, YOU.

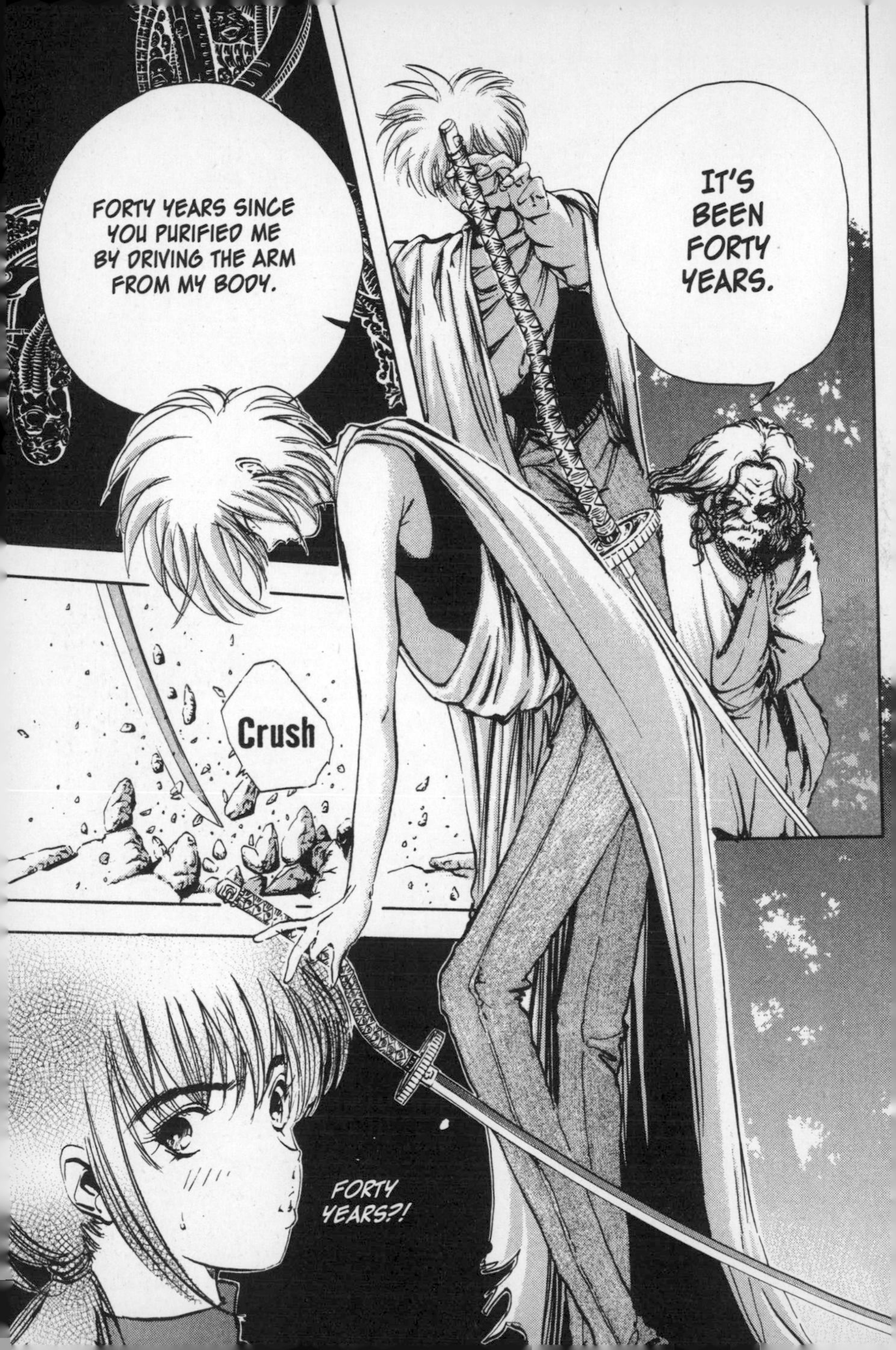
IT'S BEEN FORTY YEARS.
FORTY YEARS SINCE YOU PURIFIED ME BY DRIVING THE ARM FROM MY BODY.
Crush
FORTY YEARS?!

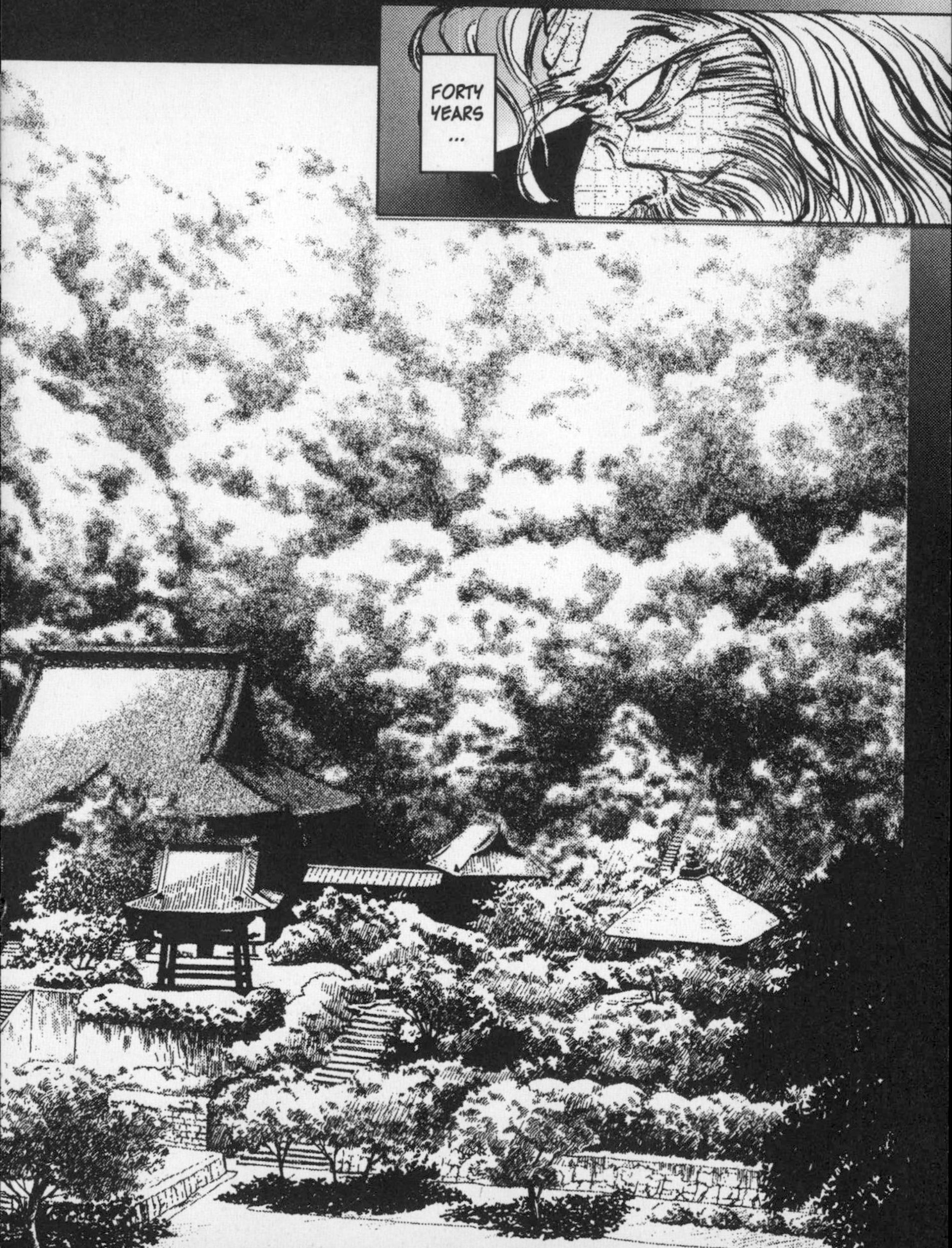
FORTY YEARS ...

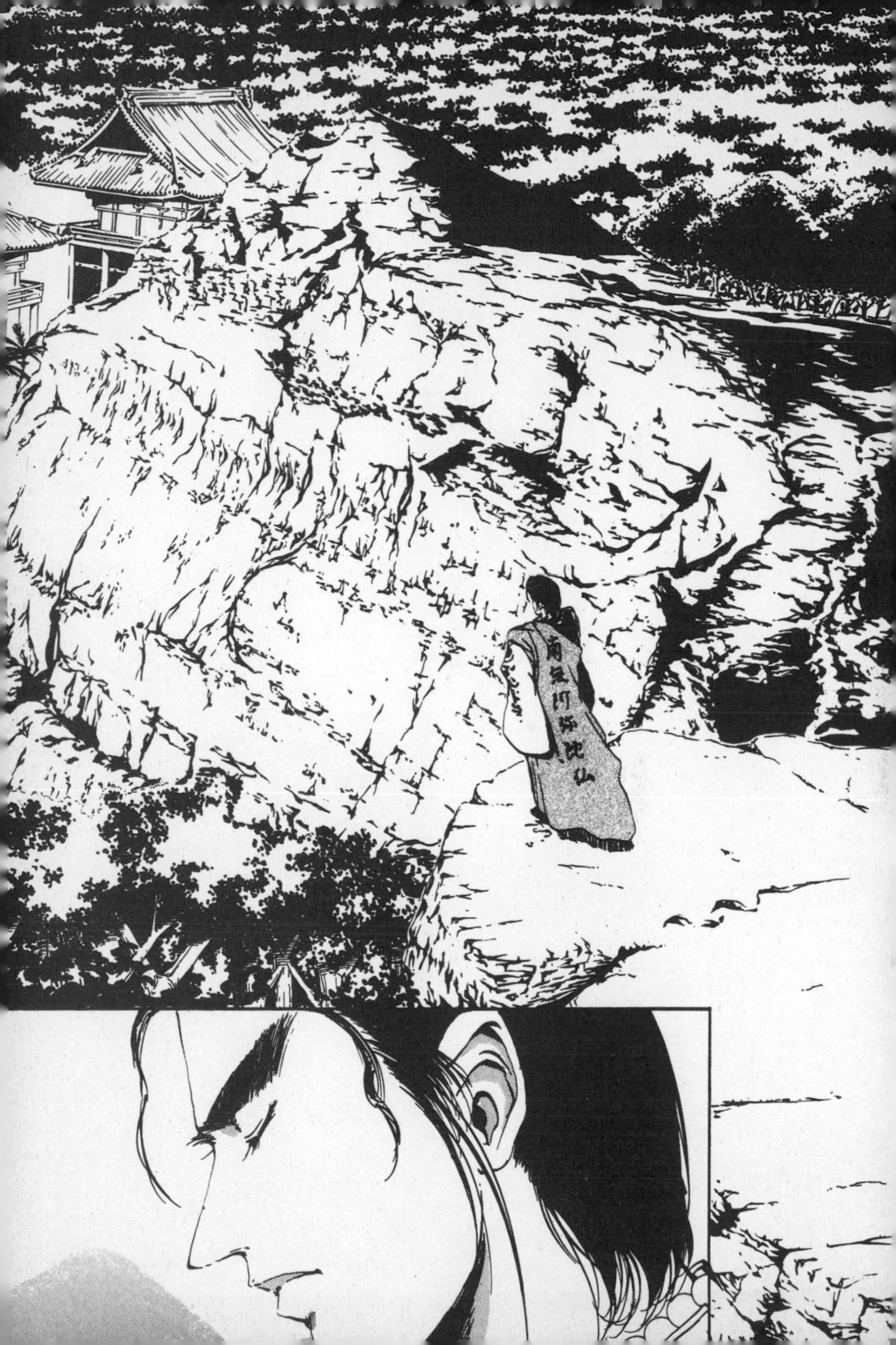
南無阿弥陀仏

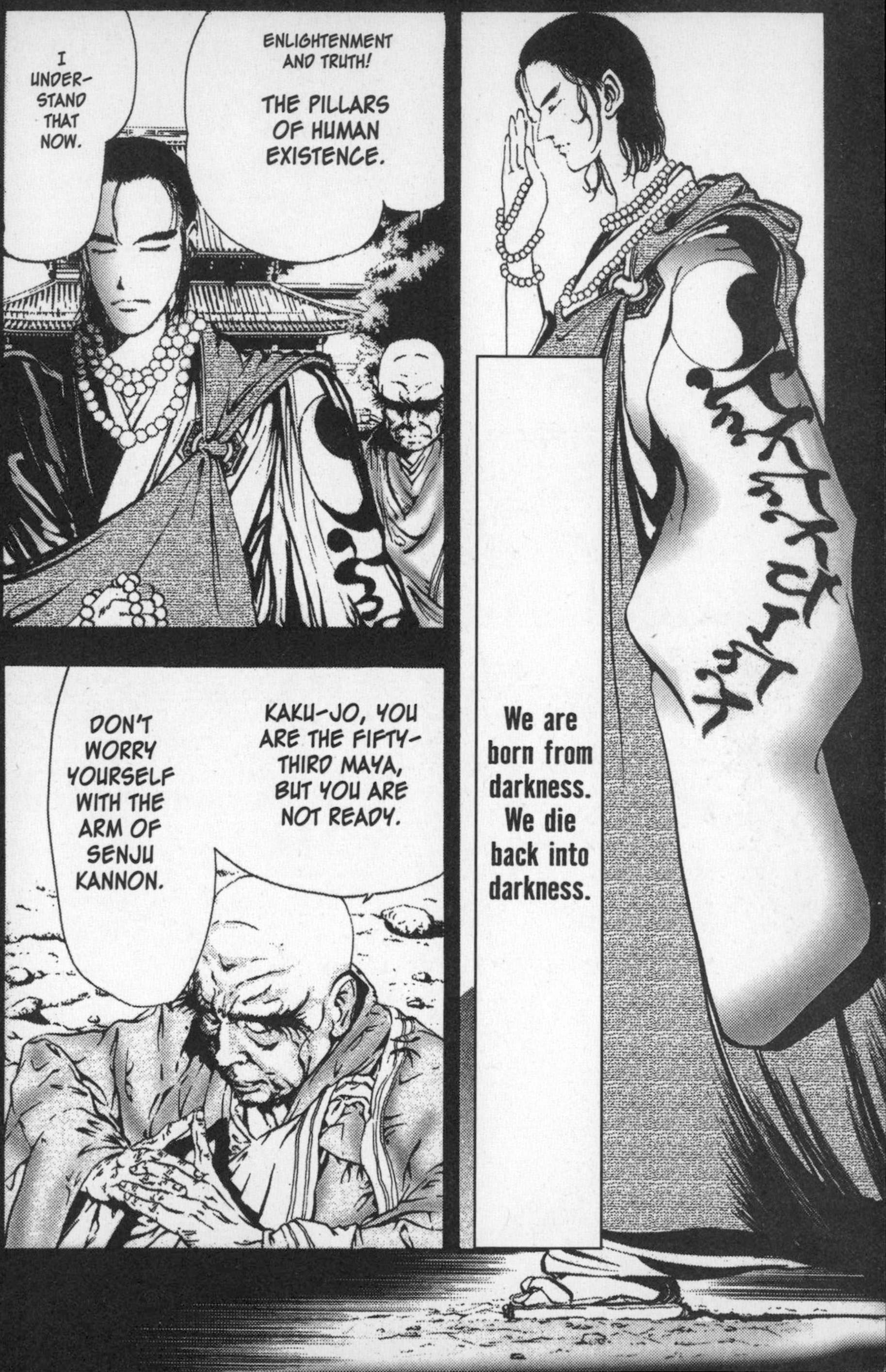
We are born from darkness. We die back into darkness.
ENLIGHTENMENT AND TRUTH!
THE PILLARS OF HUMAN EXISTENCE.
I UNDERSTAND THAT NOW.
KAKU-JO, YOU ARE THE FIFTY-THIRD MAYA, BUT YOU ARE NOT READY.
DON'T WORRY YOURSELF WITH THE ARM OF SENJU KANNON.

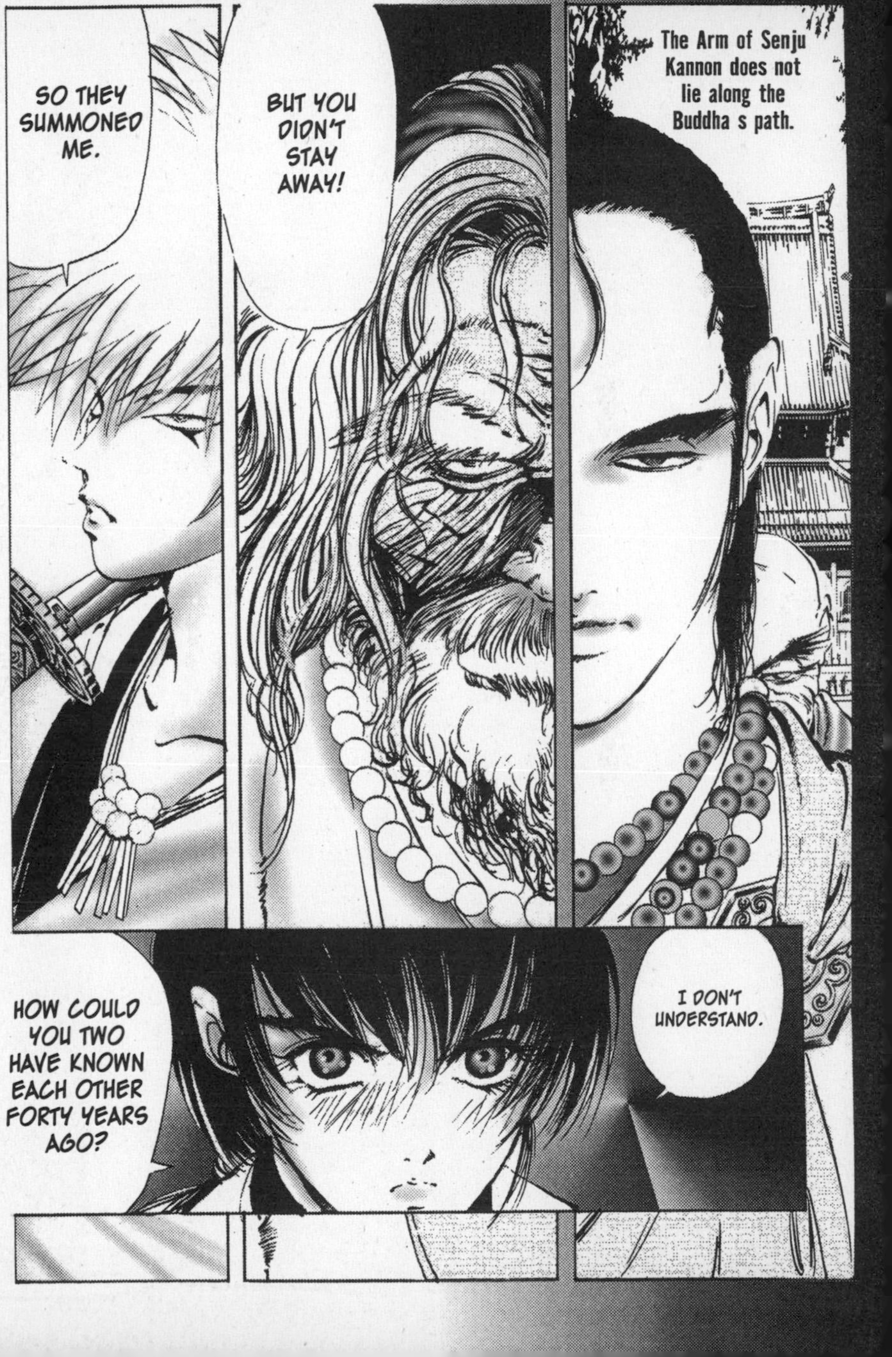
The Arm of Senju Kannon does not lie along the Buddha s path.
BUT YOU DIDN'T STAY AWAY!
SO THEY SUMMONED ME.
I DON'T UNDERSTAND.
HOW COULD YOU TWO HAVE KNOWN EACH OTHER FORTY YEARS AGO?

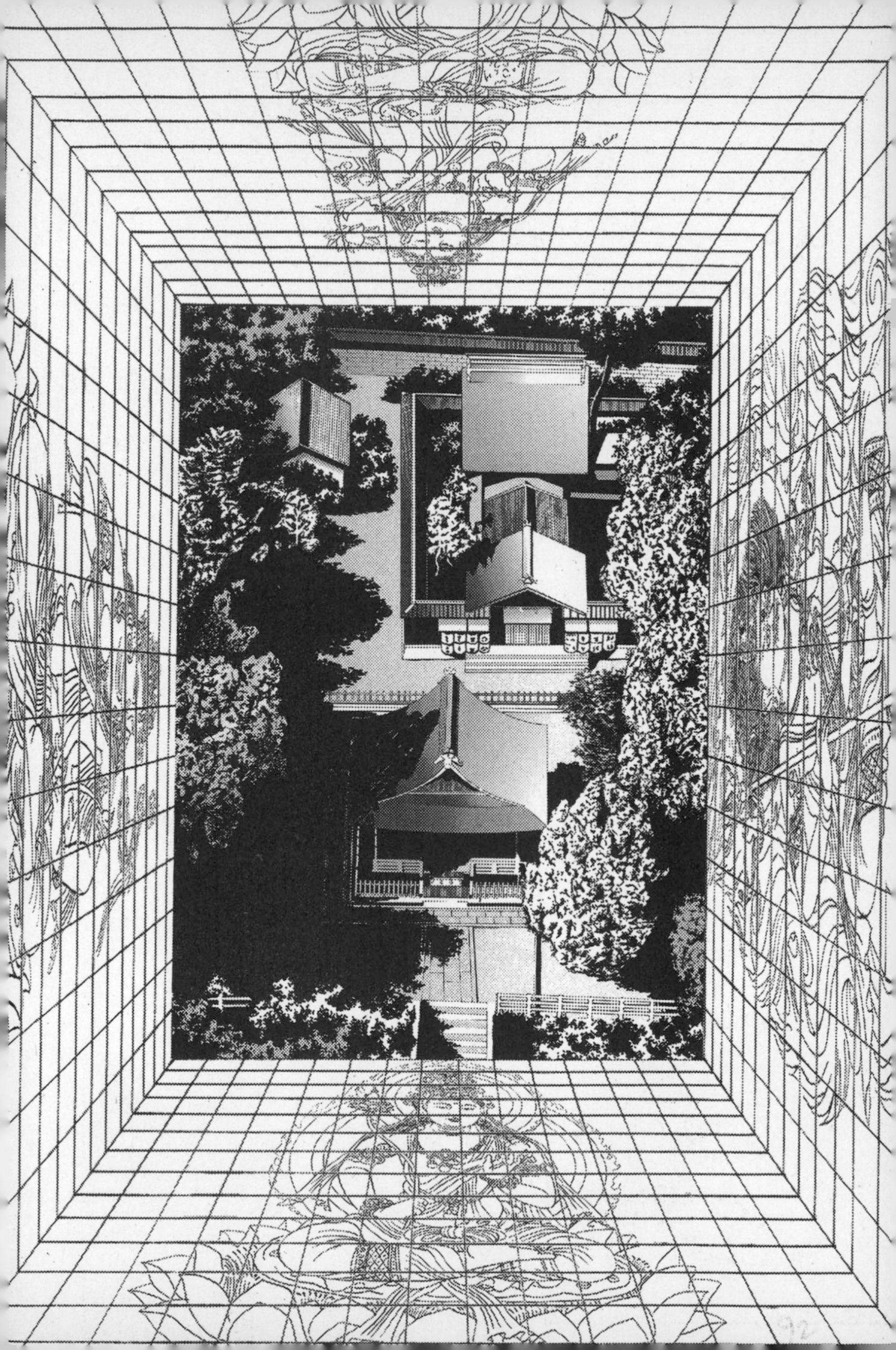

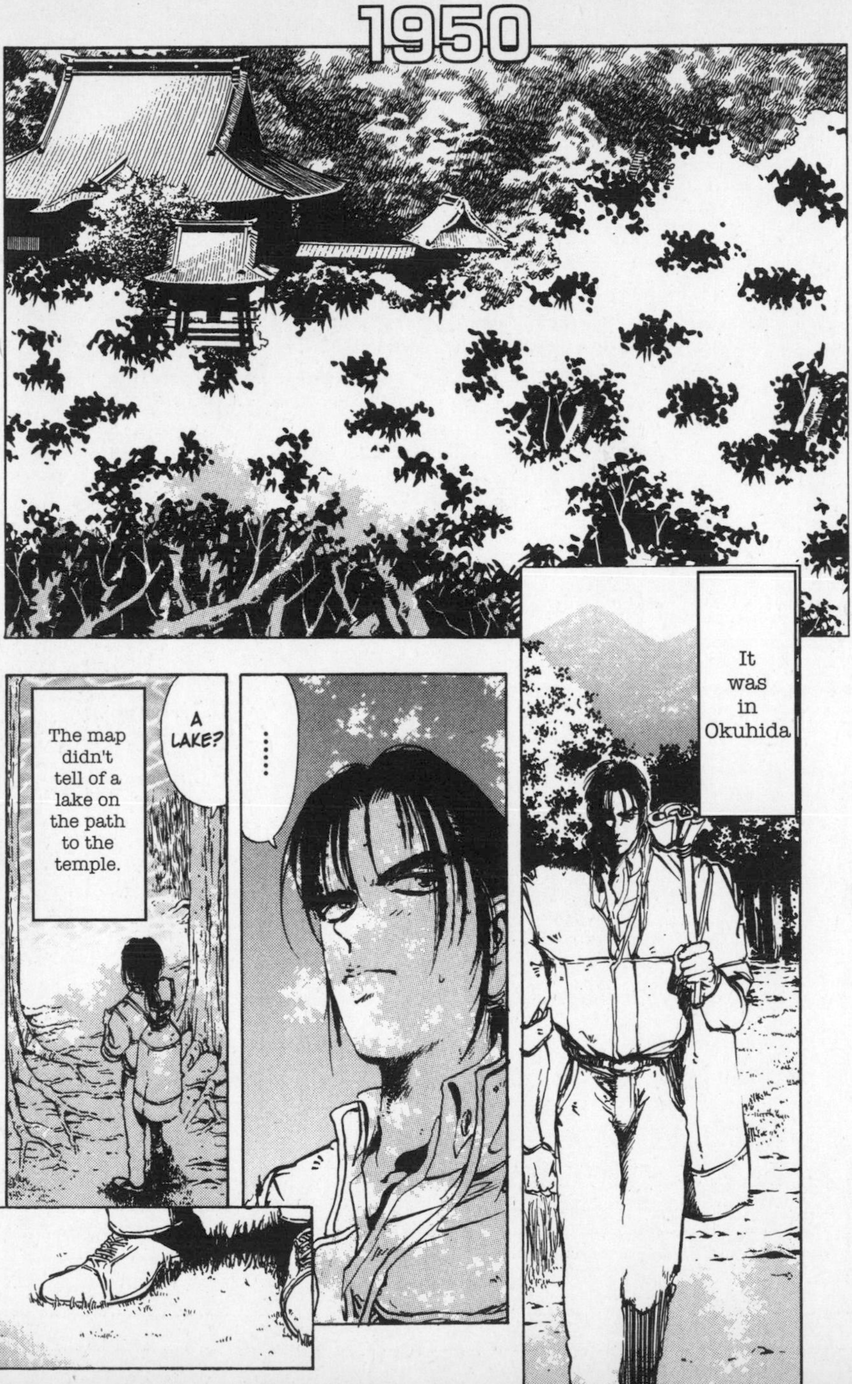
1950
It was in Okuhida
......
A LAKE?
The map didn't tell of a lake on the path to the temple.

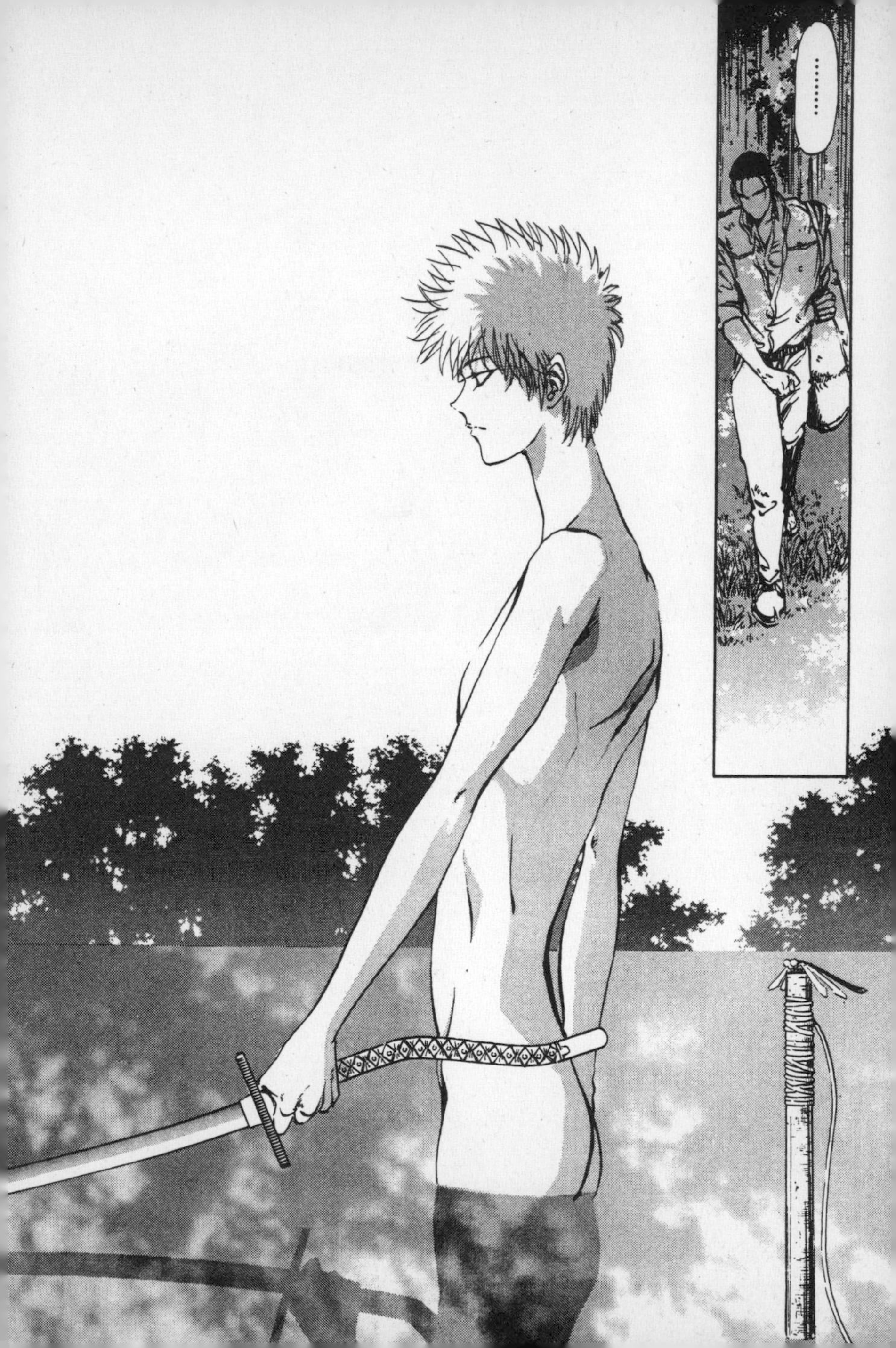
....

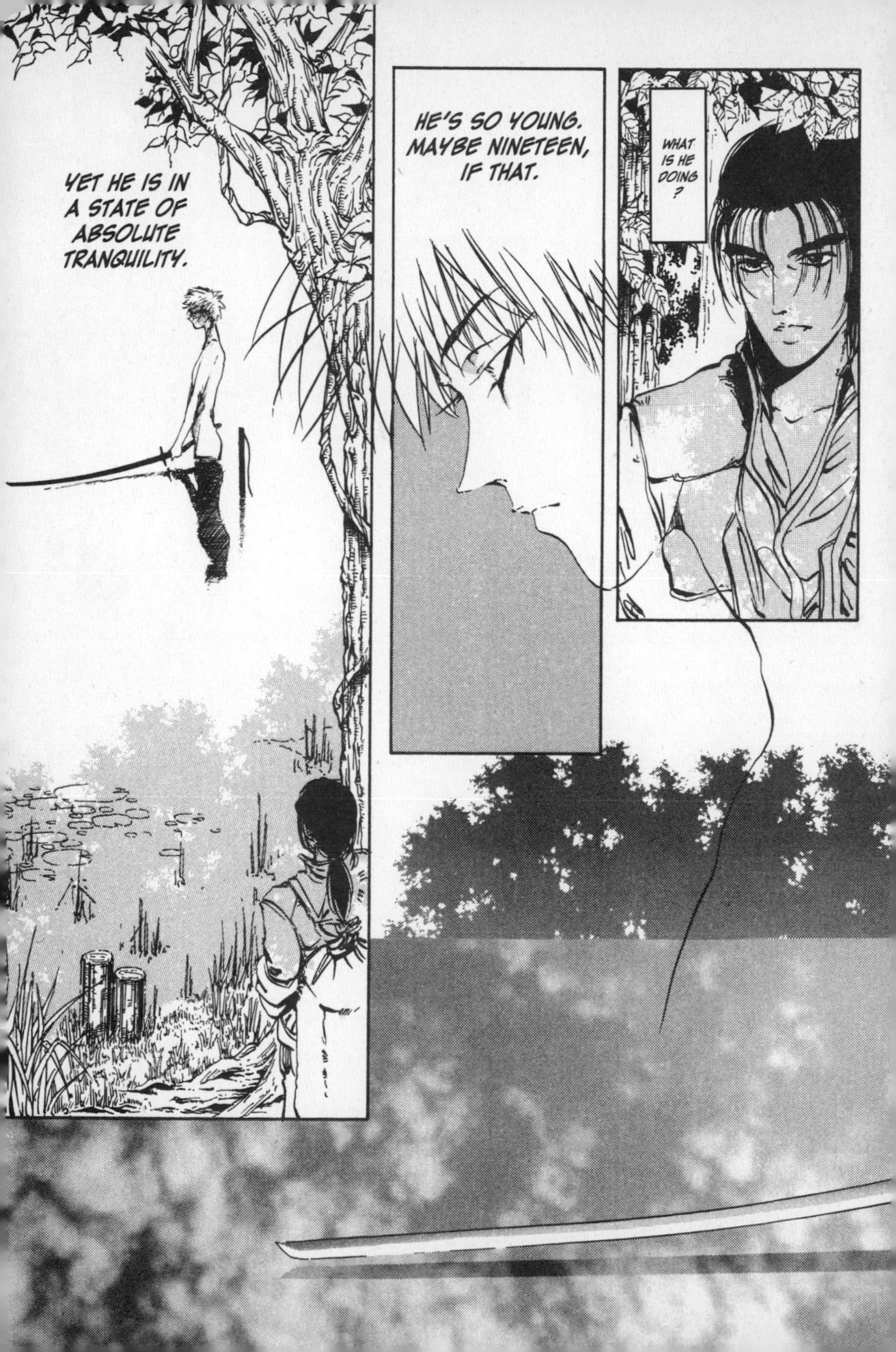
WHAT IS HE DOING?
HE'S SO YOUNG. MAYBE NINETEEN, IF THAT.
YET HE IS IN A STATE OF ABSOLUTE TRANQUILITY.

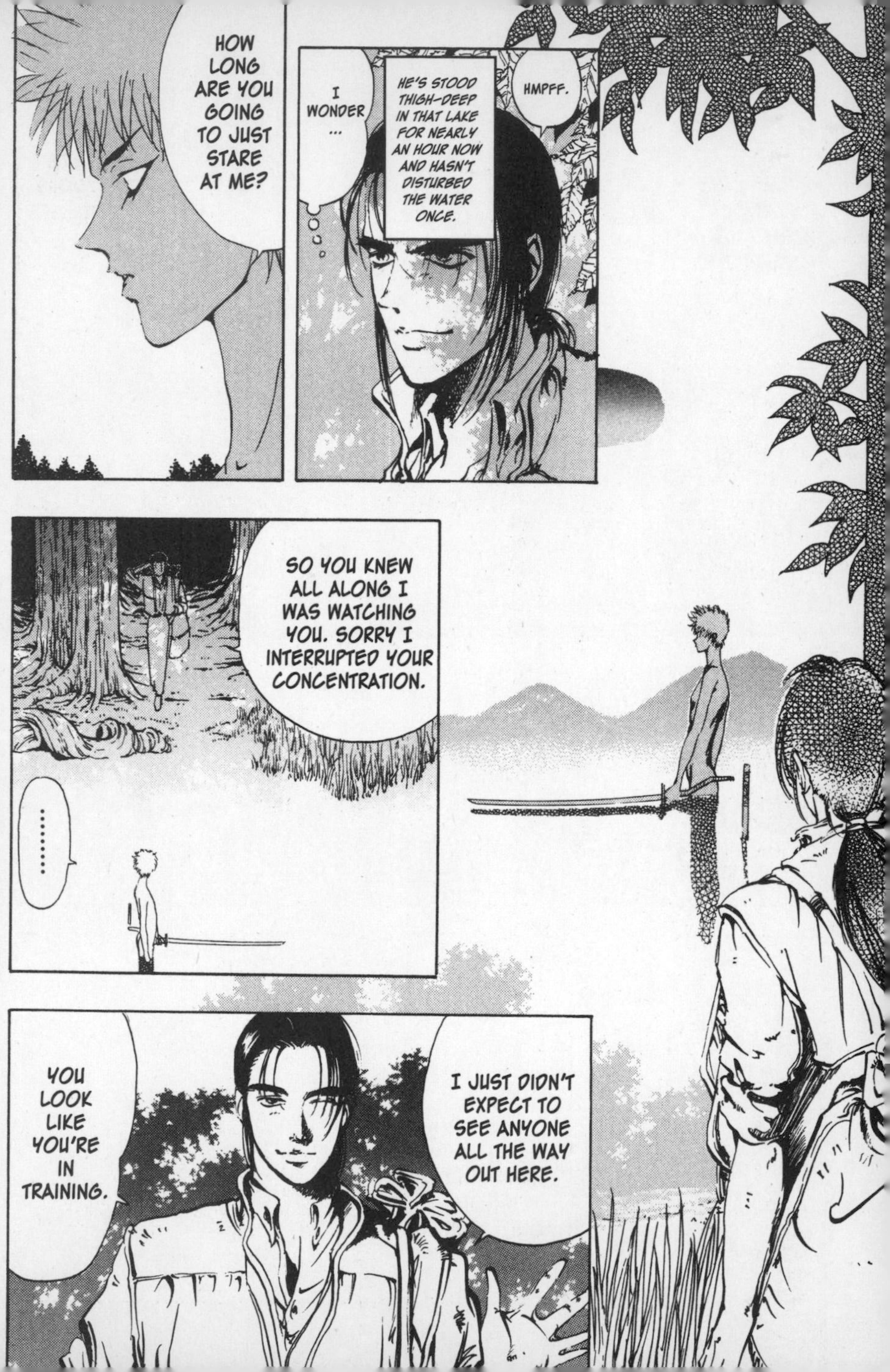
HMPFF.
HE'S STOOD THIGH-DEEP IN THAT LAKE FOR NEARLY AN HOUR NOW AND HASN'T DISTURBED THE WATER ONCE.
I WONDER ...
HOW LONG ARE YOU GOING TO JUST STARE AT ME?
SO YOU KNEW ALL ALONG I WAS WATCHING YOU. SORRY I INTERRUPTED YOUR CONCENTRATION.
......
I JUST DIDN'T EXPECT TO SEE ANYONE ALL THE WAY OUT HERE.
YOU LOOK LIKE YOU'RE IN TRAINING.

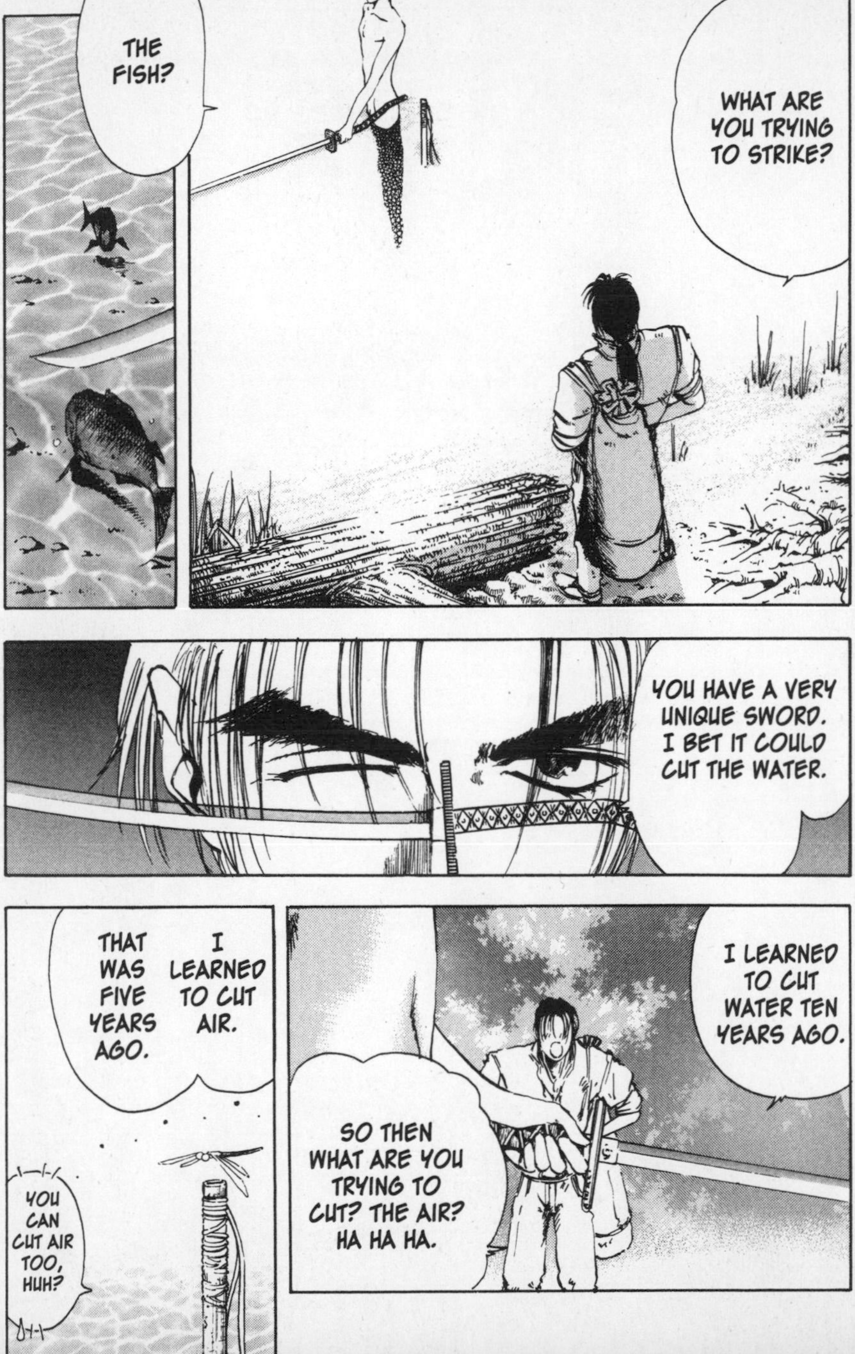
WHAT ARE YOU TRYING TO STRIKE?
THE FISH?
YOU HAVE A VERY UNIQUE SWORD. I BET IT COULD CUT THE WATER.
I LEARNED TO CUT WATER TEN YEARS AGO.
SO THEN WHAT ARE YOU TRYING TO CUT? THE AIR? HA HA HA.
I LEARNED TO CUT AIR.
THAT WAS FIVE YEARS AGO.
YOU CAN CUT AIR TOO, HUH?

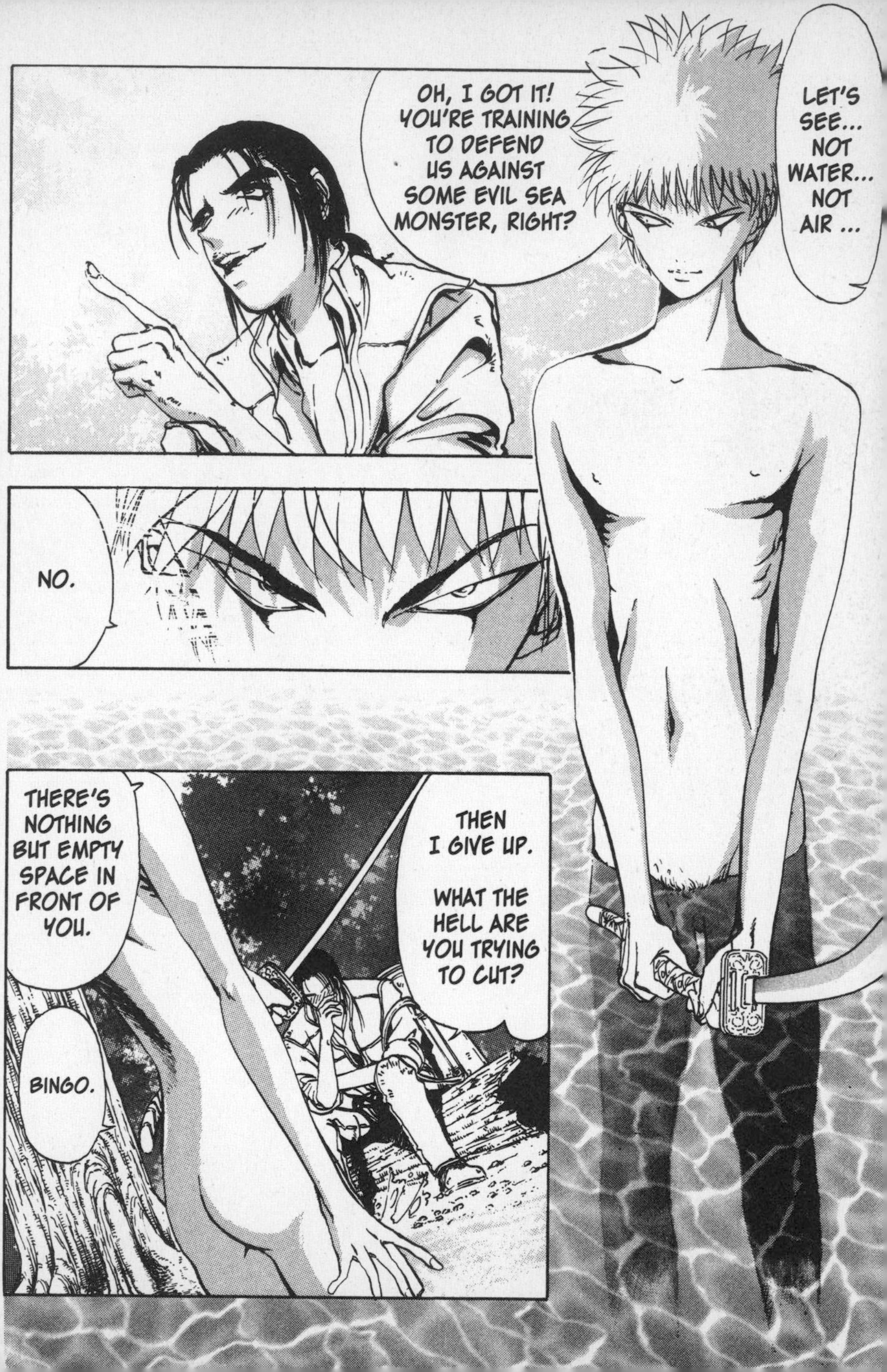
LET'S SEE... NOT WATER... NOT AIR ...
OH, I GOT IT! YOU'RE TRAINING TO DEFEND US AGAINST SOME EVIL SEA MONSTER, RIGHT?
NO.
THEN I GIVE UP.
WHAT THE HELL ARE YOU TRYING TO CUT?
THERE'S NOTHING BUT EMPTY SPACE IN FRONT OF YOU.
BINGO.

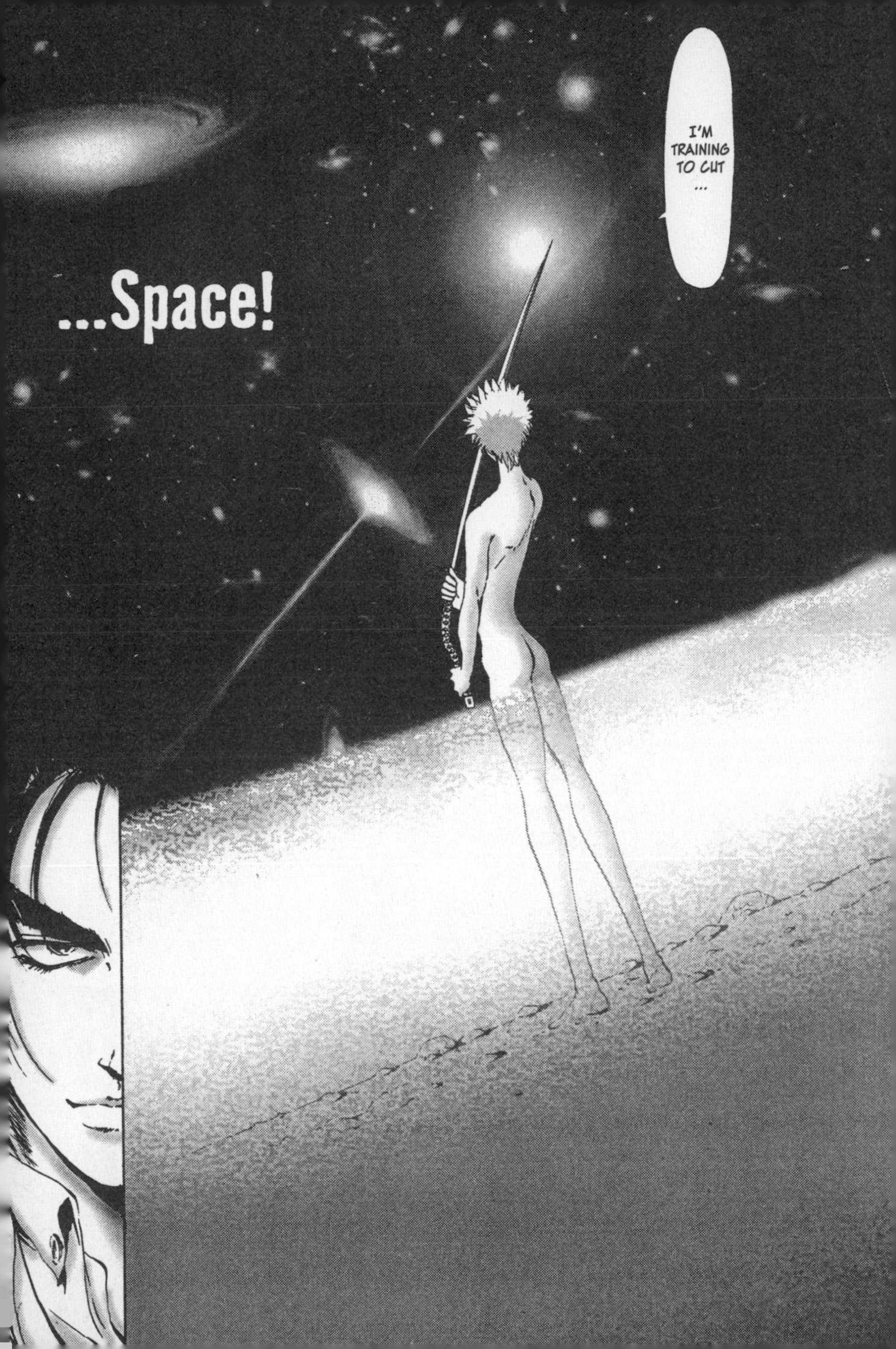

I'M TRAINING TO CUT ...
...Space!

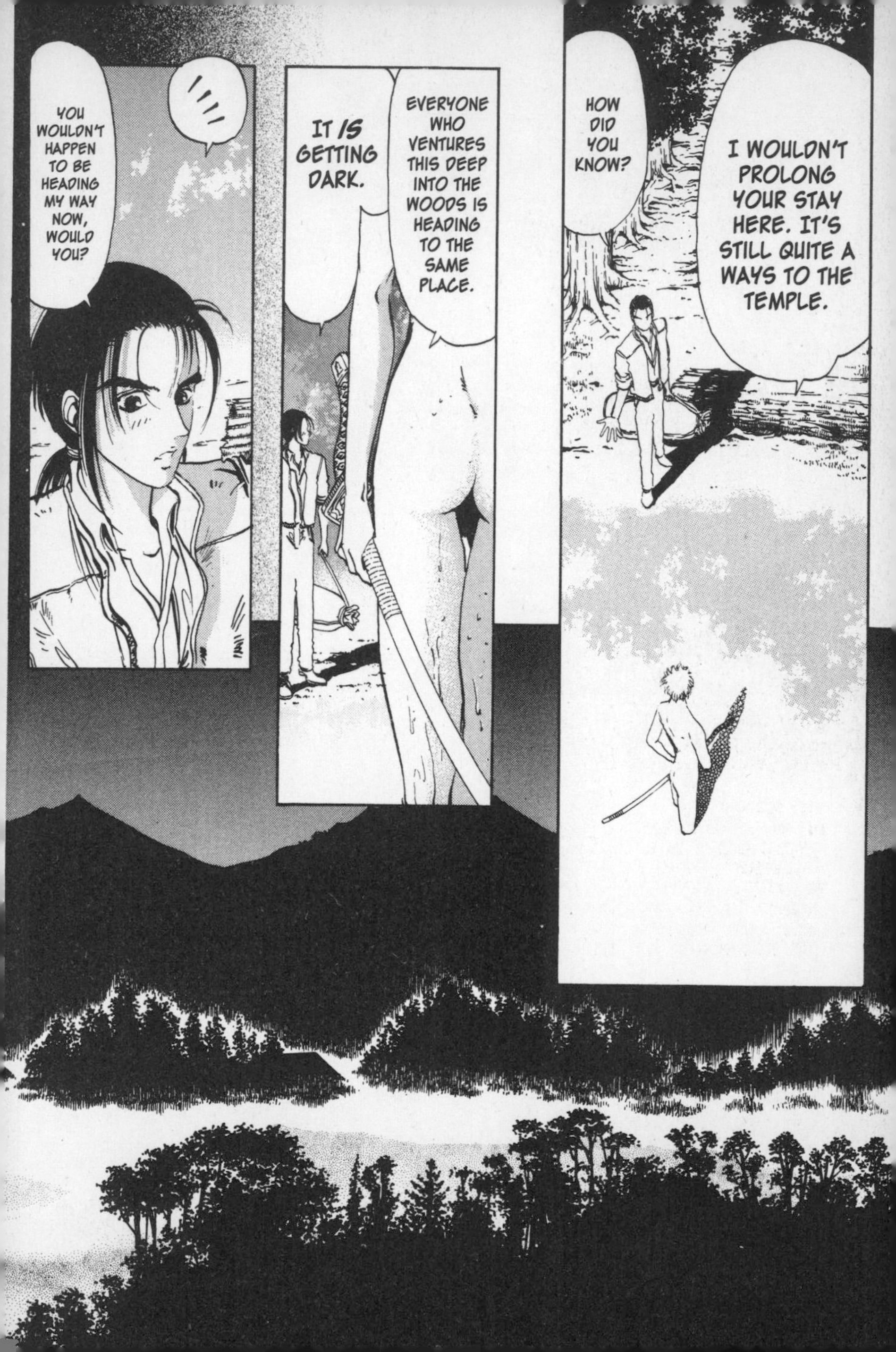
I WOULDN'T PROLONG YOUR STAY HERE. IT'S STILL QUITE A WAYS TO THE TEMPLE.
HOW DID YOU KNOW?
EVERYONE WHO VENTURES THIS DEEP INTO THE WOODS IS HEADING TO THE SAME PLACE.
IT IS GETTING DARK.
!
YOU WOULDN'T HAPPEN TO BE HEADING MY WAY NOW, WOULD YOU?

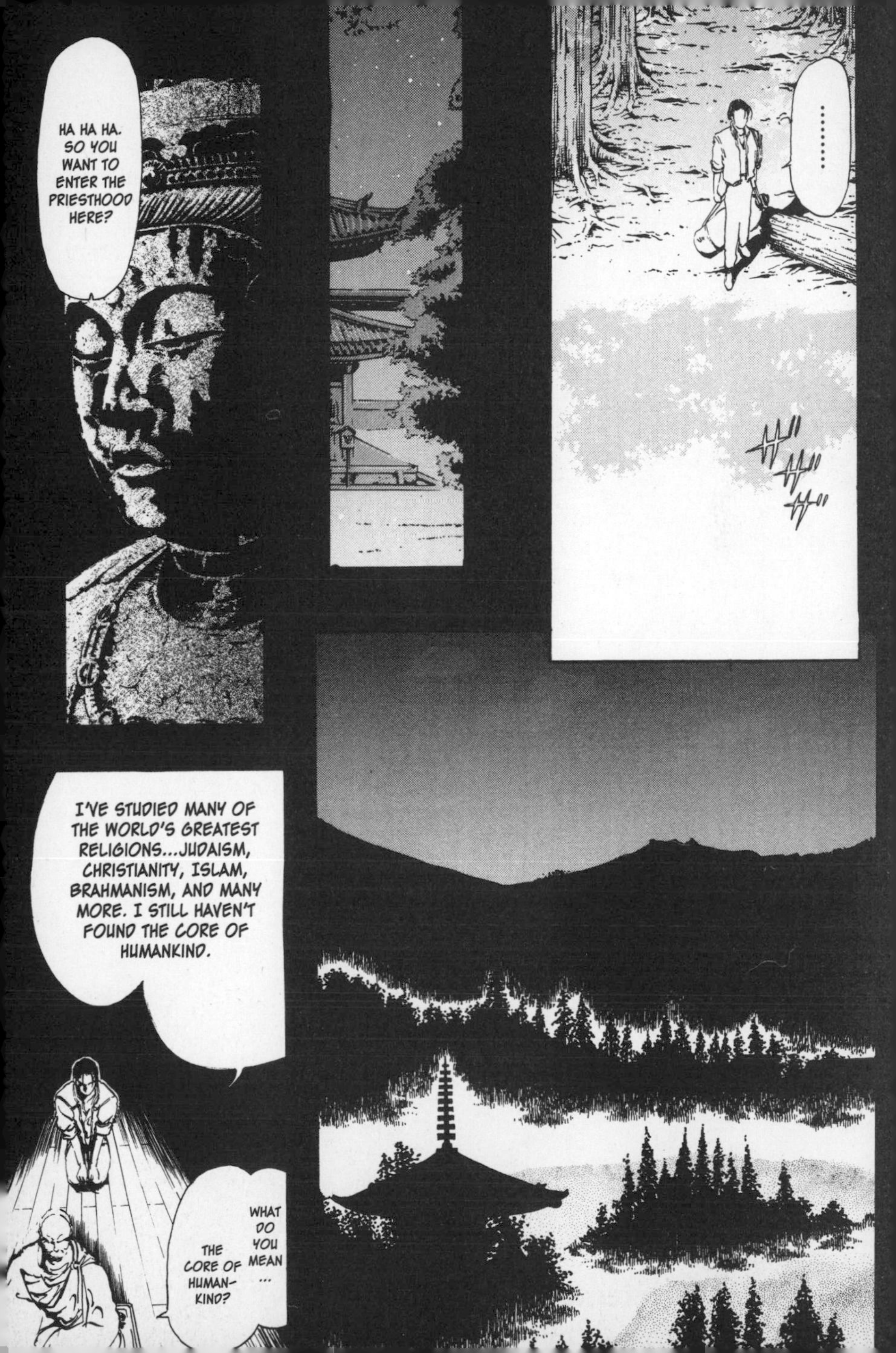
……
ザッ ザッ ザッ
HA HA HA. SO YOU WANT TO ENTER THE PRIESTHOOD HERE?
I'VE STUDIED MANY OF THE WORLD'S GREATEST RELIGIONS...JUDAISM, CHRISTIANITY, ISLAM, BRAHMANISM, AND MANY MORE. I STILL HAVEN'T FOUND THE CORE OF HUMANKIND.
WHAT DO YOU MEAN...
THE CORE OF HUMAN-KIND?

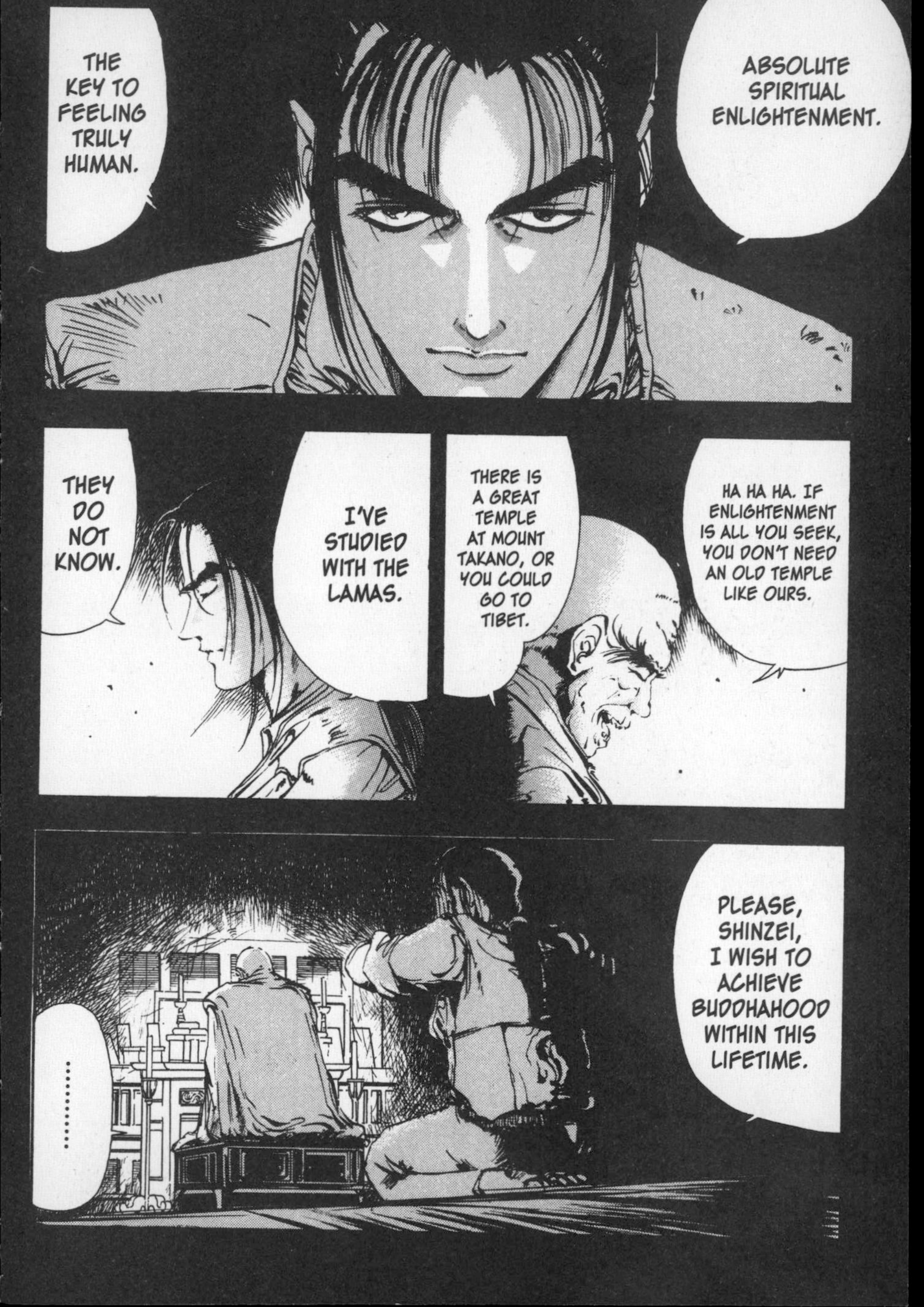
ABSOLUTE SPIRITUAL ENLIGHTENMENT.
THE KEY TO FEELING TRULY HUMAN.
HA HA HA. IF ENLIGHTENMENT IS ALL YOU SEEK, YOU DON'T NEED AN OLD TEMPLE LIKE OURS.
THERE IS A GREAT TEMPLE AT MOUNT TAKANO, OR YOU COULD GO TO TIBET.
I'VE STUDIED WITH THE LAMAS.
THEY DO NOT KNOW.
PLEASE, SHINZEI, I WISH TO ACHIEVE BUDDHAHOOD WITHIN THIS LIFETIME.
....

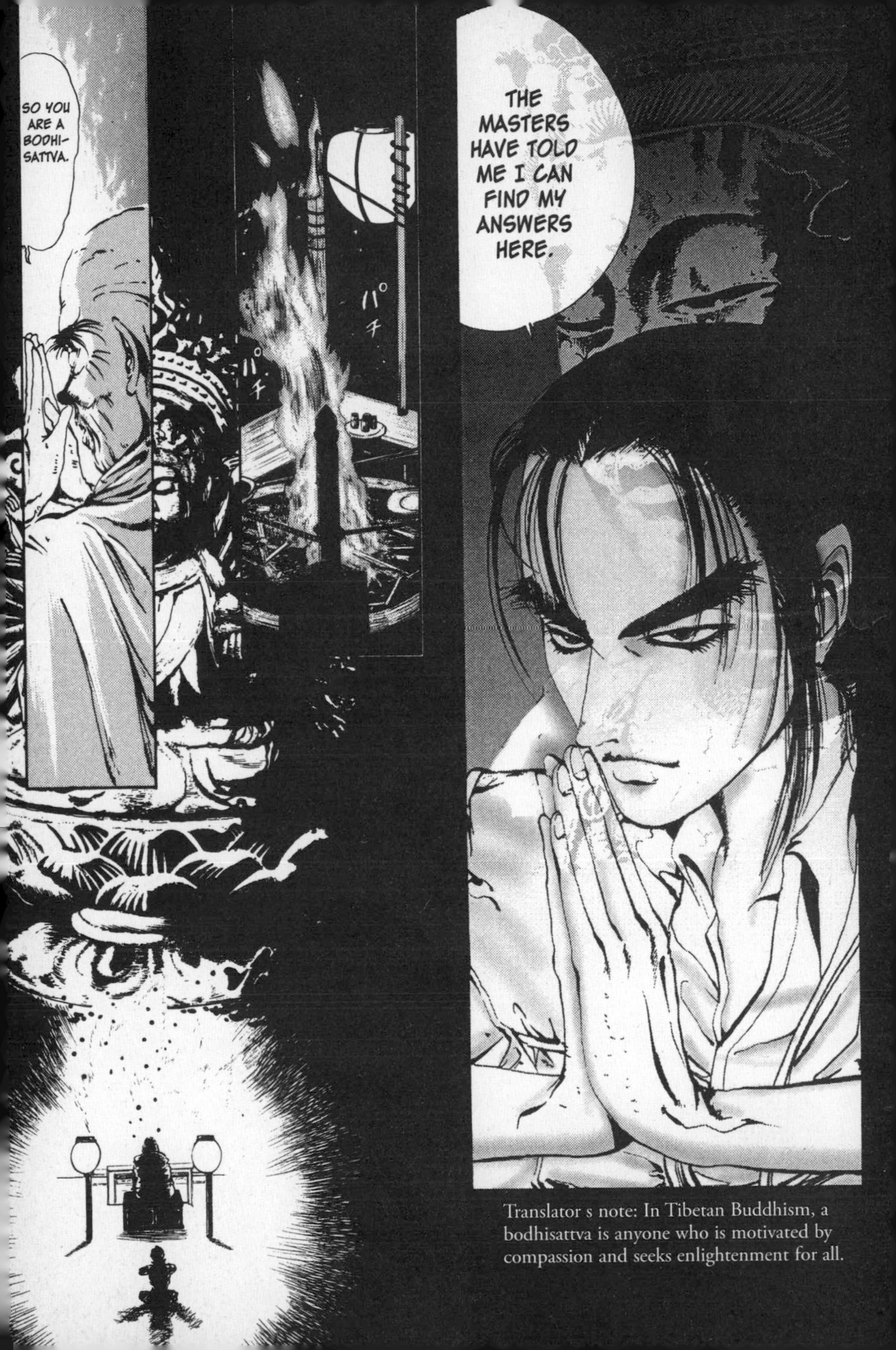
THE MASTERS HAVE TOLD ME I CAN FIND MY ANSWERS HERE.
パチ
パチ
SO YOU ARE A BODHISATTVA.

Translator s note: In Tibetan Buddhism, a bodhisattva is anyone who is motivated by compassion and seeks enlightenment for all.

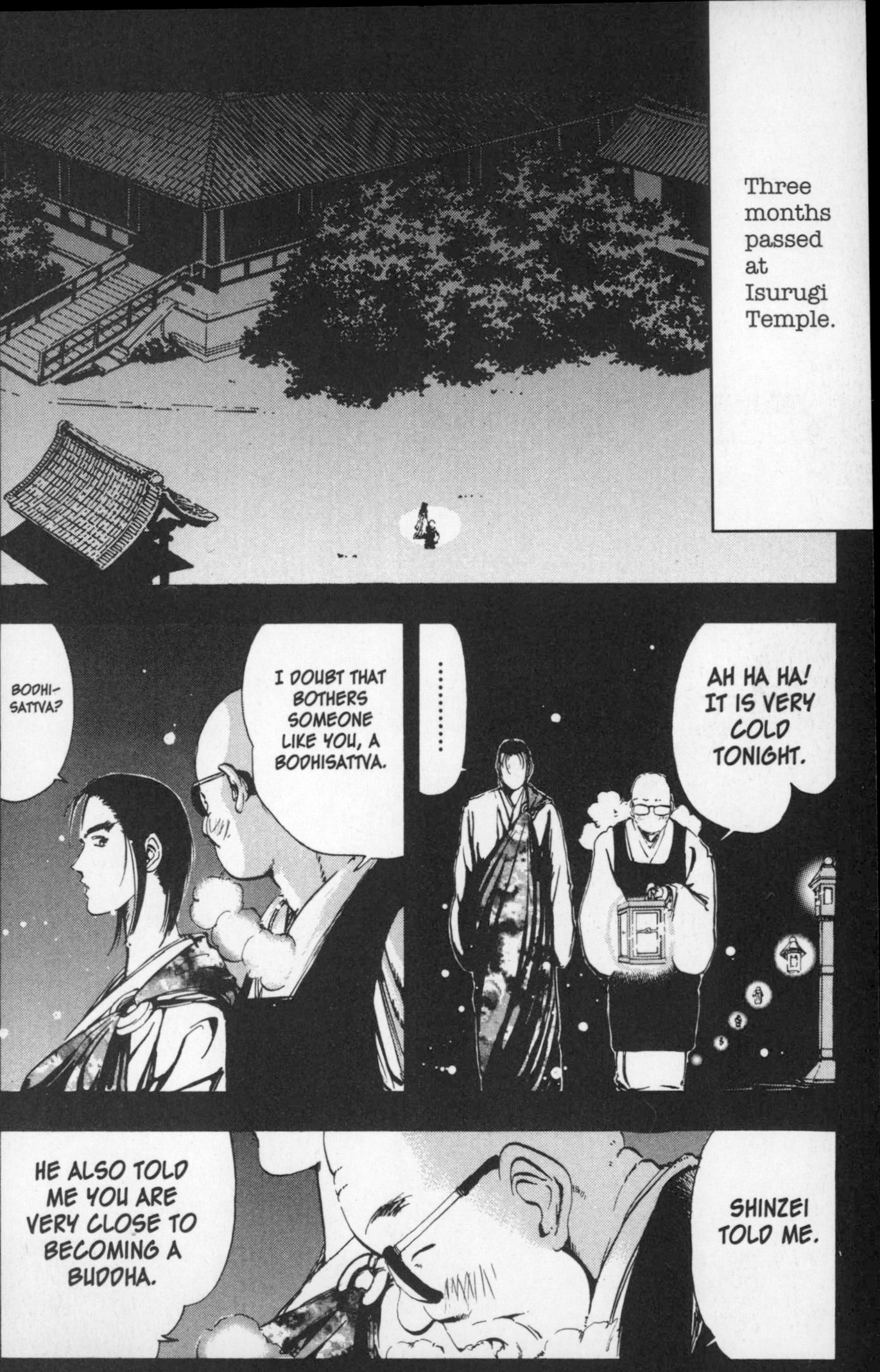
Three months passed at Isurugi Temple.
AH HA HA! IT IS VERY COLD TONIGHT.
......
I DOUBT THAT BOTHERS SOMEONE LIKE YOU, A BODHISATTVA.
BODHI-SATTVA?
SHINZEI TOLD ME.
HE ALSO TOLD ME YOU ARE VERY CLOSE TO BECOMING A BUDDHA.

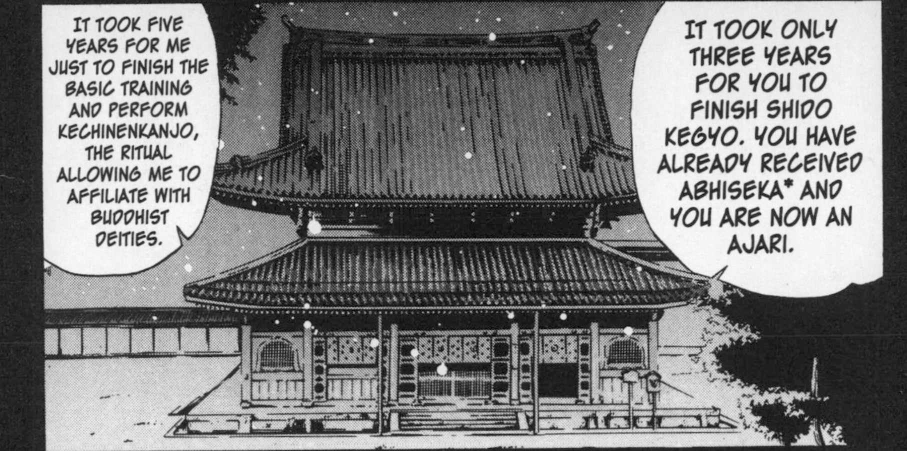
IT TOOK ONLY THREE YEARS FOR YOU TO FINISH SHIDO KEGYO. YOU HAVE ALREADY RECEIVED ABHISEKA* AND YOU ARE NOW AN AJARI.
IT TOOK FIVE YEARS FOR ME JUST TO FINISH THE BASIC TRAINING AND PERFORM KECHINENKANJO, THE RITUAL ALLOWING ME TO AFFILIATE WITH BUDDHIST DEITIES.

*Translator's note : Abhiseka is a ritual, rich with energy and insight, in which the disciple is given secret Mudras and Mantras, brought from China to Japan by Kobo Daishi.

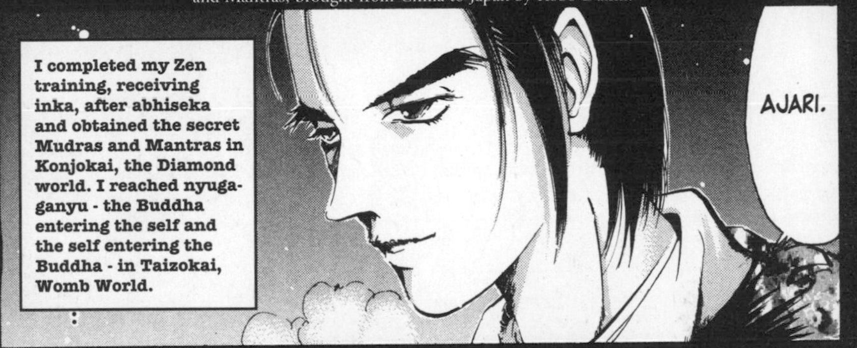
AJARI.
I completed my Zen training, receiving inka, after abhiseka and obtained the secret Mudras and Mantras in Konjokai, the Diamond world. I reached nyugaganyu - the Buddha entering the self and the self entering the Buddha - in Taizokai, Womb World.

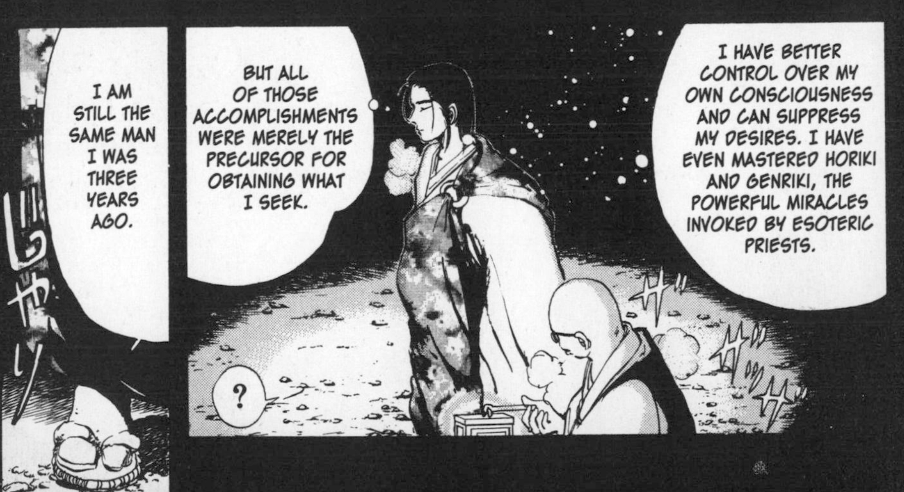
I HAVE BETTER CONTROL OVER MY OWN CONSCIOUSNESS AND CAN SUPPRESS MY DESIRES. I HAVE EVEN MASTERED HORIKI AND GENRIKI, THE POWERFUL MIRACLES INVOKED BY ESOTERIC PRIESTS.
BUT ALL OF THOSE ACCOMPLISHMENTS WERE MERELY THE PRECURSOR FOR OBTAINING WHAT I SEEK.
I AM STILL THE SAME MAN I WAS THREE YEARS AGO.
?

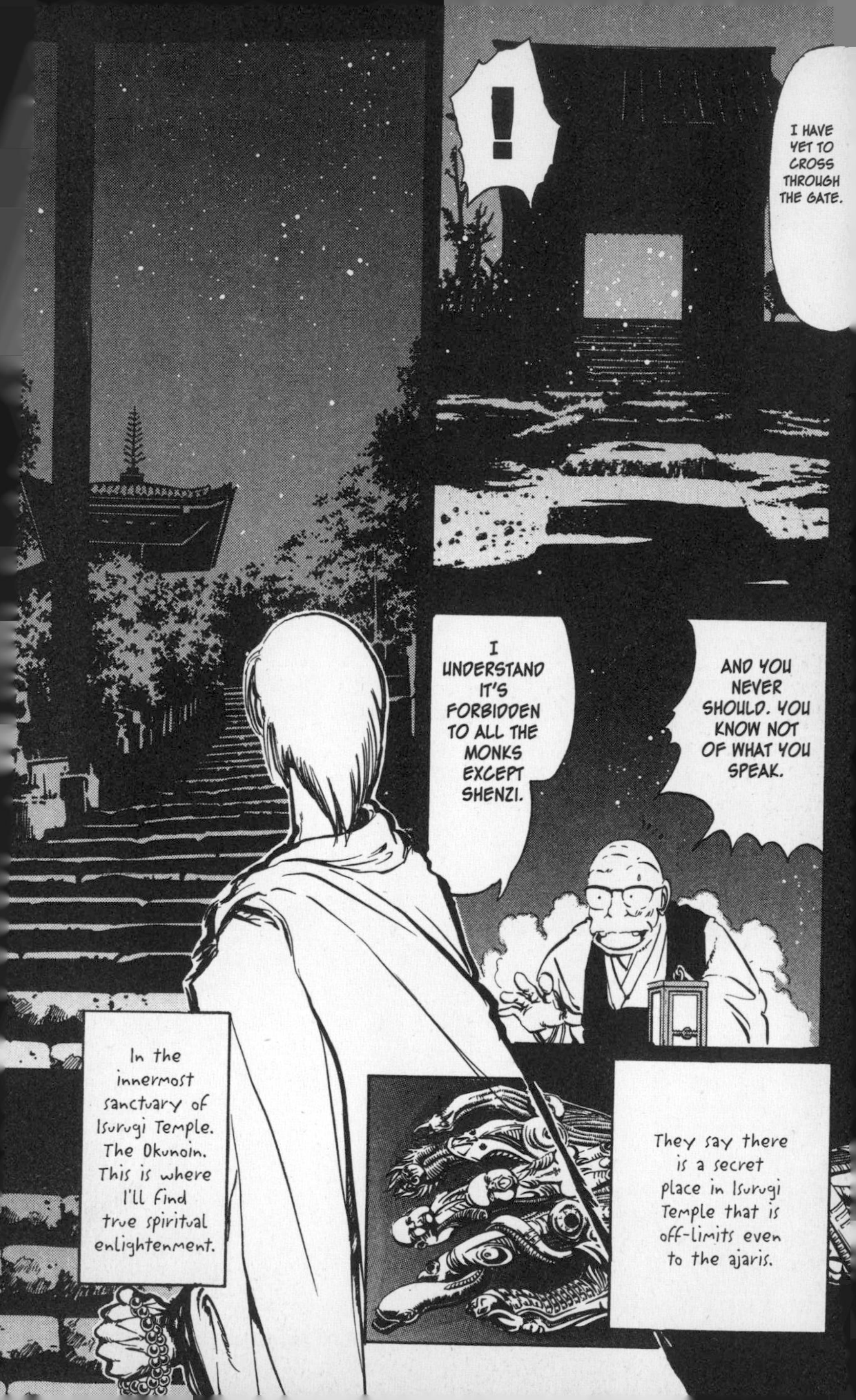

I HAVE YET TO CROSS THROUGH THE GATE.
!
AND YOU NEVER SHOULD. YOU KNOW NOT OF WHAT YOU SPEAK.
I UNDERSTAND IT'S FORBIDDEN TO ALL THE MONKS EXCEPT SHENZI.
They say there is a secret place in Isurugi Temple that is off-limits even to the ajaris.
In the innermost sanctuary of Isurugi Temple. The Okunoin. This is where I'll find true spiritual enlightenment.

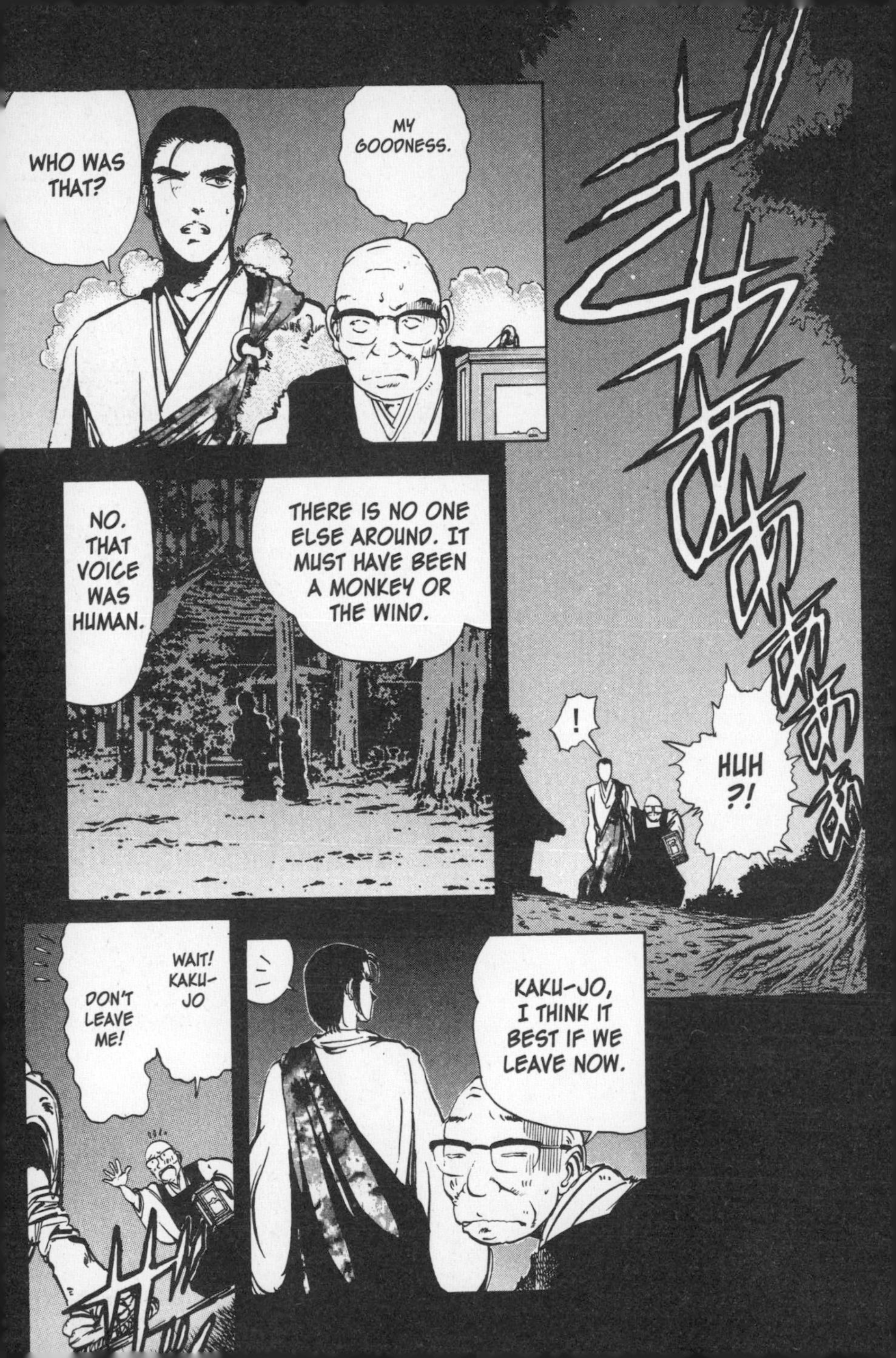
HUH ?!
!
MY GOODNESS.
WHO WAS THAT?
THERE IS NO ONE ELSE AROUND. IT MUST HAVE BEEN A MONKEY OR THE WIND.
NO. THAT VOICE WAS HUMAN.
KAKU-JO, I THINK IT BEST IF WE LEAVE NOW.
WAIT! KAKU-JO
DON'T LEAVE ME!

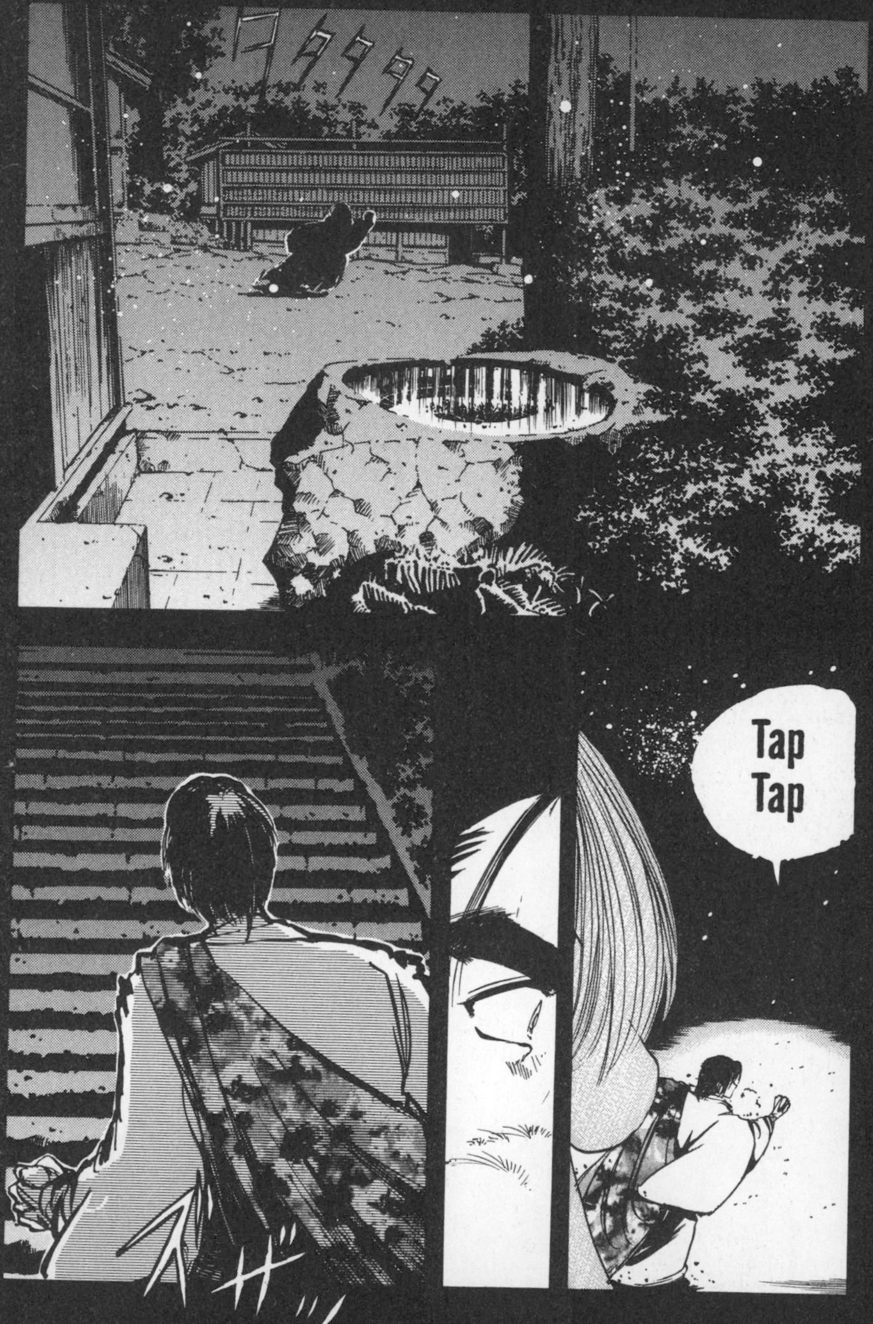
Tap Tap

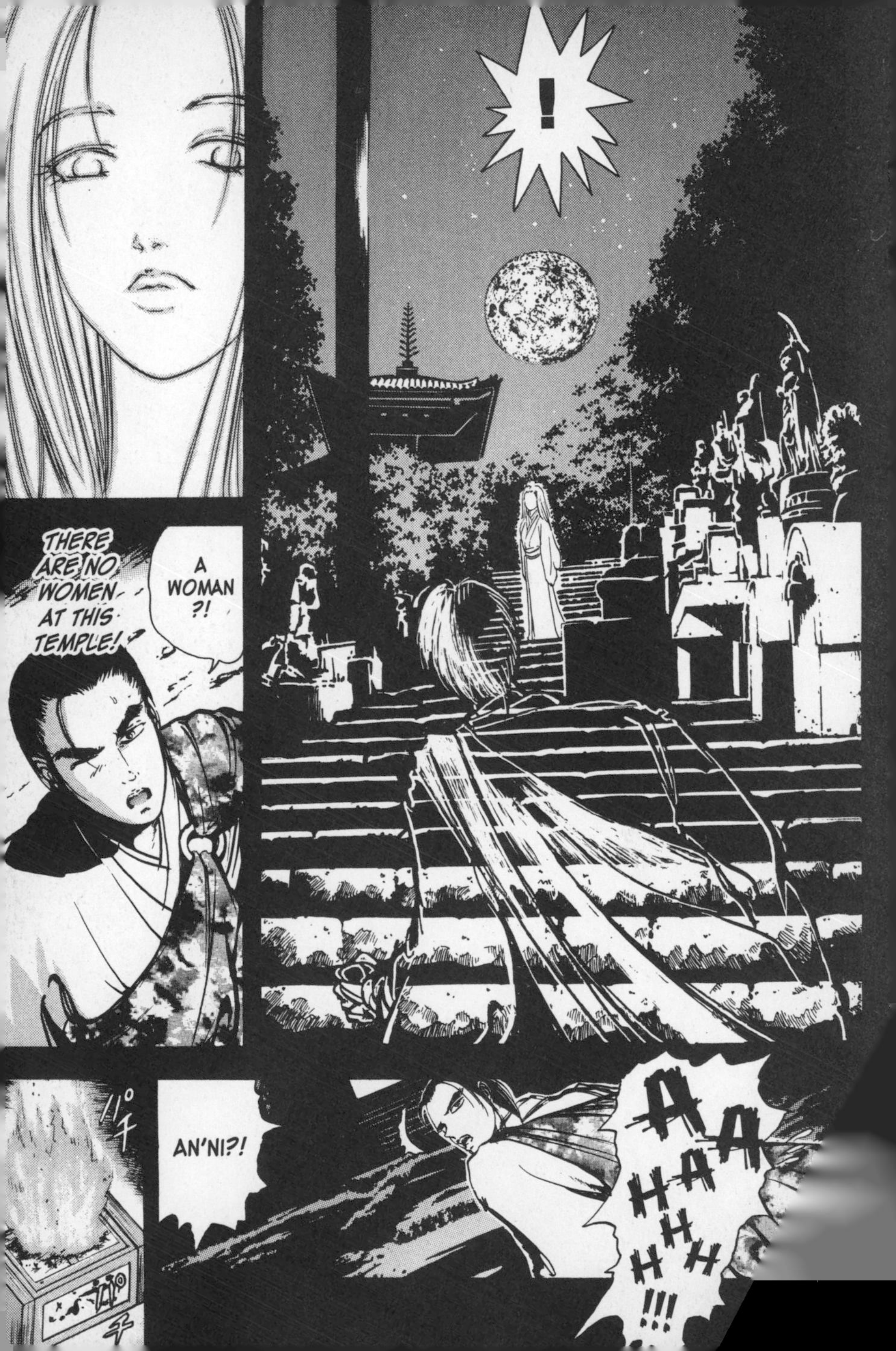
!
A WOMAN ?!
THERE ARE NO WOMEN AT THIS TEMPLE!
AAAHHHH!!!
AN'NI?!
パチ
チ

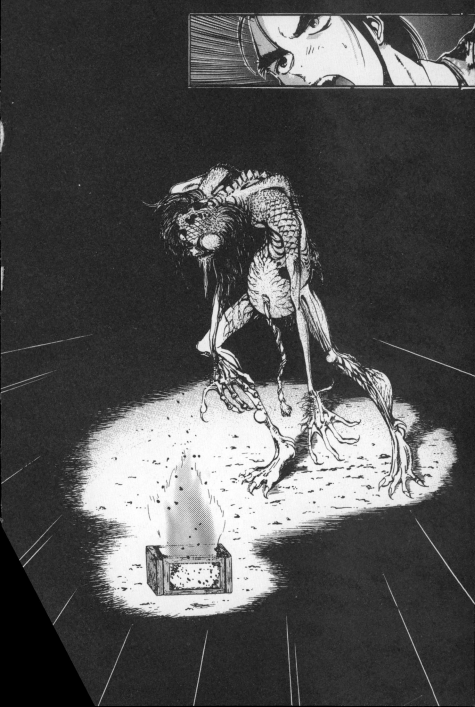

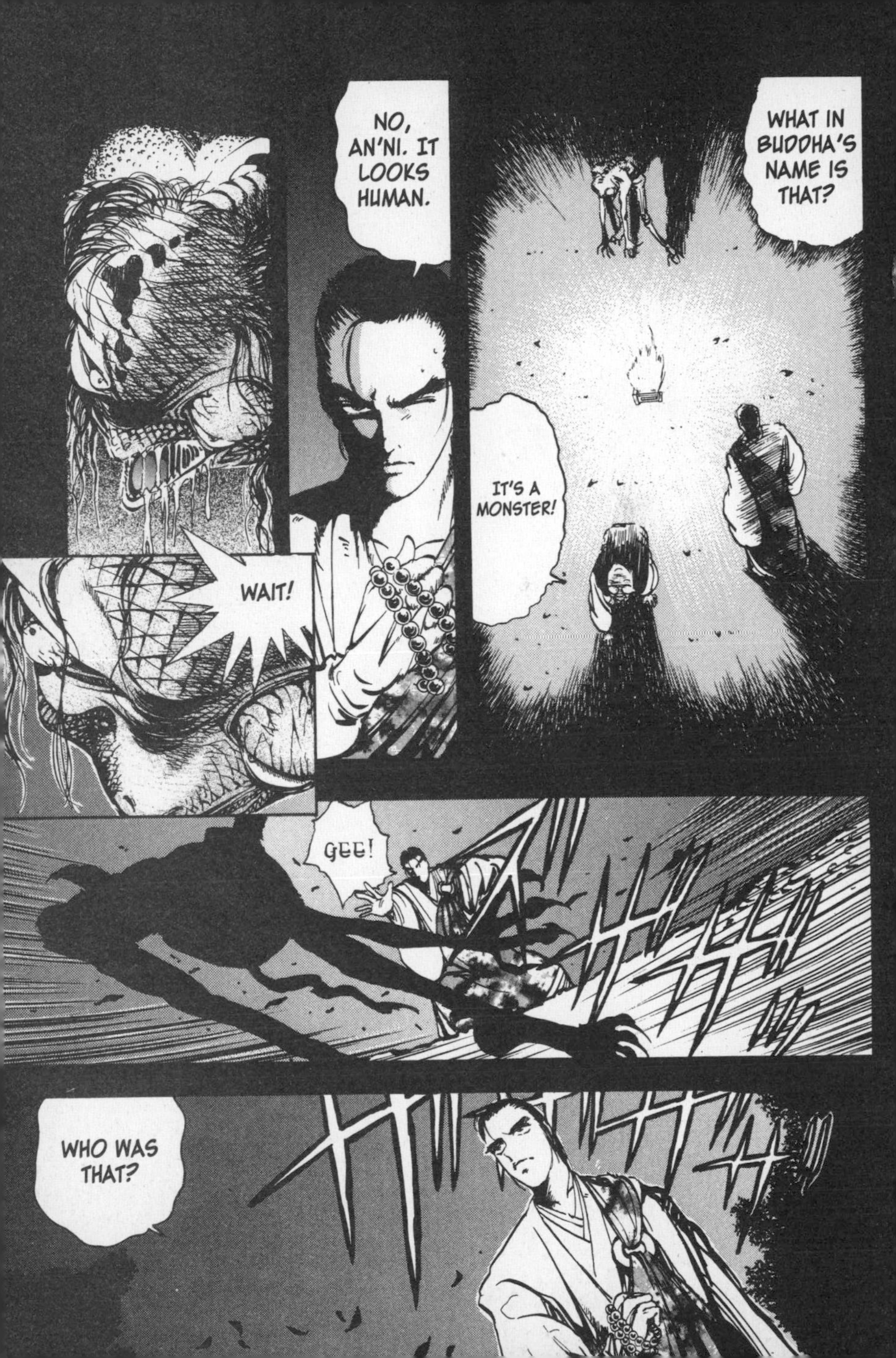
WHAT IN BUDDHA'S NAME IS THAT?
IT'S A MONSTER!
NO, AN'NI. IT LOOKS HUMAN.
WAIT!
GEE!
WHO WAS THAT?

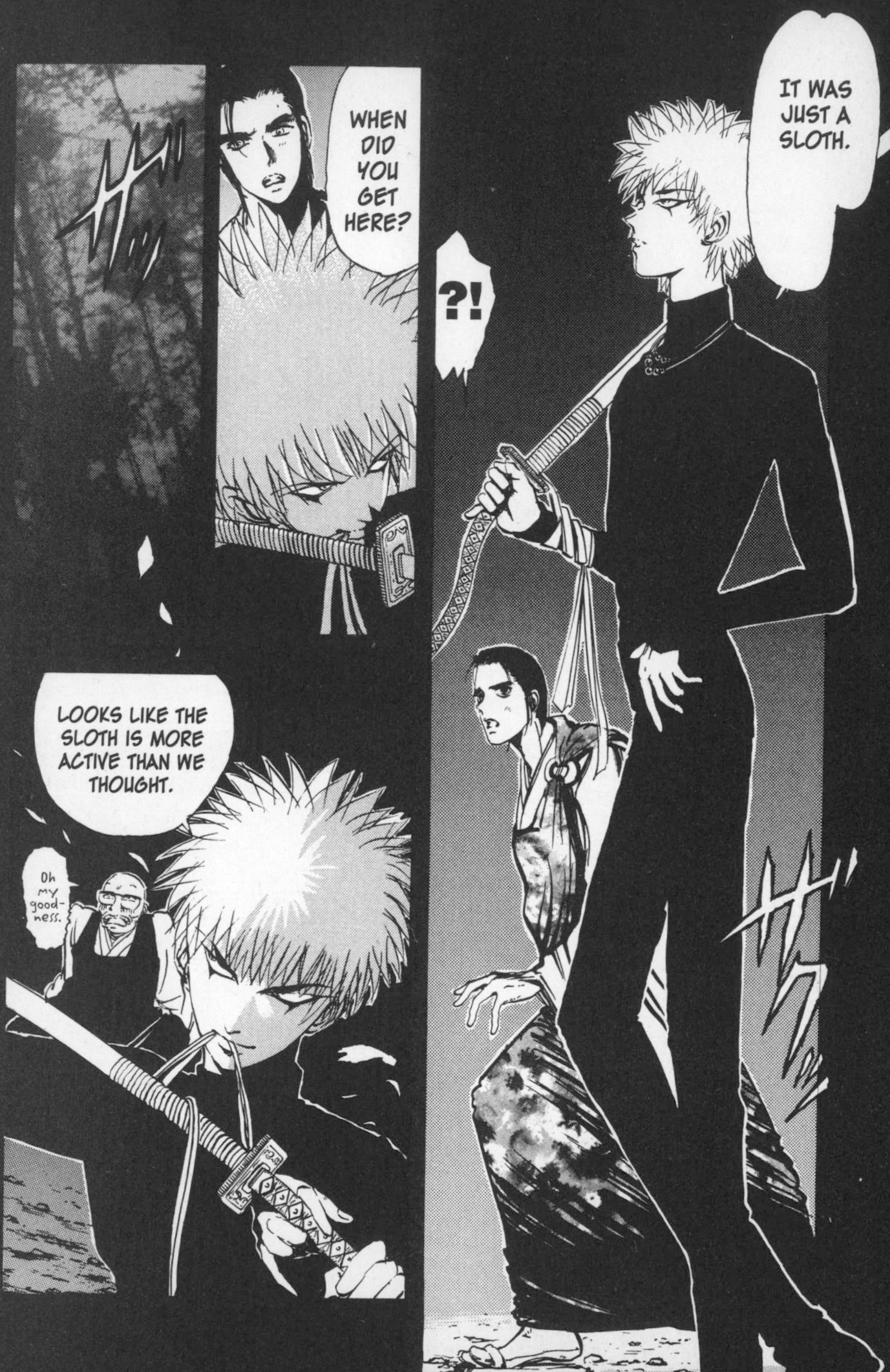
IT WAS JUST A SLOTH.
?!
WHEN DID YOU GET HERE?
LOOKS LIKE THE SLOTH IS MORE ACTIVE THAN WE THOUGHT.
Oh my goodness.

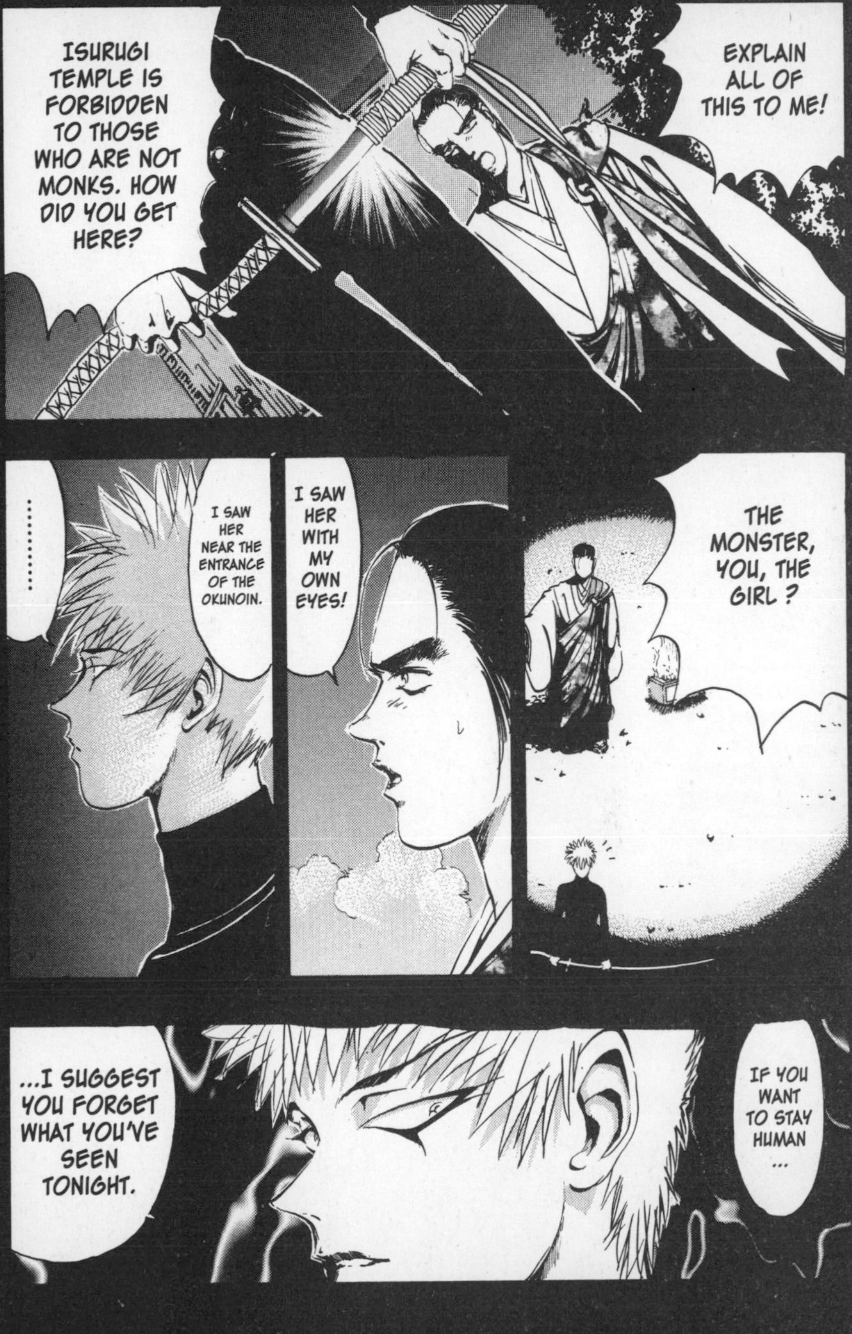
EXPLAIN ALL OF THIS TO ME!
ISURUGI TEMPLE IS FORBIDDEN TO THOSE WHO ARE NOT MONKS. HOW DID YOU GET HERE?
THE MONSTER, YOU, THE GIRL ?
I SAW HER WITH MY OWN EYES!
I SAW HER NEAR THE ENTRANCE OF THE OKUNOIN.
......
IF YOU WANT TO STAY HUMAN ...
...I SUGGEST YOU FORGET WHAT YOU'VE SEEN TONIGHT.

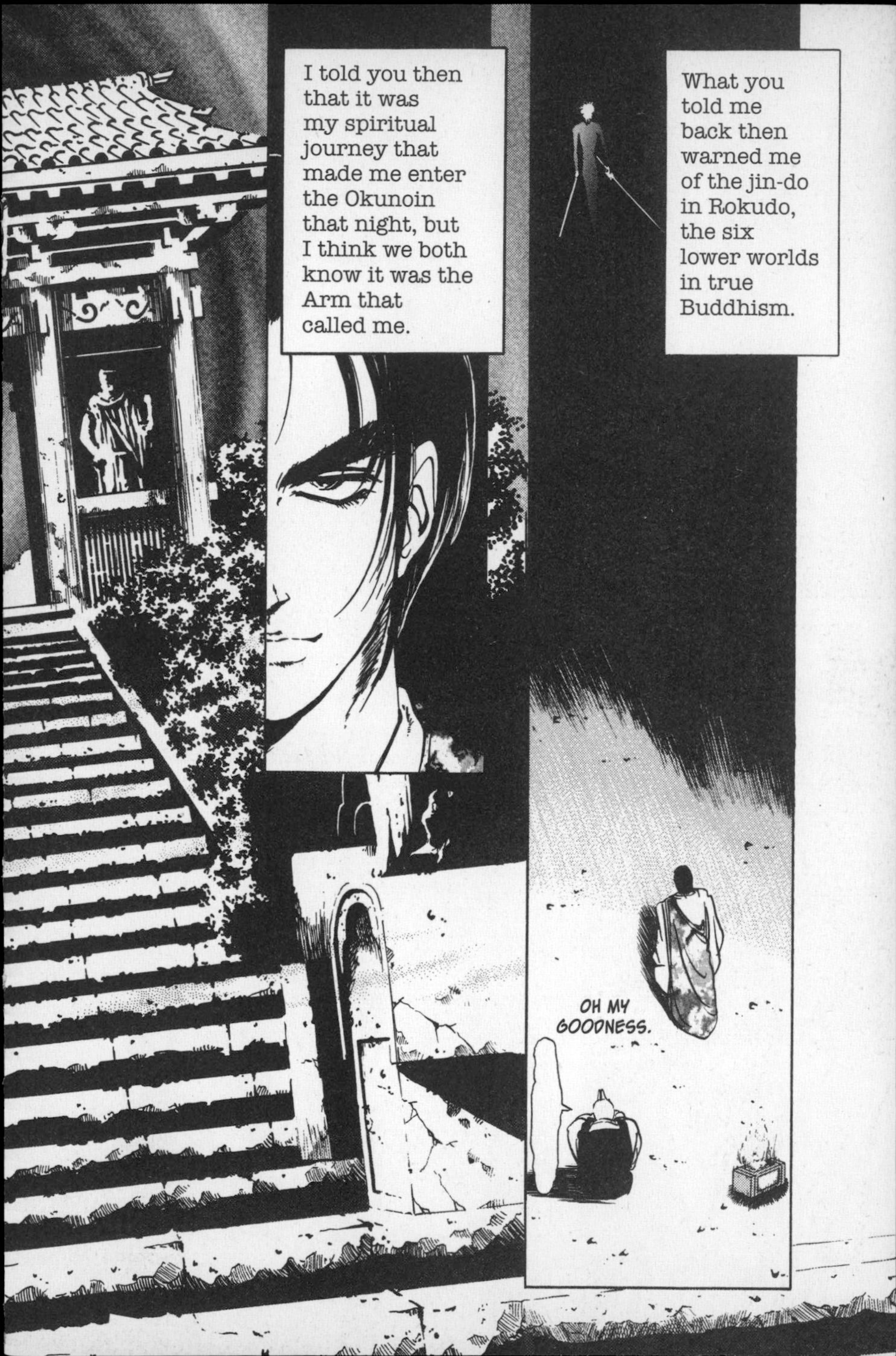
What you told me back then warned me of the jin-do in Rokudo, the six lower worlds in true Buddhism.
OH MY GOODNESS.
I told you then that it was my spiritual journey that made me enter the Okunoin that night, but I think we both know it was the Arm that called me.

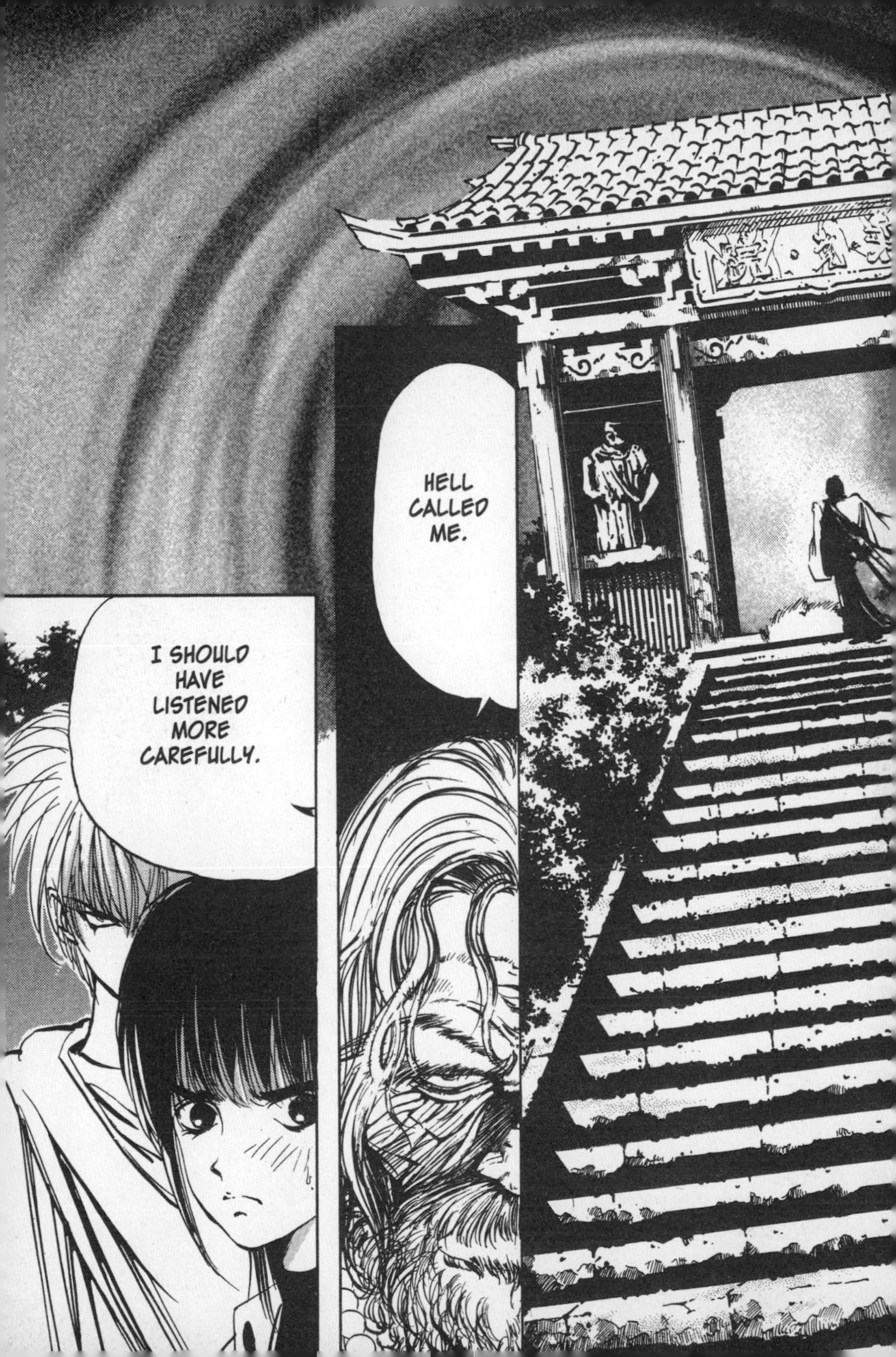
HELL CALLED ME.
I SHOULD HAVE LISTENED MORE CAREFULLY.

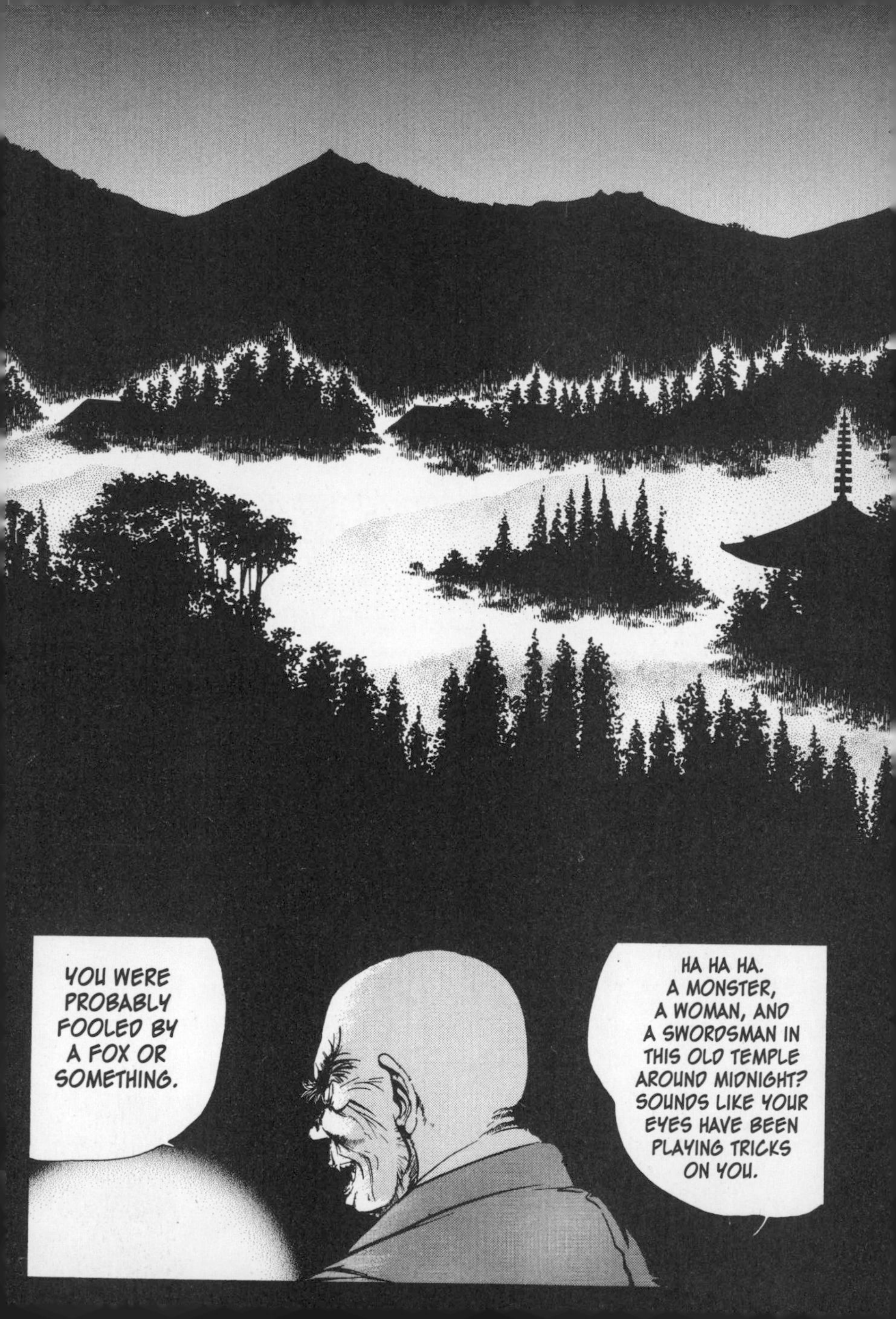
HA HA HA. A MONSTER, A WOMAN, AND A SWORDSMAN IN THIS OLD TEMPLE AROUND MIDNIGHT? SOUNDS LIKE YOUR EYES HAVE BEEN PLAYING TRICKS ON YOU.
YOU WERE PROBABLY FOOLED BY A FOX OR SOMETHING.

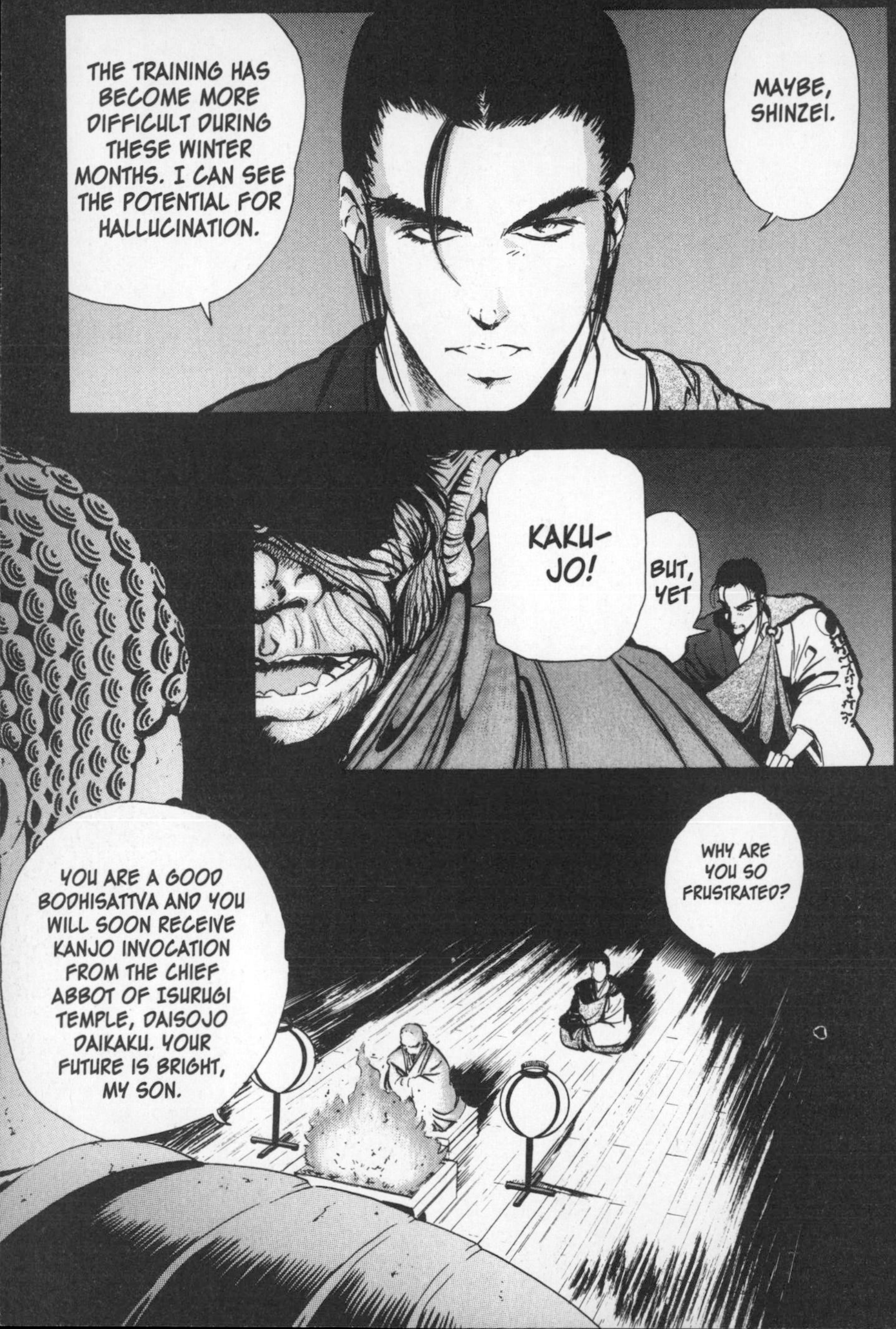
MAYBE, SHINZEI.
THE TRAINING HAS BECOME MORE DIFFICULT DURING THESE WINTER MONTHS. I CAN SEE THE POTENTIAL FOR HALLUCINATION.
BUT, YET
KAKU-JO!
WHY ARE YOU SO FRUSTRATED?
YOU ARE A GOOD BODHISATTVA AND YOU WILL SOON RECEIVE KANJO INVOCATION FROM THE CHIEF ABBOT OF ISURUGI TEMPLE, DAISOJO DAIKAKU. YOUR FUTURE IS BRIGHT, MY SON.

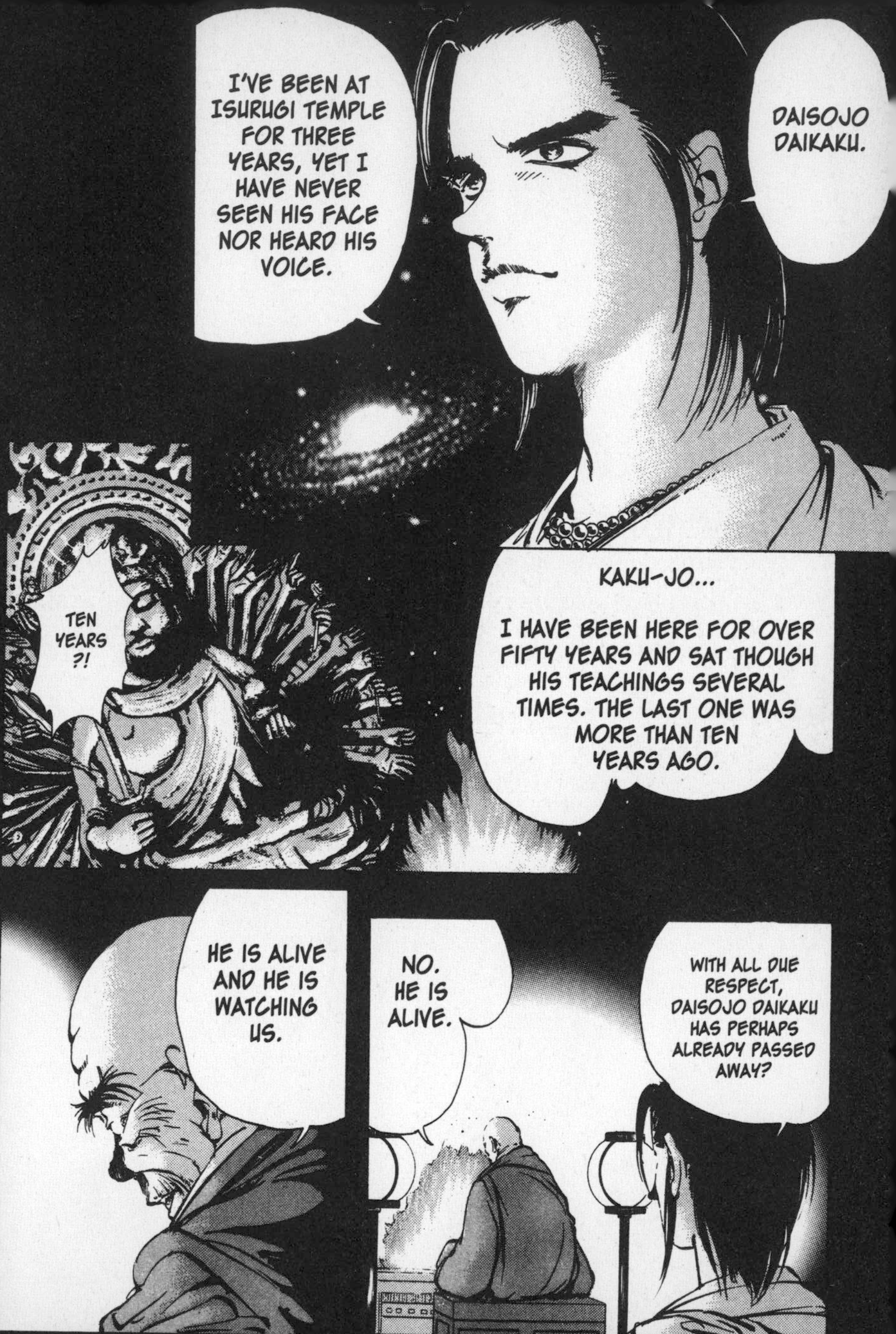
DAISOJO DAIKAKU.
I'VE BEEN AT ISURUGI TEMPLE FOR THREE YEARS, YET I HAVE NEVER SEEN HIS FACE NOR HEARD HIS VOICE.
KAKU-JO...
I HAVE BEEN HERE FOR OVER FIFTY YEARS AND SAT THOUGH HIS TEACHINGS SEVERAL TIMES. THE LAST ONE WAS MORE THAN TEN YEARS AGO.
TEN YEARS ?!
WITH ALL DUE RESPECT, DAISOJO DAIKAKU HAS PERHAPS ALREADY PASSED AWAY?
NO. HE IS ALIVE.
HE IS ALIVE AND HE IS WATCHING US.

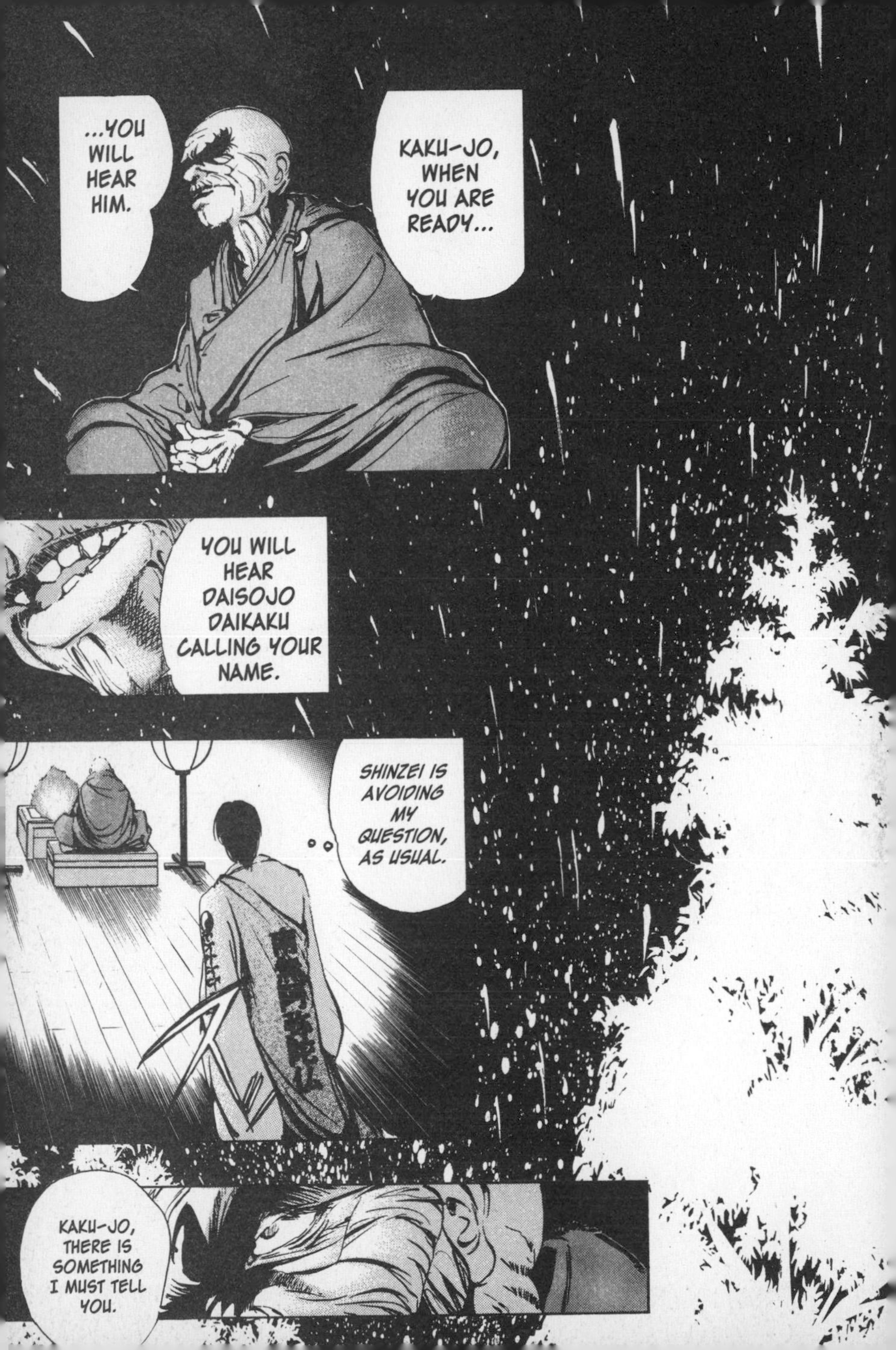
KAKU-JO, WHEN YOU ARE READY...
...YOU WILL HEAR HIM.
YOU WILL HEAR DAISOJO DAIKAKU CALLING YOUR NAME.
SHINZEI IS AVOIDING MY QUESTION, AS USUAL.
KAKU-JO, THERE IS SOMETHING I MUST TELL YOU.

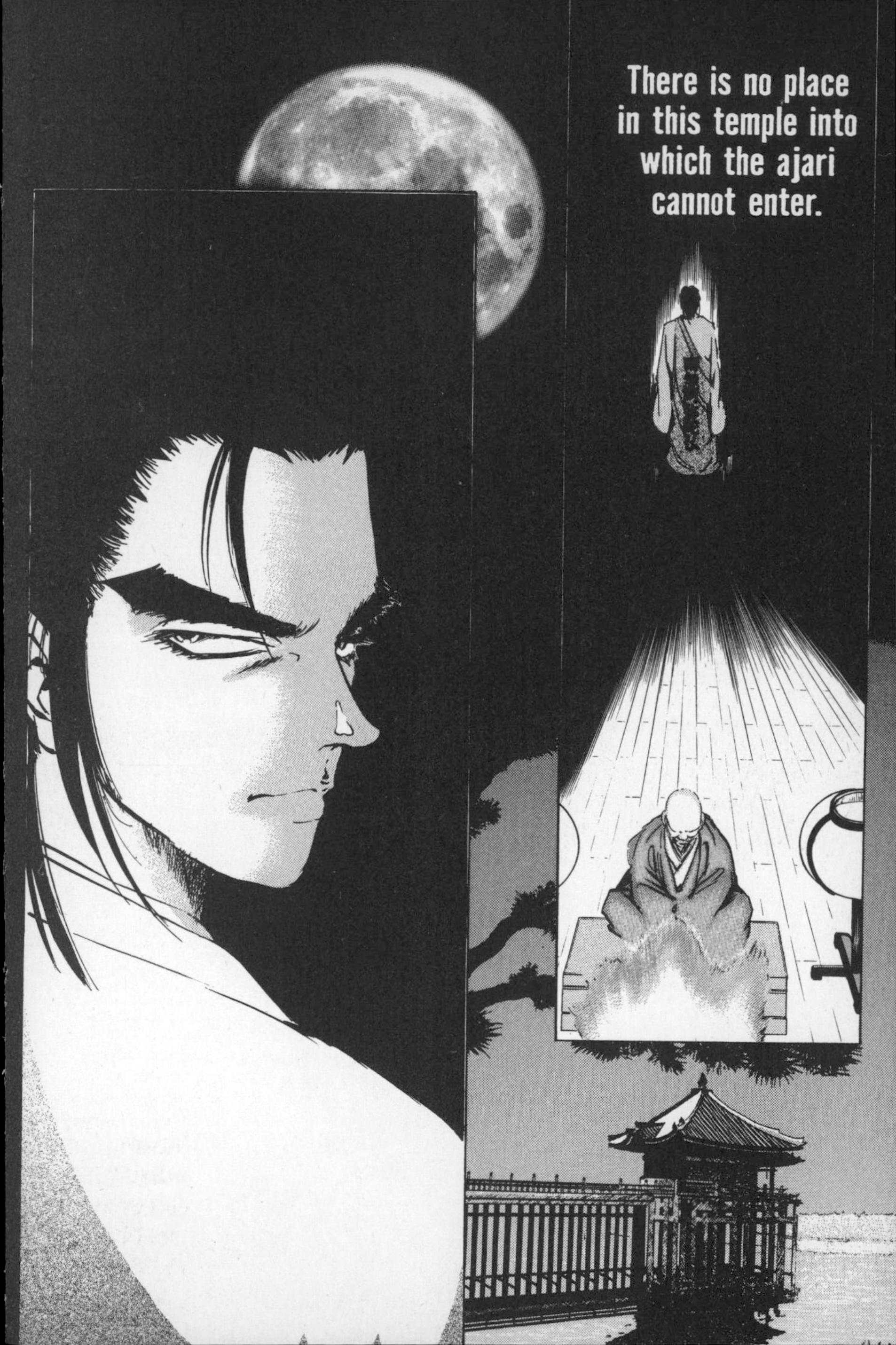
There is no place in this temple into which the ajari cannot enter.

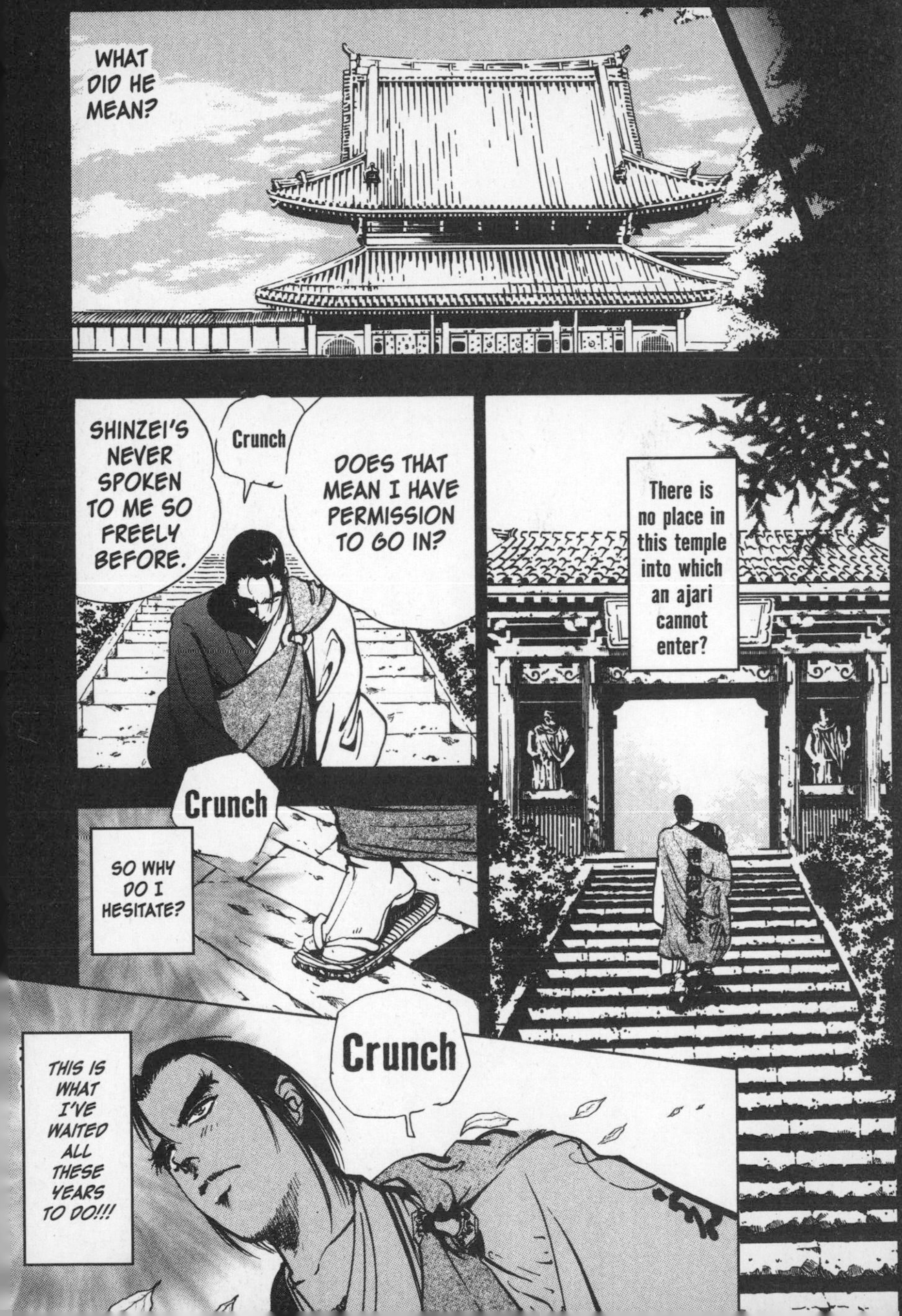
WHAT DID HE MEAN?
There is no place in this temple into which an ajari cannot enter?
DOES THAT MEAN I HAVE PERMISSION TO GO IN?
Crunch
SHINZEI'S NEVER SPOKEN TO ME SO FREELY BEFORE.
Crunch
SO WHY DO I HESITATE?
Crunch
THIS IS WHAT I'VE WAITED ALL THESE YEARS TO DO!!!

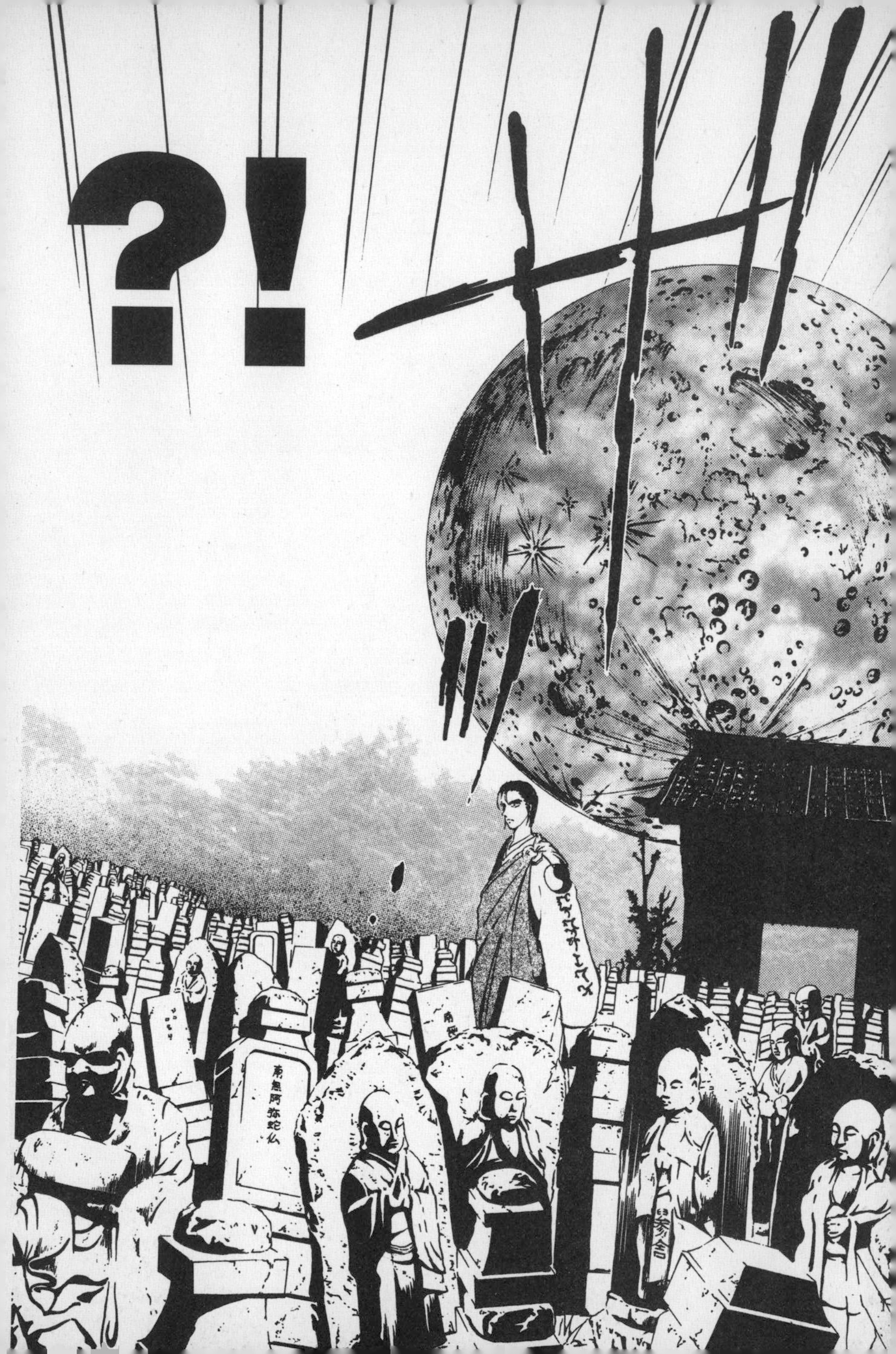
?!

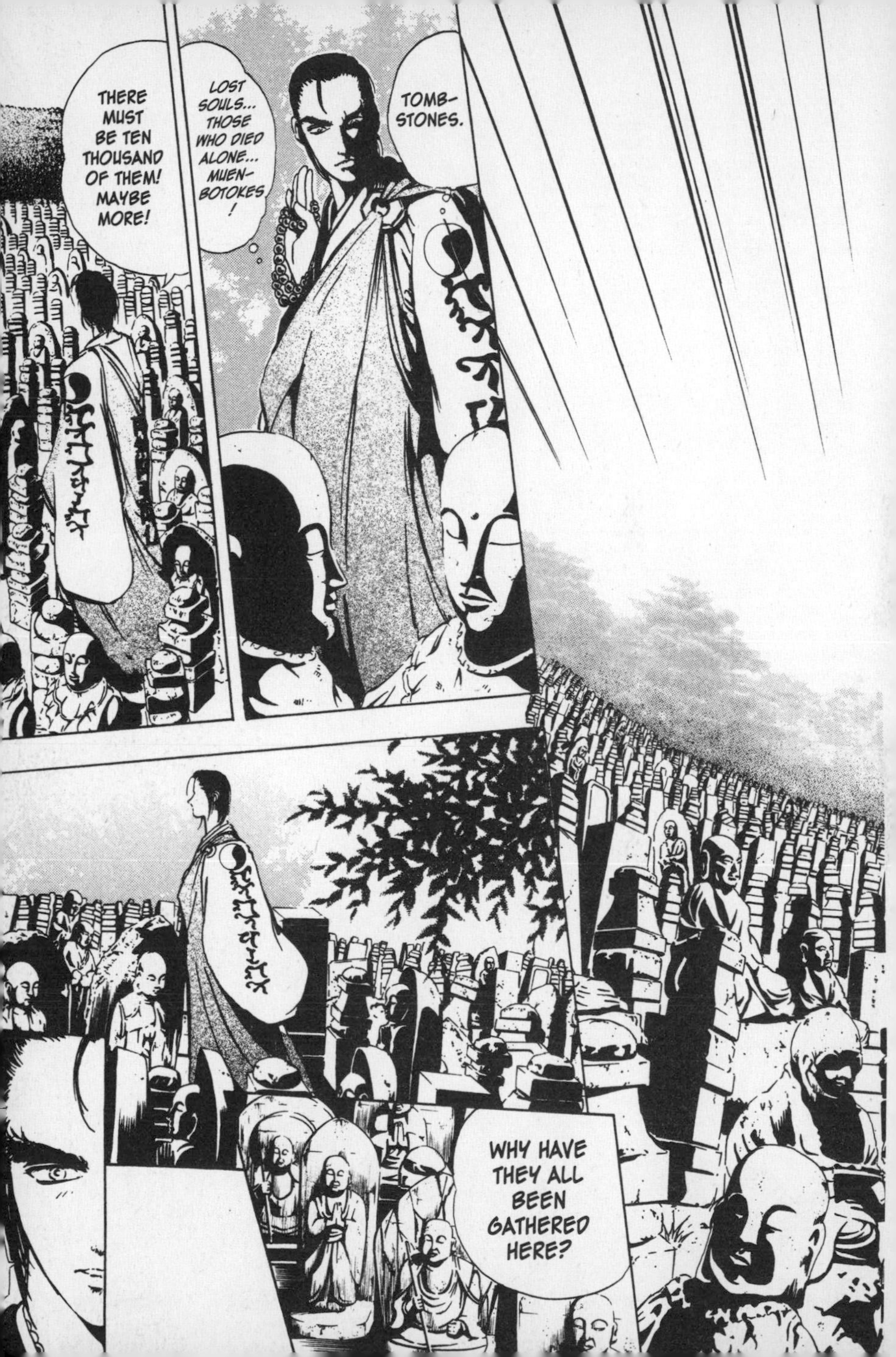
TOMB-STONES.
LOST SOULS... THOSE WHO DIED ALONE... MUEN-BOTOKES!
THERE MUST BE TEN THOUSAND OF THEM! MAYBE MORE!
WHY HAVE THEY ALL BEEN GATHERED HERE?

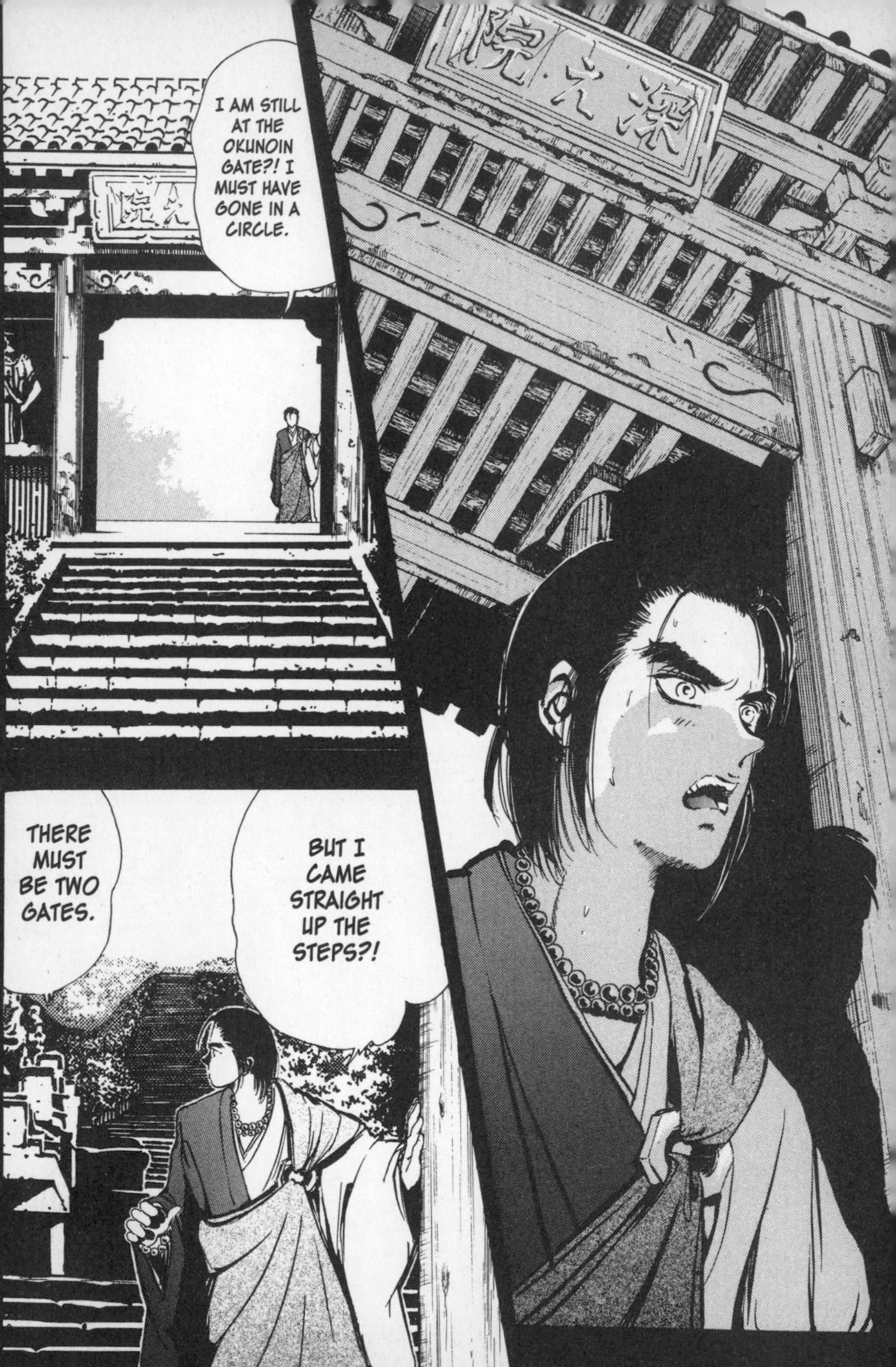

I AM STILL AT THE OKUNOIN GATE?! I MUST HAVE GONE IN A CIRCLE.
BUT I CAME STRAIGHT UP THE STEPS?!
THERE MUST BE TWO GATES.

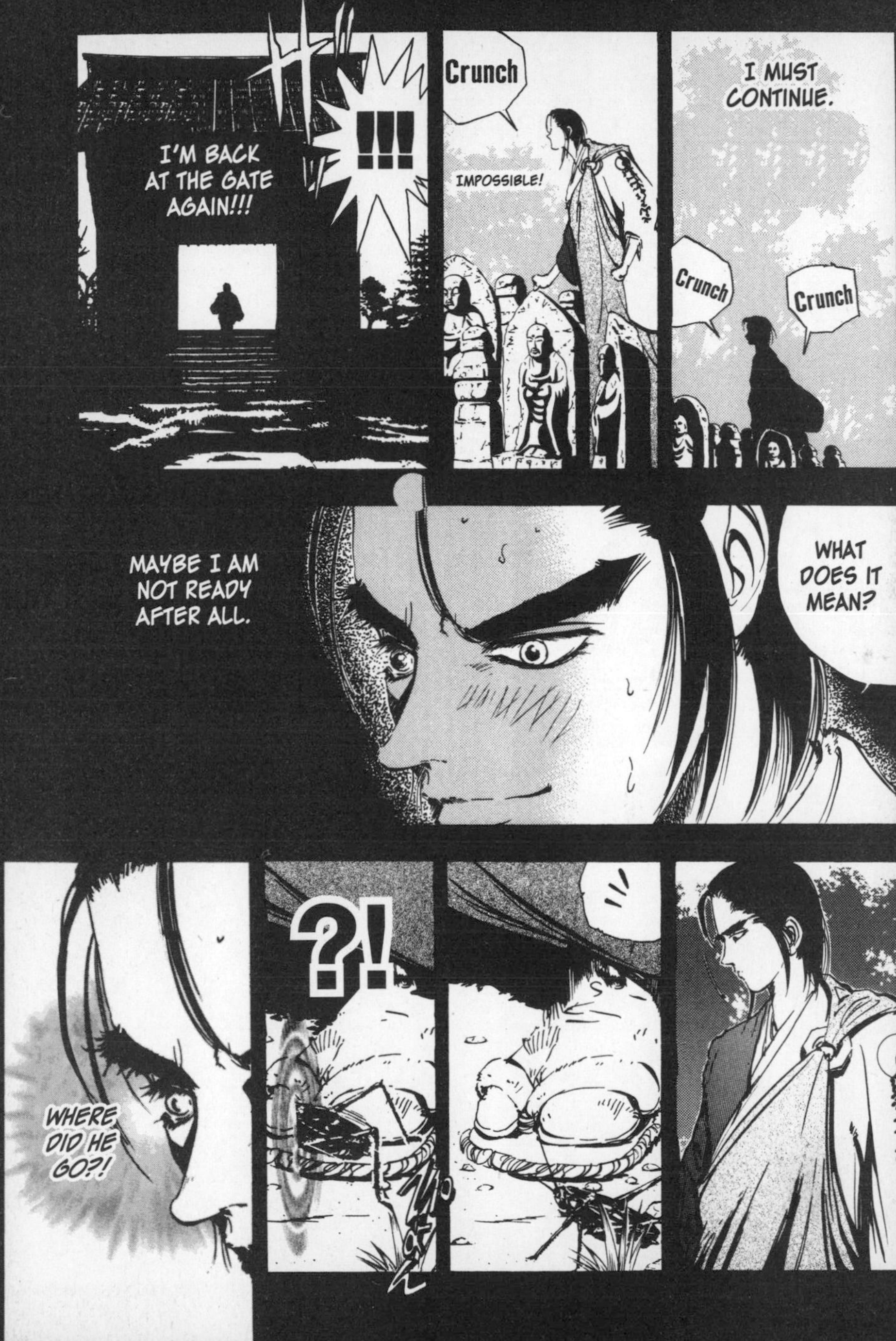
I MUST CONTINUE.
Crunch
Crunch
Crunch
IMPOSSIBLE!
!!!
I'M BACK AT THE GATE AGAIN!!!
WHAT DOES IT MEAN?
MAYBE I AM NOT READY AFTER ALL.
?!
WHERE DID HE GO?!

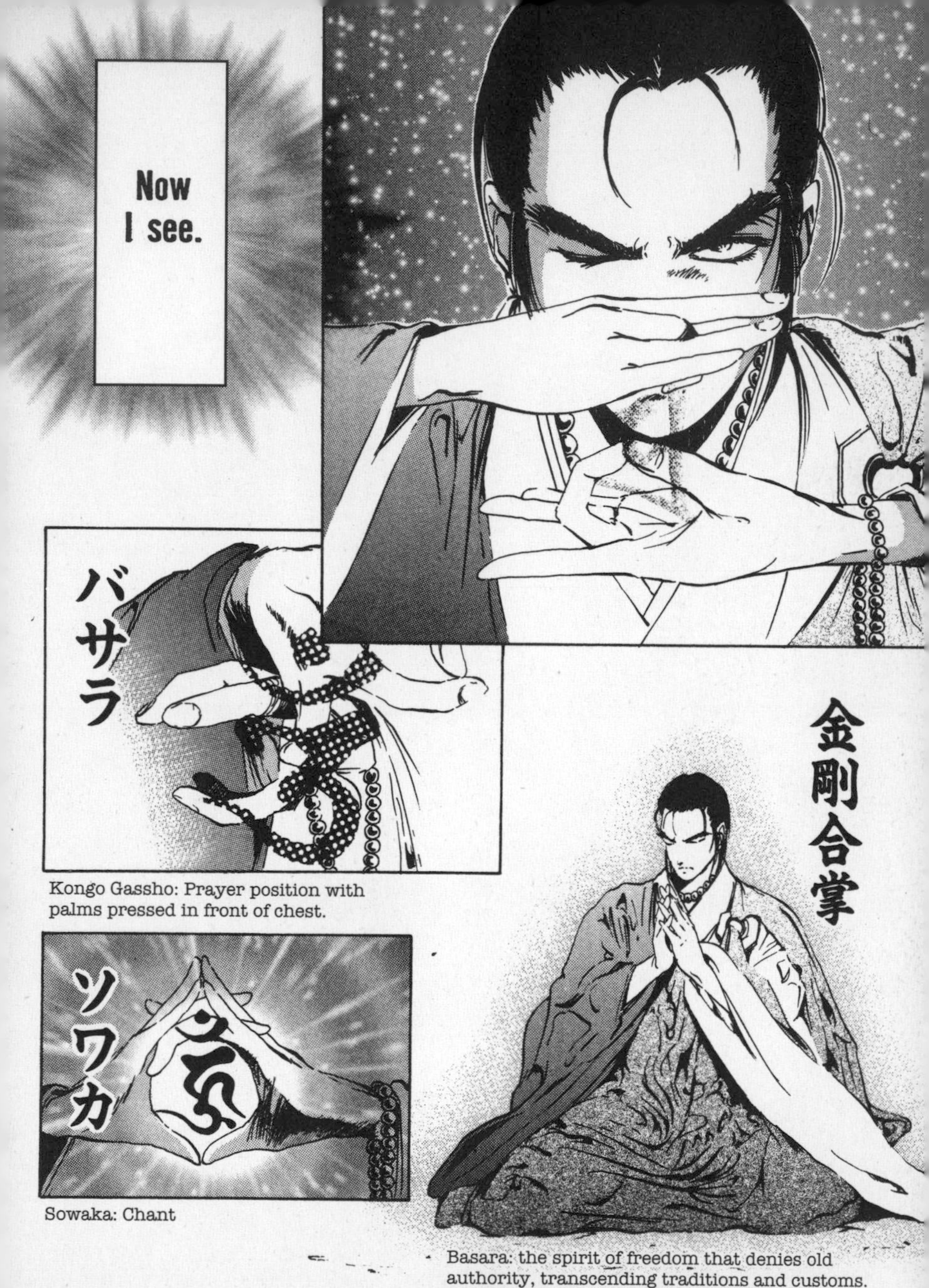

Now I see.
金剛合掌
バサラ
ソワカ

Kongo Gassho: Prayer position with palms pressed in front of chest.

Sowaka: Chant

Basara: the spirit of freedom that denies old authority, transcending traditions and customs. Derived from the Sanskrit word "vajra," which means, among other things, an indestructible substance, it is usually represented by a diamond or a thunderbolt.

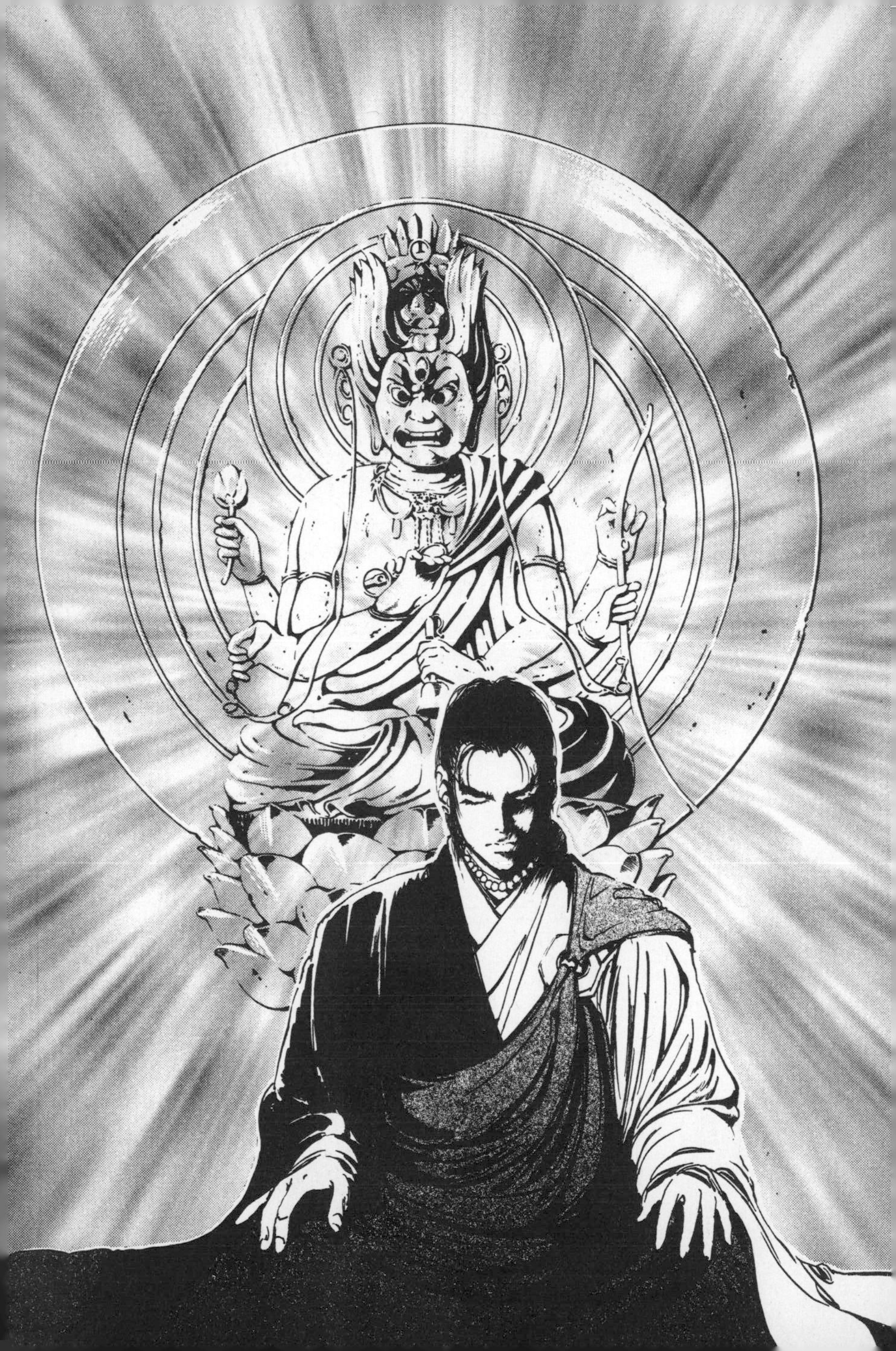

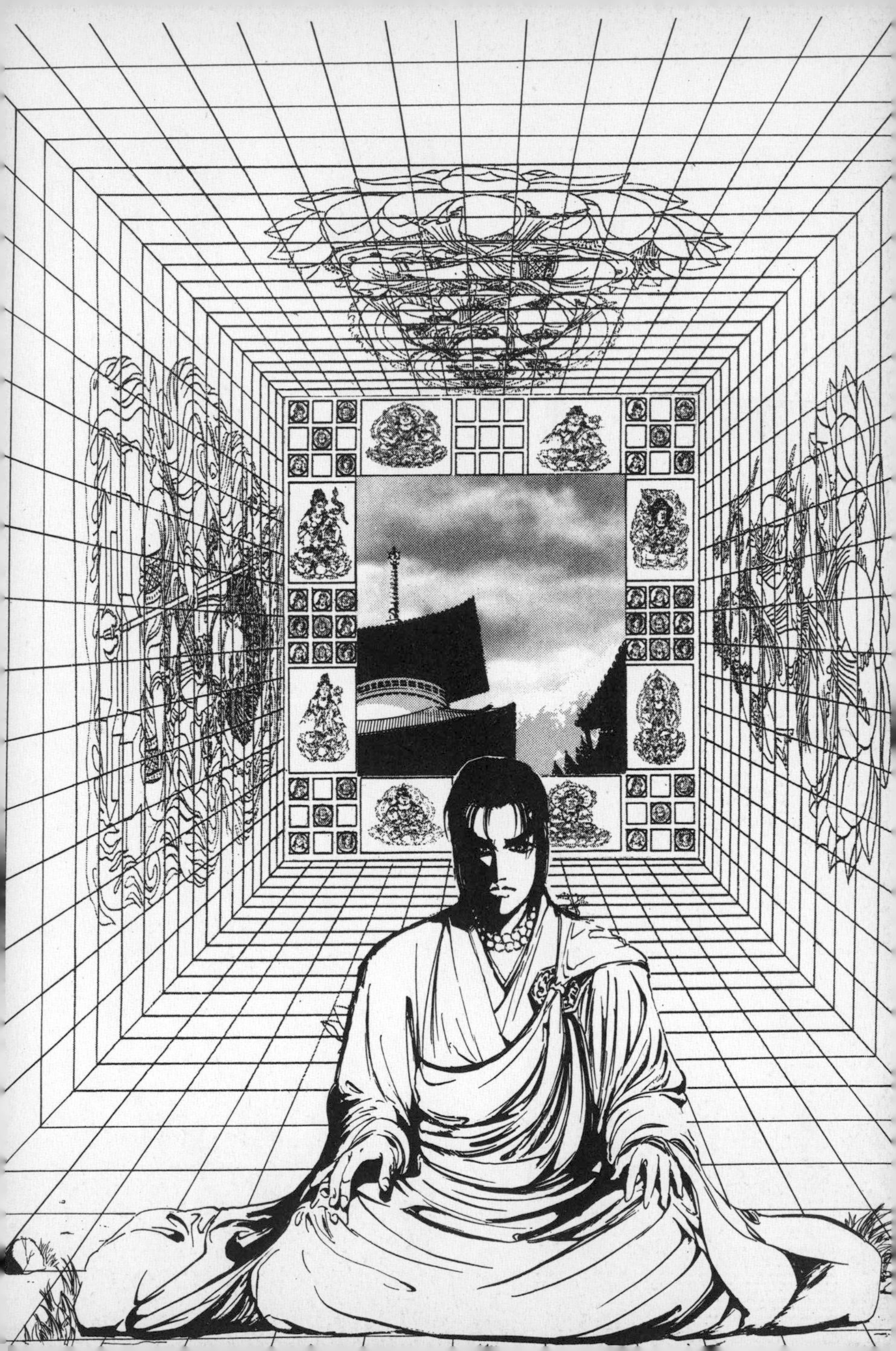

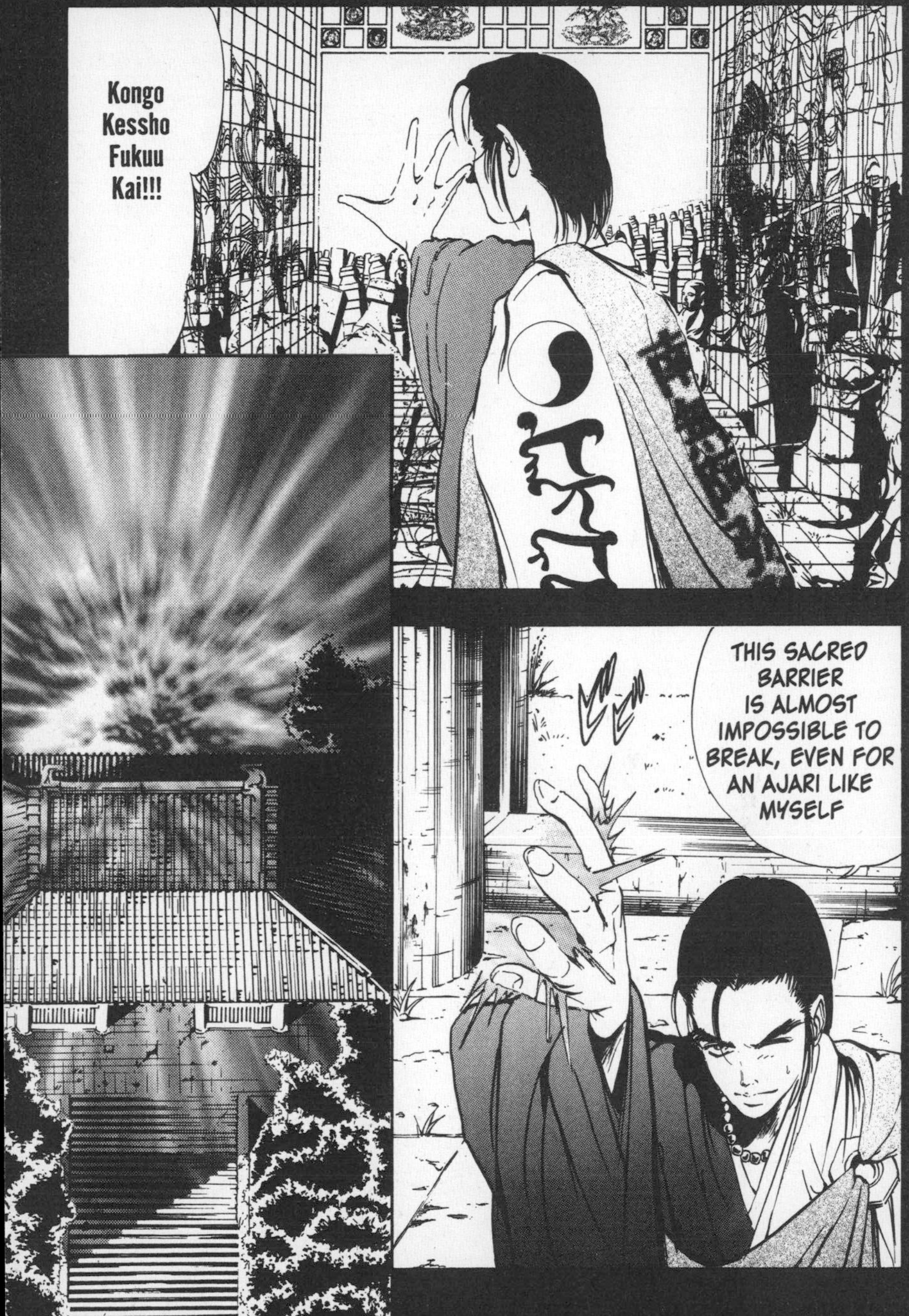
Kongo Kessho Fukuu Kai!!!
THIS SACRED BARRIER IS ALMOST IMPOSSIBLE TO BREAK, EVEN FOR AN AJARI LIKE MYSELF

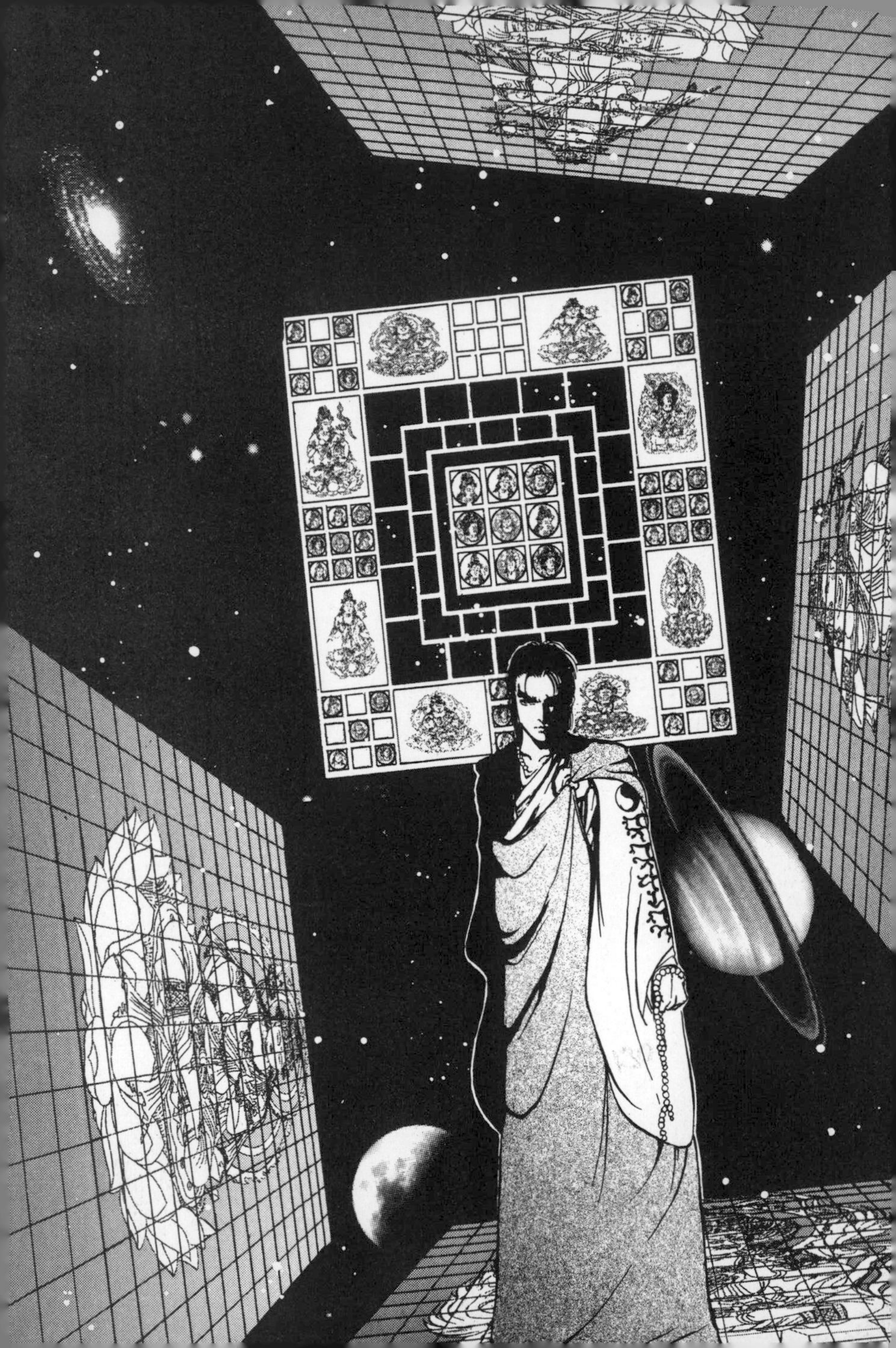

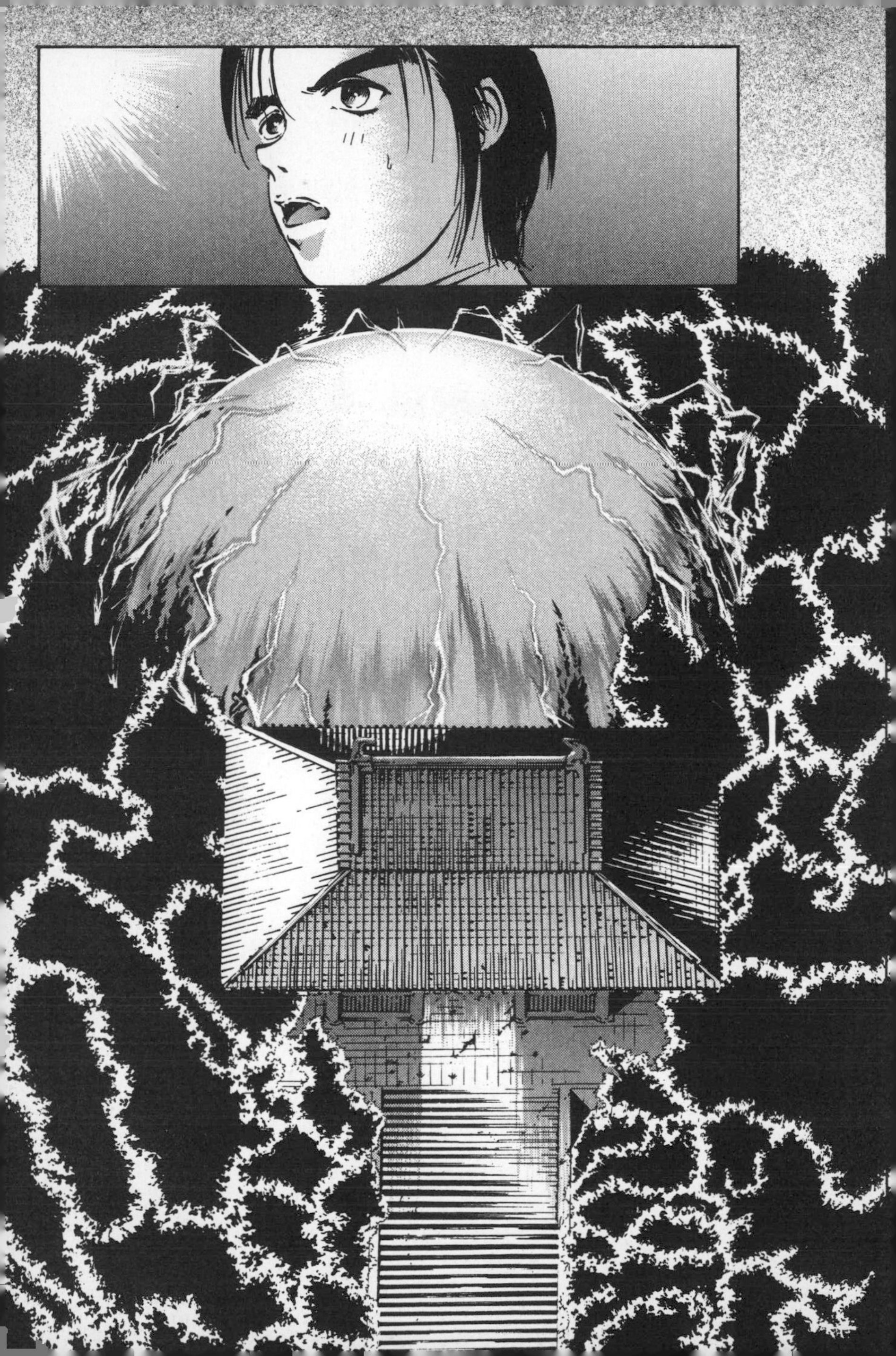

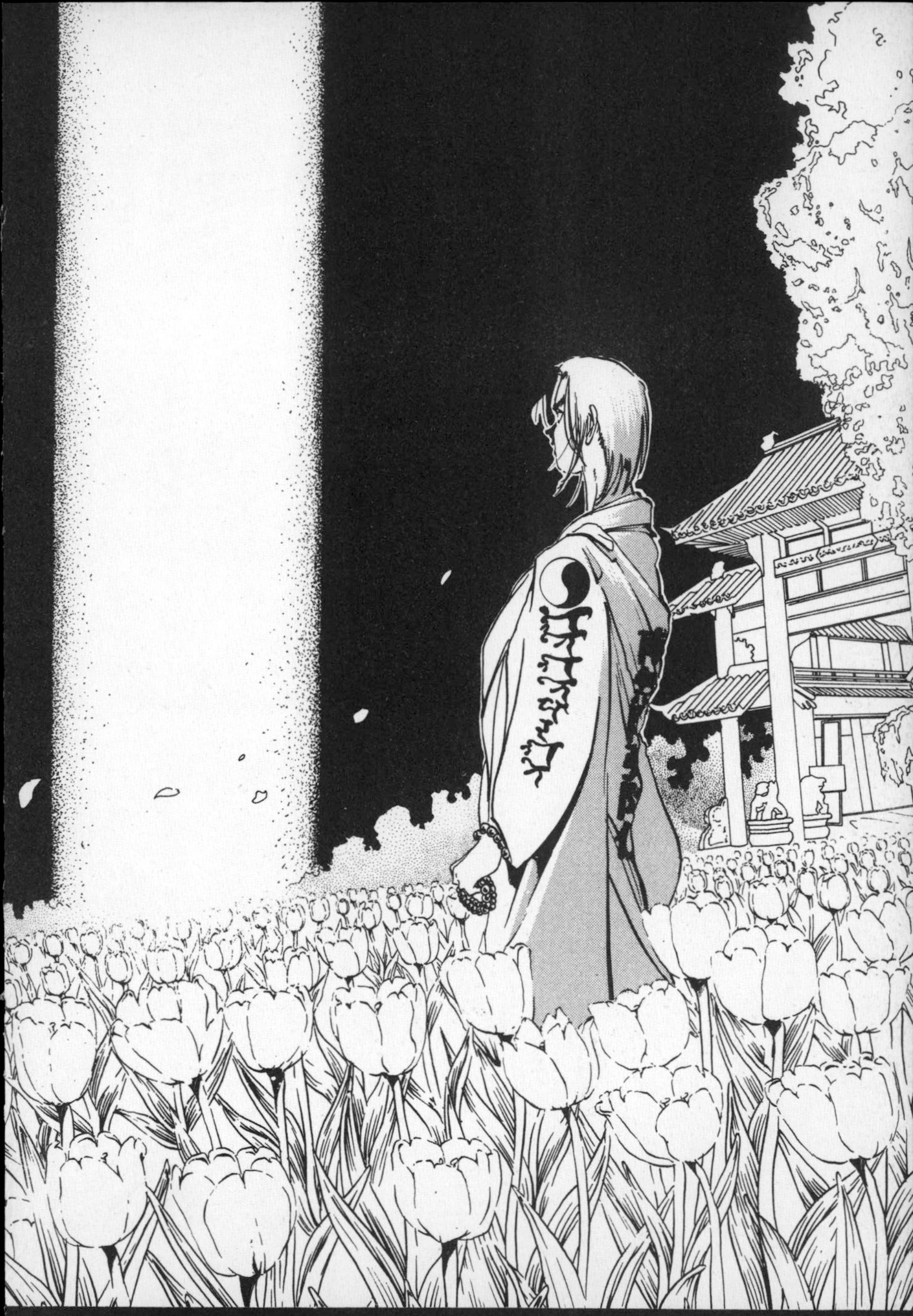

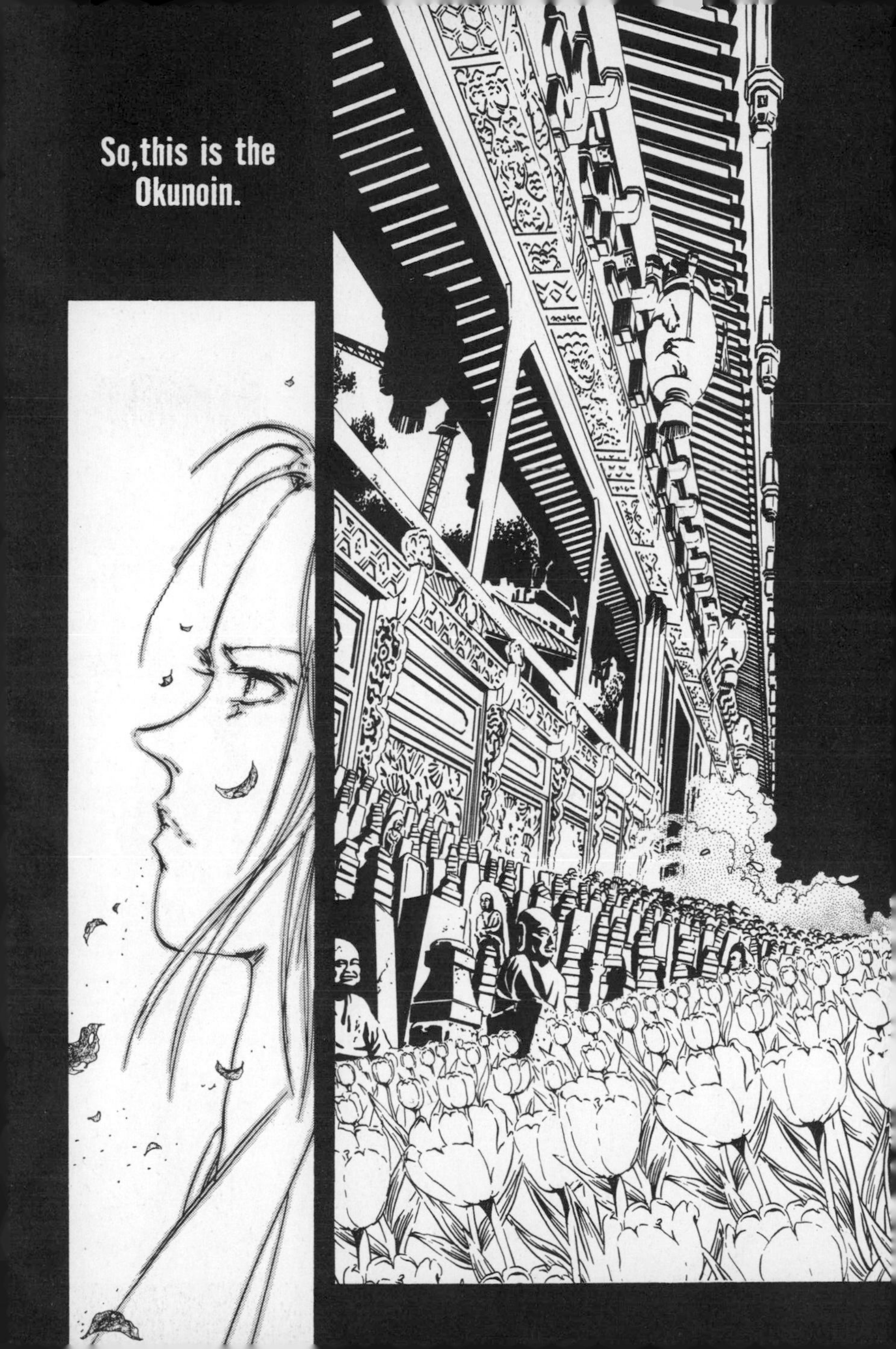
So, this is the Okunoin.

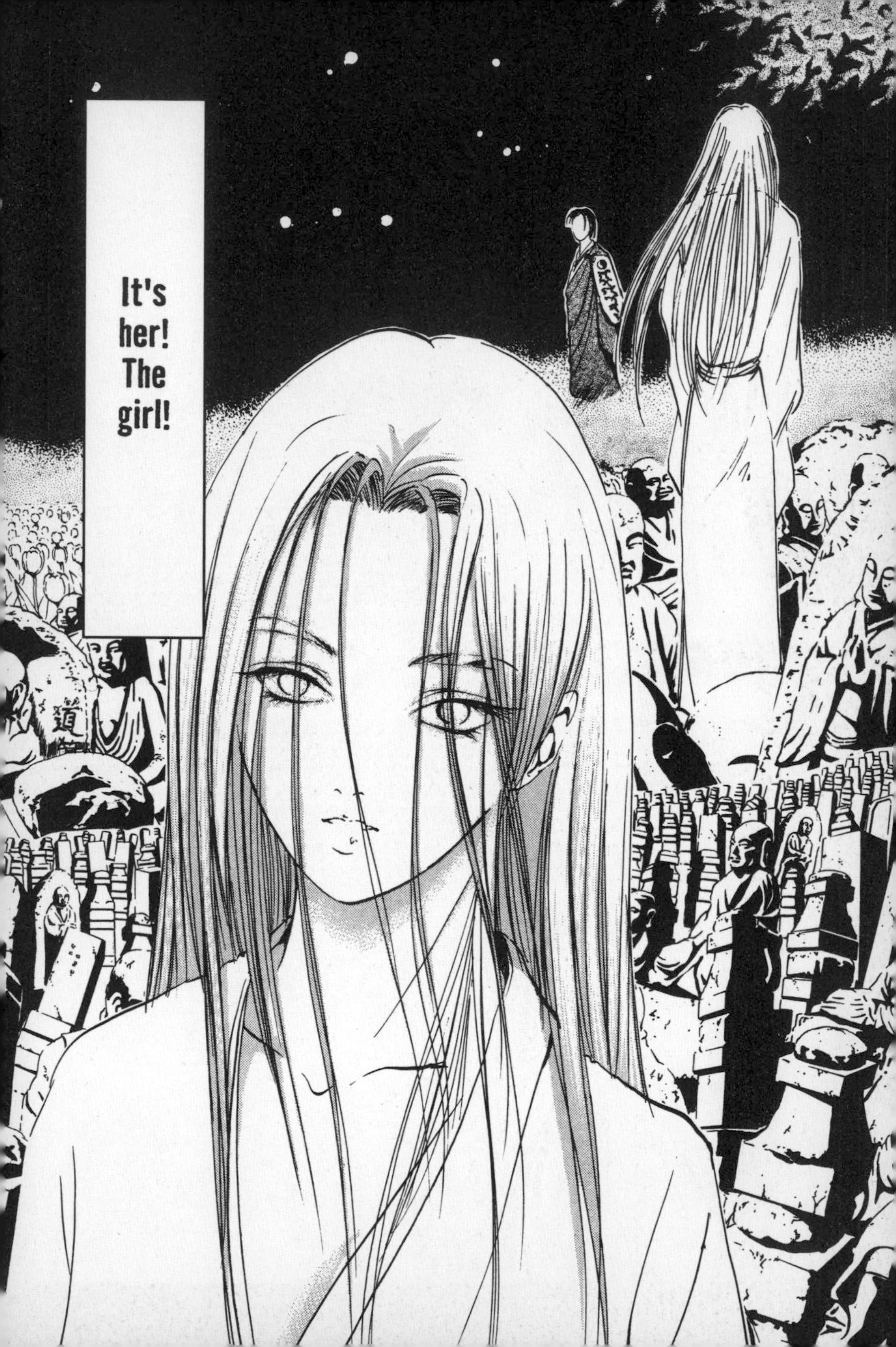
It's her! The girl!
道

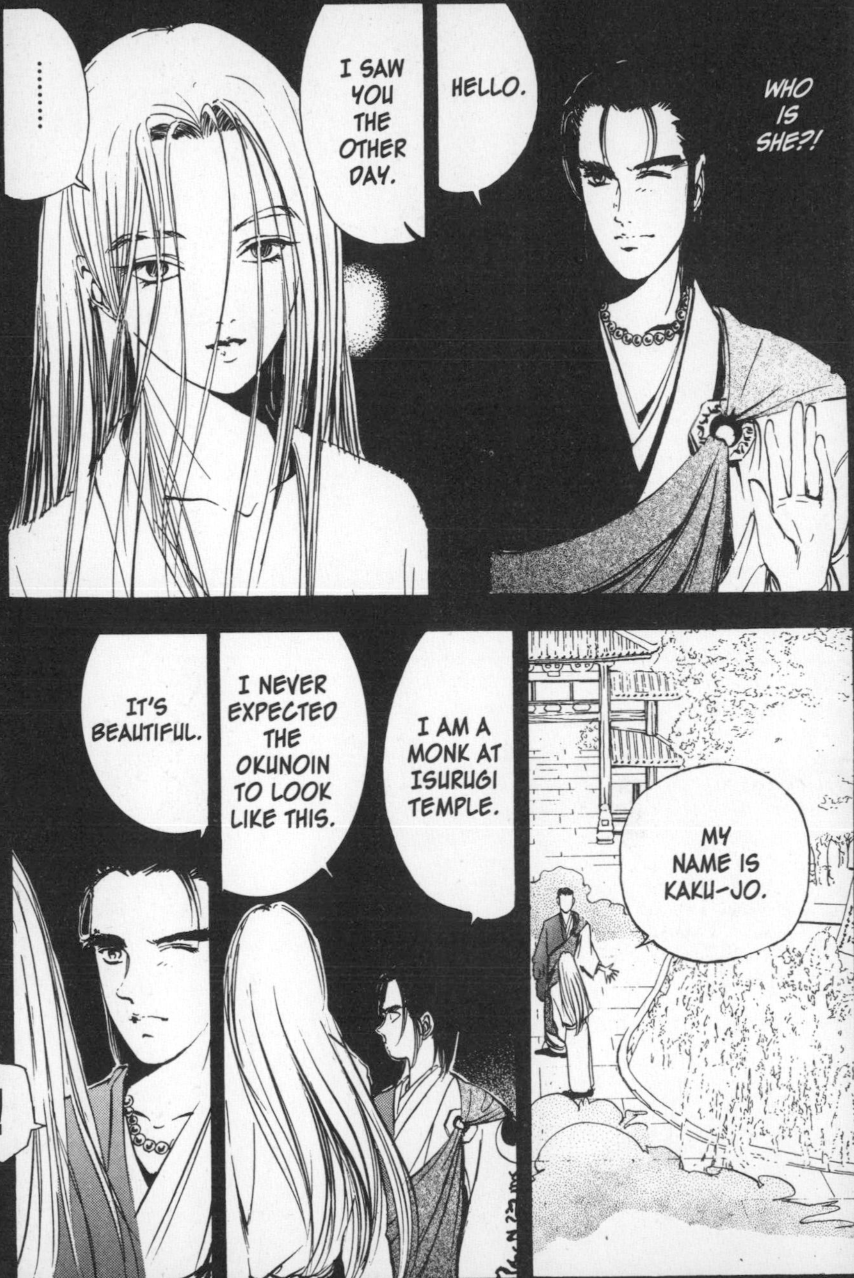
WHO IS SHE?!
HELLO.
I SAW YOU THE OTHER DAY.
......
MY NAME IS KAKU-JO.
I AM A MONK AT ISURUGI TEMPLE.
I NEVER EXPECTED THE OKUNOIN TO LOOK LIKE THIS.
IT'S BEAUTIFUL.
!

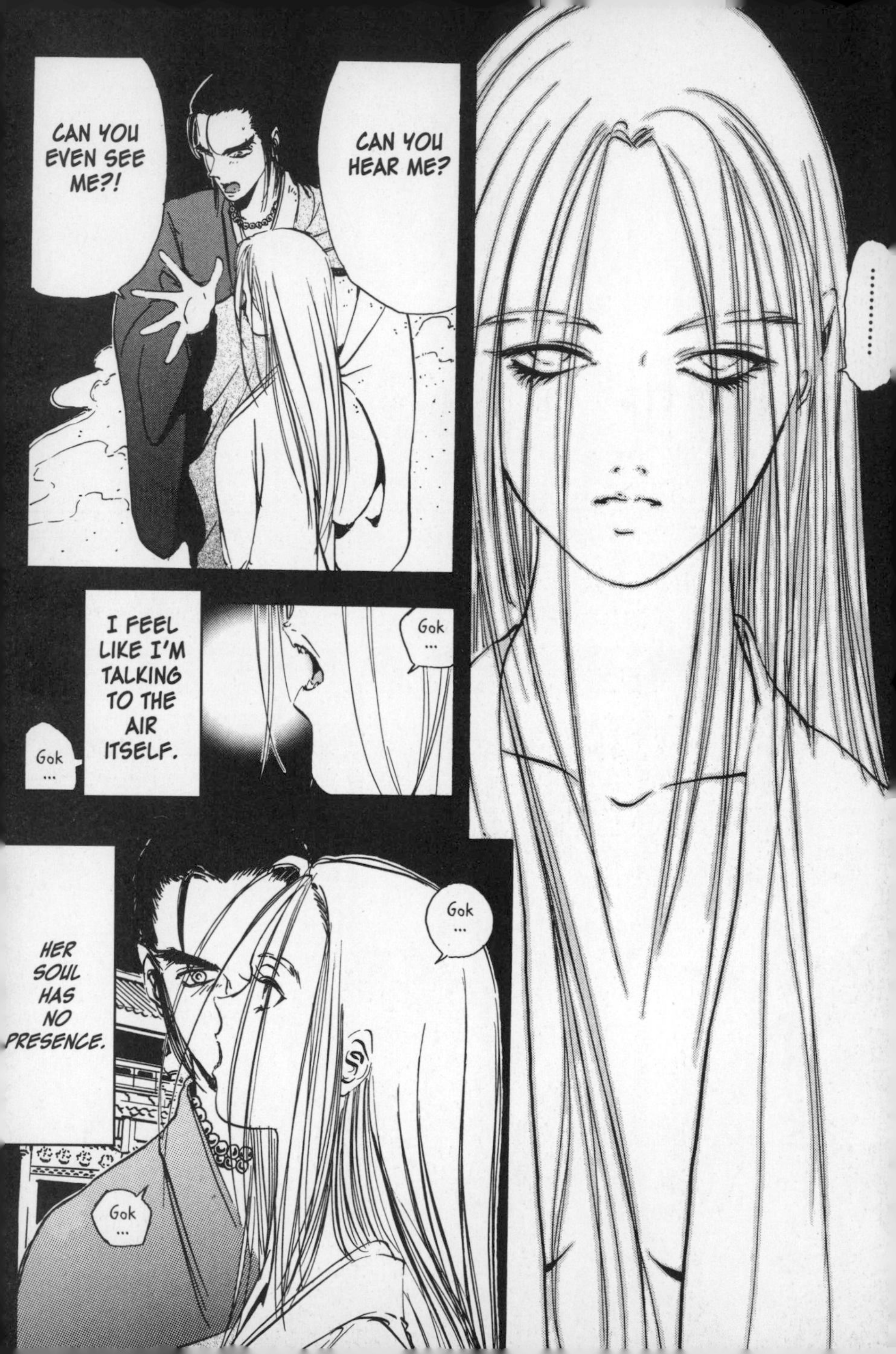
......
CAN YOU HEAR ME?
CAN YOU EVEN SEE ME?!
Gok ...
I FEEL LIKE I'M TALKING TO THE AIR ITSELF.
Gok ...
Gok ...
HER SOUL HAS NO PRESENCE.
Gok ...

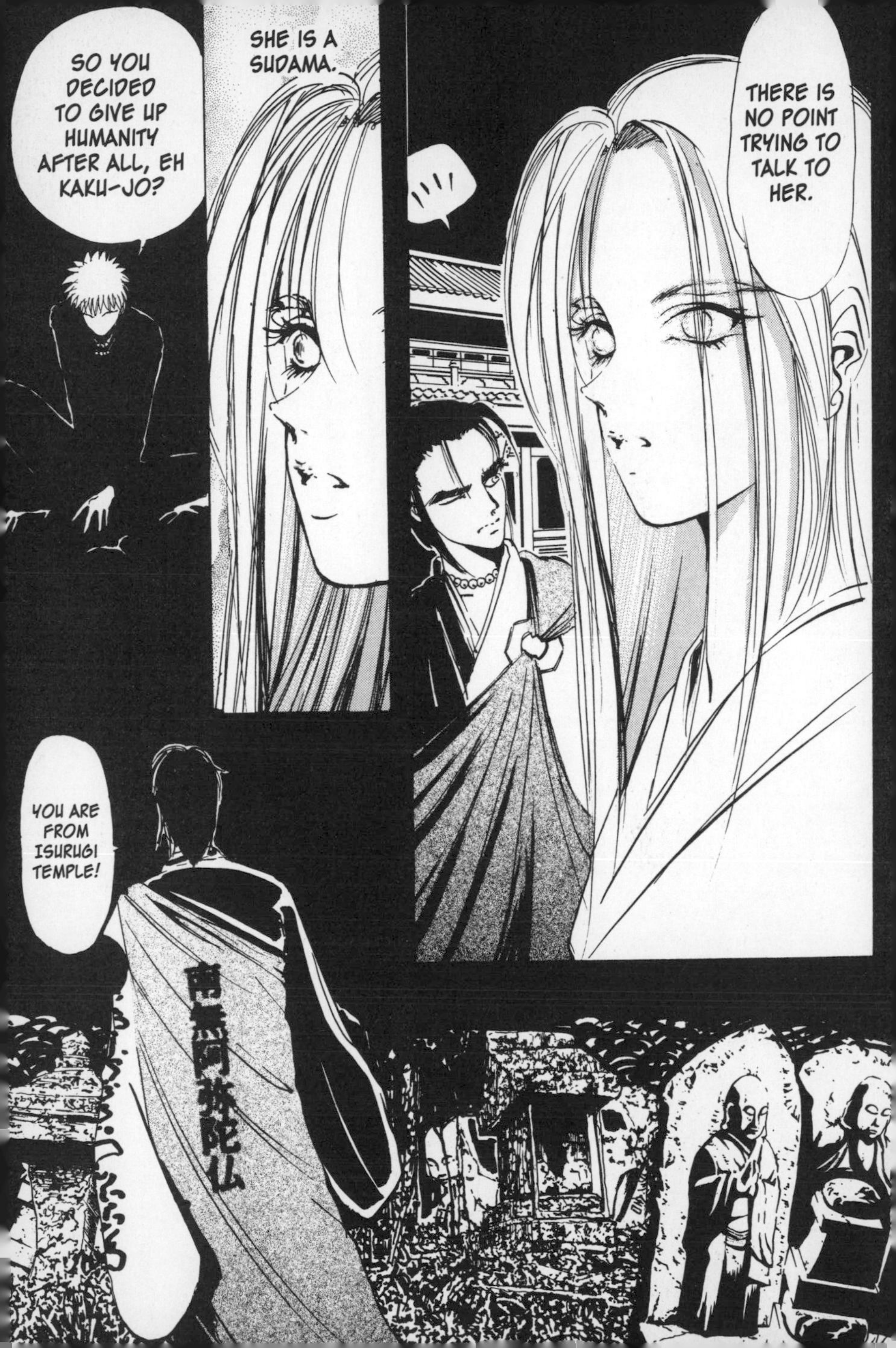
THERE IS NO POINT TRYING TO TALK TO HER.
...
SHE IS A SUDAMA.
SO YOU DECIDED TO GIVE UP HUMANITY AFTER ALL, EH KAKU-JO?
YOU ARE FROM ISURUGI TEMPLE!
南無阿弥陀仏

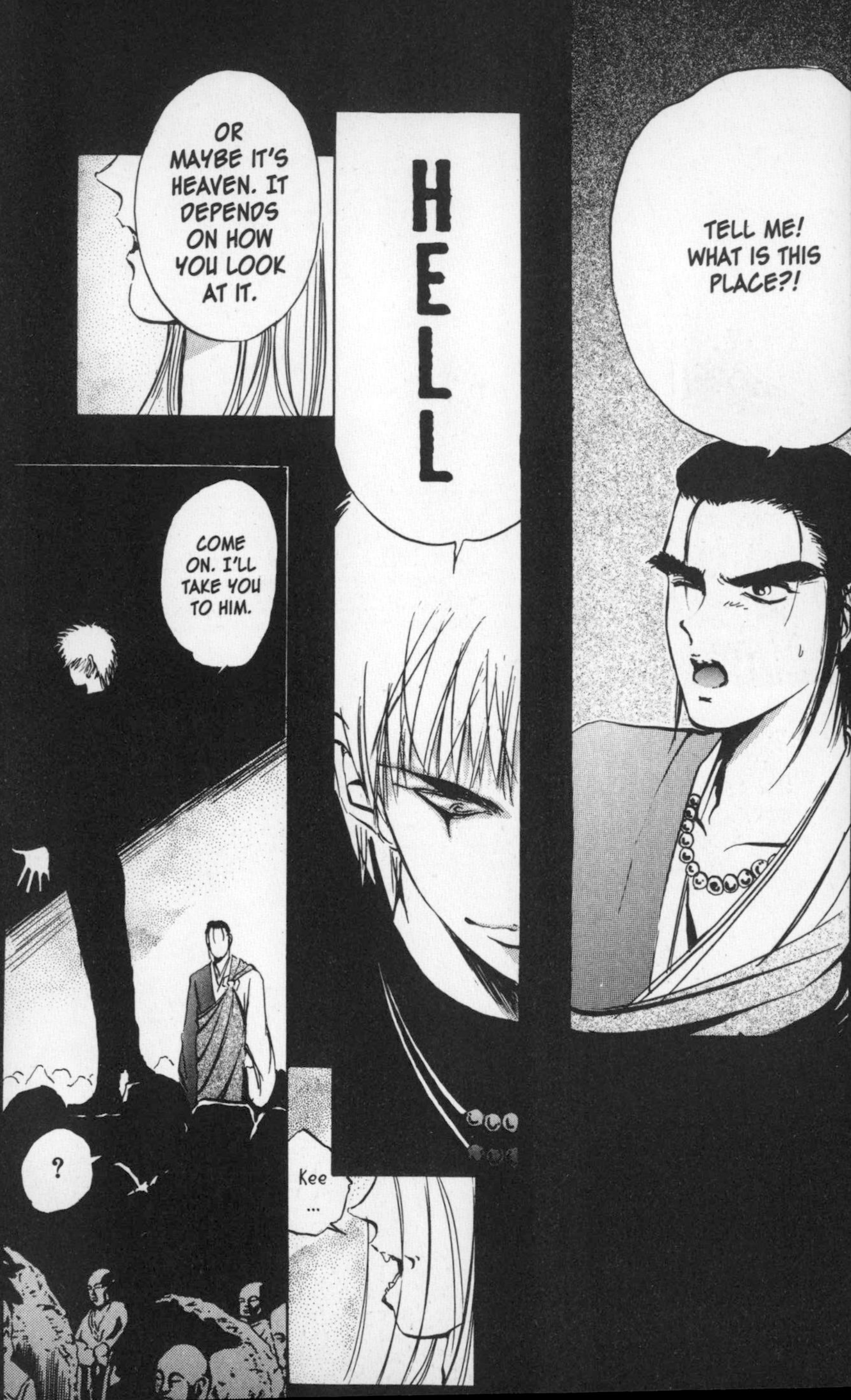
TELL ME! WHAT IS THIS PLACE?!
HELL
OR MAYBE IT'S HEAVEN. IT DEPENDS ON HOW YOU LOOK AT IT.
Kee ...
COME ON. I'LL TAKE YOU TO HIM.
?

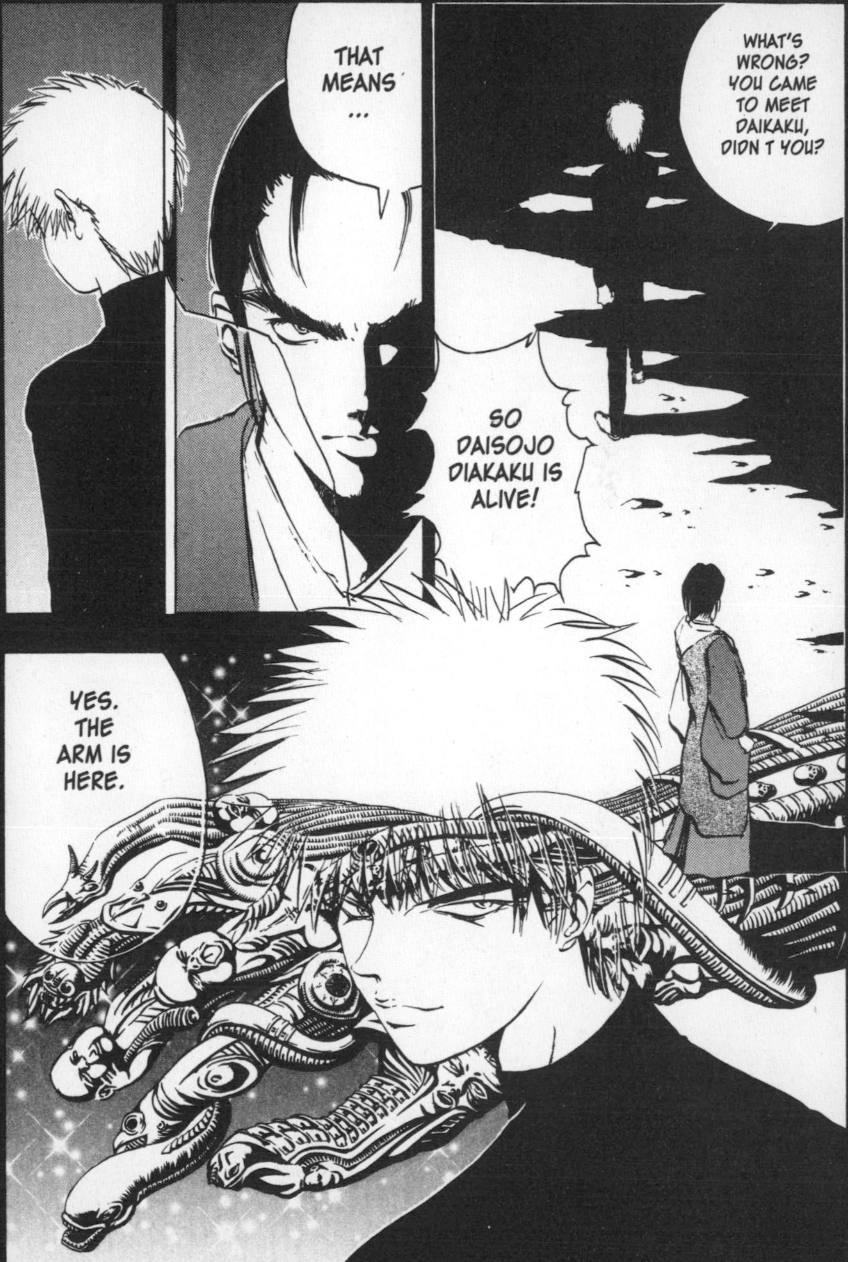
WHAT'S WRONG? YOU CAME TO MEET DAIKAKU, DIDN T YOU?
SO DAISOJO DIAKAKU IS ALIVE!
THAT MEANS ...
YES. THE ARM IS HERE.

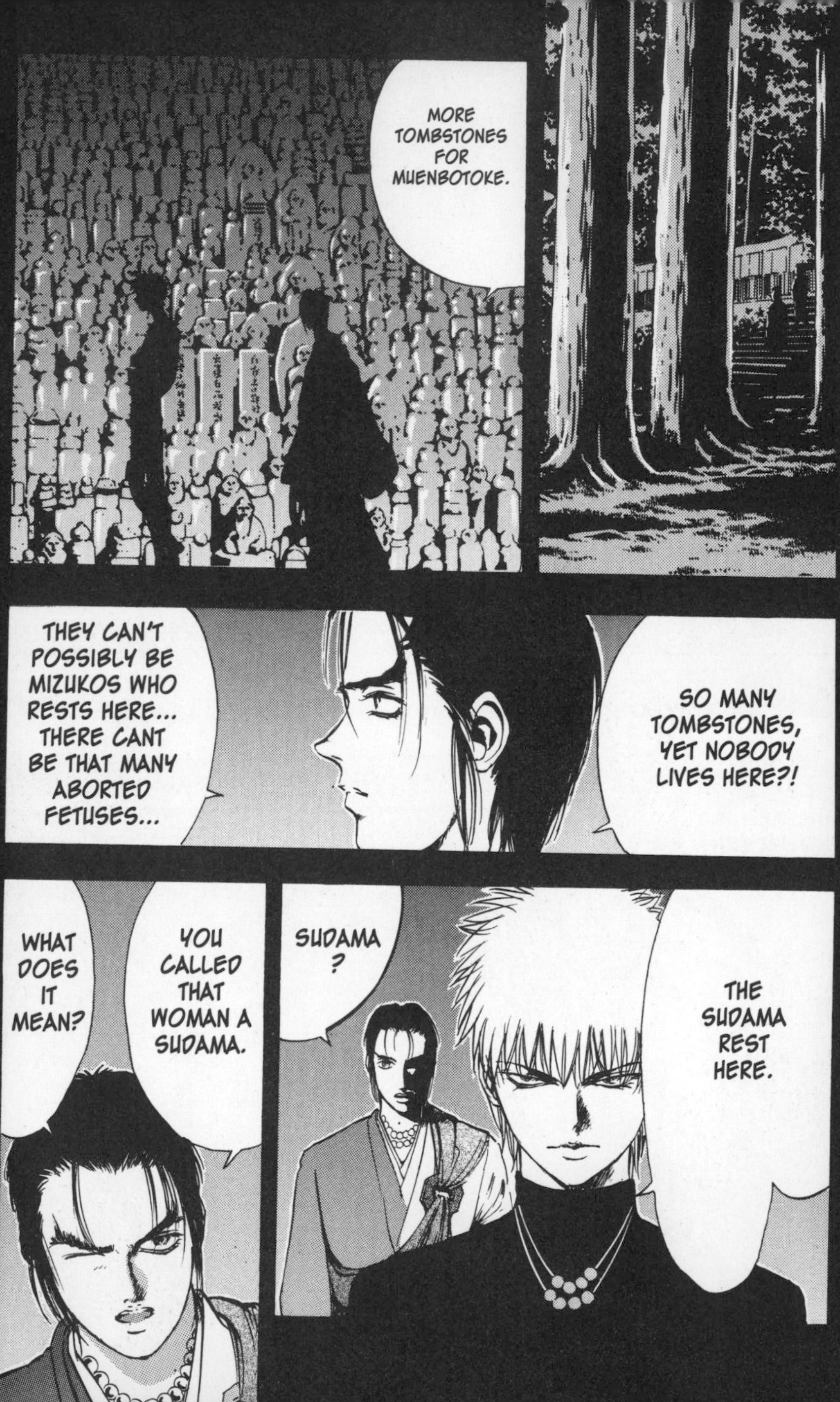
MORE TOMBSTONES FOR MUENBOTOKE.
SO MANY TOMBSTONES, YET NOBODY LIVES HERE?!
THEY CAN'T POSSIBLY BE MIZUKOS WHO RESTS HERE... THERE CANT BE THAT MANY ABORTED FETUSES...
THE SUDAMA REST HERE.
SUDAMA ?
YOU CALLED THAT WOMAN A SUDAMA.
WHAT DOES IT MEAN?

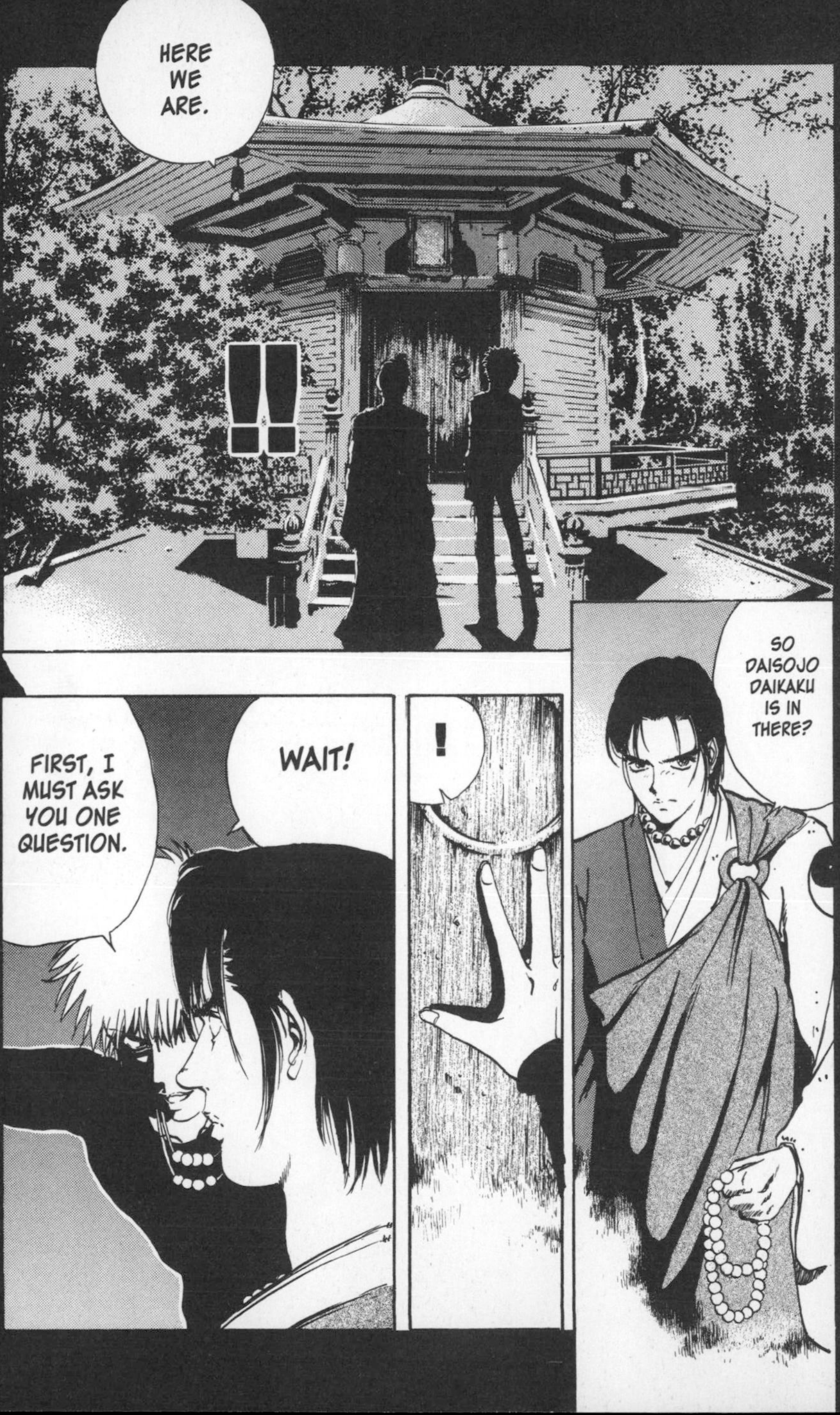
HERE WE ARE.
!!
SO DAISOJO DAIKAKU IS IN THERE?
!
WAIT!
FIRST, I MUST ASK YOU ONE QUESTION.

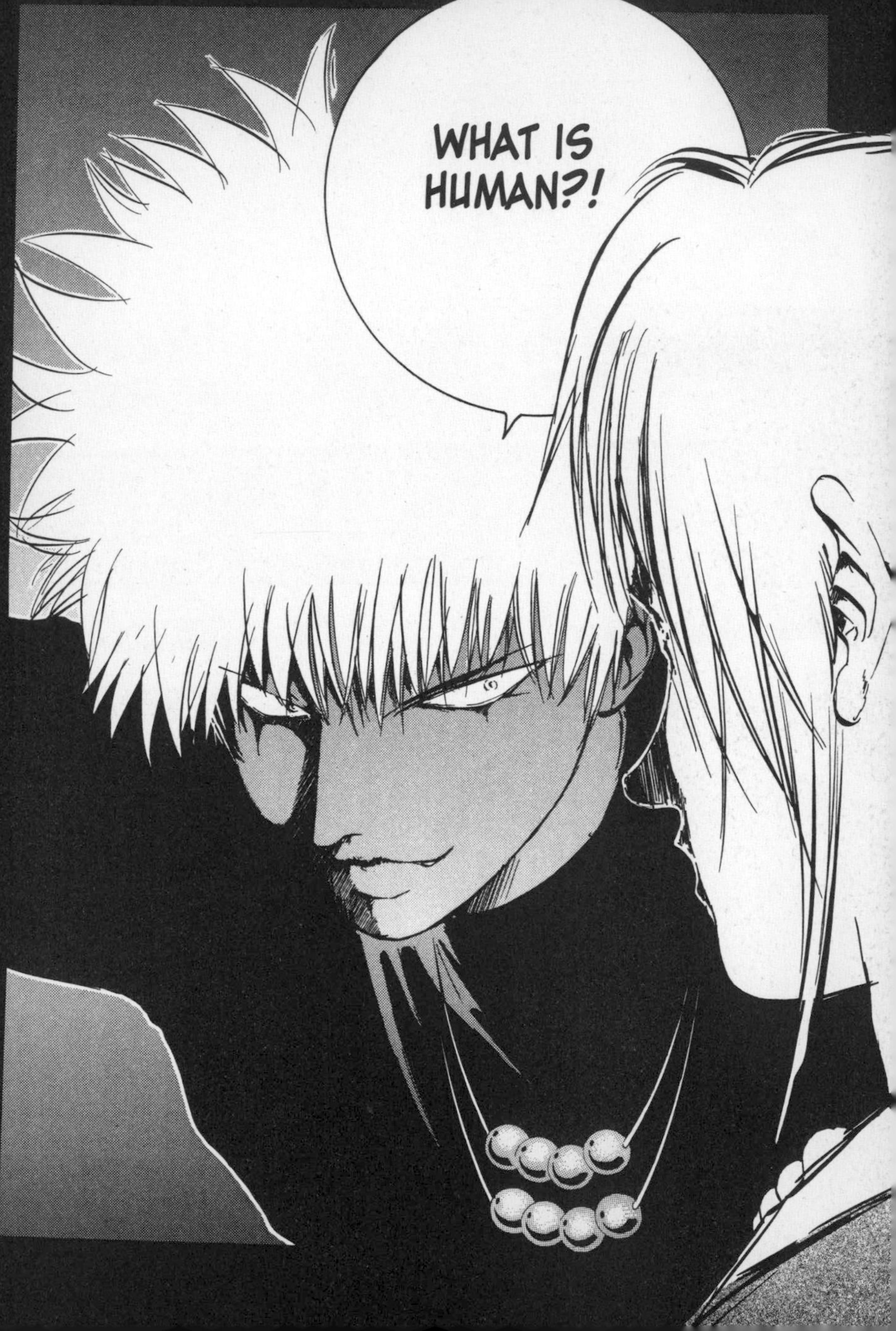
WHAT IS HUMAN?!

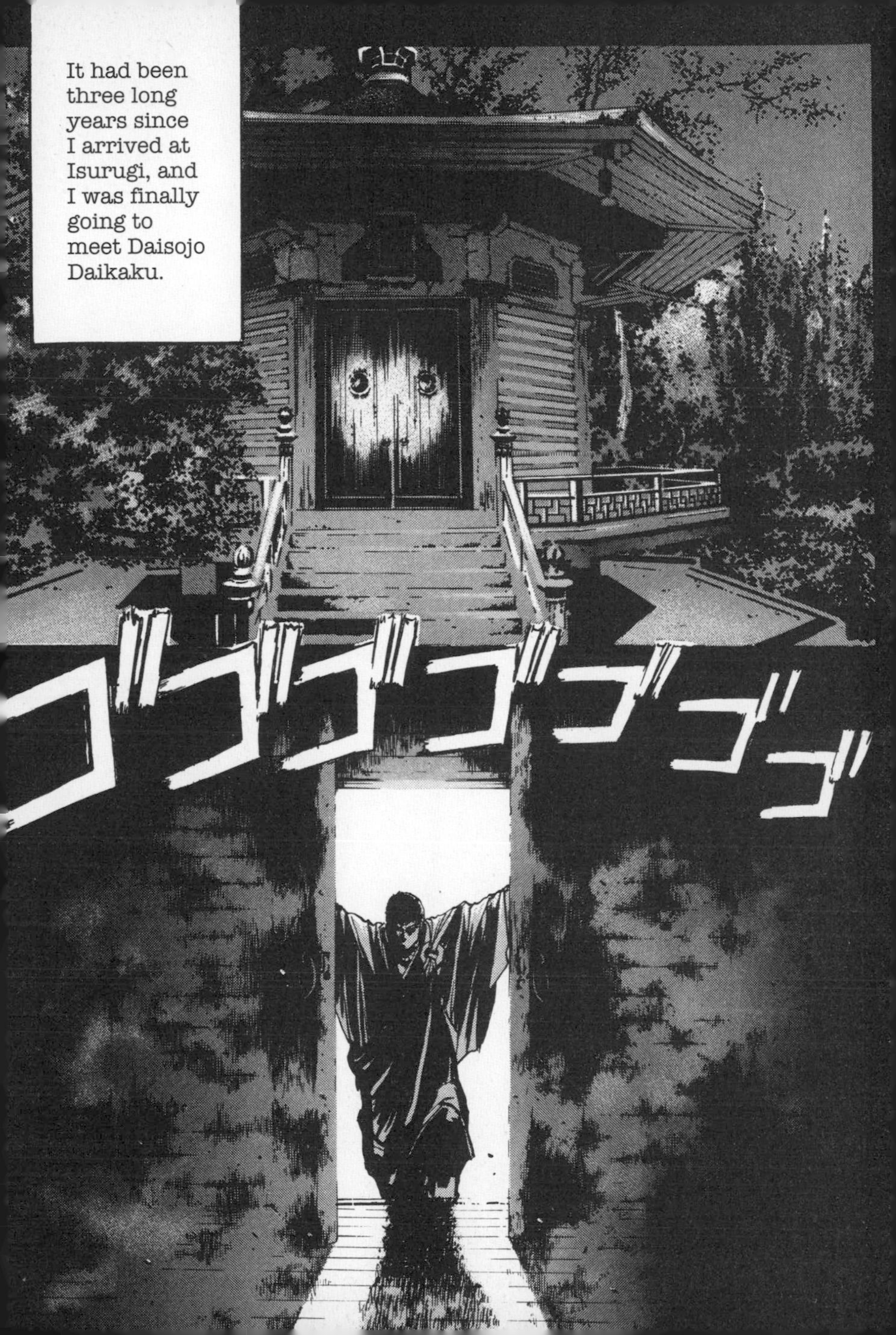
It had been three long years since I arrived at Isurugi, and I was finally going to meet Daisojo Daikaku.
ゴゴゴゴゴゴゴ

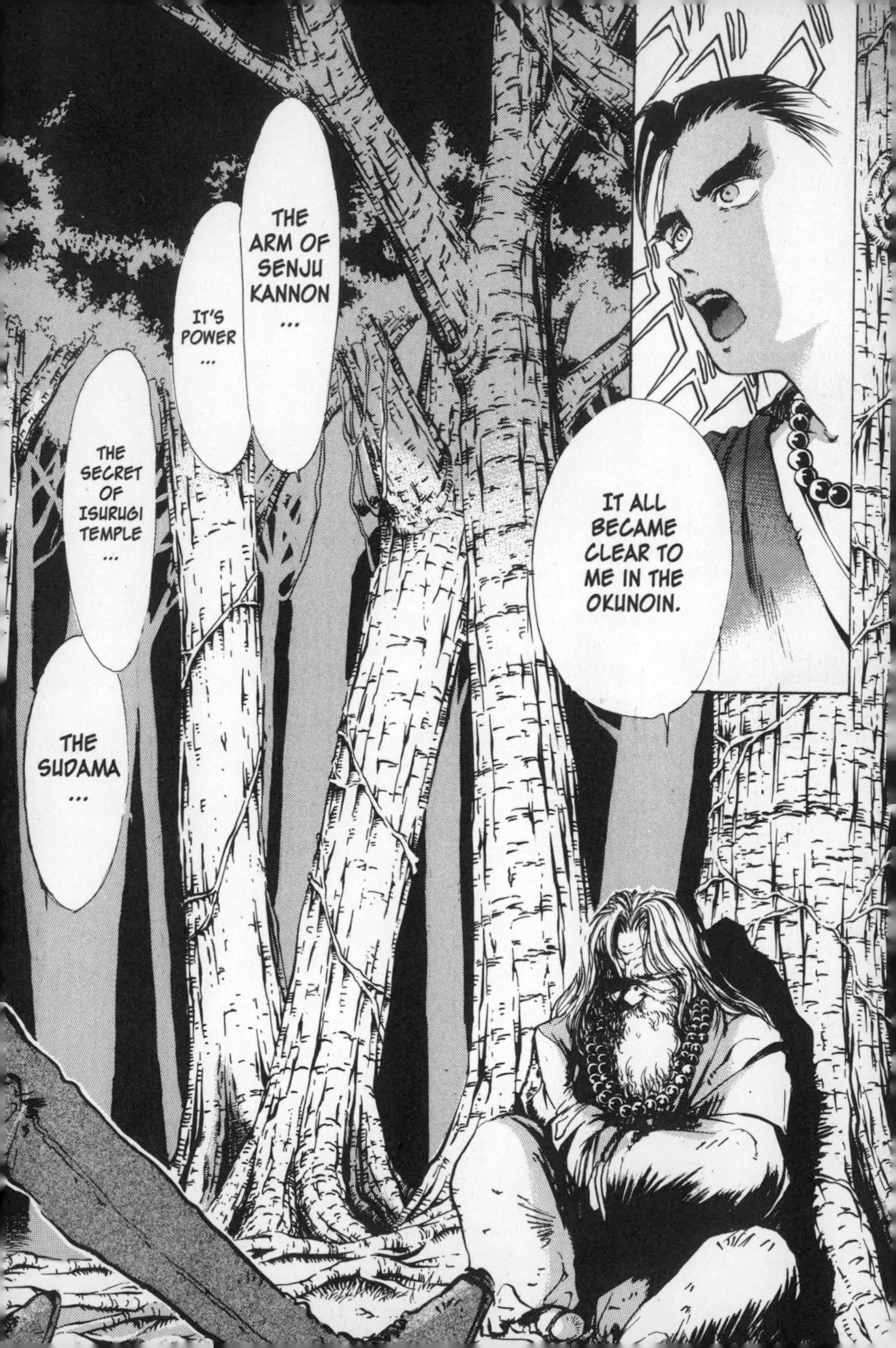
IT ALL BECAME CLEAR TO ME IN THE OKUNOIN.
THE ARM OF SENJU KANNON ...
IT'S POWER ...
THE SECRET OF ISURUGI TEMPLE ...
THE SUDAMA ...

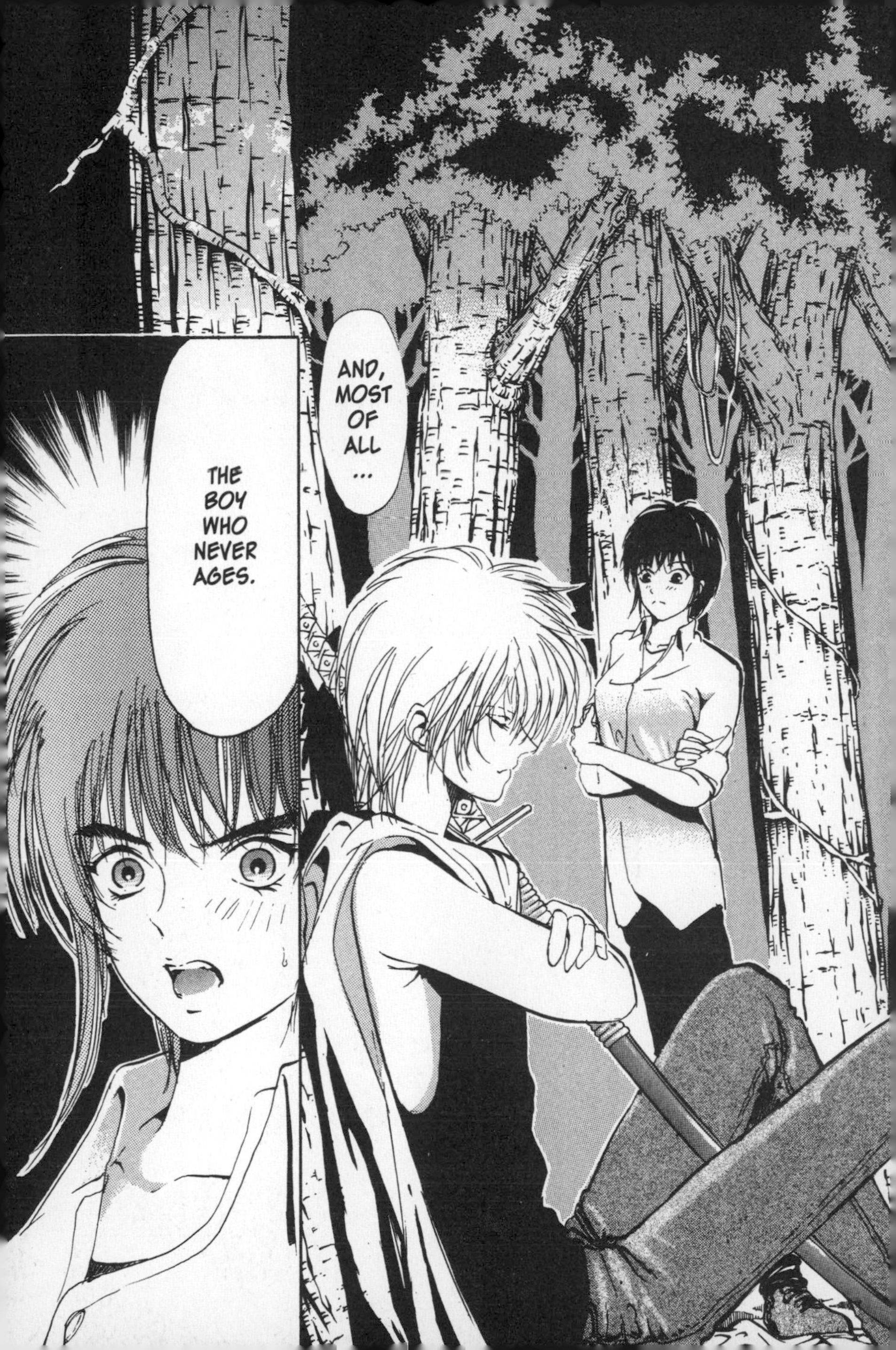
AND, MOST OF ALL ...
THE BOY WHO NEVER AGES.

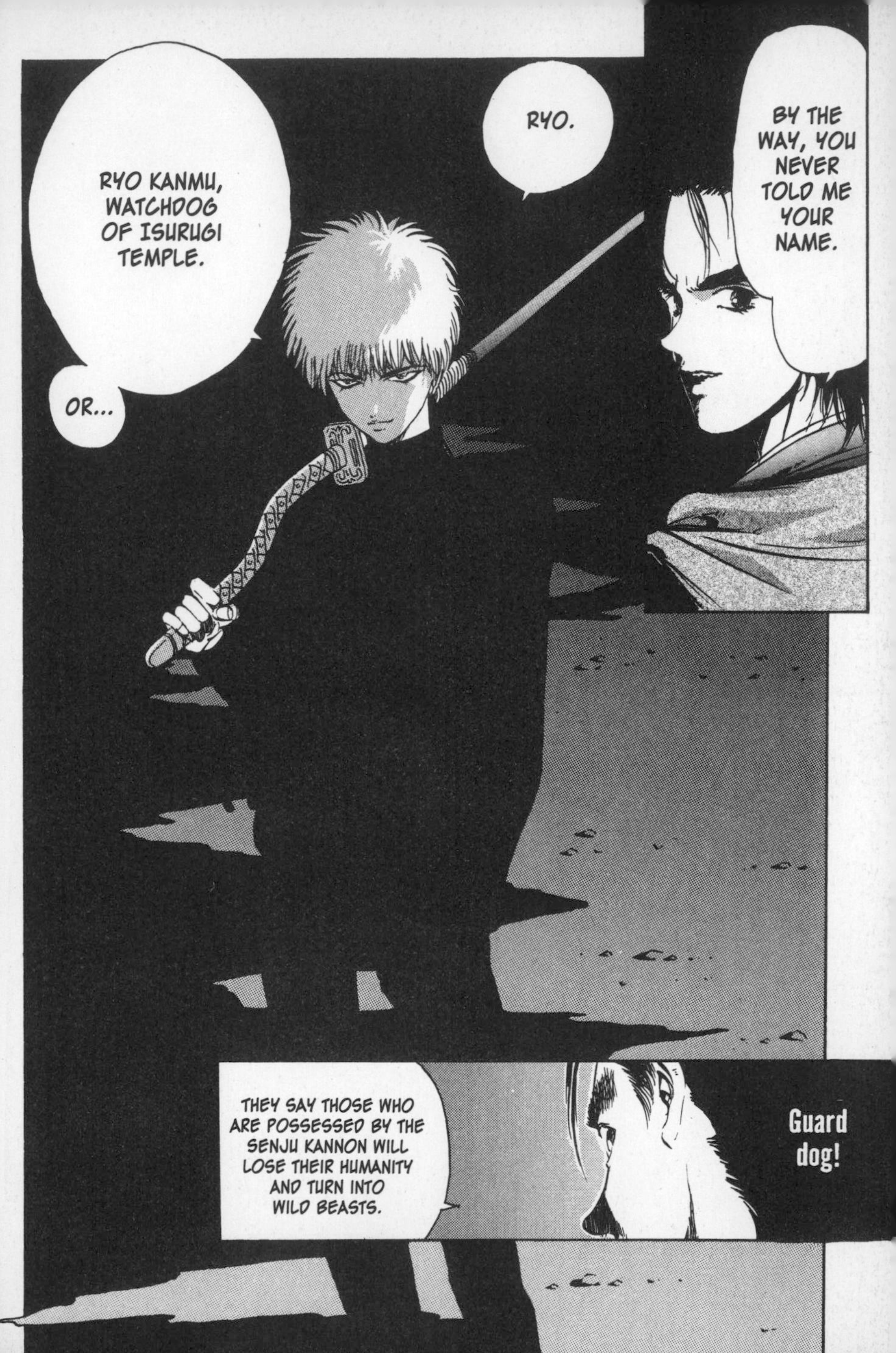
BY THE WAY, YOU NEVER TOLD ME YOUR NAME.
RYO.
RYO KANMU, WATCHDOG OF ISURUGI TEMPLE.
OR...
Guard dog!
THEY SAY THOSE WHO ARE POSSESSED BY THE SENJU KANNON WILL LOSE THEIR HUMANITY AND TURN INTO WILD BEASTS.

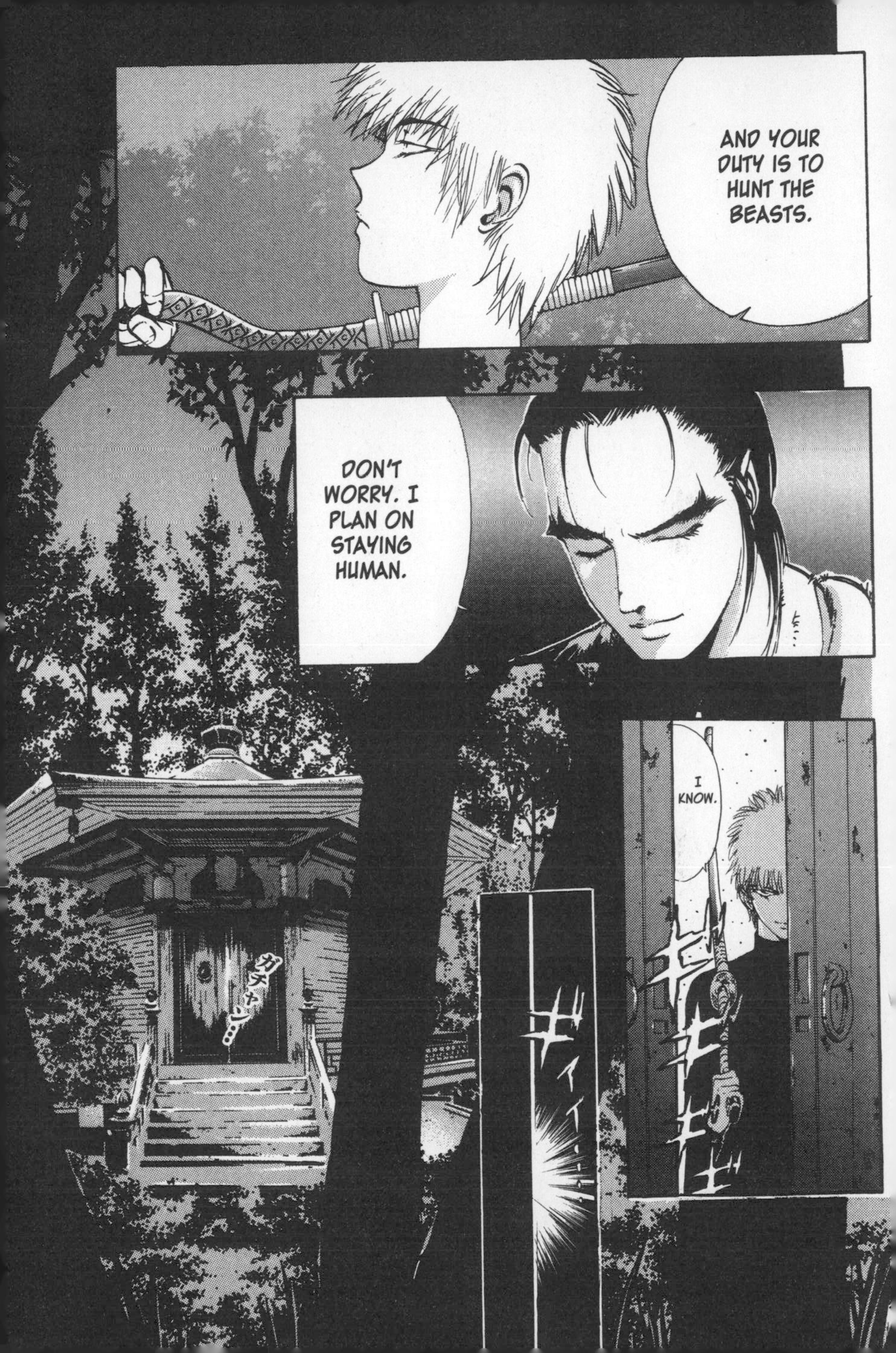
AND YOUR DUTY IS TO HUNT THE BEASTS.
DON'T WORRY. I PLAN ON STAYING HUMAN.
I KNOW.
ガチャン…
ギィィ…

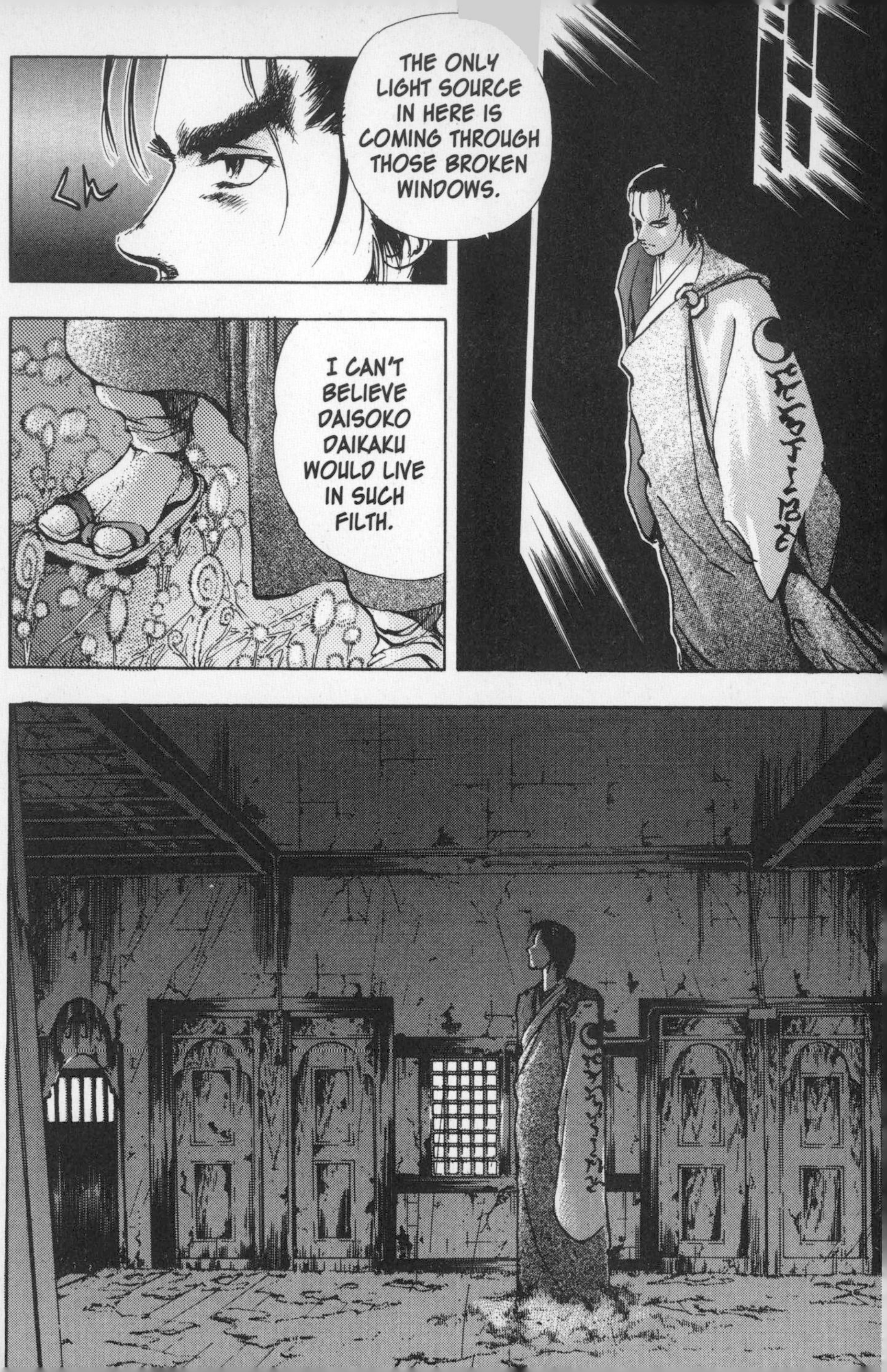
THE ONLY LIGHT SOURCE IN HERE IS COMING THROUGH THOSE BROKEN WINDOWS.
しん
I CAN'T BELIEVE DAISOKO DAIKAKU WOULD LIVE IN SUCH FILTH.

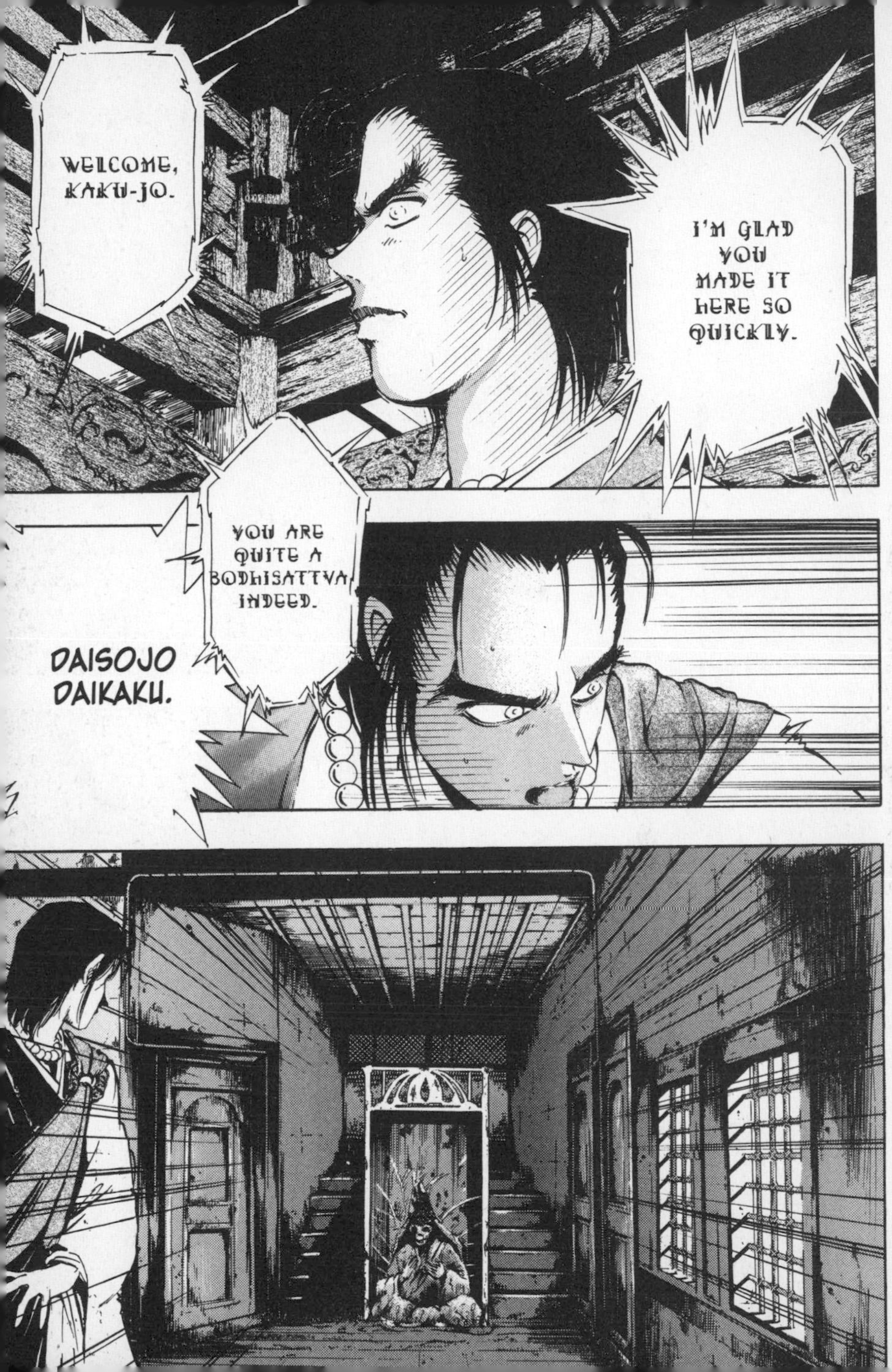
I'M GLAD YOU MADE IT HERE SO QUICKLY.
WELCOME, KAKU-JO.
YOU ARE QUITE A BODHISATTVA INDEED.
DAISOJO DAIKAKU.

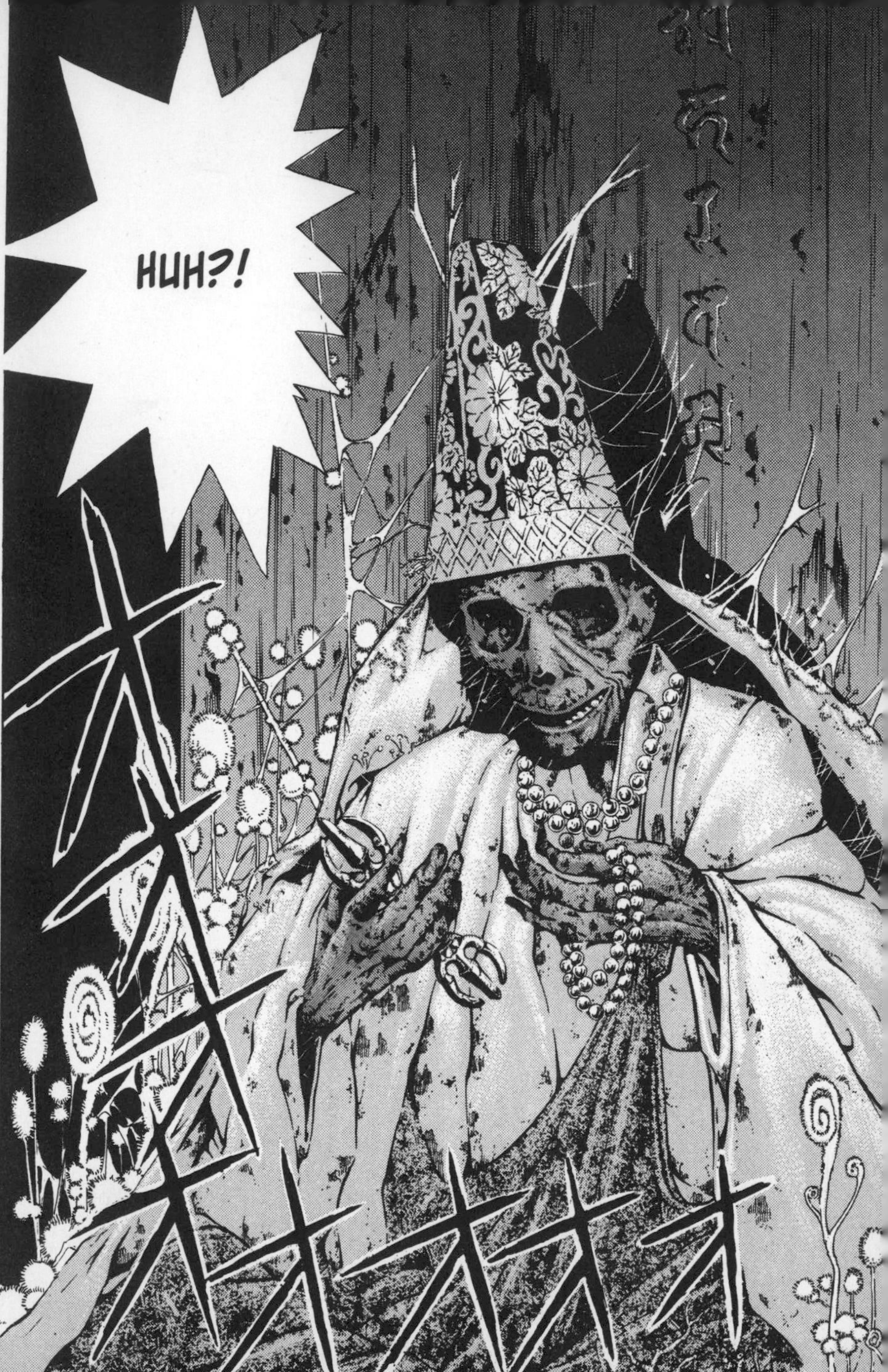
HUH?!

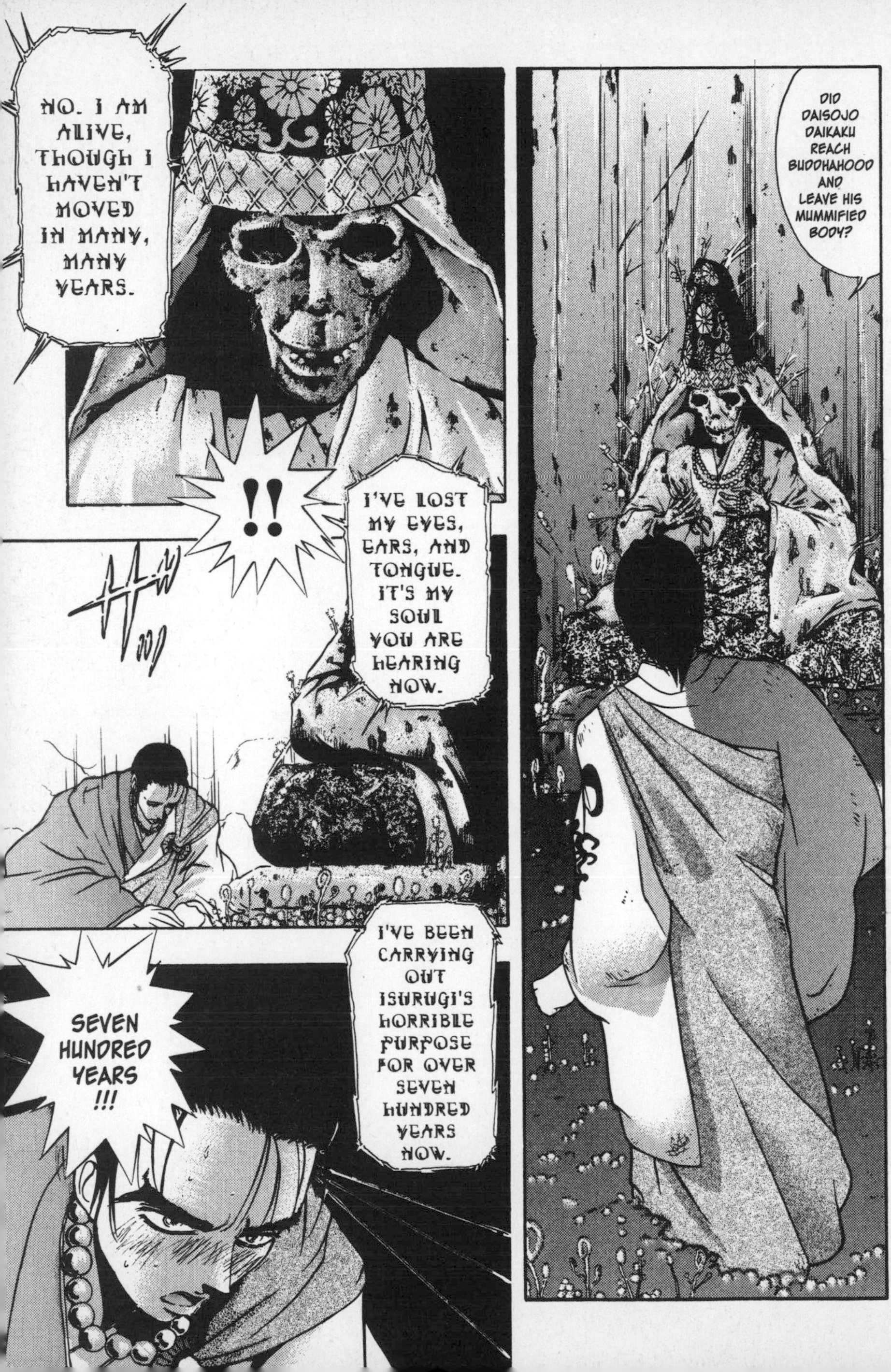

DID DAISOJO DAIKAKU REACH BUDDHAHOOD AND LEAVE HIS MUMMIFIED BODY?
NO. I AM ALIVE, THOUGH I HAVEN'T MOVED IN MANY, MANY YEARS.
!!
I'VE LOST MY EYES, EARS, AND TONGUE. IT'S MY SOUL YOU ARE HEARING NOW.
I'VE BEEN CARRYING OUT ISURUGI'S HORRIBLE PURPOSE FOR OVER SEVEN HUNDRED YEARS NOW.
SEVEN HUNDRED YEARS !!!

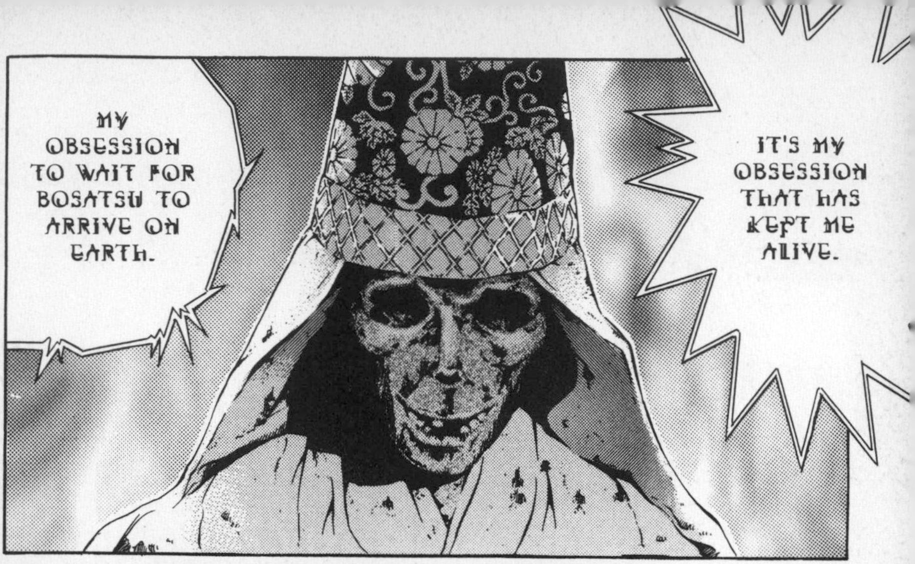
IT'S MY OBSESSION THAT HAS KEPT ME ALIVE.
MY OBSESSION TO WAIT FOR BOSATSU TO ARRIVE ON EARTH.

Translator's note: Bosatsu is a manifestation of the Buddha in the past, present or future.

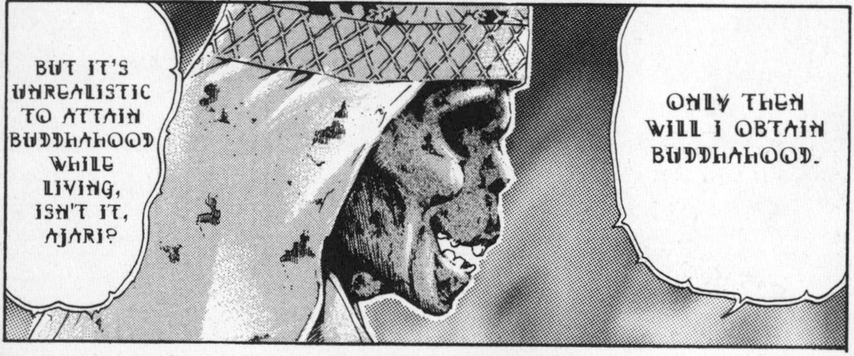
ONLY THEN WILL I OBTAIN BUDDHAHOOD.
BUT IT'S UNREALISTIC TO ATTAIN BUDDHAHOOD WHILE LIVING, ISN'T IT, AJARI?

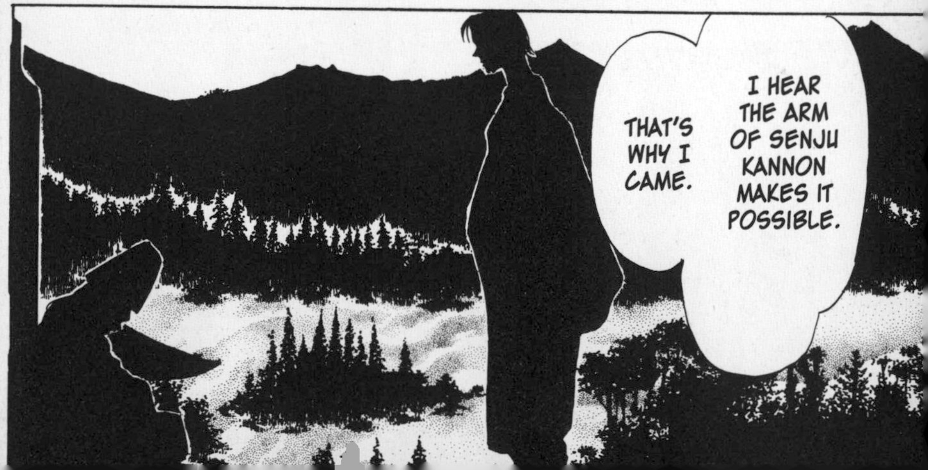
I HEAR THE ARM OF SENJU KANNON MAKES IT POSSIBLE.
THAT'S WHY I CAME.

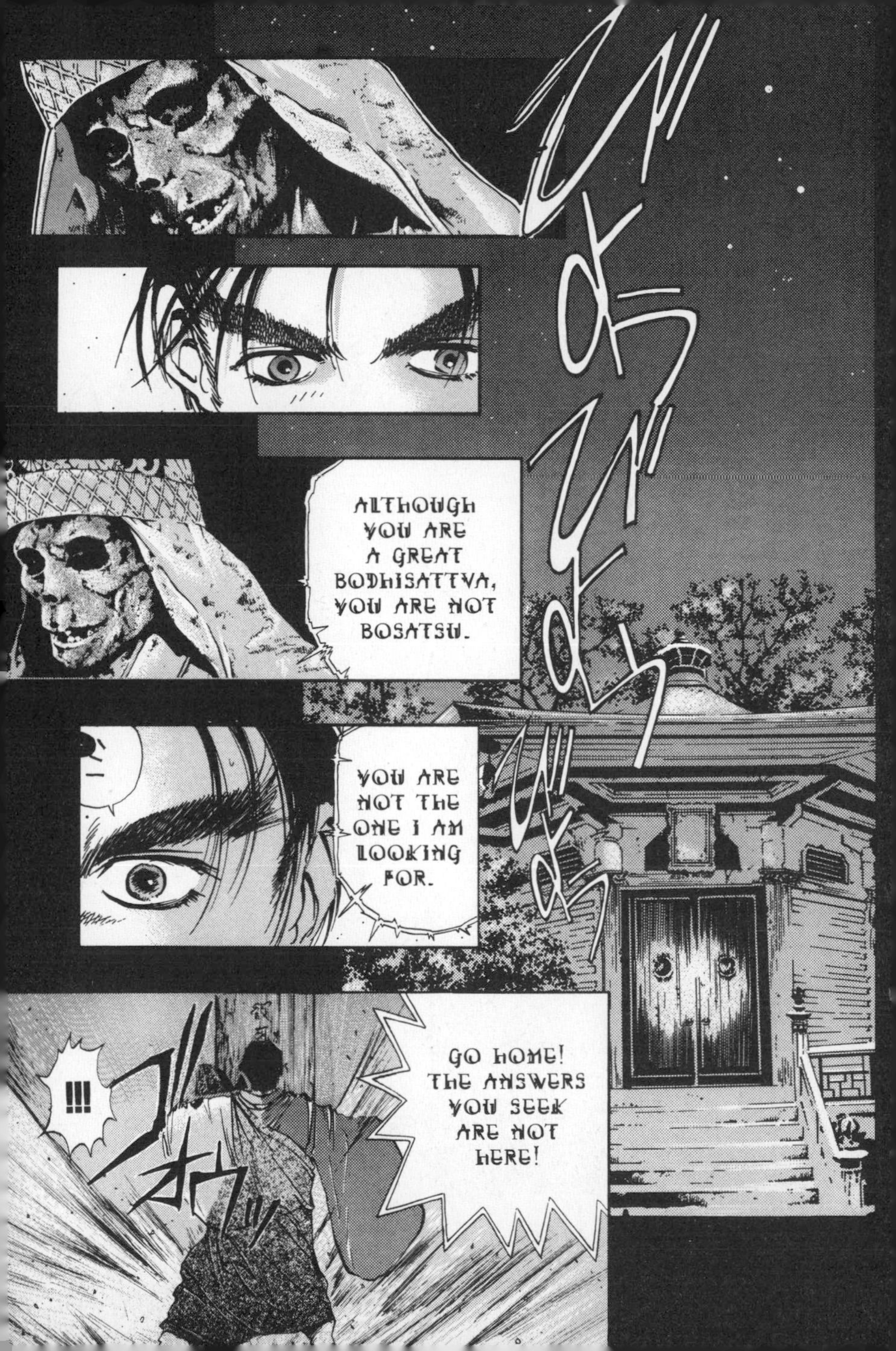
ALTHOUGH YOU ARE A GREAT BODHISATTVA, YOU ARE NOT BOSATSU.
YOU ARE NOT THE ONE I AM LOOKING FOR.
GO HOME! THE ANSWERS YOU SEEK ARE NOT HERE!
!!!

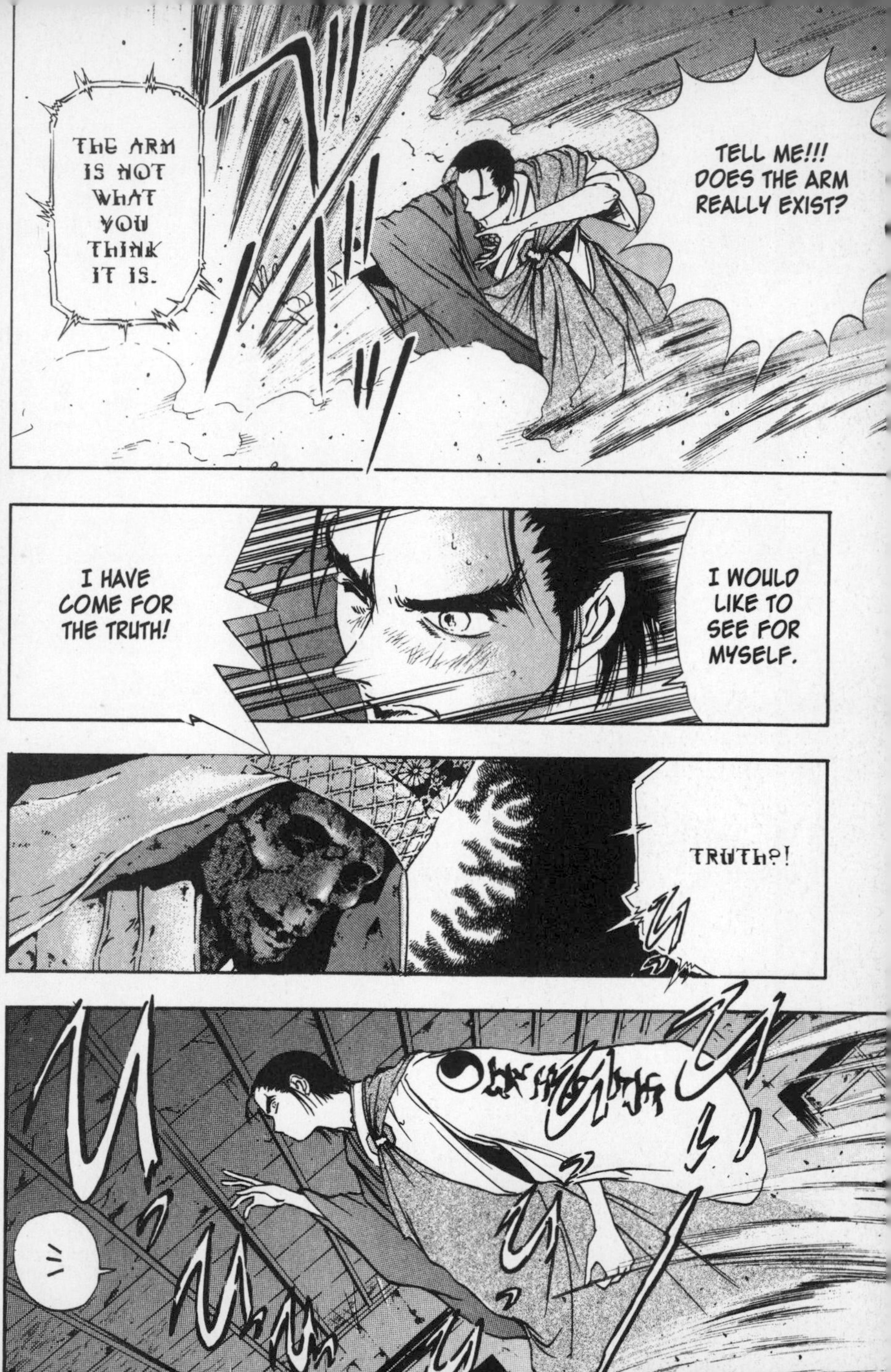
TELL ME!!! DOES THE ARM REALLY EXIST?
THE ARM IS NOT WHAT YOU THINK IT IS.
I WOULD LIKE TO SEE FOR MYSELF.
I HAVE COME FOR THE TRUTH!
TRUTH?!

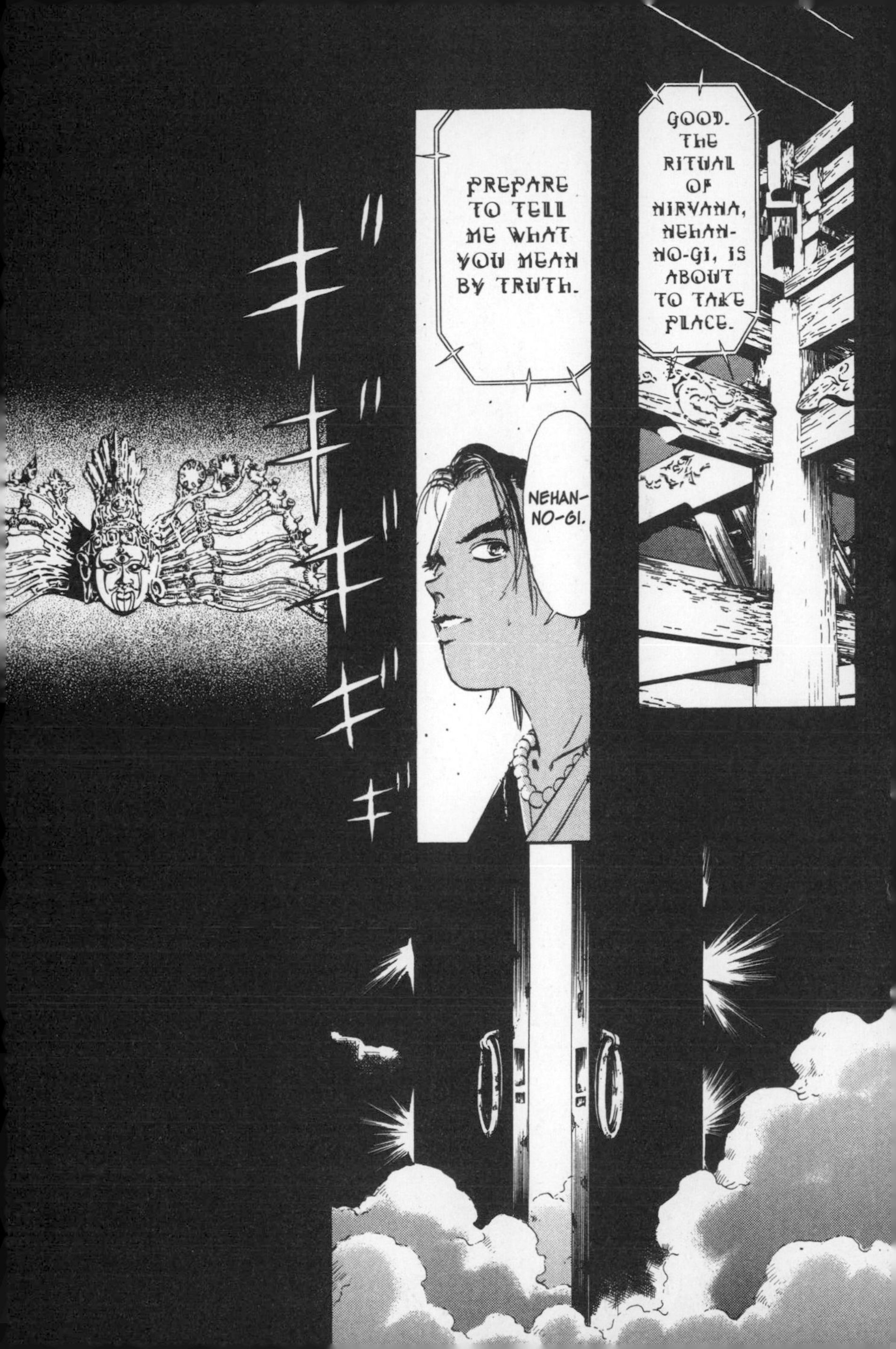
GOOD. THE RITUAL OF NIRVANA, NEHAN-NO-GI, IS ABOUT TO TAKE PLACE.
PREPARE TO TELL ME WHAT YOU MEAN BY TRUTH.
NEHAN-NO-GI.

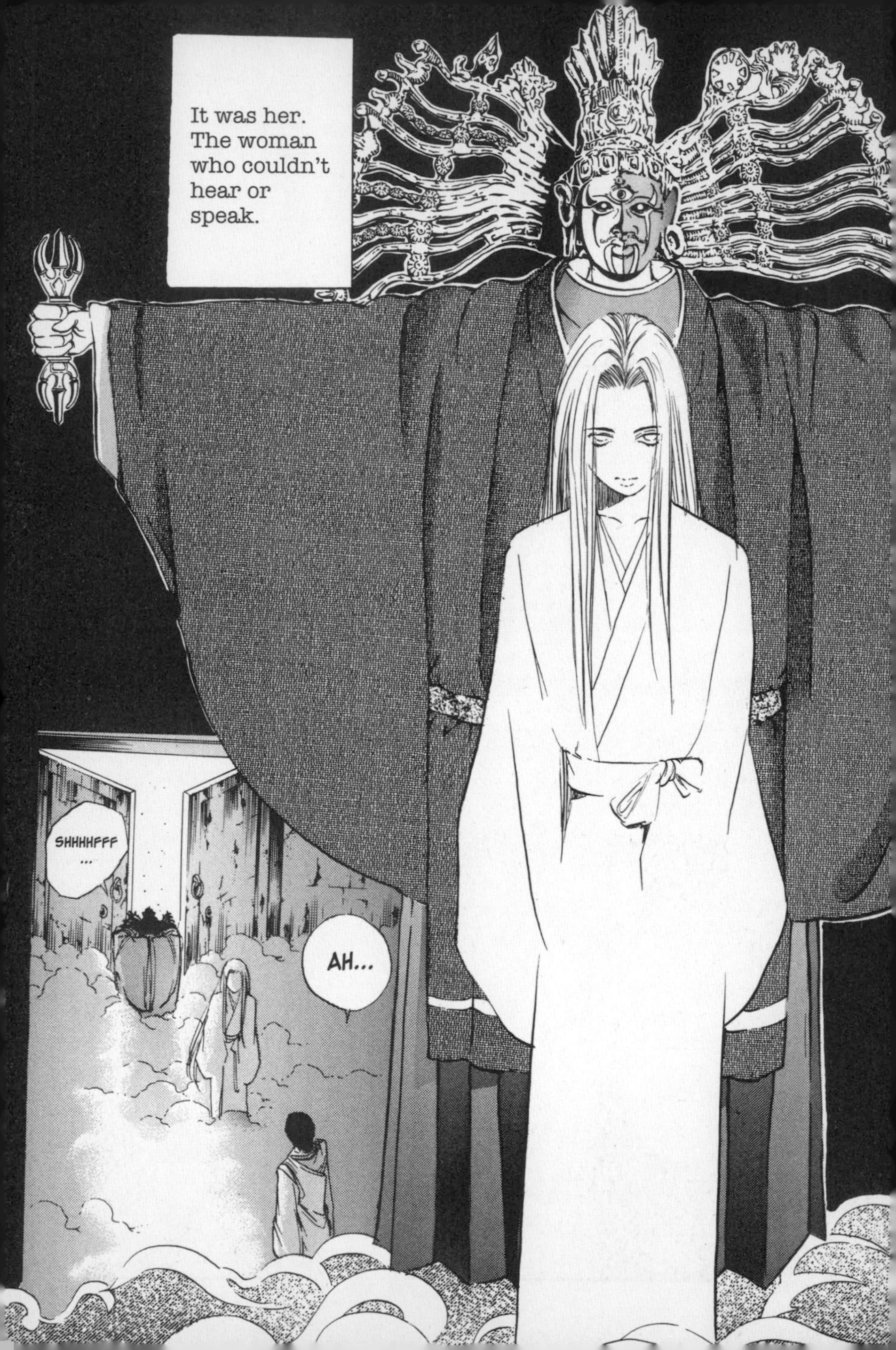
It was her. The woman who couldn't hear or speak.
SHHHHFFF ...
AH...

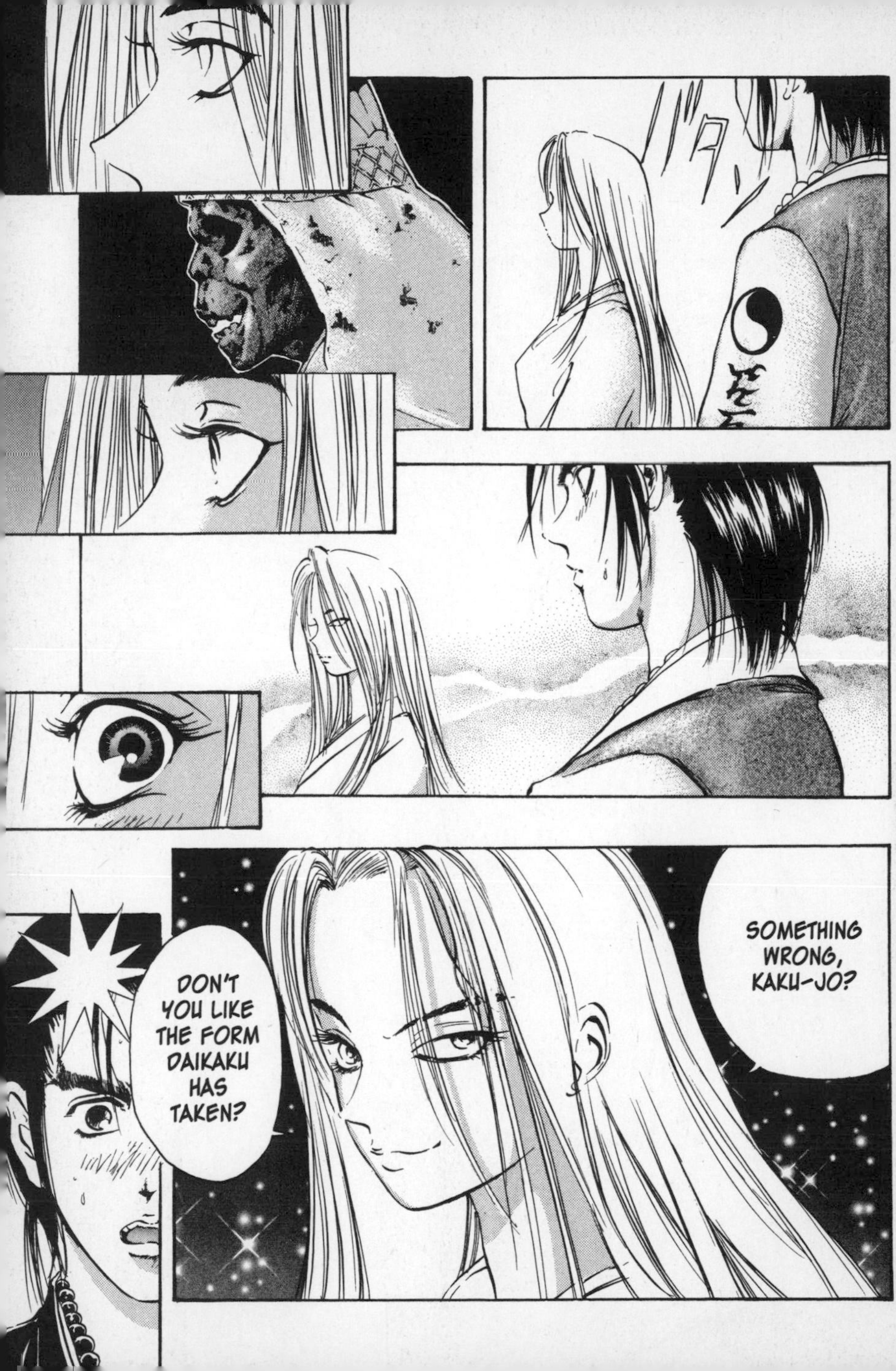
バタ
SOMETHING WRONG, KAKU-JO?
DON'T YOU LIKE THE FORM DAIKAKU HAS TAKEN?

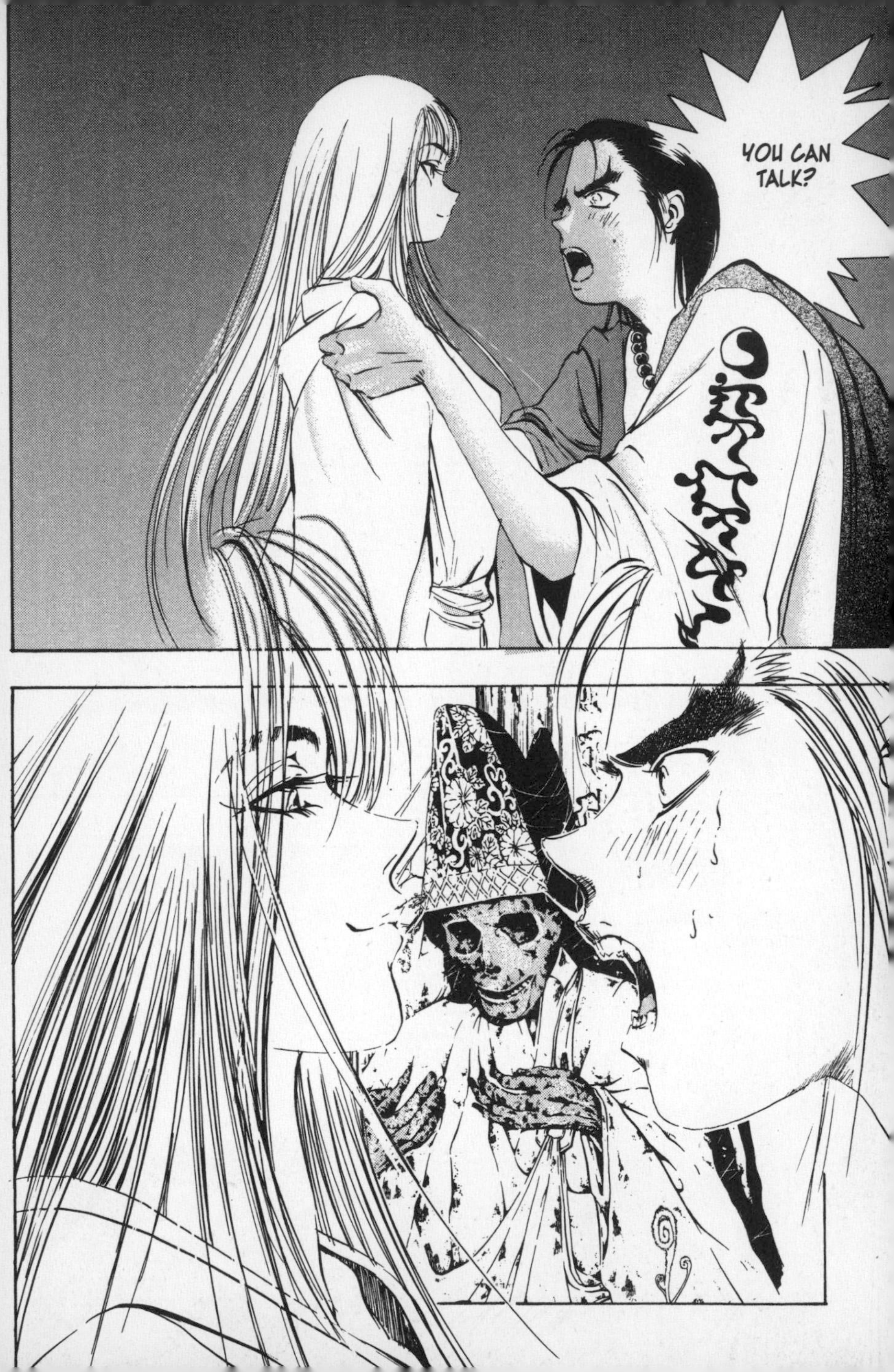
YOU CAN TALK?

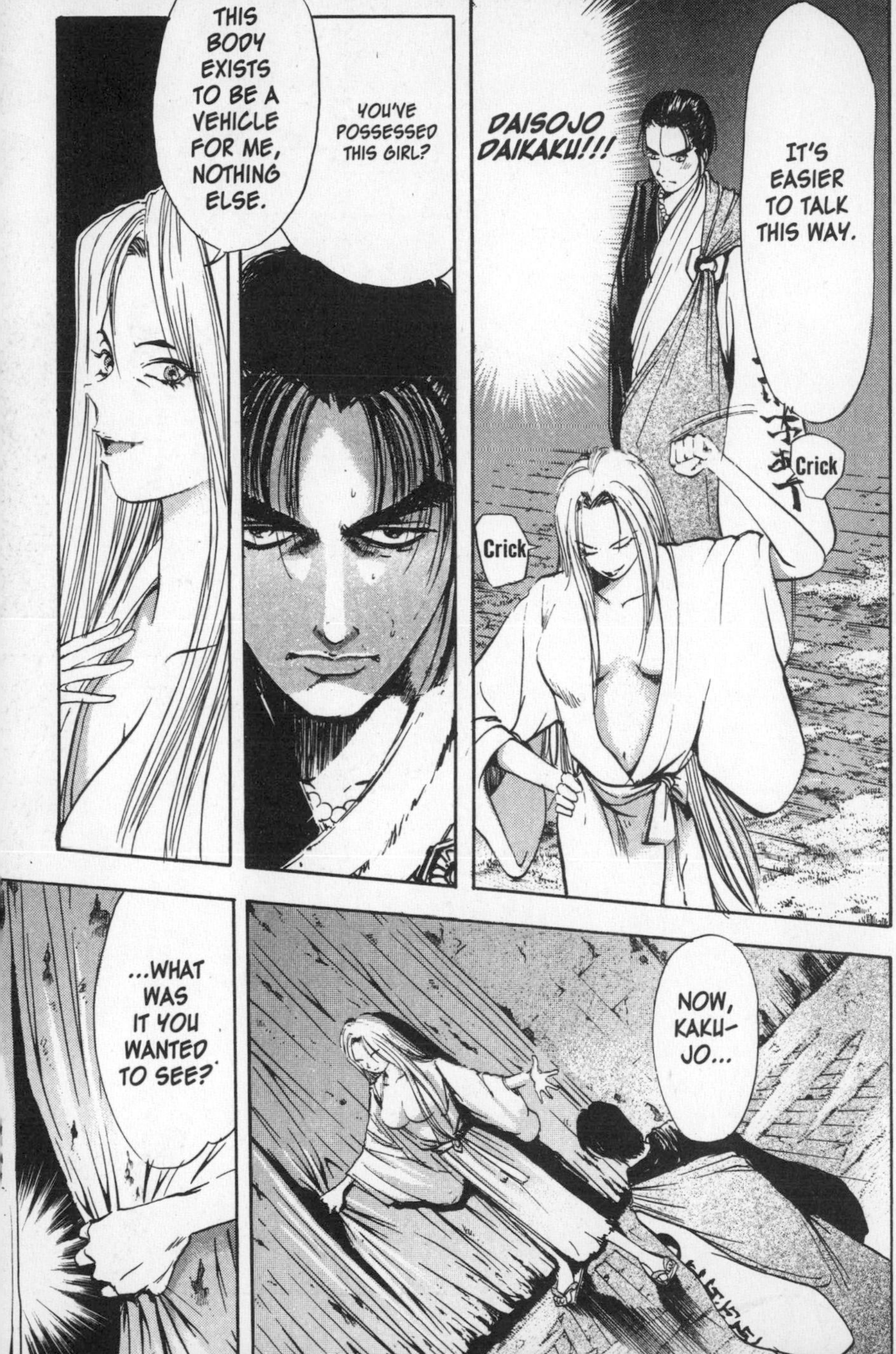
IT'S EASIER TO TALK THIS WAY.
DAISOJO DAIKAKU!!!
Crick
Crick
YOU'VE POSSESSED THIS GIRL?
THIS BODY EXISTS TO BE A VEHICLE FOR ME, NOTHING ELSE.
NOW, KAKU-JO...
...WHAT WAS IT YOU WANTED TO SEE?

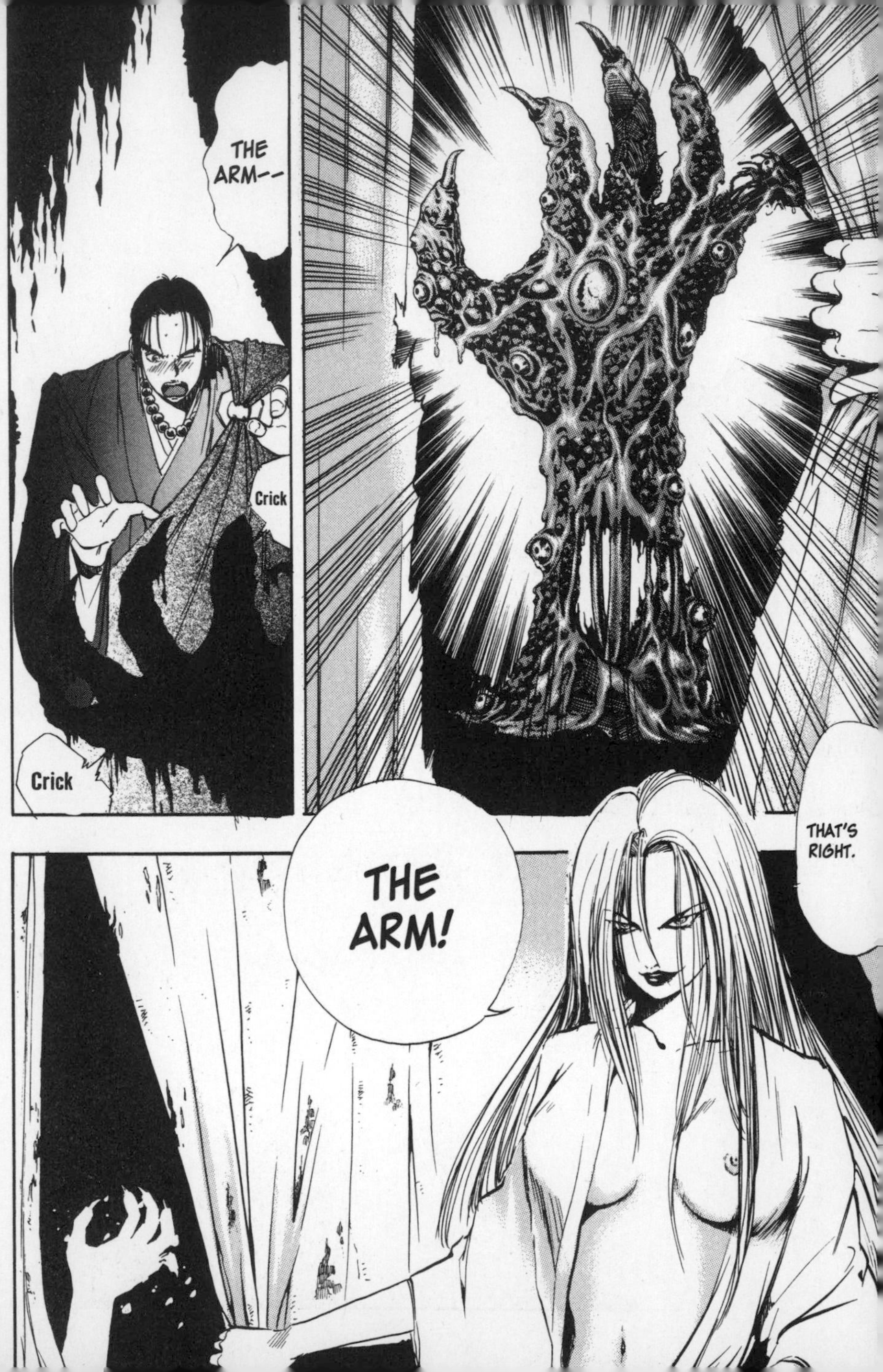
THE ARM--
Crick
Crick
THAT'S RIGHT.
THE ARM!

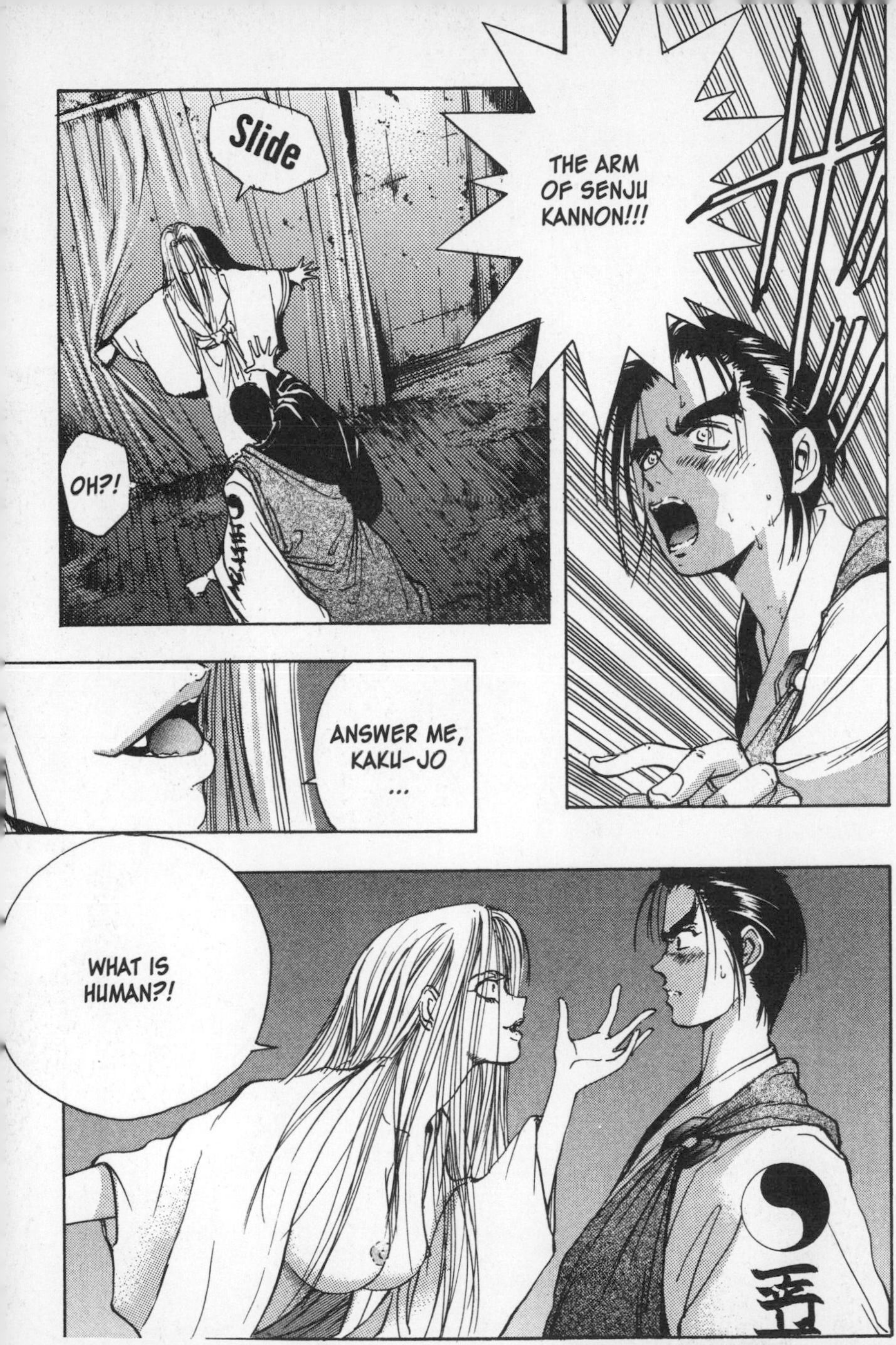

THE ARM OF SENJU KANNON!!!
Slide
OH?!
ANSWER ME, KAKU-JO ...
WHAT IS HUMAN?!

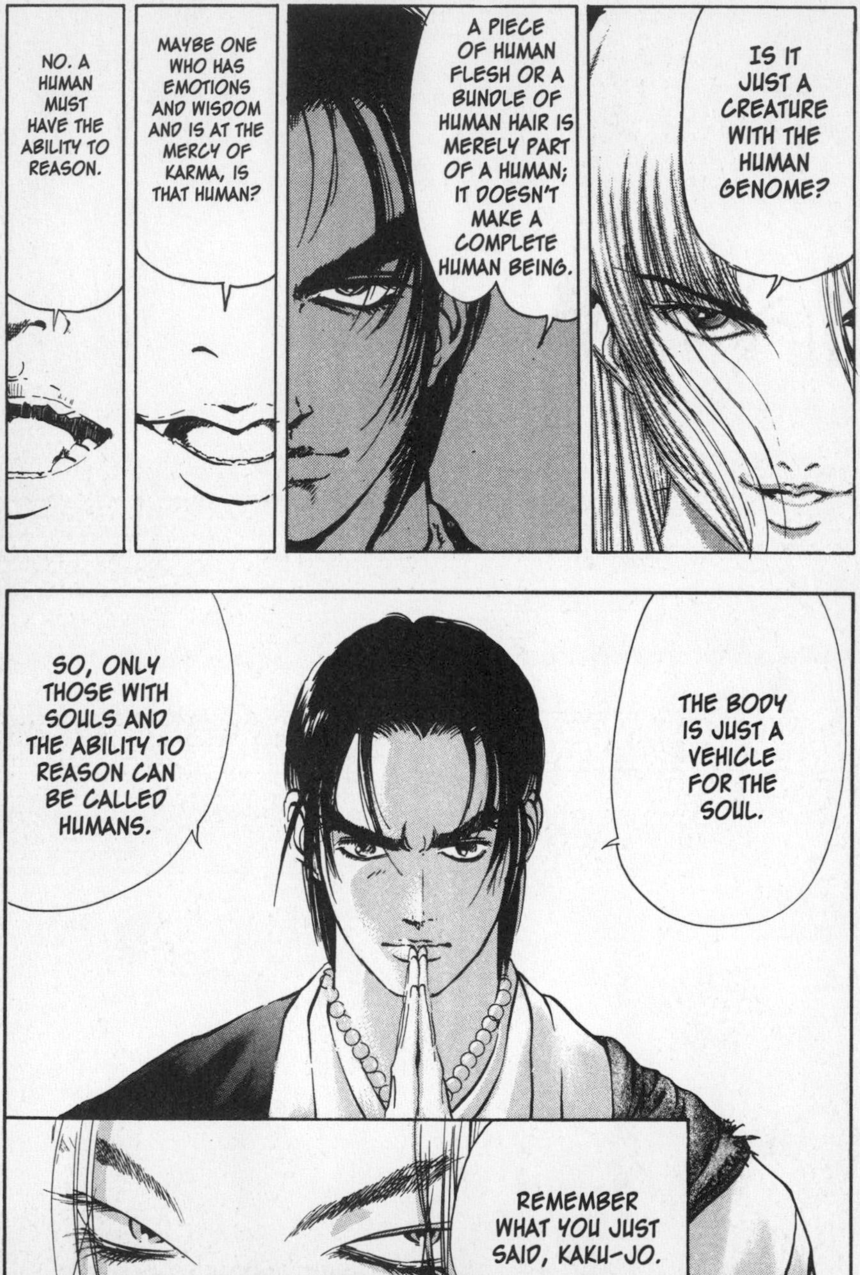
IS IT JUST A CREATURE WITH THE HUMAN GENOME?
A PIECE OF HUMAN FLESH OR A BUNDLE OF HUMAN HAIR IS MERELY PART OF A HUMAN; IT DOESN'T MAKE A COMPLETE HUMAN BEING.
MAYBE ONE WHO HAS EMOTIONS AND WISDOM AND IS AT THE MERCY OF KARMA, IS THAT HUMAN?
NO. A HUMAN MUST HAVE THE ABILITY TO REASON.
THE BODY IS JUST A VEHICLE FOR THE SOUL.
SO, ONLY THOSE WITH SOULS AND THE ABILITY TO REASON CAN BE CALLED HUMANS.
REMEMBER WHAT YOU JUST SAID, KAKU-JO.

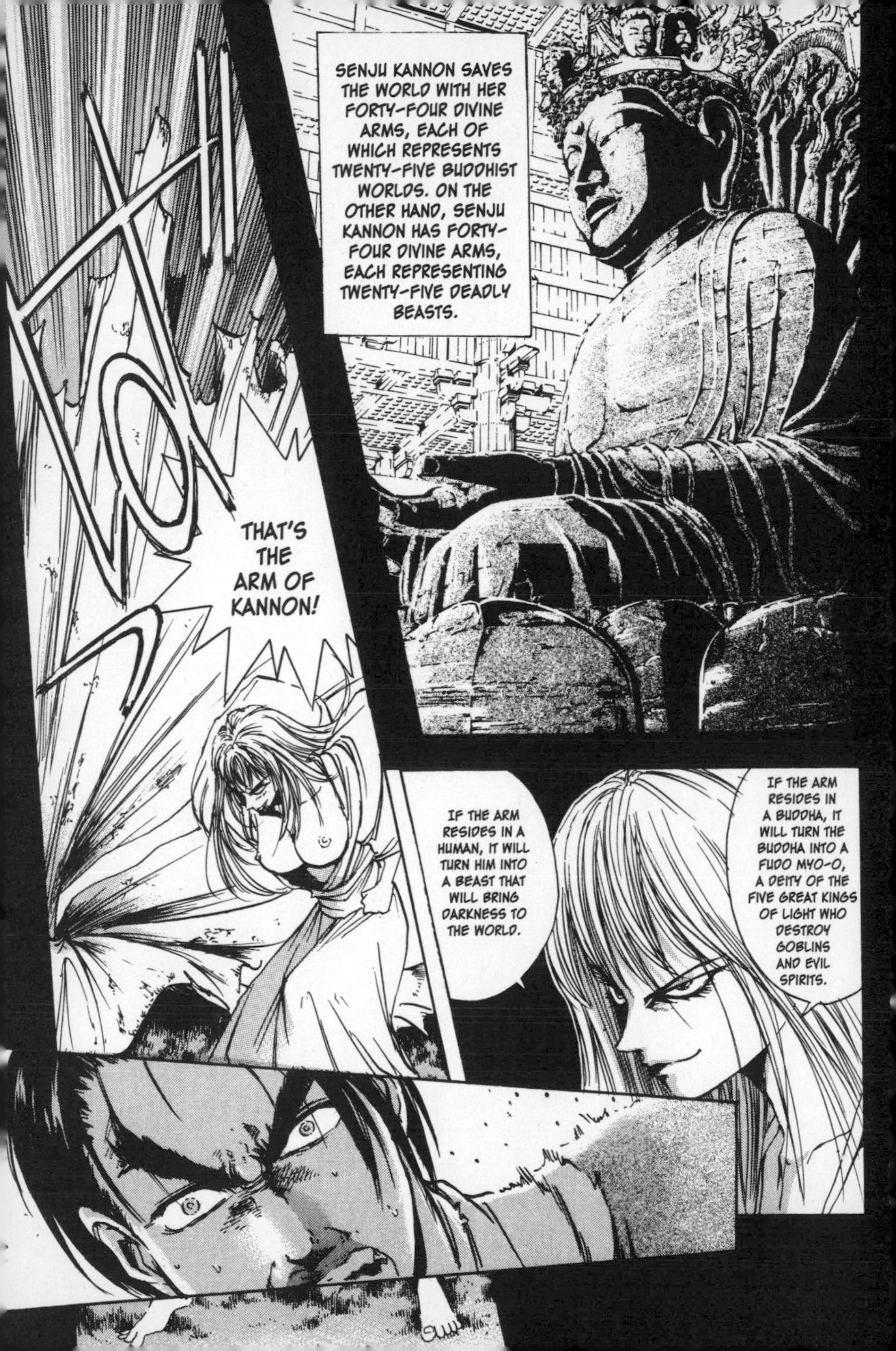
SENJU KANNON SAVES THE WORLD WITH HER FORTY-FOUR DIVINE ARMS, EACH OF WHICH REPRESENTS TWENTY-FIVE BUDDHIST WORLDS. ON THE OTHER HAND, SENJU KANNON HAS FORTY-FOUR DIVINE ARMS, EACH REPRESENTING TWENTY-FIVE DEADLY BEASTS.
THAT'S THE ARM OF KANNON!
IF THE ARM RESIDES IN A BUDDHA, IT WILL TURN THE BUDDHA INTO A FUDO MYO-O, A DEITY OF THE FIVE GREAT KINGS OF LIGHT WHO DESTROY GOBLINS AND EVIL SPIRITS.
IF THE ARM RESIDES IN A HUMAN, IT WILL TURN HIM INTO A BEAST THAT WILL BRING DARKNESS TO THE WORLD.

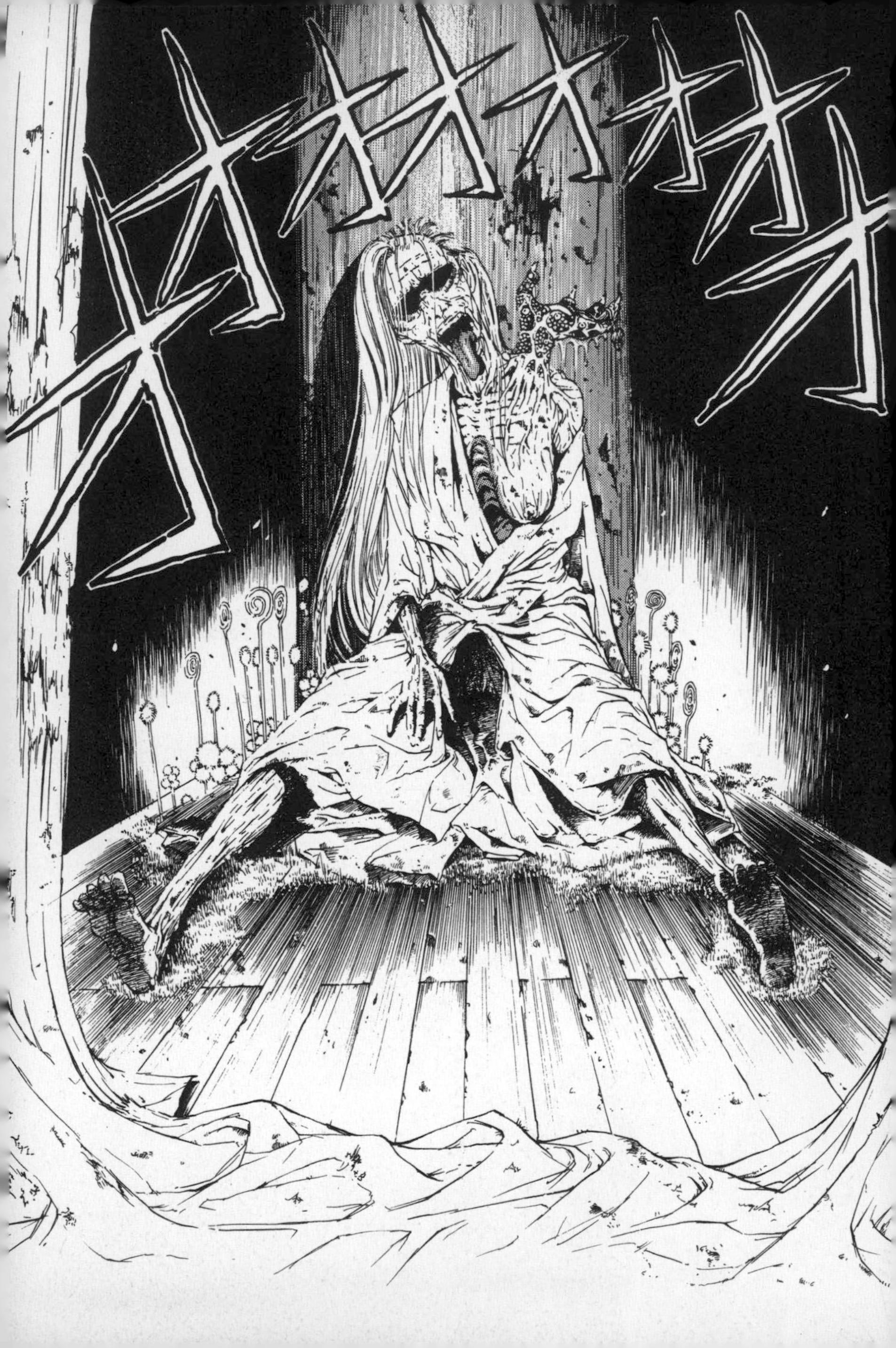

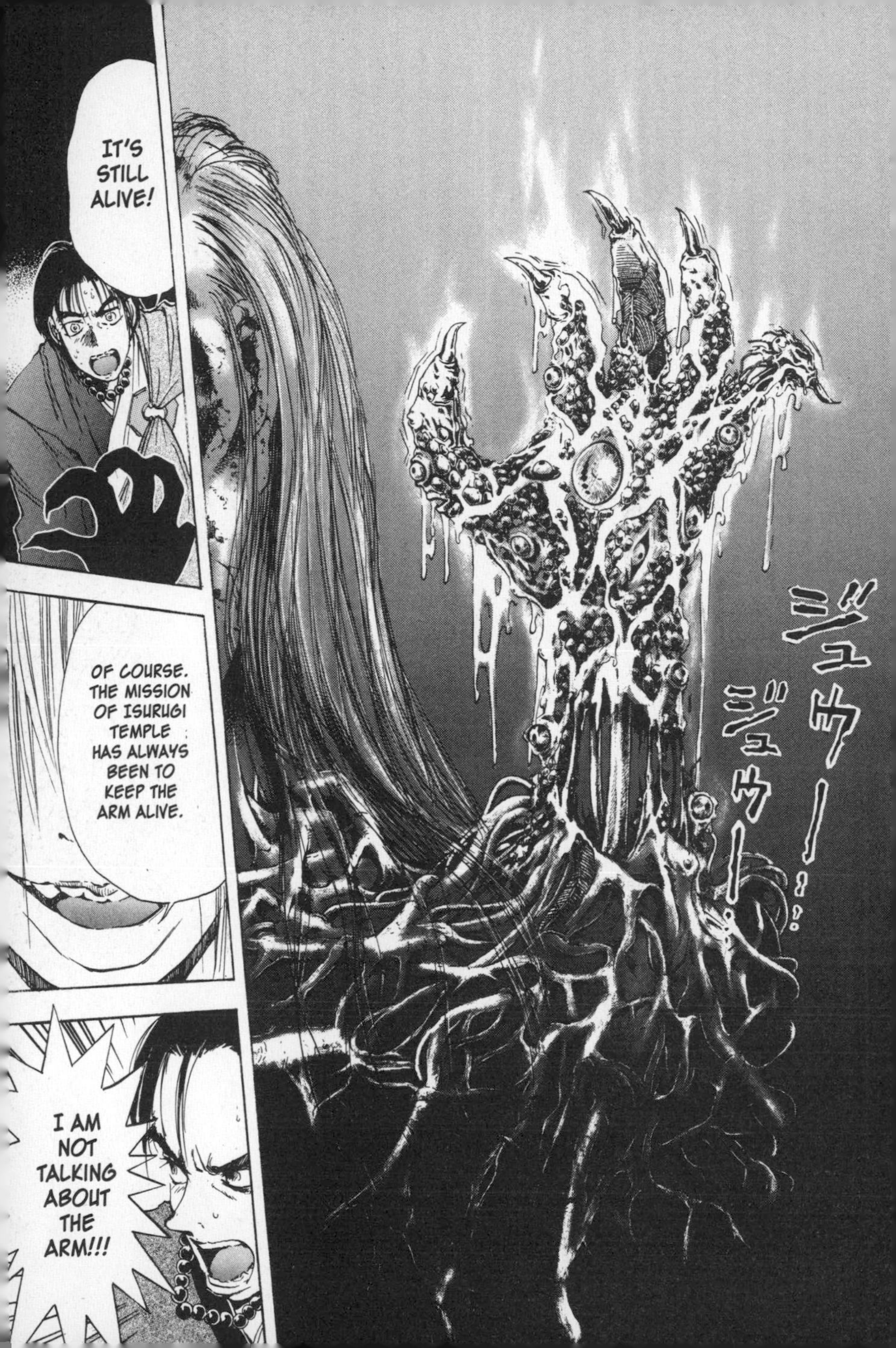
ジュウー!?
ジュウー…
IT'S STILL ALIVE!
OF COURSE. THE MISSION OF ISURUGI TEMPLE HAS ALWAYS BEEN TO KEEP THE ARM ALIVE.
I AM NOT TALKING ABOUT THE ARM!!!

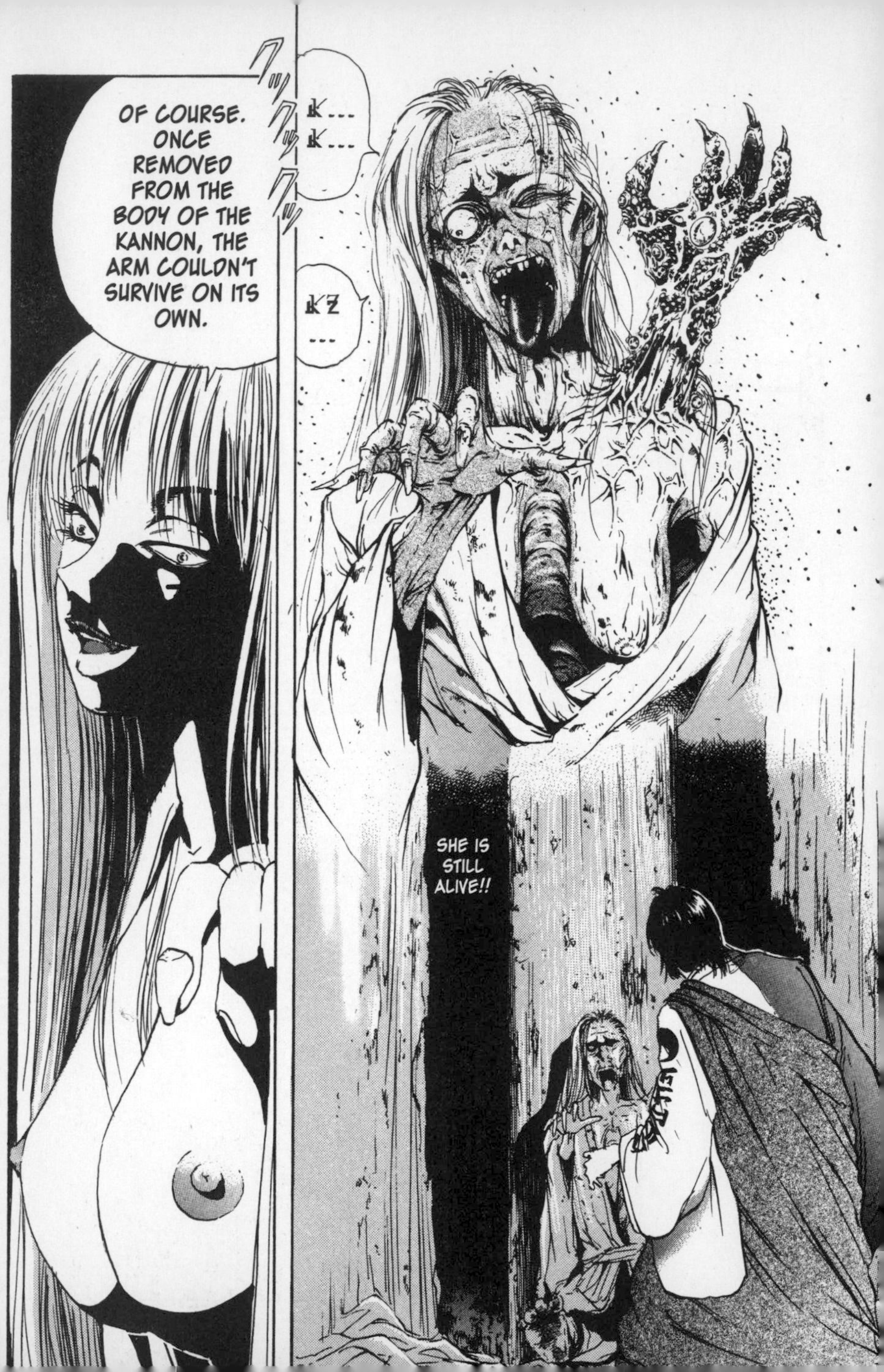
K... K...
KZ ...
SHE IS STILL ALIVE!!
クッ クッ クッ
OF COURSE. ONCE REMOVED FROM THE BODY OF THE KANNON, THE ARM COULDN'T SURVIVE ON ITS OWN.

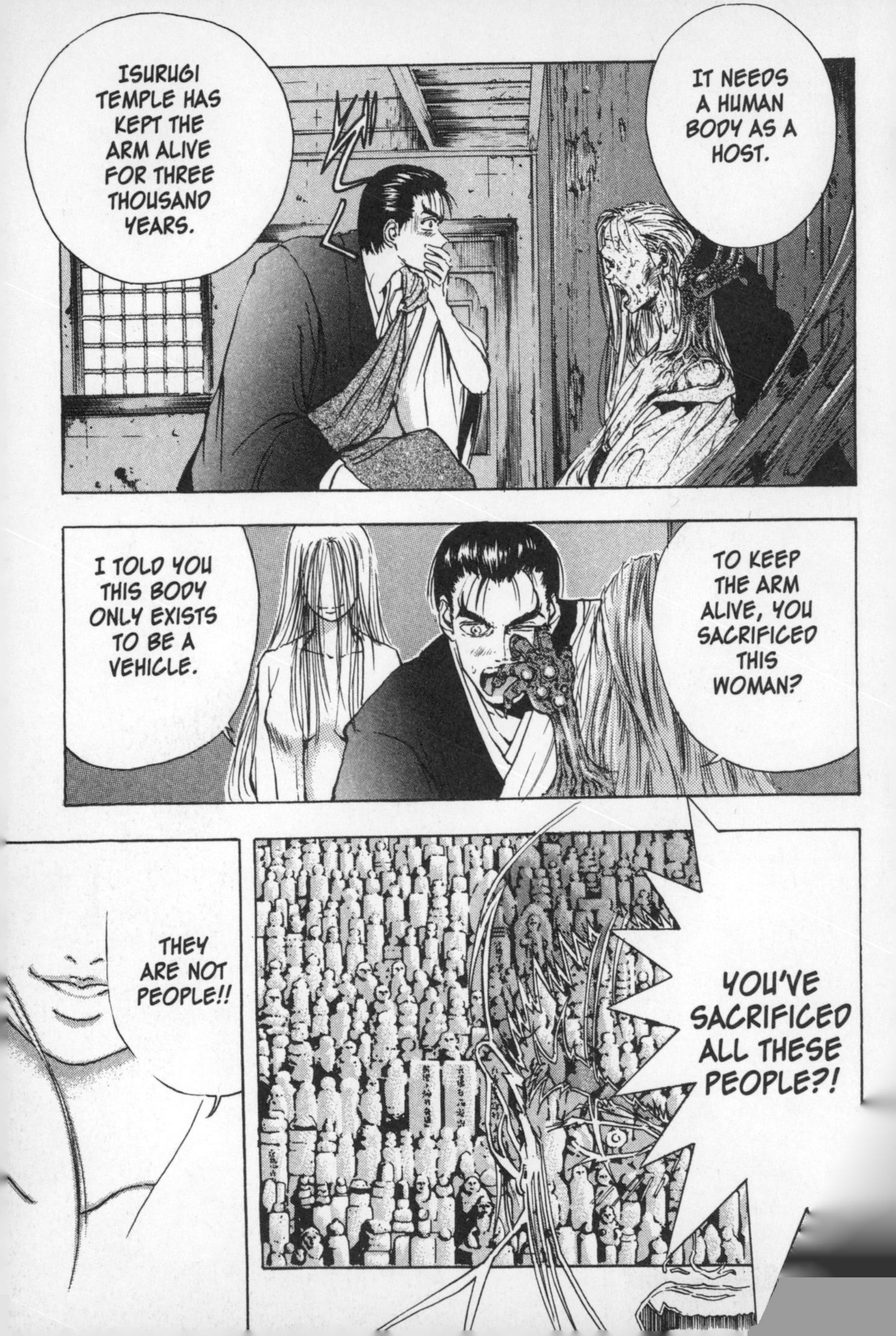
IT NEEDS A HUMAN BODY AS A HOST.
ISURUGI TEMPLE HAS KEPT THE ARM ALIVE FOR THREE THOUSAND YEARS.
TO KEEP THE ARM ALIVE, YOU SACRIFICED THIS WOMAN?
I TOLD YOU THIS BODY ONLY EXISTS TO BE A VEHICLE.
YOU'VE SACRIFICED ALL THESE PEOPLE?!
THEY ARE NOT PEOPLE!!

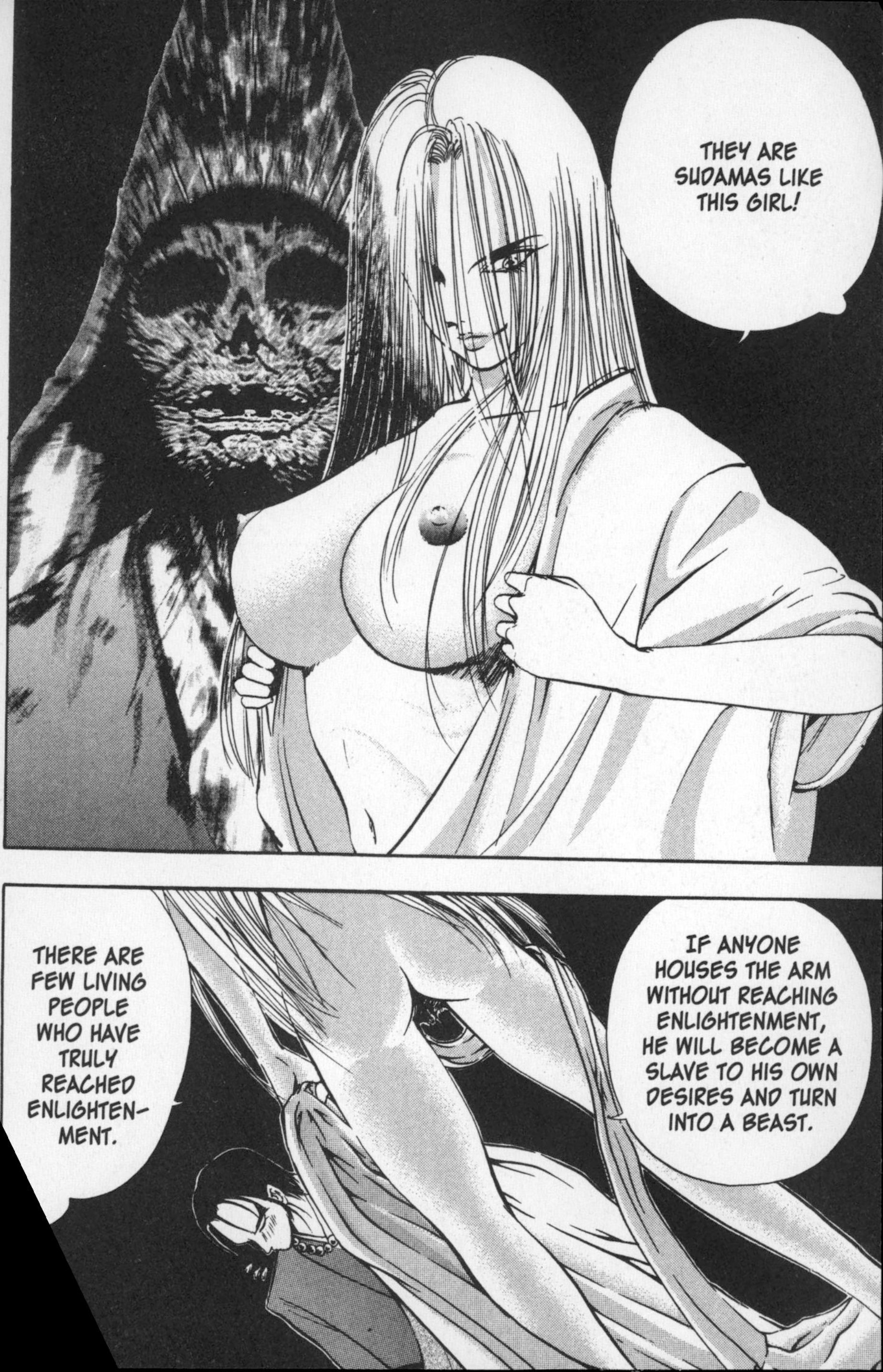
THEY ARE SUDAMAS LIKE THIS GIRL!
IF ANYONE HOUSES THE ARM WITHOUT REACHING ENLIGHTENMENT, HE WILL BECOME A SLAVE TO HIS OWN DESIRES AND TURN INTO A BEAST.
THERE ARE FEW LIVING PEOPLE WHO HAVE TRULY REACHED ENLIGHTEN-MENT.

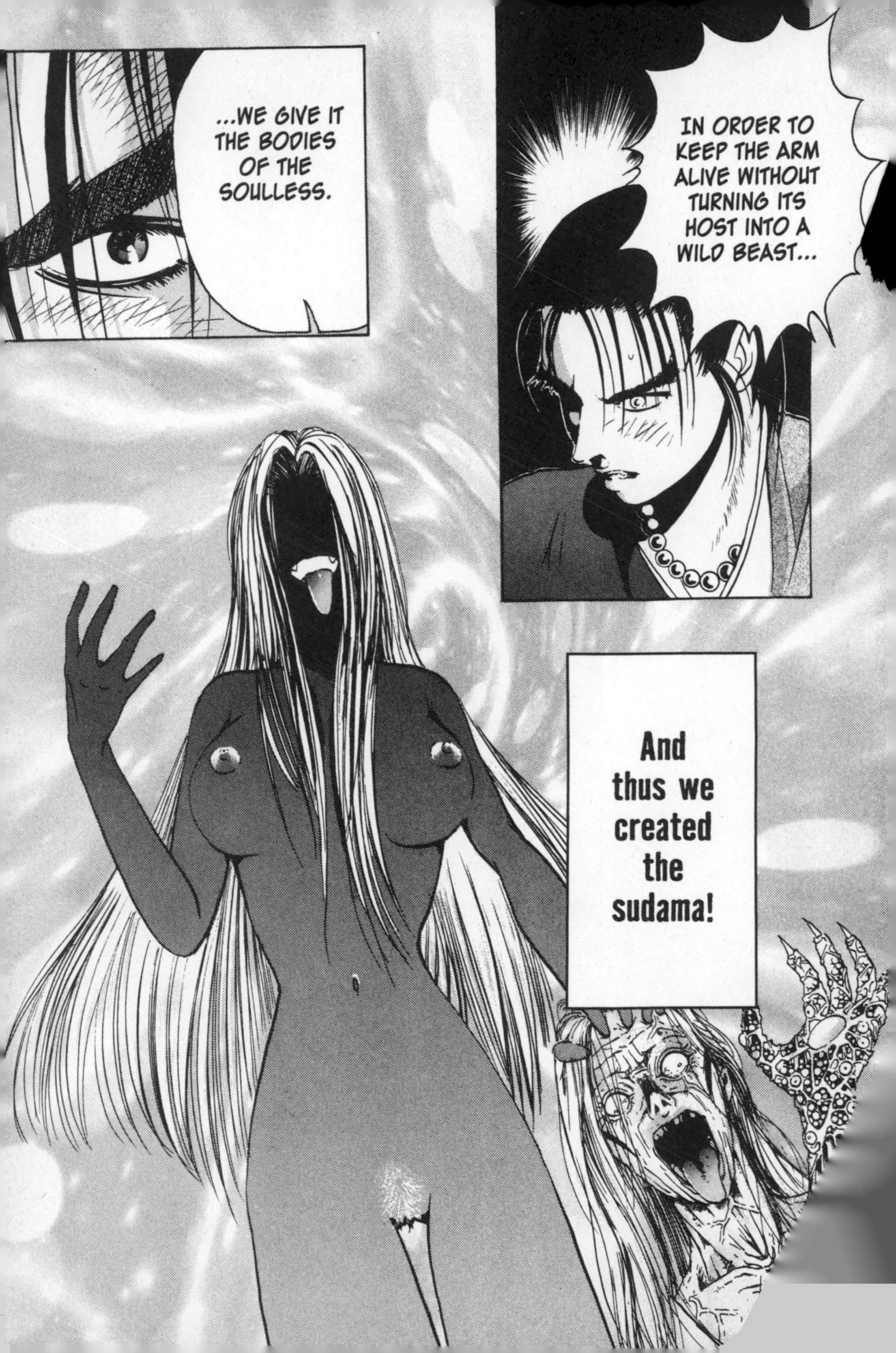
IN ORDER TO KEEP THE ARM ALIVE WITHOUT TURNING ITS HOST INTO A WILD BEAST...
...WE GIVE IT THE BODIES OF THE SOULLESS.
And thus we created the sudama!

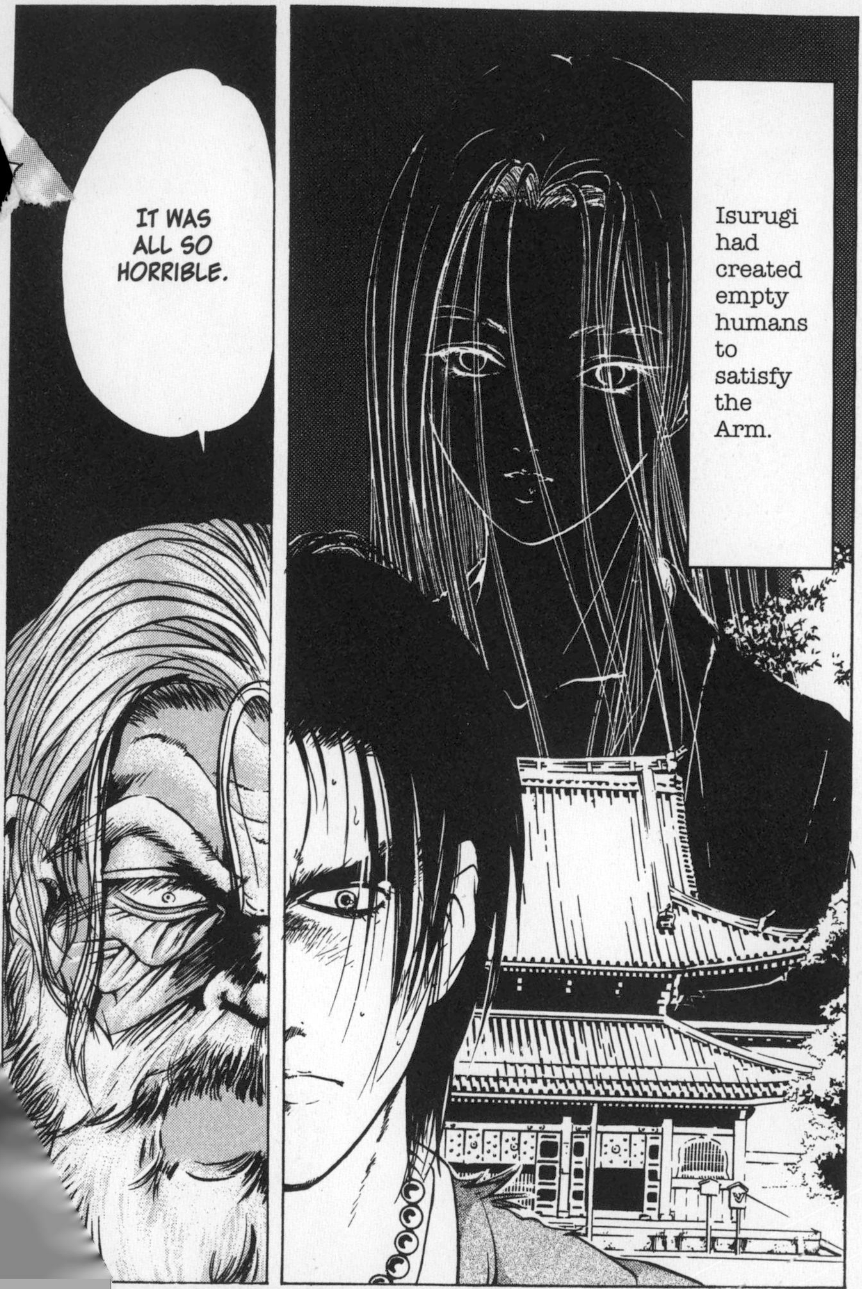
Isurugi had created empty humans to satisfy the Arm.
IT WAS ALL SO HORRIBLE.

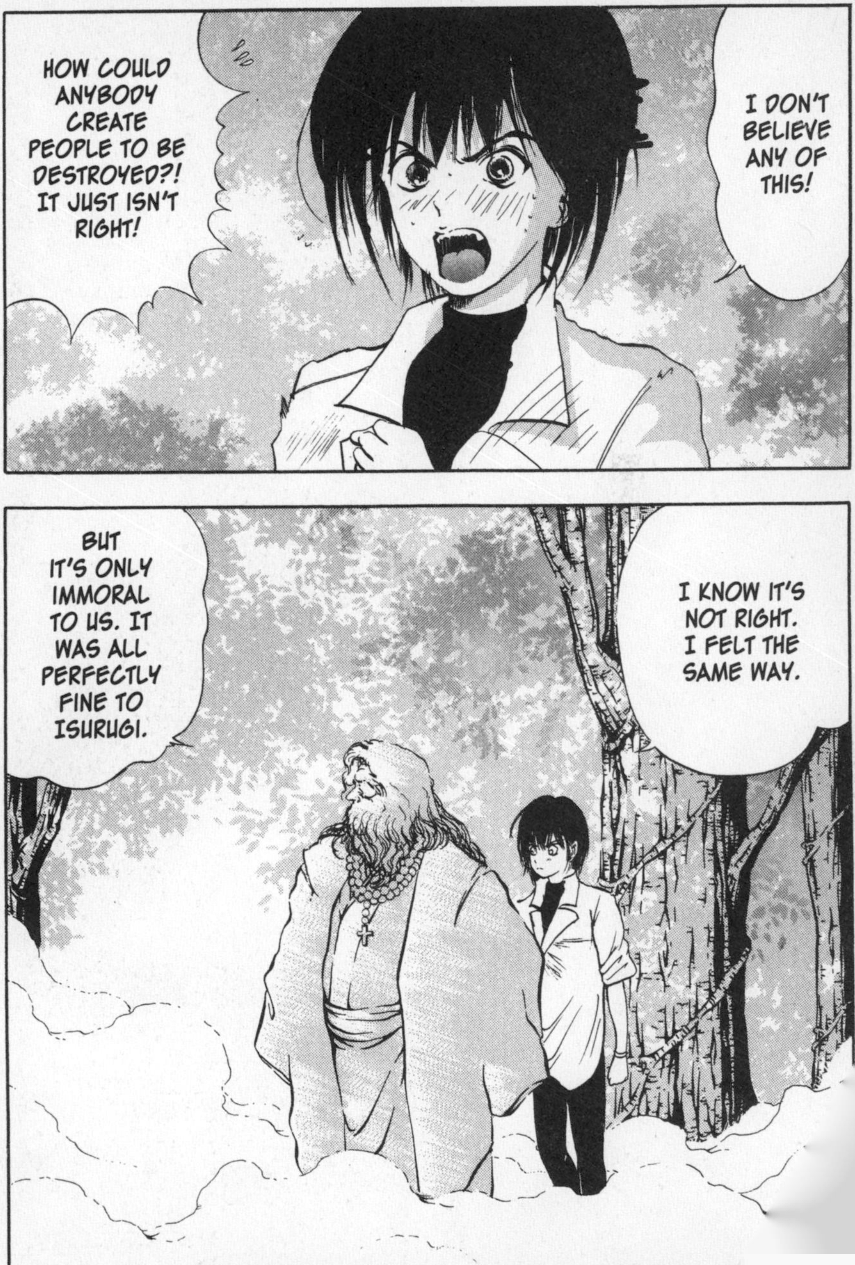
I DON'T BELIEVE ANY OF THIS!
HOW COULD ANYBODY CREATE PEOPLE TO BE DESTROYED?! IT JUST ISN'T RIGHT!
I KNOW IT'S NOT RIGHT. I FELT THE SAME WAY.
BUT IT'S ONLY IMMORAL TO US. IT WAS ALL PERFECTLY FINE TO ISURUGI.

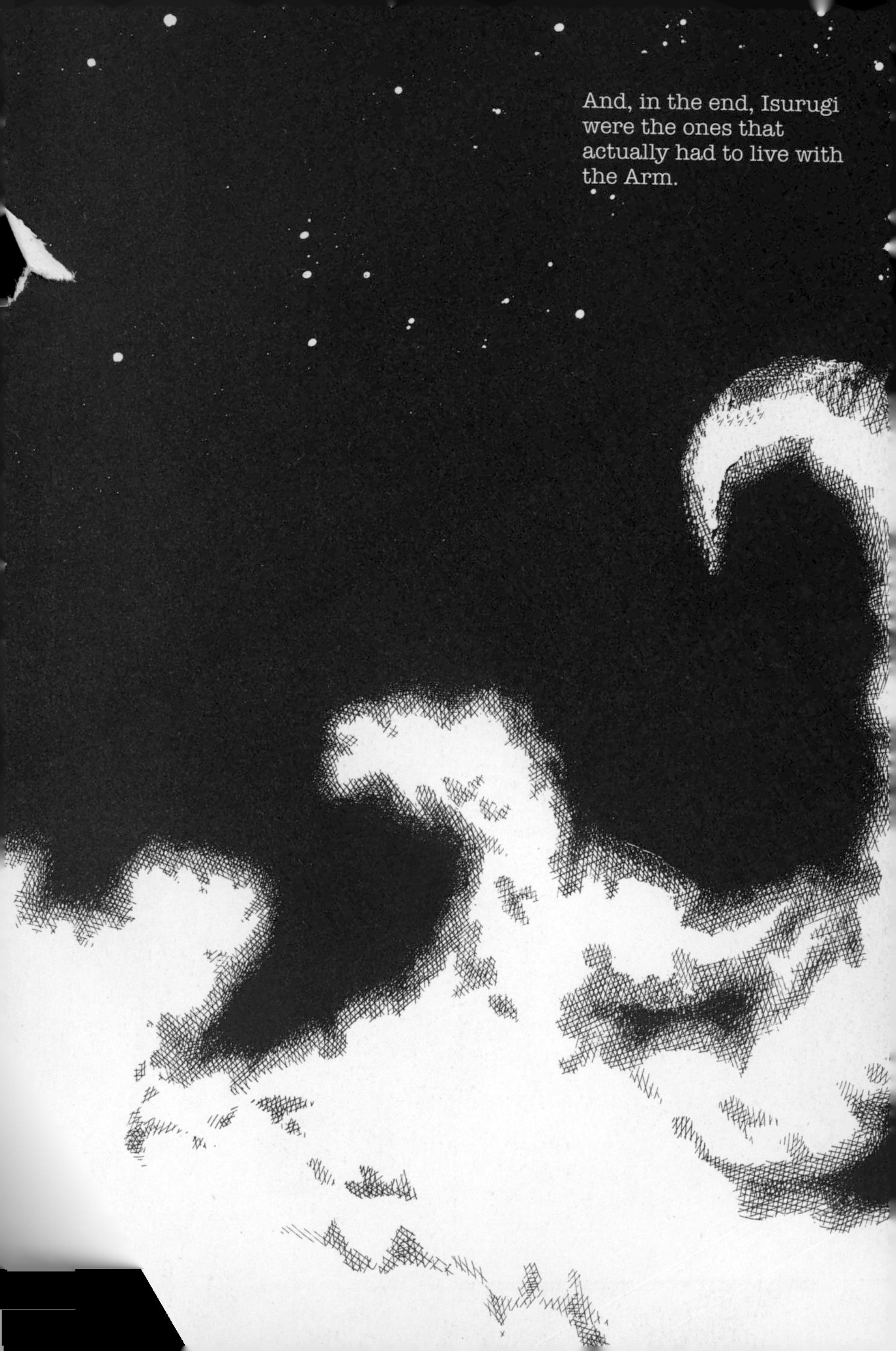
And, in the end, Isurugi were the ones that actually had to live with the Arm.

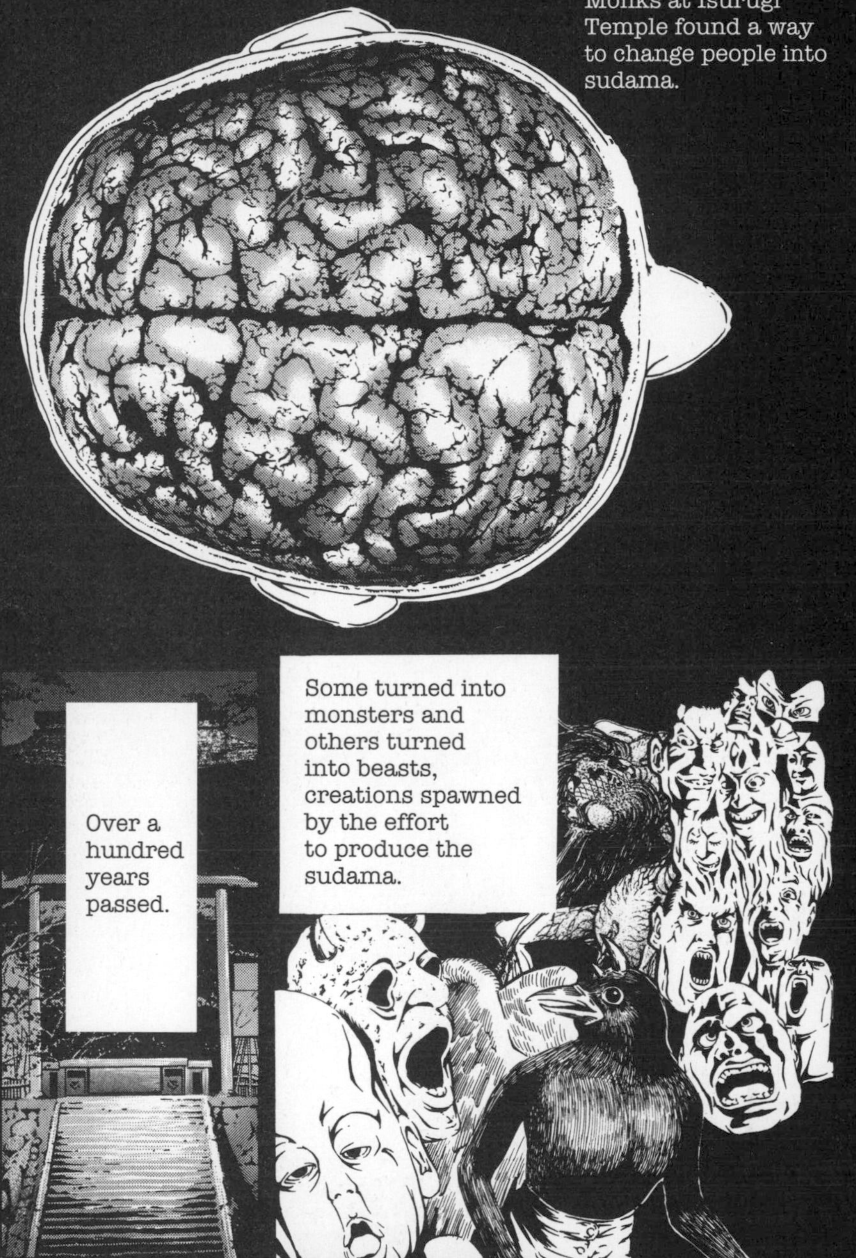
Monks at Isurugi Temple found a way to change people into sudama.
Some turned into monsters and others turned into beasts, creations spawned by the effort to produce the sudama.
Over a hundred years passed.

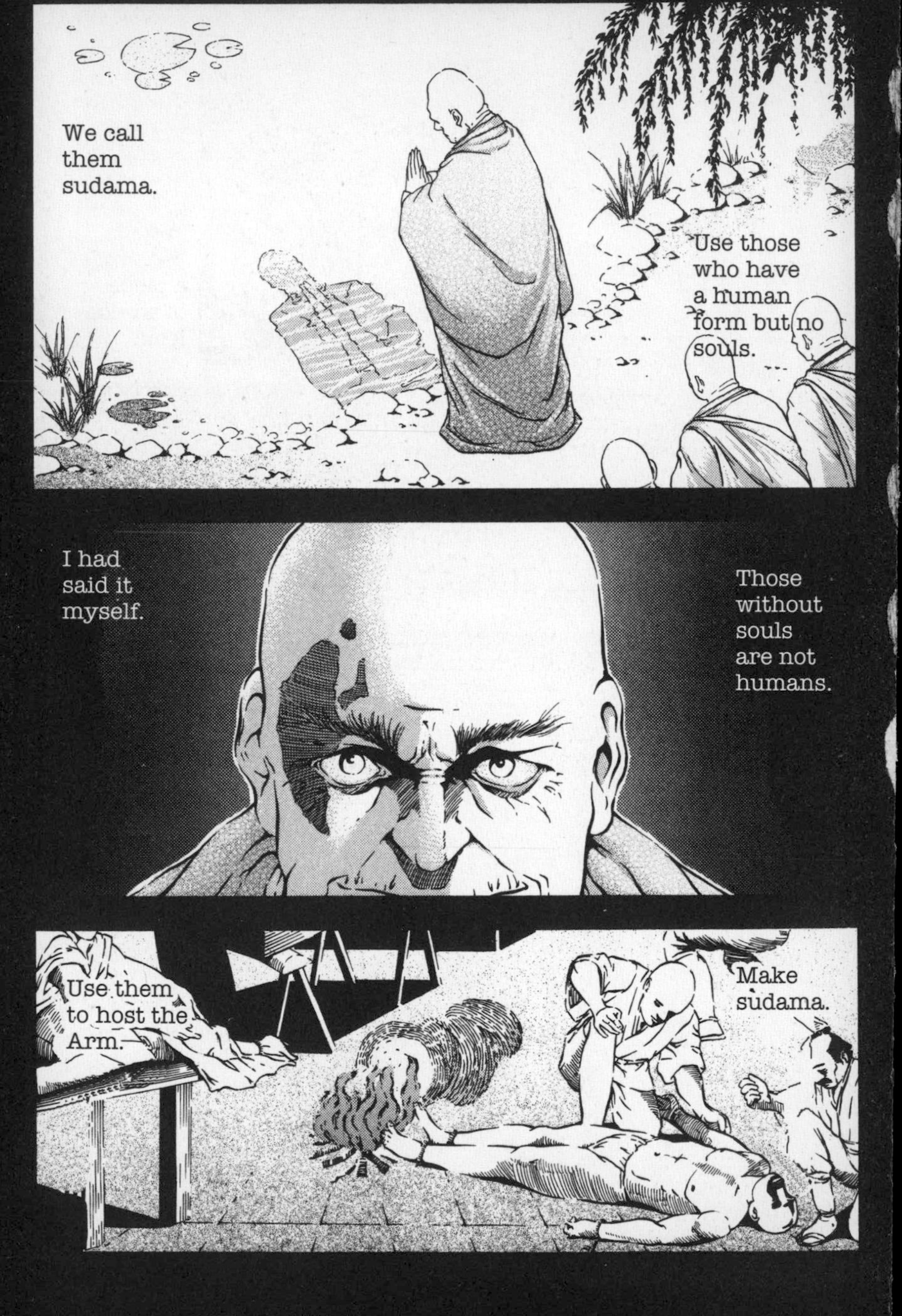
Use those who have a human form but no souls.
We call them sudama.
Those without souls are not humans.
I had said it myself.
Make sudama.
Use them to host the Arm.

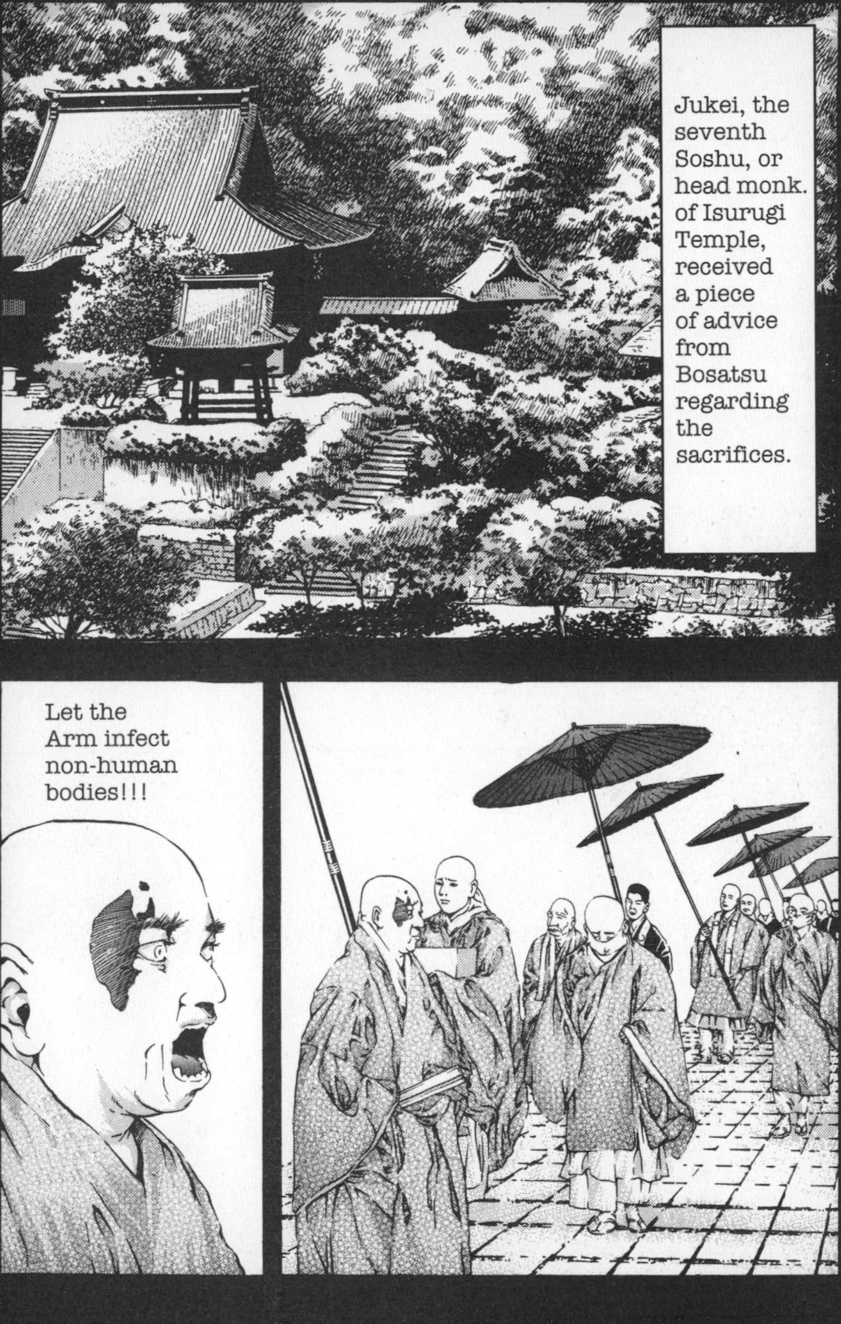
Jukei, the seventh Soshu, or head monk. of Isurugi Temple, received a piece of advice from Bosatsu regarding the sacrifices.
Let the Arm infect non-human bodies!!!

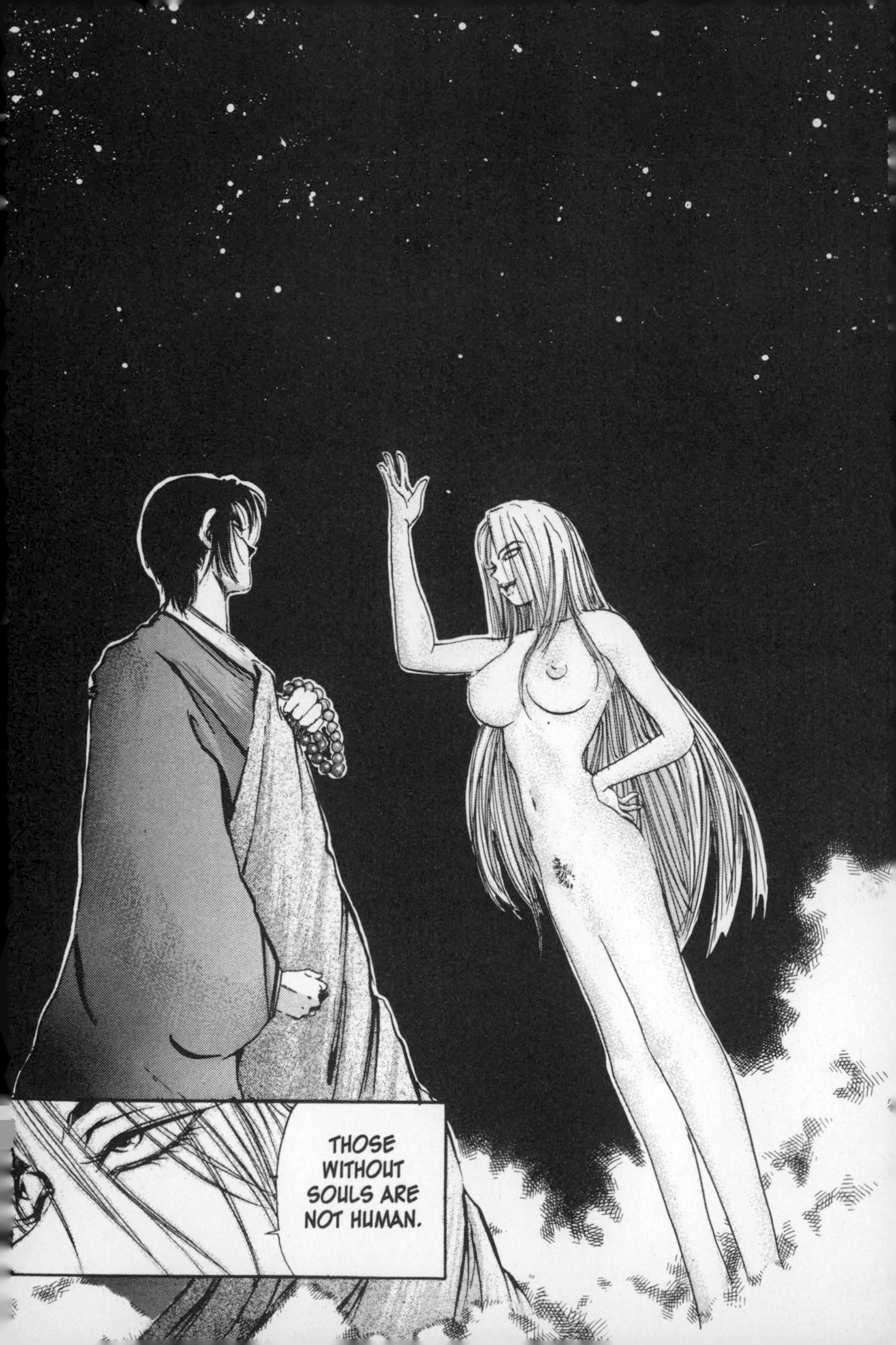
THOSE WITHOUT SOULS ARE NOT HUMAN.

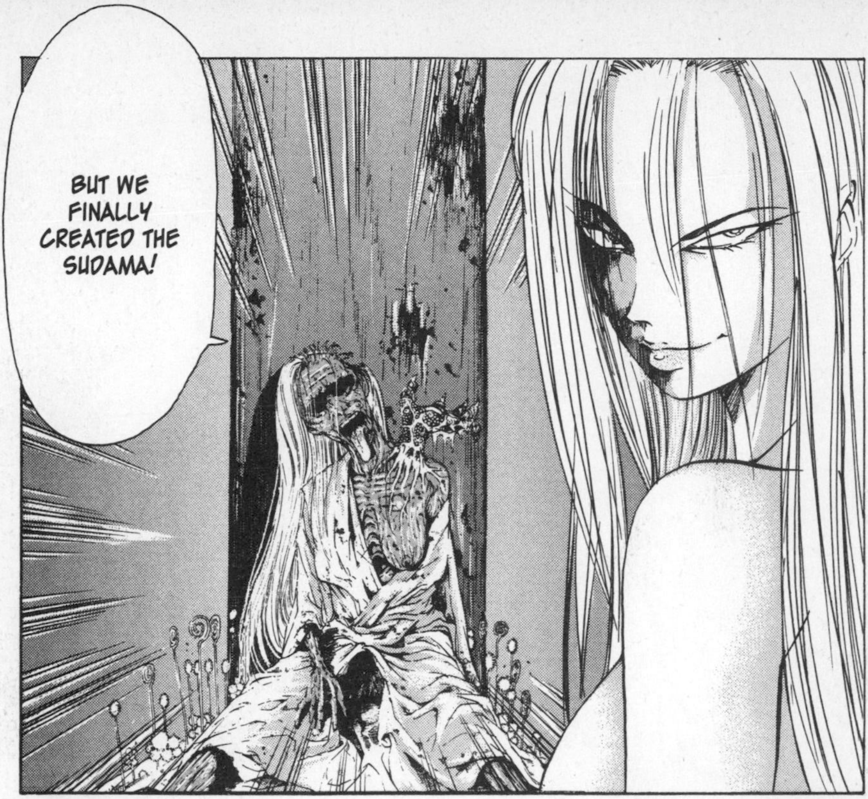
BUT WE FINALLY CREATED THE SUDAMA!

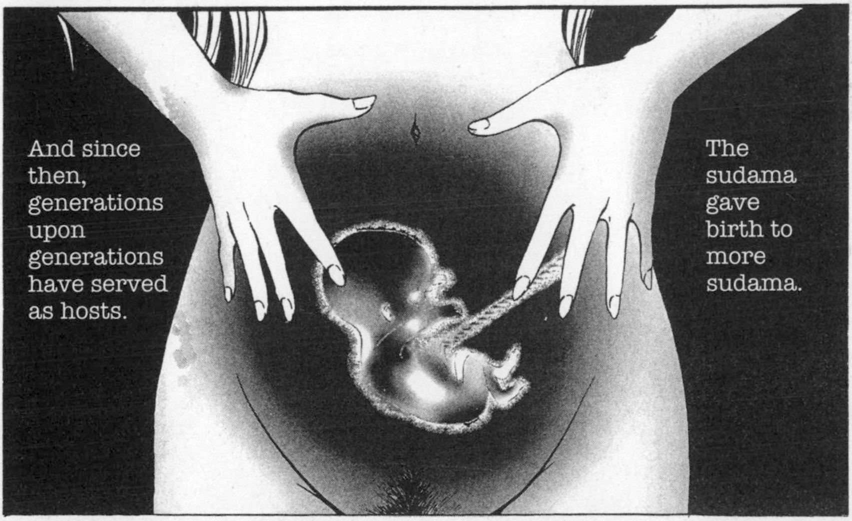
The sudama gave birth to more sudama.
And since then, generations upon generations have served as hosts.

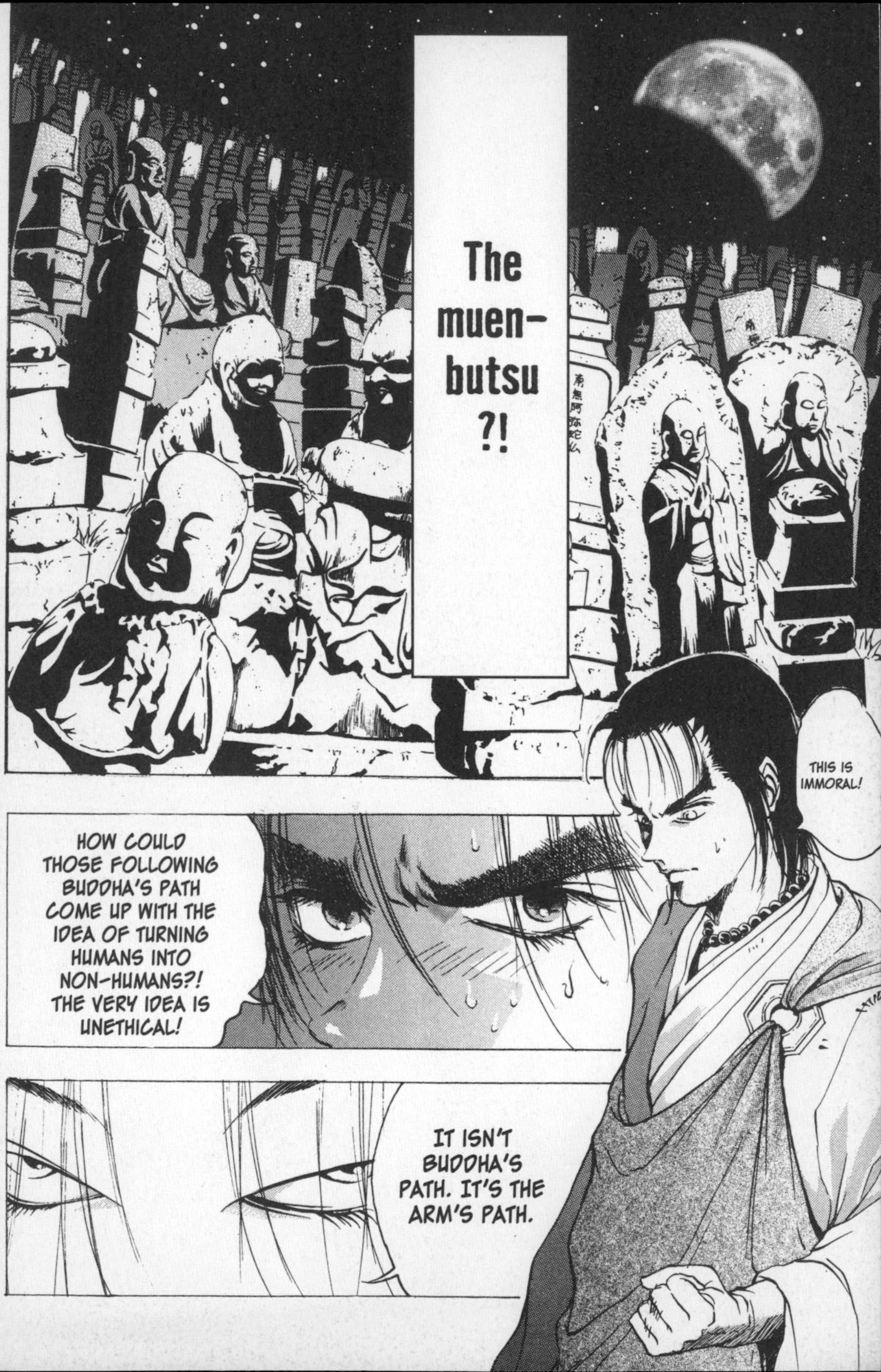

南無阿弥陀仏
The muen-butsu ?!
THIS IS IMMORAL!
HOW COULD THOSE FOLLOWING BUDDHA'S PATH COME UP WITH THE IDEA OF TURNING HUMANS INTO NON-HUMANS?! THE VERY IDEA IS UNETHICAL!
IT ISN'T BUDDHA'S PATH. IT'S THE ARM'S PATH.

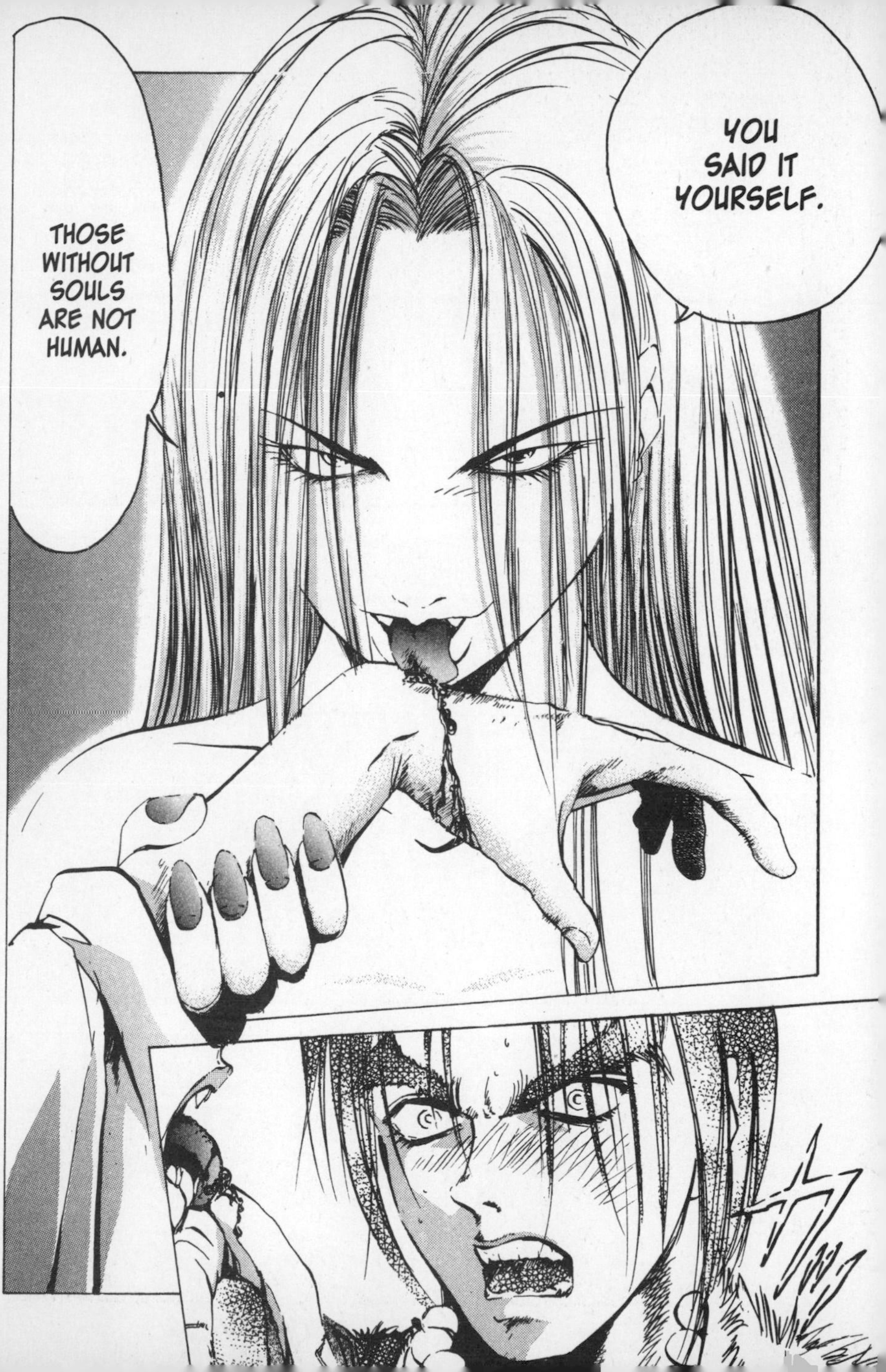
YOU SAID IT YOURSELF.
THOSE WITHOUT SOULS ARE NOT HUMAN.

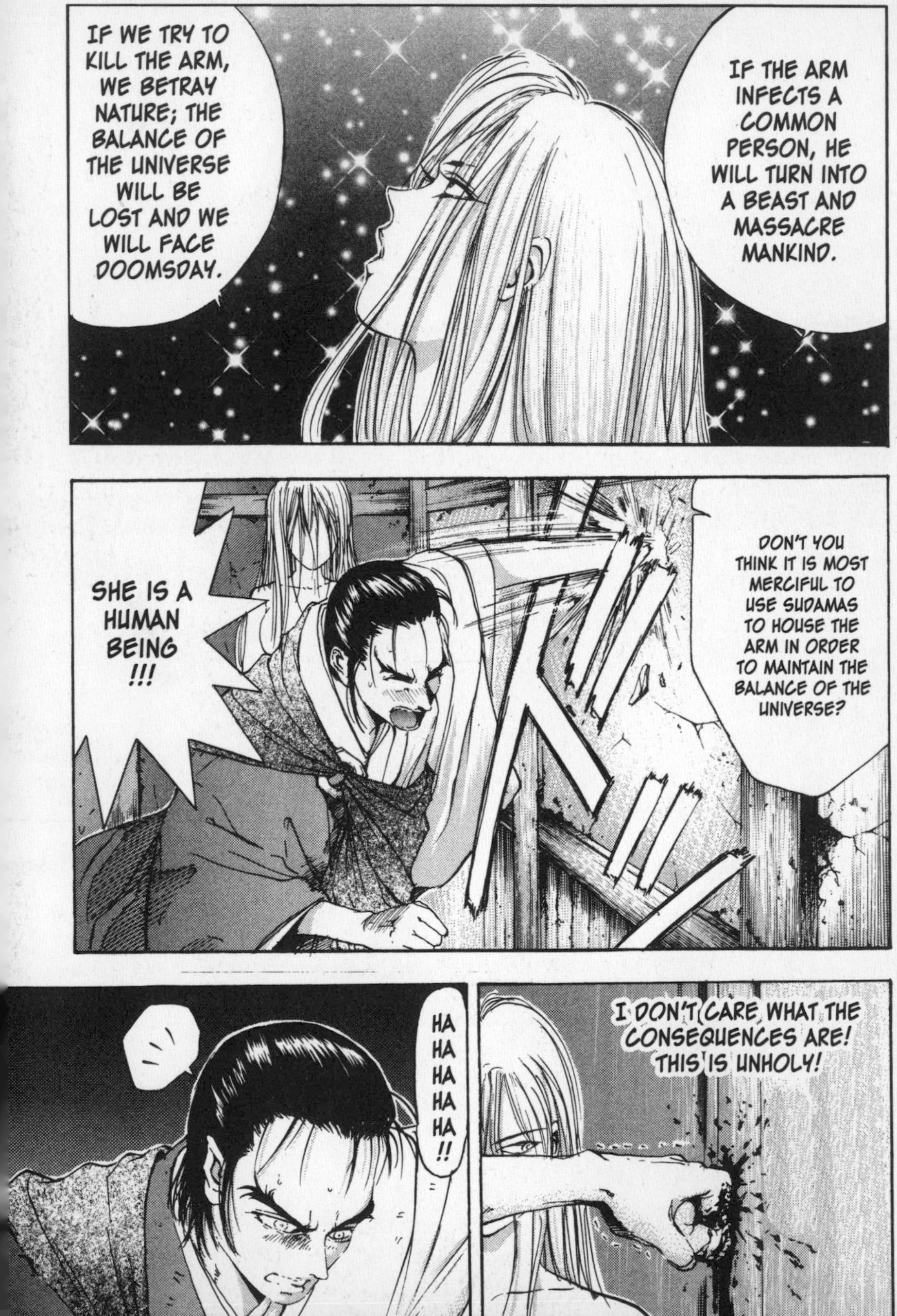
IF THE ARM INFECTS A COMMON PERSON, HE WILL TURN INTO A BEAST AND MASSACRE MANKIND.
IF WE TRY TO KILL THE ARM, WE BETRAY NATURE; THE BALANCE OF THE UNIVERSE WILL BE LOST AND WE WILL FACE DOOMSDAY.
DON'T YOU THINK IT IS MOST MERCIFUL TO USE SUDAMAS TO HOUSE THE ARM IN ORDER TO MAINTAIN THE BALANCE OF THE UNIVERSE?
SHE IS A HUMAN BEING!!!
I DON'T CARE WHAT THE CONSEQUENCES ARE! THIS IS UNHOLY!
HA HA HA HA HA!!
...

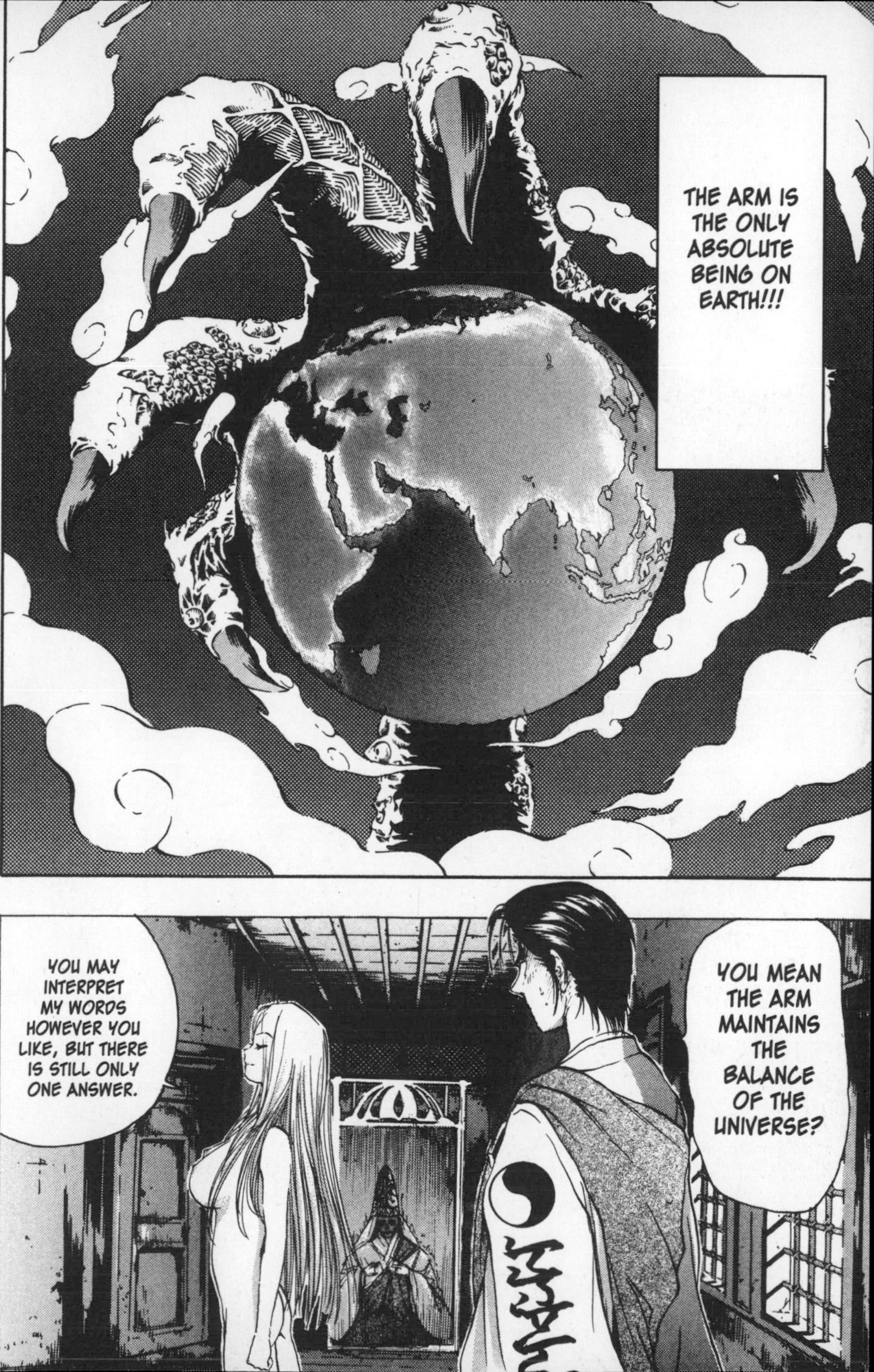
THE ARM IS THE ONLY ABSOLUTE BEING ON EARTH!!!
YOU MEAN THE ARM MAINTAINS THE BALANCE OF THE UNIVERSE?
YOU MAY INTERPRET MY WORDS HOWEVER YOU LIKE, BUT THERE IS STILL ONLY ONE ANSWER.

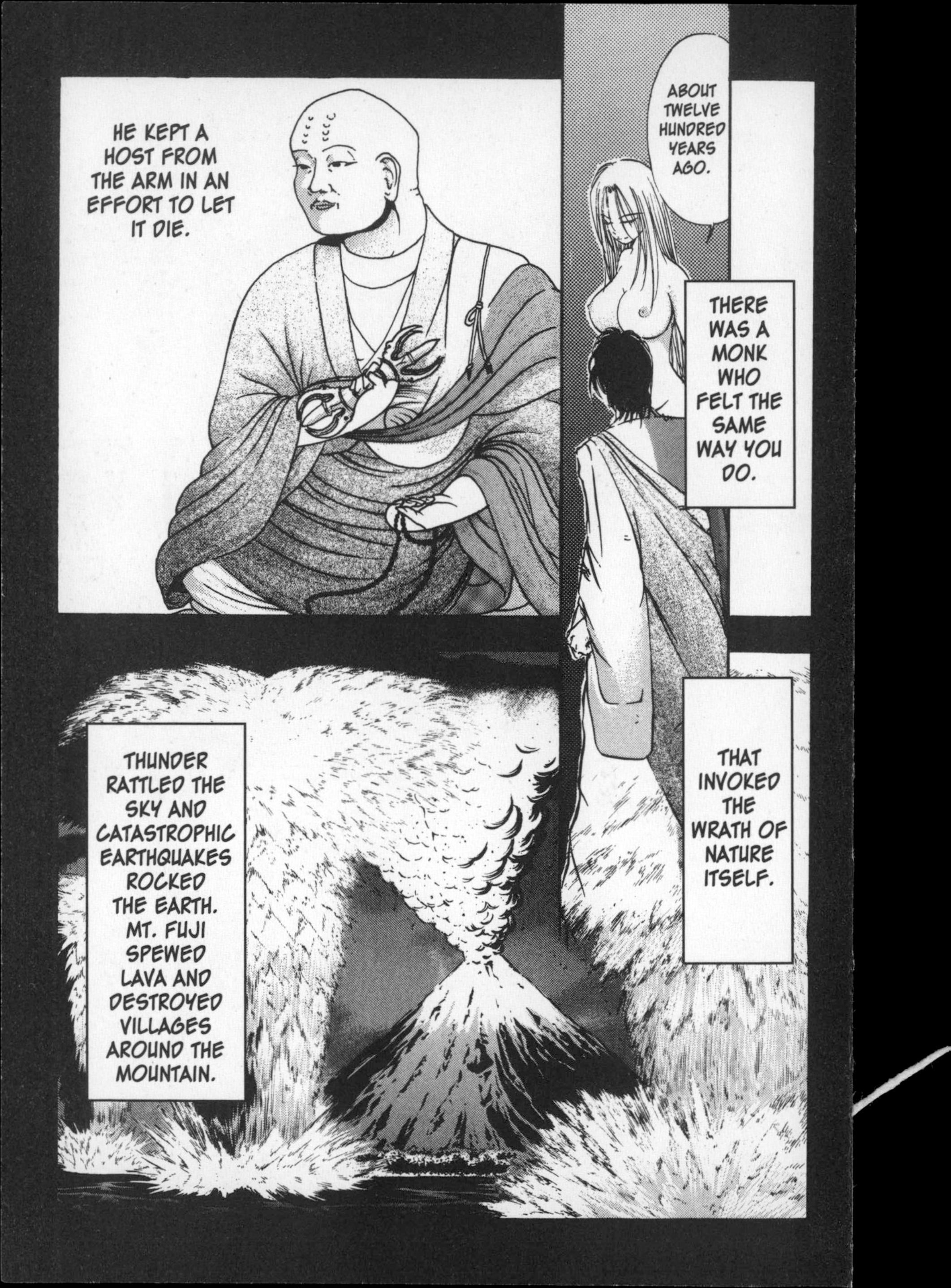
ABOUT TWELVE HUNDRED YEARS AGO.
THERE WAS A MONK WHO FELT THE SAME WAY YOU DO.
HE KEPT A HOST FROM THE ARM IN AN EFFORT TO LET IT DIE.
THAT INVOKED THE WRATH OF NATURE ITSELF.
THUNDER RATTLED THE SKY AND CATASTROPHIC EARTHQUAKES ROCKED THE EARTH. MT. FUJI SPEWED LAVA AND DESTROYED VILLAGES AROUND THE MOUNTAIN.

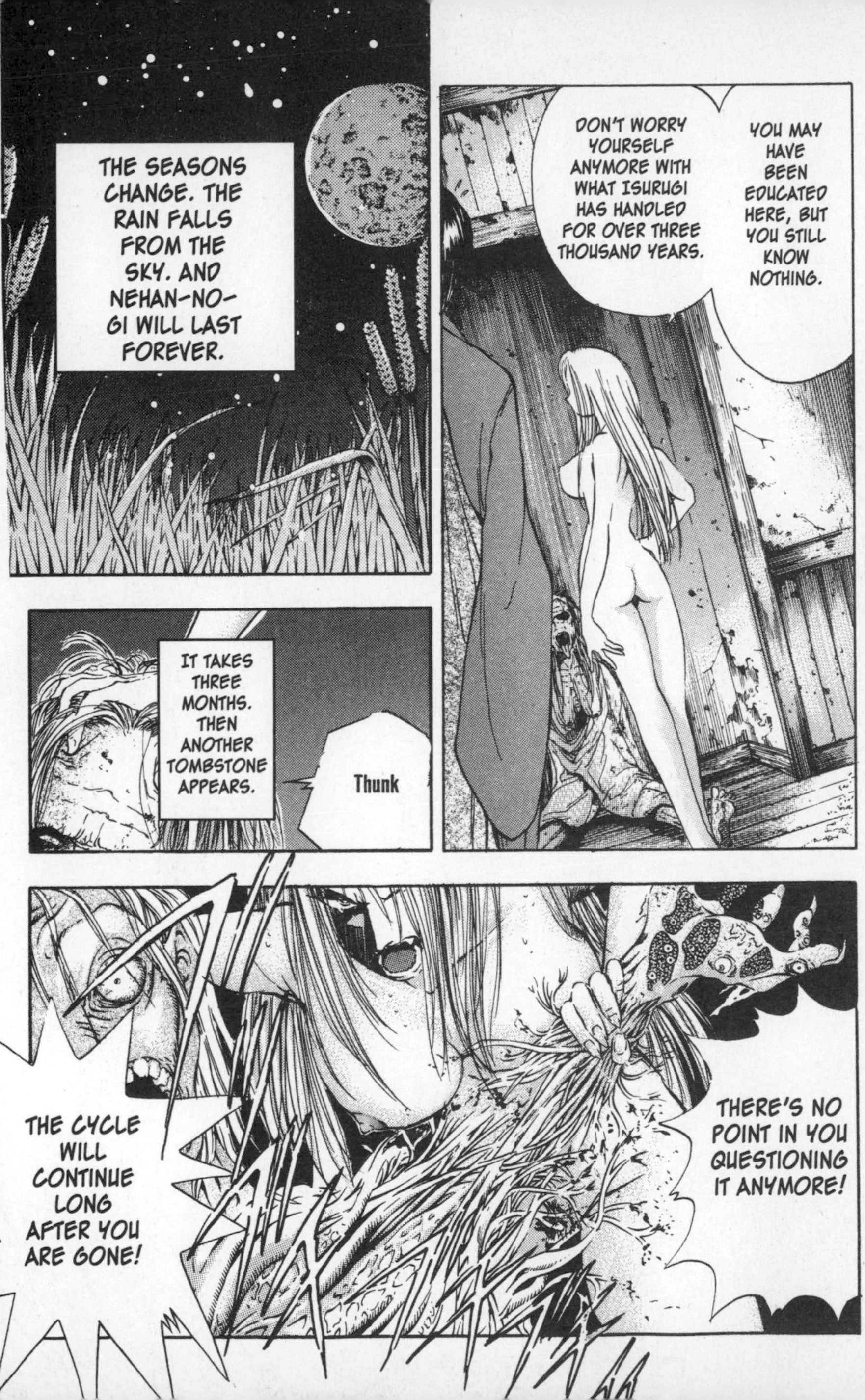
YOU MAY HAVE BEEN EDUCATED HERE, BUT YOU STILL KNOW NOTHING.
DON'T WORRY YOURSELF ANYMORE WITH WHAT ISURUGI HAS HANDLED FOR OVER THREE THOUSAND YEARS.
THE SEASONS CHANGE. THE RAIN FALLS FROM THE SKY. AND NEHAN-NO-GI WILL LAST FOREVER.
IT TAKES THREE MONTHS. THEN ANOTHER TOMBSTONE APPEARS.
Thunk
THERE'S NO POINT IN YOU QUESTIONING IT ANYMORE!
THE CYCLE WILL CONTINUE LONG AFTER YOU ARE GONE!

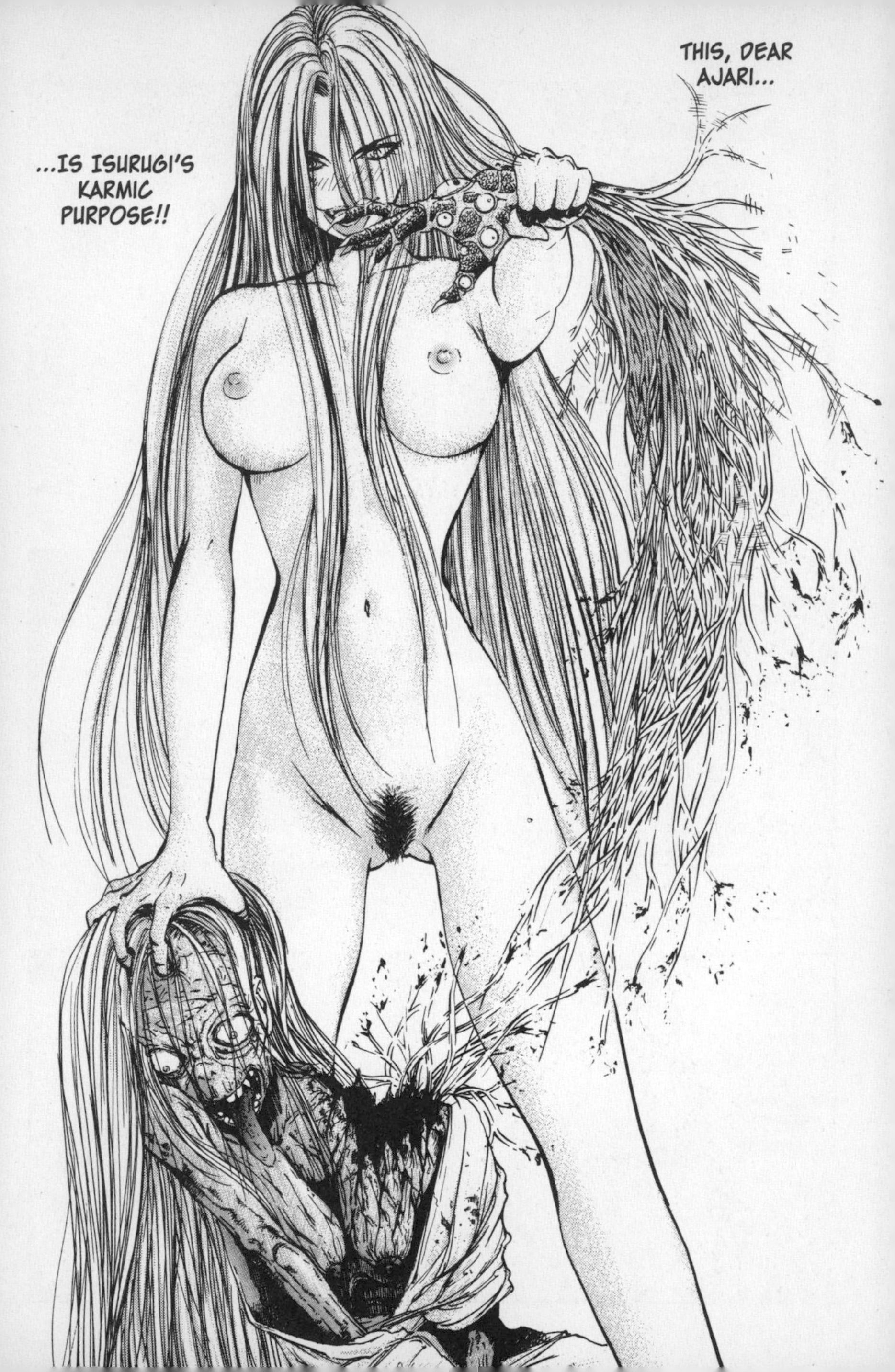
THIS, DEAR AJARI...
...IS ISURUGI'S KARMIC PURPOSE!!

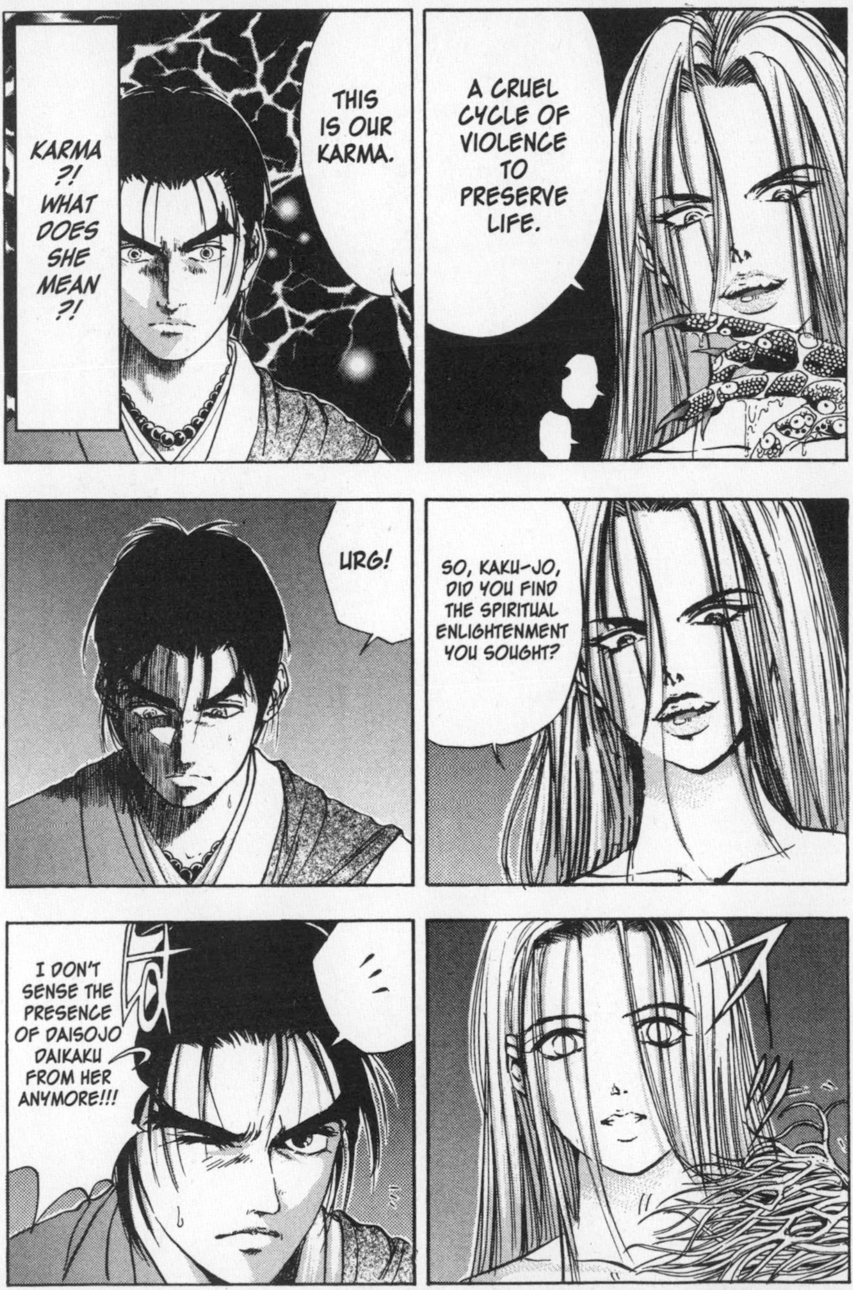
A CRUEL CYCLE OF VIOLENCE TO PRESERVE LIFE.
THIS IS OUR KARMA.
KARMA?! WHAT DOES SHE MEAN?!
SO, KAKU-JO, DID YOU FIND THE SPIRITUAL ENLIGHTENMENT YOU SOUGHT?
URG!
I DON'T SENSE THE PRESENCE OF DAISOJO DAIKAKU FROM HER ANYMORE!!!

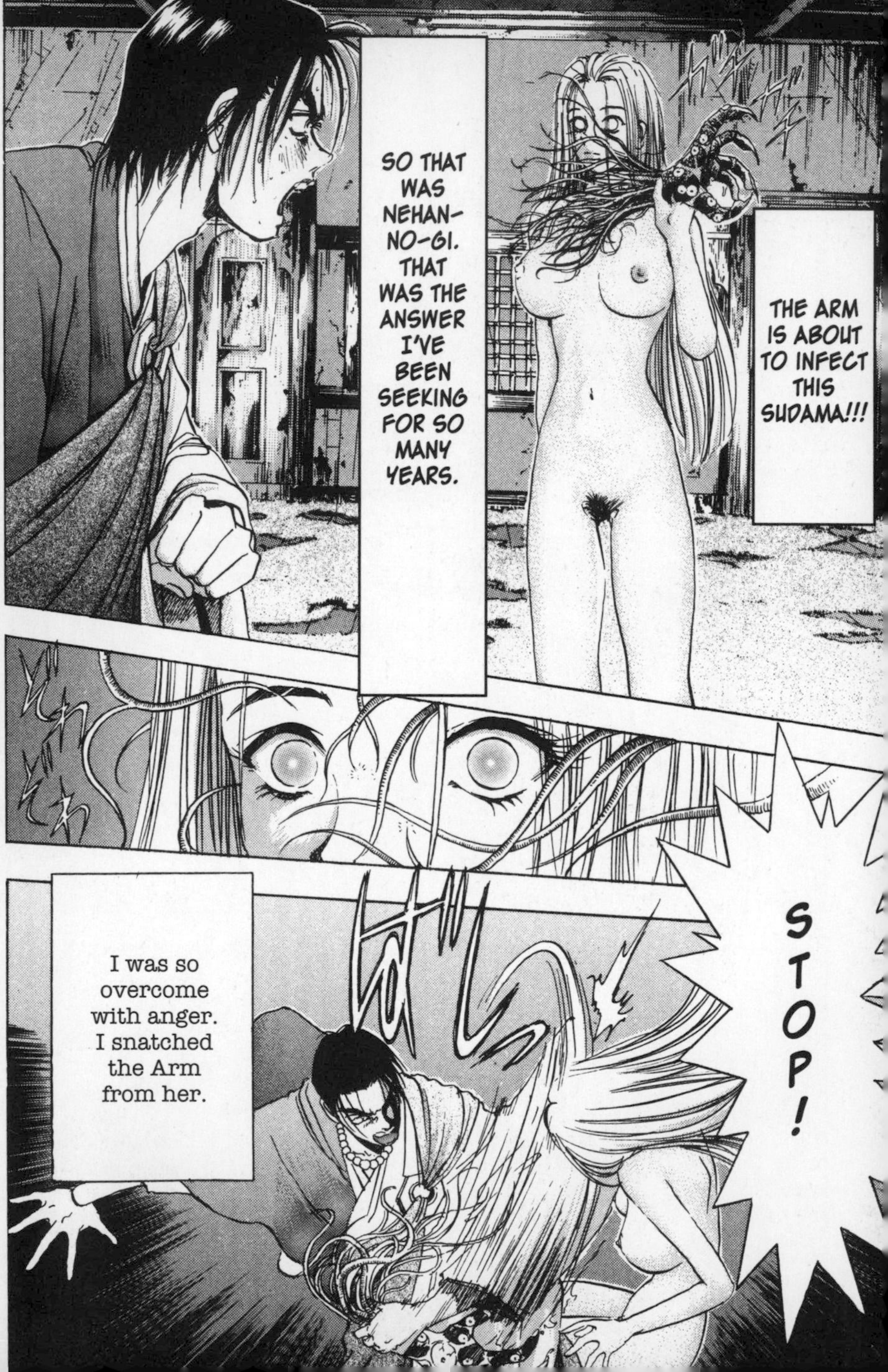
THE ARM IS ABOUT TO INFECT THIS SUDAMA!!!
SO THAT WAS NEHAN-NO-GI. THAT WAS THE ANSWER I'VE BEEN SEEKING FOR SO MANY YEARS.
STOP!
I was so overcome with anger. I snatched the Arm from her.

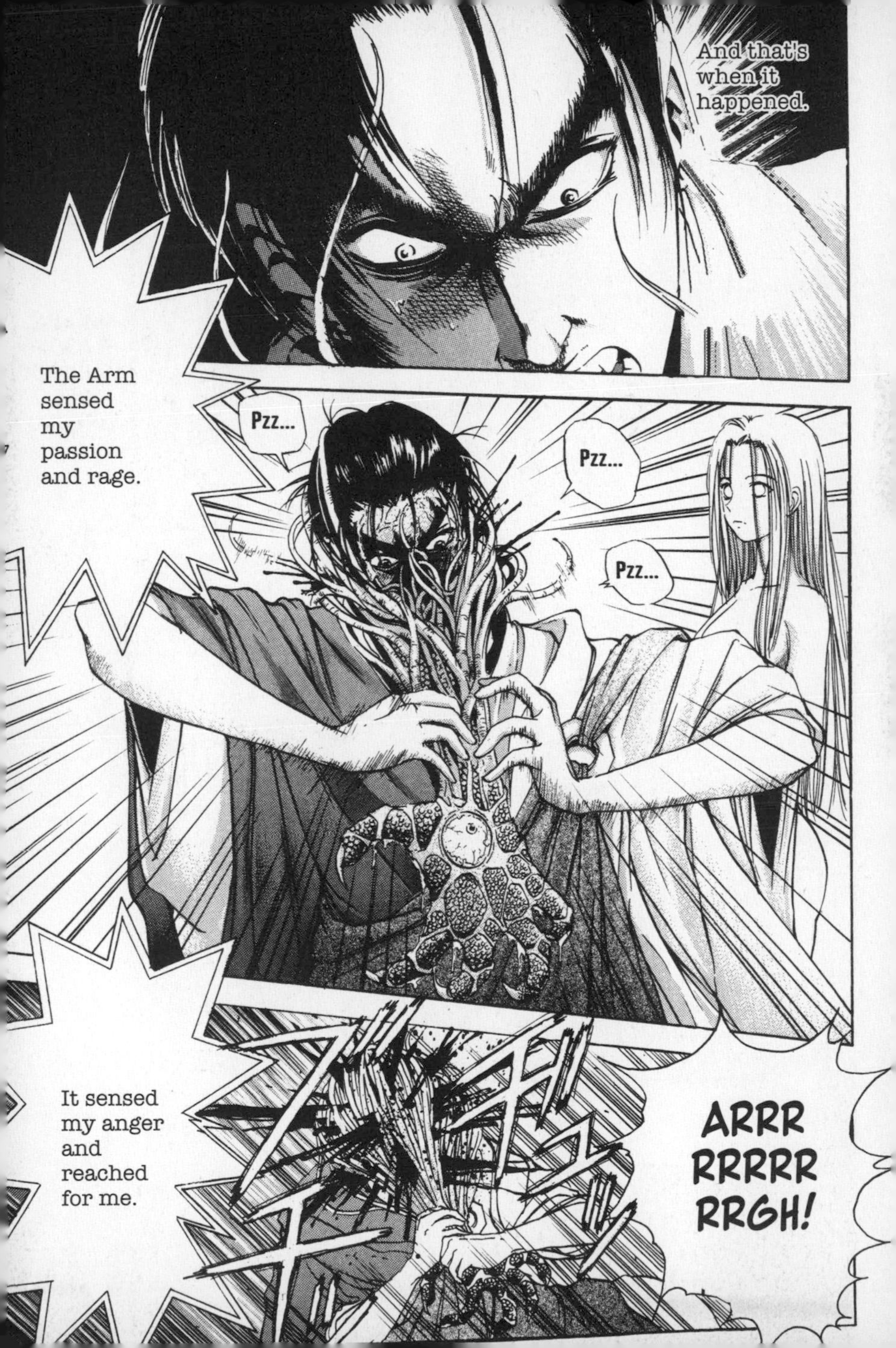
And that's when it happened.
The Arm sensed my passion and rage.
Pzz...
Pzz...
Pzz...
ARRR RRRRR RRGH!
It sensed my anger and reached for me.

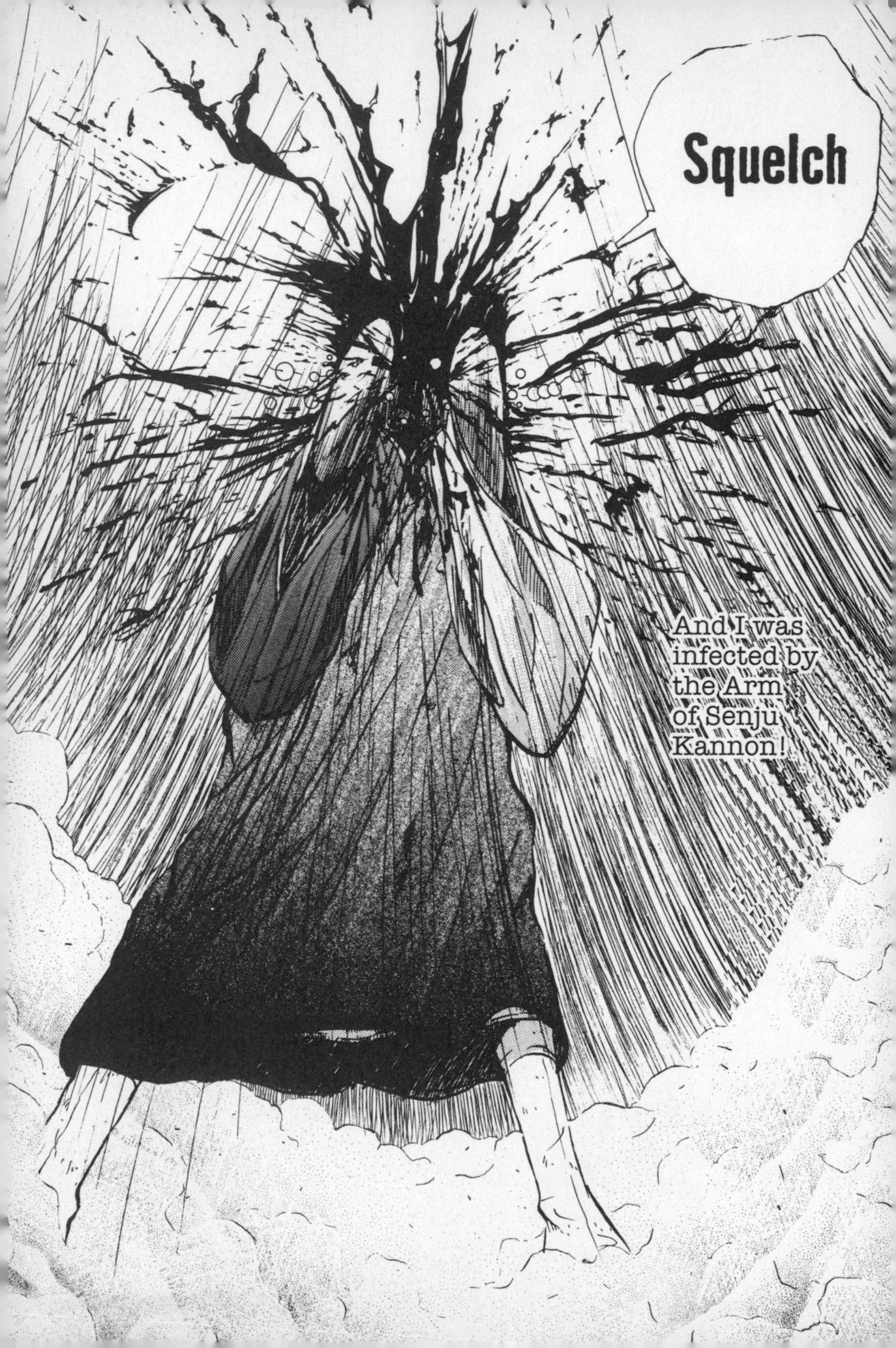
Squelch
And I was infected by the Arm of Senju Kannon!

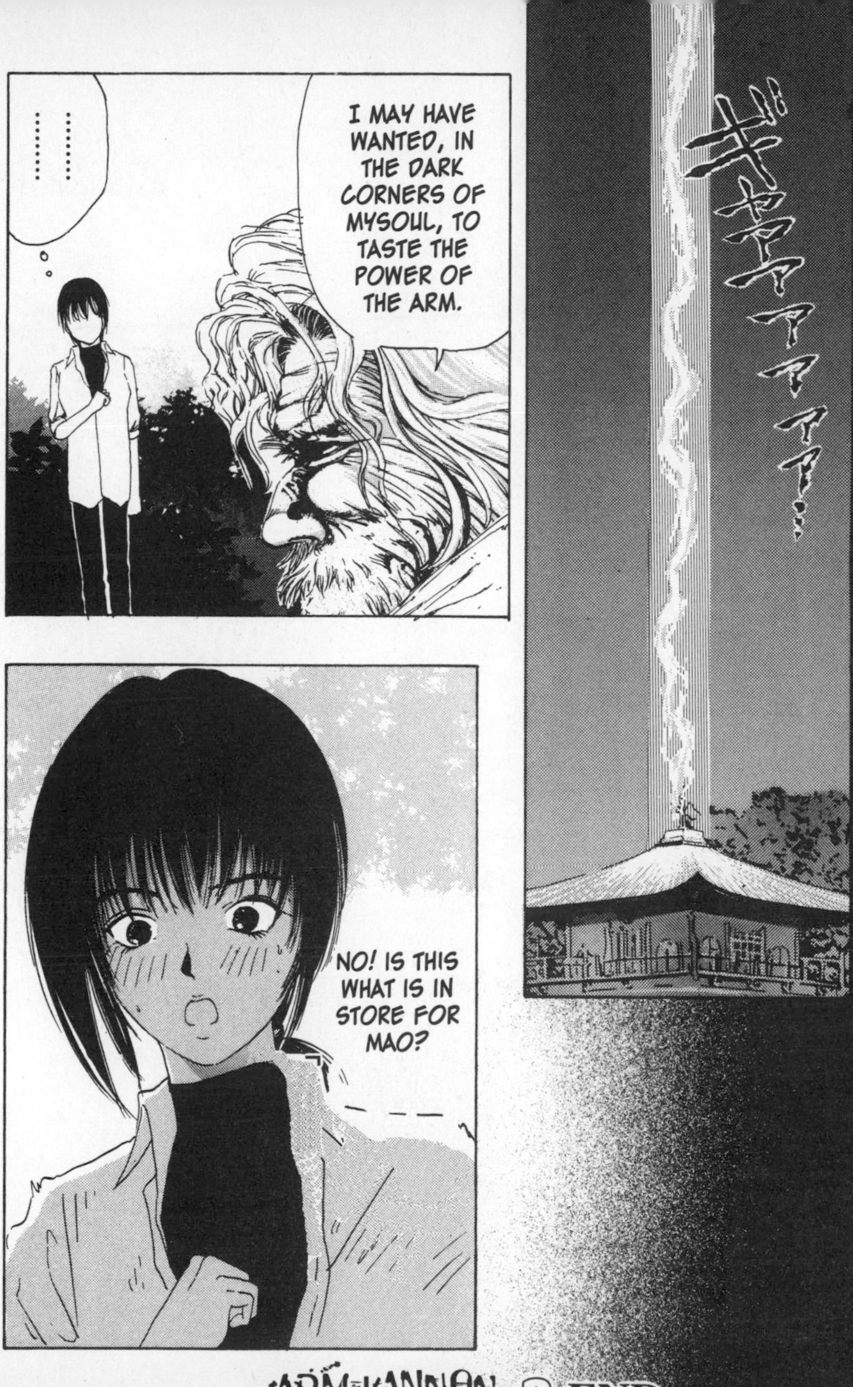
ギャアアアアア…
I MAY HAVE WANTED, IN THE DARK CORNERS OF MYSOUL, TO TASTE THE POWER OF THE ARM.
……
NO! IS THIS WHAT IS IN STORE FOR MAO?

ARM OF KANNON 3 END

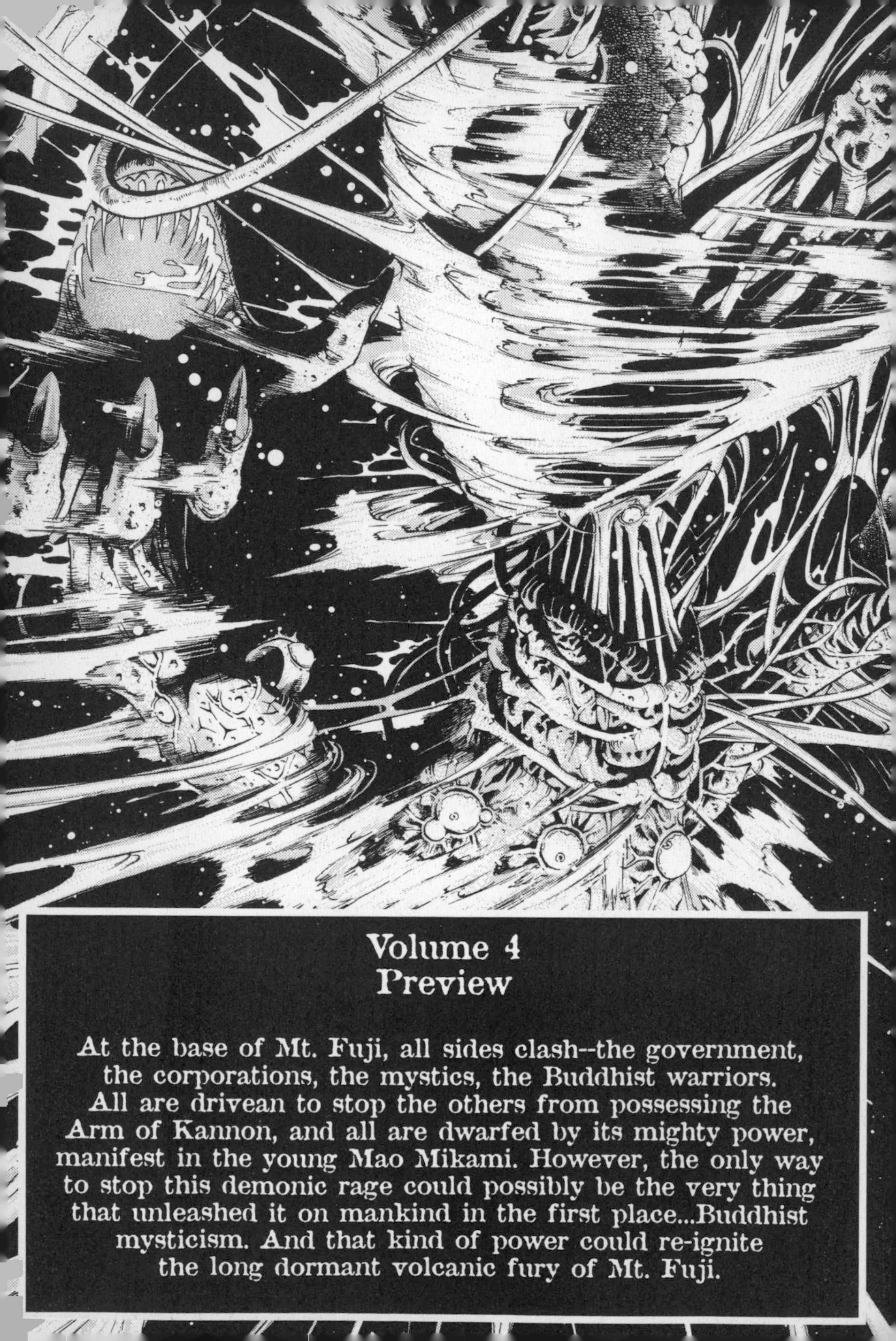

Volume 4
Preview

At the base of Mt. Fuji, all sides clash--the government, the corporations, the mystics, the Buddhist warriors. All are drivean to stop the others from possessing the Arm of Kannon, and all are dwarfed by its mighty power, manifest in the young Mao Mikami. However, the only way to stop this demonic rage could possibly be the very thing that unleashed it on mankind in the first place...Buddhist mysticism. And that kind of power could re-ignite the long dormant volcanic fury of Mt. Fuji.

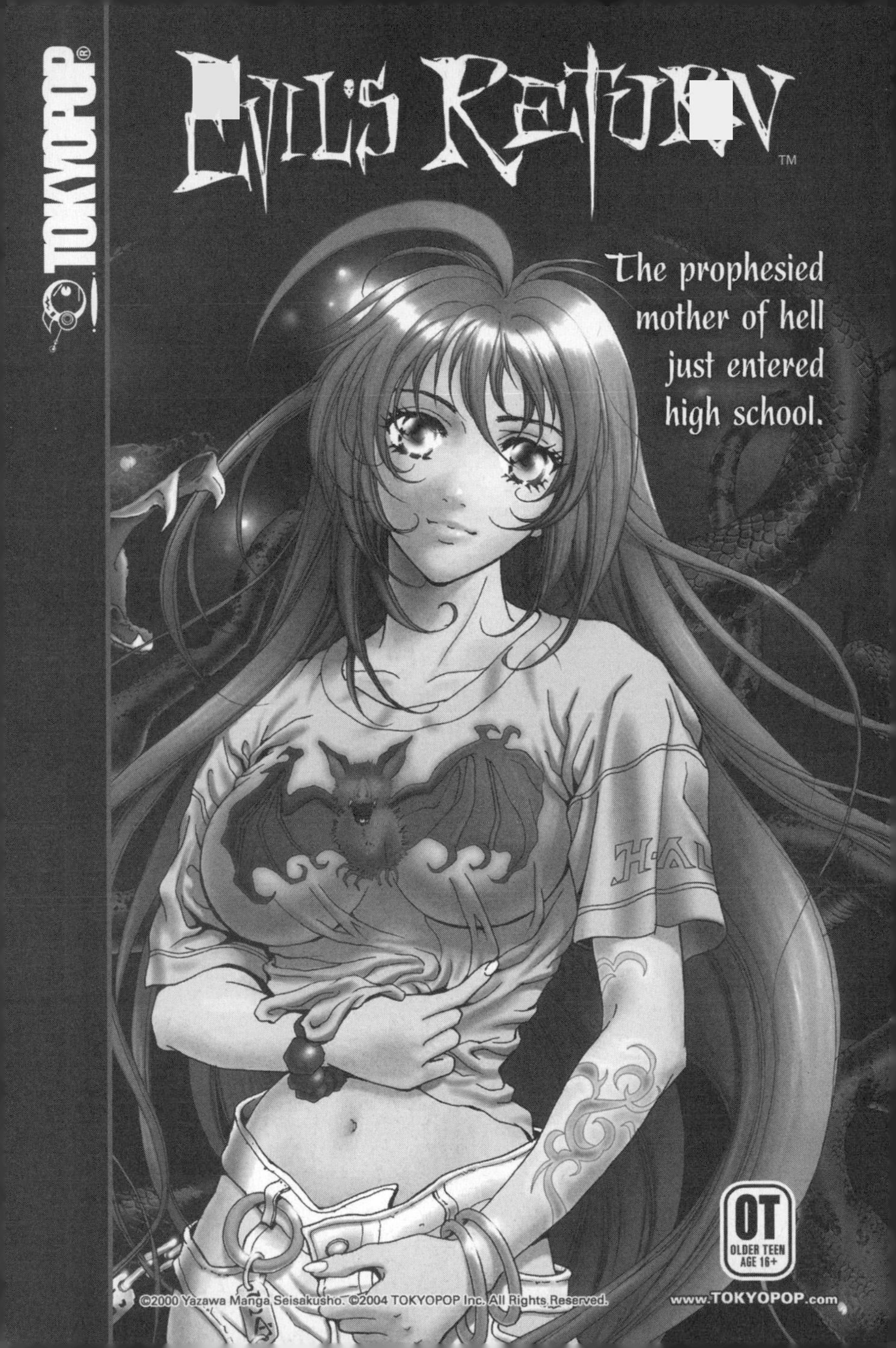
TOKYOPOP®
EVIL'S RETURN™
The prophesied
mother of hell
just entered
high school.
OT
OLDER TEEN
AGE 16+
©2000 Yazawa Manga Seisakusho. ©2004 TOKYOPOP Inc. All Rights Reserved.
www.TOKYOPOP.com

ALSO AVAILABLE FROM TOKYOPOP®

MANGA

.HACK//LEGEND OF THE TWILIGHT
@LARGE
ABENOBASHI: MAGICAL SHOPPING ARCADE
A.I. LOVE YOU
AI YORI AOSHI
ANGELIC LAYER
ARM OF KANNON
BABY BIRTH
BATTLE ROYALE
BATTLE VIXENS
BRAIN POWERED
BRIGADOON
B'TX
CANDIDATE FOR GODDESS, THE
CARDCAPTOR SAKURA
CARDCAPTOR SAKURA - MASTER OF THE CLOW
CHOBITS
CHRONICLES OF THE CURSED SWORD
CLAMP SCHOOL DETECTIVES
CLOVER
COMIC PARTY
CONFIDENTIAL CONFESSIONS
CORRECTOR YUI
COWBOY BEBOP
COWBOY BEBOP: SHOOTING STAR
CRAZY LOVE STORY
CRESCENT MOON
CROSS
CULDCEPT
CYBORG 009
D•N•ANGEL
DEMON DIARY
DEMON ORORON, THE
DEUS VITAE
DIABOLO
DIGIMON
DIGIMON TAMERS
DIGIMON ZERO TWO
DOLL
DRAGON HUNTER
DRAGON KNIGHTS
DRAGON VOICE
DREAM SAGA
DUKLYON: CLAMP SCHOOL DEFENDERS
EERIE QUEERIE!
ERICA SAKURAZAWA: COLLECTED WORKS
ET CETERA
ETERNITY
EVIL'S RETURN
FAERIES' LANDING
FAKE
FLCL
FLOWER OF THE DEEP SLEEP
FORBIDDEN DANCE
FRUITS BASKET
G GUNDAM

GATEKEEPERS
GETBACKERS
GIRL GOT GAME
GIRLS EDUCATIONAL CHARTER
GRAVITATION
GTO
GUNDAM BLUE DESTINY
GUNDAM SEED ASTRAY
GUNDAM WING
GUNDAM WING: BATTLEFIELD OF PACIFISTS
GUNDAM WING: ENDLESS WALTZ
GUNDAM WING: THE LAST OUTPOST (G-UNIT)
GUYS' GUIDE TO GIRLS
HANDS OFF!
HAPPY MANIA
HARLEM BEAT
HYPER RUNE
I.N.V.U.
IMMORTAL RAIN
INITIAL D
INSTANT TEEN: JUST ADD NUTS
ISLAND
JING: KING OF BANDITS
JING: KING OF BANDITS - TWILIGHT TALES
JULINE
KARE KANO
KILL ME, KISS ME
KINDAICHI CASE FILES, THE
KING OF HELL
KODOCHA: SANA'S STAGE
LAMENT OF THE LAMB
LEGAL DRUG
LEGEND OF CHUN HYANG, THE
LES BIJOUX
LOVE HINA
LUPIN III
LUPIN III: WORLD'S MOST WANTED
MAGIC KNIGHT RAYEARTH I
MAGIC KNIGHT RAYEARTH II
MAHOROMATIC: AUTOMATIC MAIDEN
MAN OF MANY FACES
MARMALADE BOY
MARS
MARS: HORSE WITH NO NAME
MINK
MIRACLE GIRLS
MIYUKI-CHAN IN WONDERLAND
MODEL
MOURYOU KIDEN
MY LOVE
NECK AND NECK
ONE
ONE I LOVE, THE
PARADISE KISS
PARASYTE
PASSION FRUIT
PEACH GIRL
PEACH GIRL: CHANGE OF HEART

05.26.04T

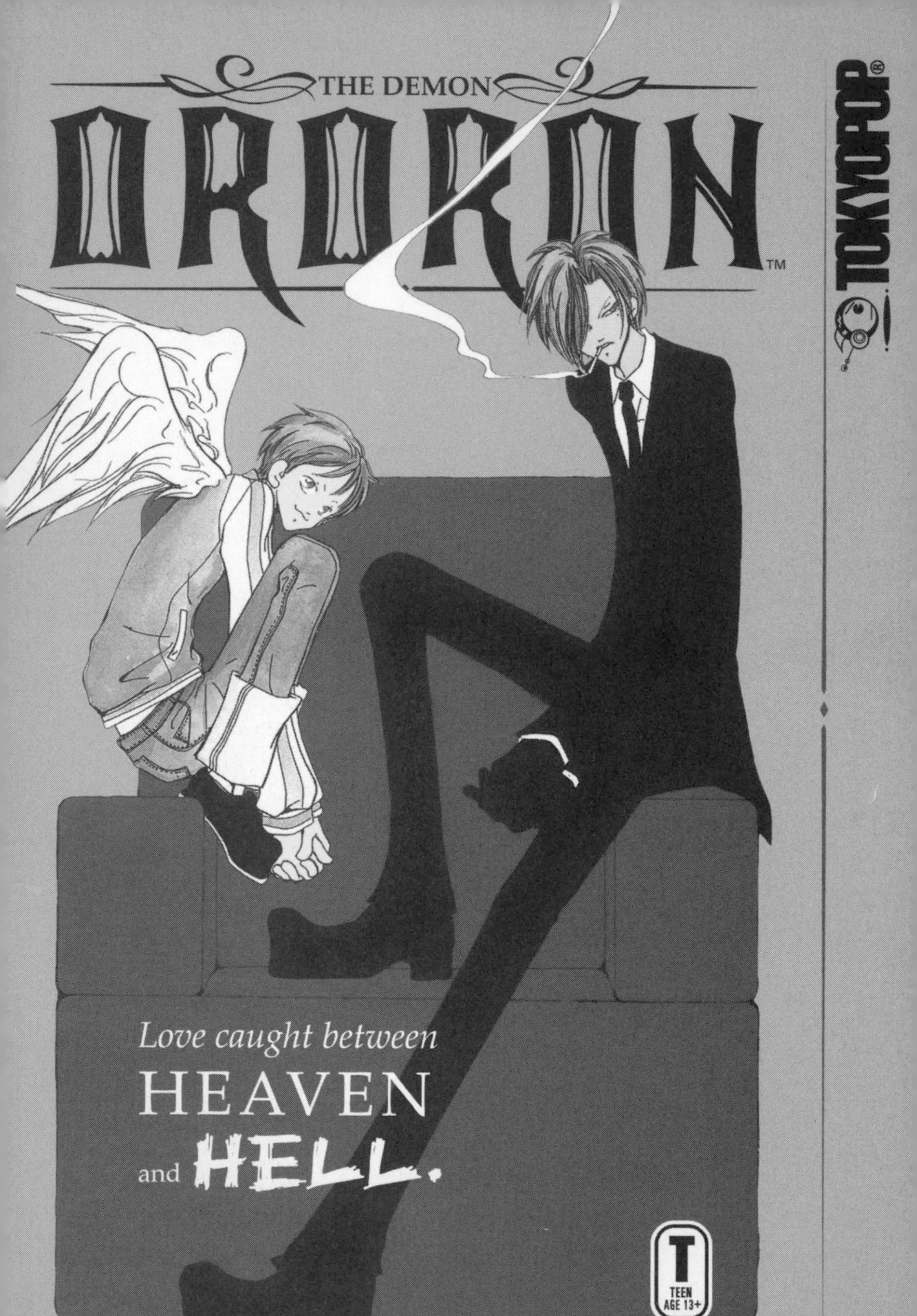
THE DEMON
ORORON™
TOKYOPOP®
Love caught between
HEAVEN
and HELL.
T
TEEN
AGE 13+

STOP!

This is the back of the book.
You wouldn't want to spoil a great ending!

This book is printed "manga-style," in the authentic Japanese right-to-left format. Since none of the artwork has been flipped or altered, readers get to experience the story just as the creator intended. You've been asking for it, so TOKYOPOP® delivered: authentic, hot-off-the-press, and far more fun!

DIRECTIONS

If this is your first time reading manga-style, here's a quick guide to help you understand how it works.

It's easy... just start in the top right panel and follow the numbers. Have fun, and look for more 100% authentic manga from TOKYOPOP®!

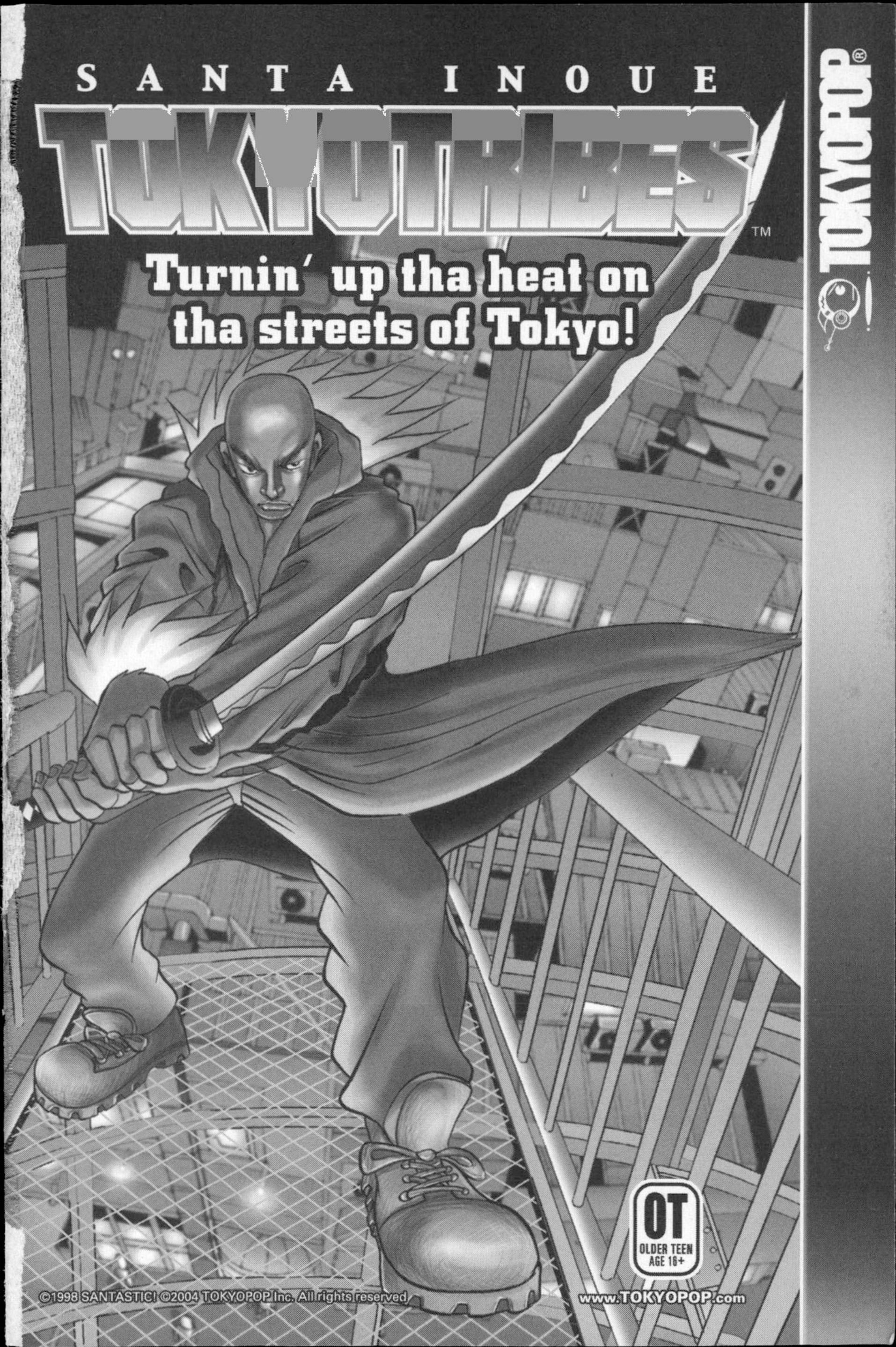
SANTA INOUE
TOKYO TRIBES™
Turnin' up tha heat on tha streets of Tokyo!
TOKYOPOP®
OT
OLDER TEEN AGE 16+
©1998 SANTASTIC! ©2004 TOKYOPOP Inc. All rights reserved.
www.TOKYOPOP.com

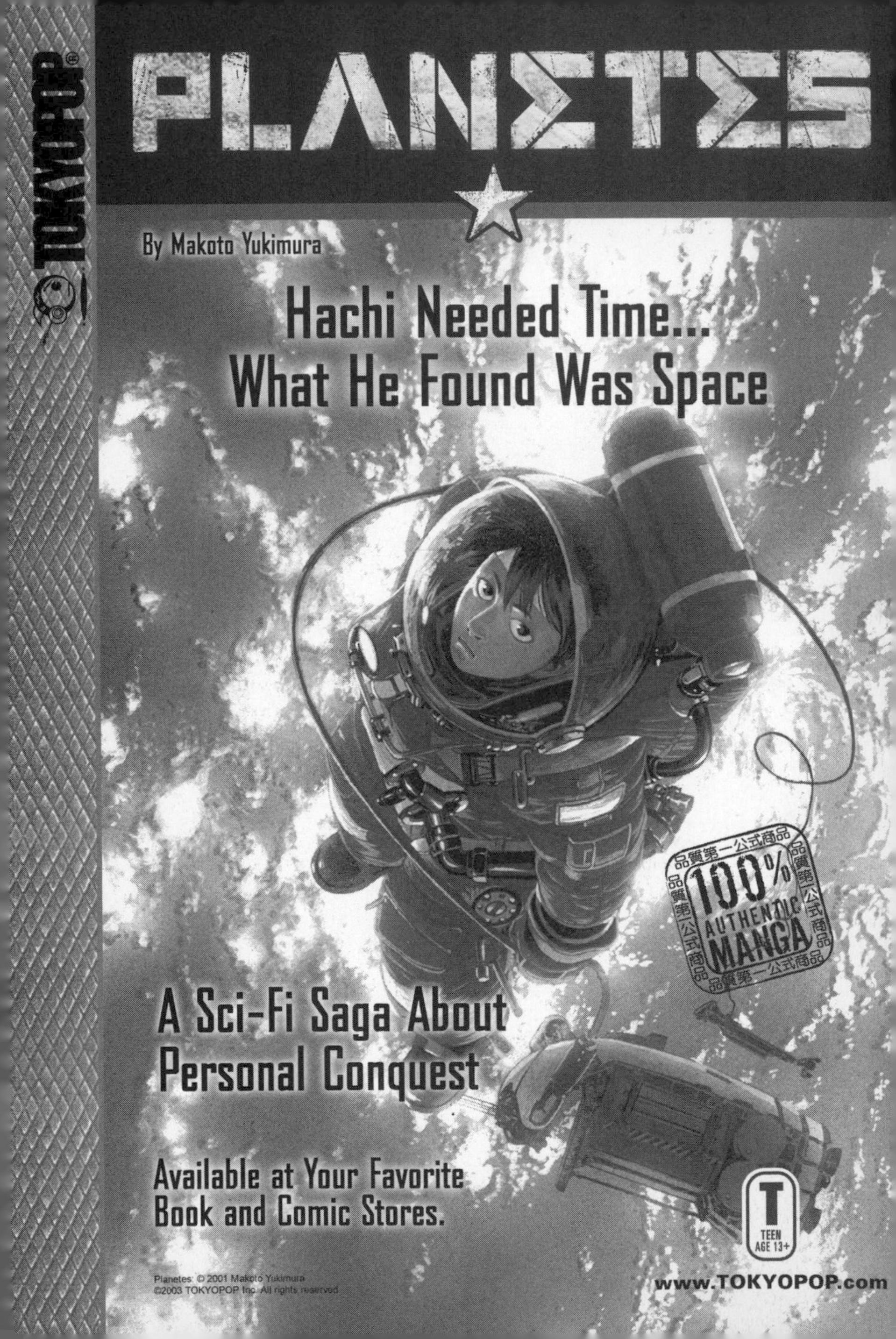

By Makoto Yukimura

Hachi Needed Time...
What He Found Was Space

100% AUTHENTIC MANGA

A Sci-Fi Saga About Personal Conquest

Available at Your Favorite Book and Comic Stores.

T TEEN AGE 13+

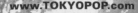